Going to the Source

The Bedford Reader in American History

Principles for Interrogating Sources

Every object produced by human beings is a potential source of information about the past. Historians must coax the past out of every source by asking it the right questions. In *Going to the Source,* you will interrogate sources by asking the same questions historians ask:

■ When was this source produced and under what circumstances?

■ Who produced this source? And why? What purpose was this source created to serve?

■ Who was the audience for this source? Who was meant to use it?

■ What is the point of view in this source? What does the inherent bias of the source reveal about this source's past and purpose?

Principles for Interpreting Sources

After interrogating sources, historians must provide an *interpretation* of the sources to make an argument about what these sources mean and what story they reveal. In *Going to the Source,* you will interpret evidence by following the same principles that historians follow:

■ Sources are incomplete. You will never have all the sources for any single moment, and no single source can tell the whole story.

■ Sources have limits to what they can tell you. You must consider what you can and cannot logically conclude from a source.

■ Sources have biases, which must be accounted for. Do not dismiss the source's bias or adopt it in your interpretation. Instead, identify the bias and use it as evidence of one viewpoint.

■ Sources can conflict. Never hide or dismiss sources that complicate or contradict your interpretation. Either revise your interpretation or explain why conflicting evidence does not alter your interpretation.

Brief Contents

SECOND EDITION

Going to the Source

The Bedford Reader in American History

VOLUME 2: SINCE 1865

Victoria Bissell Brown

Grinnell College

Timothy J. Shannon

Gettysburg College

Bedford / St. Martin's   Boston ◆ New York

To our students, who have taught us so much

For Bedford/St. Martin's
Executive Editor for History: Mary Dougherty
Director of Development for History: Jane Knetzger
Senior Developmental Editor: Sara Wise
Senior Production Editor: Bridget Leahy
Production Supervisor: Jennifer Peterson
Executive Marketing Manager: Jenna Bookin Barry
Associate Editor: Marissa Zannetti
Copyeditor: Linda McLatchie
Text Design: Claire Seng-Niemoeller
Indexer: Steve Csipke
Cover Design: Billy Boardman
Cover Art: California by Maxine Albro, ca. 1934. © Morton Beebe/CORBIS. 1929 Cover of *The New York Times* newspaper. Page one of *The New York Times* October 30, 1929. "Stocks collapse but rally at close, cheers brokers. Bankers optimistic to continue aid." © Bettmann/CORBIS.
Cartography: Mapping Specialists, Ltd.
Composition: Pine Tree Composition, Inc.
Printing and Binding: R.R. Donnelley & Sons Company

President: Joan E. Feinberg
Editorial Director: Denise B. Wydra
Director of Marketing: Karen Melton Soeltz
Director of Editing, Design, and Production: Marcia Cohen
Managing Editor: Elizabeth M. Schaaf

Library of Congress Control Number: 2007927403

Manufactured in the United States of America.

1   0   9   8   7
f   e   d   c   b   a

For information, write: Bedford/St. Martin's, 75 Arlington Street, Boston, MA 02116
(617-399-4000)

ISBN-10: 0–312–44823–6
ISBN-13: 978–0–312–44823–3

Acknowledgments

Chapter 1
   Page 3 (Figure 1.1): Thomas Nast, "The Union as it was. The Lost Cause, worse than slavery." Library of Congress, LC-USZ62-128619.

Chapter 2
   Page 36: Detail from "Blackfeet Performance," c. 1930. Great Northern Railway Company Advertising and Publicity Department Photos, Minnesota Historical Society.
   Page 40 (Source 1): "Greetings from Glacier National Park," c. 1920. Great Northern Railway Company Advertising and Publicity Department Photos, Minnesota Historical Society.
   Page 41 (Source 2): "Great Northern Railway Calendar," 1923. Great Northern Railway Company Advertising and Publicity Department Photos, Minnesota Historical Society.
   Page 42 (Source 3): "Blackfeet and Park Golfers," c. 1930. Great Northern Railway Company Advertising and Publicity Department Photos, Minnesota Historical Society.
   Page 43 (Source 4): "Spearfishing in Glacier National Park," date unknown. Great Northern Railway Company Advertising and Publicity Department Photos, Minnesota Historical Society.

Acknowledgments and copyrights are continued at the back of the book on pages 365–67, which constitute an extension of the copyright page. It is a violation of the law to reproduce these selections by any means whatsoever without the written permission of the copyright holder.

Preface for Instructors

In the course of writing and revising *Going to the Source*, we have heard from many instructors about how they use primary and secondary documents in their history classes. Many instructors focus on the goal of providing lively historical content; they appreciate the way in which a letter from a Lowell mill worker, for example, can bring to life the feel of nineteenth-century New England. We were looking for something more. We wanted students to move beyond empathizing with folks in the past to engaging in *analysis* the way that historians do. However, we wanted to train our students in critical thinking by addressing them not as historians-in-the-making, but as consumers of information; as people who have to think about the reliability of sources of information all the time. Most survey students will never become historians, but they will have to act on sources to cast a vote or make a major decision.

We provide a range of sources for students to examine. The sources in each volume are personal and public; they run the gamut from popular to official, from obvious to obscure. In satisfying our own interest in Americans' struggle to realize democratic ideals out of undemocratic realities, we have provided sources from the margins of society as well as the centers of power. By including documents that balance a bottom-up with a top-down approach to U.S. history, we seek to remind students that the nation's conflicts over democratic ideals have not been confined to marginal communities or anonymous voices. By exposing students to elite or official documents as well as private or anonymous ones, we seek to remind them that influence can arise from humble communities in America, that centers of power cannot be ignored when writing the history of American democracy, and that marginal people have had to learn about elite institutions in order to influence the powerful. We also seek to remind students of the range of sources a historian can draw upon to capture U.S. history and to convince them of their ability to understand—and their right to access—a vast array of documentary material so that they can become more critical consumers of all types of information.

In *Going to the Source* we hope to provide students and instructors with a way to discuss historical content while experiencing hands-on work in historical source analysis. Our goal in writing this reader is to provide consideration of a particular topic while blending in a healthy portion of historical thinking about the nature of different types of sources, be they newspapers, letters, paintings, statistical data, or scholars' secondary writing. To achieve these aims, we've designed each chapter around one historical topic and one type of source in order to allow for focused student reading and engaging assignments and to enrich classroom discussion on the various processes that go into researching and reconstructing the past.

Each chapter in *Going to the Source* is designed to expose students to historians' processes and to encourage active interrogation of the sources at hand. Each chapter begins with an introduction that sets the stage for the case study that will unfold in the documents. Following the introduction, a "Using the Source" section examines the advantages and disadvantages inherent in the particular type of source on display and provides pertinent questions to ask of all sources of the type under discussion. A "Source Analysis Table" follows, providing students with a template for organizing the evidence they glean from the documents. The central portion of each chapter is "The Source," the documents or images that draw from a single source or single type of source. It is followed by a set of questions for analysis that include ideas for written assignments or class discussion. To provide closure on the case study, "The Rest of the Story" explains later developments in the chapter's story and connects it to larger themes in U.S. history. The concluding section, "To Find out More," points students to additional primary, secondary, and online sources for further study.

NEW TO THE SECOND EDITION

This new edition of *Going to the Source* reflects several changes in the book's content and structure inspired by feedback we received from instructors and students who used the first edition. Many instructors liked the reader but wanted it to mesh more fully with their survey course. With that goal in mind, we have revised and rewritten each chapter extensively. Every chapter makes explicit links to important survey topics and themes, and each volume includes several all-new chapters that introduce students to additional popular types of sources, such as political cartoons, biographies, and diaries.

The new chapters cover topics that instructors commonly teach and that are certain to capture the attention of students taking a U.S. history survey course. For example, in responding to requests for a chapter on environmental history, we discovered that some of the most interesting recent work written by environmental historians on early America deals with human–animal relations. We coupled that idea with the plan for an opening chapter that dealt with visual sources so that students would have a comparatively lighter reading load for the first week of the semester. The new chapter examines the precolonial environment of the New World through European depictions of animals. Their visual interpretations of an exotic new world reveal as much about Europeans' own mental framework as about the landscape itself. As the first chapter it also eases students' way into the book's methods and purposes by using an accessible but especially engaging source. Other new chapters in Volume 1 address Indian captivity and John Brown's raid on Harpers Ferry.

In Volume 2, we have written a new chapter on World War I soldiers' diaries and we have completely revised the post-1945 section. Chapter 10 uses transcripts of the presidential recordings from the Cuban Missile Crisis to underscore Cold War tensions; in Chapter 13, student protest manifestos provide a window into the tumult of the 1960s; and the chapter on the Reagan-Gorbachev era uses political cartoons as a fun and creative way to examine cracks in the Cold War order—they combine presentations of Ronald Reagan that range from lovable leader to foolish ideologue. At the end of the semester, when everyone is feeling a bit weary, we hope the editorial cartoons will provide a welcome stimulus to class discussion.

We have also increased our emphasis on helping students understand why each type of document works well for each topic under examination. The sections explaining the advantages and disadvantages of a particular source prompt students to think about what types of sources might best suit their own research and help them become more critical consumers of all types of information—skills that are important not just for budding historians, but for all productive citizens.

To make it easier for students to navigate each chapter, we have streamlined the reader's prose and heading structure. In addition, we added a new subsection, "Questions to Ask," which comes at the end of each "Using the Source" section to summarize key issues in bulleted points for students just before they delve into the source material. The Source Analysis Tables have also been redesigned and expanded to provide more room for note-taking.

A new appendix on avoiding plagiarism augments the popular "Documenting the Source" appendix, which shows students how to document the sources included in these volumes according to the *Chicago Manual of Style*.

The second edition of *Going to the Source* also features a supporting Web site where students or instructors can download the Source Analysis Tables for each chapter to complete electronically and email back to their instructor. Students will also find links to Web-based resources mentioned in the chapters, additional links, and related research and documentation aids. Instructors who wish to arrange homework or research assignments around the book's chapters will find these tools especially useful for integrating their students' use of *Going to the Source* with the rest of their coursework.

ACKNOWLEDGMENTS

We would like to thank the following reviewers who guided us in our revisions with their suggestions and comments: Jonathan Bass, Samford University; Steven Boyd, University of Texas at San Antonio; Rowland Brucken, Norwich University; Marius Carriere, Christian Brothers University; Paul Clemens, Rutgers University; Kendrick Clements, University of South Carolina; Elizabeth Crosman, University of Delaware; Douglas Cupples, University of Memphis; Suzanne DeLuca, Northern Kentucky University; Darren Dochuk, Purdue University; Douglas Dodd, California State University, Bakersfield; Vicki Eaklor, Alfred University; Van Forsyth, Clark College; George Geib, Butler University; Terrell Goddard, Northwest Vista College; Larry Dana Goodrich, Northwest Vista College; Joseph Hawes, University of Memphis; Dwight Henderson, University of Texas at San Antonio; Kurt Hohenstein, Hampden-Sydney College; John Johnson, University of Northern Iowa; Carol Keller, San Antonio College; Kevin Kern, University of Akron; Daniel Kotzin, Kutztown University; Jessica Kross, University of South Carolina; David Krugler, University of Wisconsin–Platteville; Michelle Kuhl, University of Wisconsin–Oshkosh; Janice

Leone, Middle Tennessee State University; Sheila McIntyre, The State University of New York at Potsdam; John Mack, Labette Community College; Gordon Marshall, Brock University; Lawrence Mastroni, University of Oklahoma; Eric Morser, University of New Mexico; Earl Mulderink, Southern Utah University; James O'Donnell, Marietta College; Ami Pflugrad-Jackisch, University at Buffalo; Richard Pointer, Westmont College; Louis Potts, University of Missouri–Kansas City; Caroline Pruden, North Carolina State University; Sandra Pryor, University of Delaware; Yasmin Rahman, University of Colorado at Boulder; Sonya Ramsey, University of Texas Arlington; Roger Robins, Marymount College; Thomas Rust, Montana State University Billings; Brett Schmoll, California State University, Bakersfield; Jeff Seiken, Ohio State University; Ashley Sousa, West Valley College; Joan Supplee, Baylor University; Paul Sutter, University of Georgia; Sean Taylor, Minnesota State University Moorhead; Melissa Teed, Saginaw Valley State University; Vincent Vinikas, University of Arkansas at Little Rock; John Gregory Whitesides, University of Colorado; Cynthia Van Zandt, University of New Hampshire; and four reviewers who chose to remain anonymous.

We extend our thanks to the editorial staff at Bedford/St. Martin's: Joan E. Feinberg, president; Mary Dougherty, publisher for history; Jane Knetzger, director of development for history; Sara Wise, our appropriately named editor for this edition; Marissa Zanetti, our deft editorial assistant; and Bridget Leahy, our efficient production editor. We continue to thank Laura Arcari, our developmental editor on the first edition; Heidi Hood, the developmental editor who guided the plan for the second edition; our copyeditor, Linda McLatchie, and the book's designer, Clare Seng-Neimoeller. A very special thanks also to Katherine Kurzman, our original sponsoring editor. This book never would have happened without her impetus and the sponsorship of Charles H. Christensen, former president of Bedford Books.

We were greatly aided in our endeavors by the librarians at Gettysburg College, including Chris Amadure, Karen Drickamer, Linda Isenberger, and Susan Roach, as well as the Government Documents librarians at the University of Iowa, Marianne Mason and John Elson, and the staff in the archives section of the Minnesota Historical Society. Staff assistance from Carla Pavlick, Rebecca Barth, and Linda Ludwig is gratefully acknowledged, as is the advice we received from colleagues who answered questions and read drafts of chapters. We are particularly grateful to Gabor Boritt, Joe Coohill, Brendan Cushing-Daniels, William Farr, Keith Fitzgerald, Matt Gallman, Jim Jacobs, Mary Lou Locke, Gerald Markowitz, Barbara Sommer, Mark Weitz, and Robert Wright. The assistance of students and former students was invaluable in this project, and we owe much to Maggie Campbell, Katie Mears, Amy Scott, Jason Stohler, Matthew Raw, and Lauren Rocco.

Finally, of course, we owe thanks to our families, who encouraged us throughout this process and regularly offered much-needed relaxation from our labors. Thanks to Jim, Colleen, Caroline, Daniel, and both of our Elizabeths.

Victoria Bissell Brown
Timothy J. Shannon

About the Editors

Victoria Bissell Brown is the L.F. Parker Professor of History at Grinnell College, where she teaches Modern U.S. History, U.S. Women's History, and U.S. Immigration History. She is the author of *The Education of Jane Addams* (2003) and the editor of the Bedford/St. Martin's edition of Jane Addams's *Twenty Years at Hull-House* (1999). Her articles have appeared in *Feminist Studies*, *The Journal of Women's History*, and *The Journal of the Illinois State Historical Society*. She has served as a Book Review Editor for *The Journal of the Gilded Age and Progressive Era* and for the Women and Social Movements website.

Timothy J. Shannon is an associate professor at Gettysburg College, where he teaches Early American and Native American History. His other books include *Atlantic Lives: A Comparative Approach to Early America* (2004) and *Indians and Colonists at the Crossroads of Empire: The Albany Congress of 1754* (2000), which received the Dixon Ryan Fox Prize from the New York State Historical Association and the Distinguished Book Award from the Society of Colonial Wars. His articles have appeared in the *William and Mary Quarterly*, *Ethnohistory*, and the *New England Quarterly*, and he has been a research fellow at the Huntington Library and John Carter Brown Library.

Contents

<table>
<tr><td>

3

</td><td>

**Reading the 1894 Pullman Strike:
Chicago's Daily Papers Report
the News   54**

</td><td>

</td></tr>
</table>

| 8 | **Painting a New Deal: U.S. Post Office Murals from the Great Depression   173** |

CHAPTER 1

Political Terrorism during Reconstruction

Congressional Hearings and Reports on the Ku Klux Klan

E lias Thomson was an old man in 1871. Born a slave in Spartanburg County, South Carolina, he had lived his entire life on the plantation of Dr. and Mrs. Vernon. When he gained his freedom in 1865, he continued to live there, farming land he rented from his former masters. Thomson's daily life after the war must have gone on much the same as it did before, but freedom did bring some opportunities he was anxious to seize, even at his advanced age. In particular, the ratification of the Fifteenth Amendment in March 1870 guaranteed him the right to vote. Thomson exercised that right in the fall of 1870, casting his ballot in the state and congressional elections for the Republican ticket.

Late one night the following May, a group of men disguised in hoods appeared on his doorstep. They dragged him from his home and told him to start praying, for "your time is short." When Thomson refused, they pointed pistols at his head and asked him, "Who did you vote for?" Thomson responded that he had voted for Claudius Turner, a neighbor whom he held in high esteem. The disguised men told him he had made the wrong choice and whipped him. They told Thomson to remain silent about what had happened and left him with a final warning: "We will have this country right before we get through."

Elias Thomson was one of many Southern men and women to suffer at the hands of the Ku Klux Klan between 1867 and 1871. In fact, his home in Spartanburg, South Carolina, was at the center of one of the most violent and prolonged outbreaks of Klan activity during Reconstruction. The Klan had first appeared there in 1868, using intimidation, arson, whippings, sexual assault, and murder to keep potential Republican voters away from the polls in that year's election. Despite such efforts, the state government remained in the hands of the Republicans, and the Klan temporarily receded as a public threat.

Klan violence rose again, however, with the next election in 1870 and became more intense as white and black Republicans tried to mobilize the vote. In addition to intimidation and physical assaults on potential black voters, Klansmen burned black churches, schools, and homes and murdered black men who had enrolled in the state militia. In several counties of the Carolina up-country, the inland piedmont region, where white and black populations were roughly equal or whites held a slight majority, the Klan conducted these crimes without fear of prosecution. Local sheriffs failed to make arrests, and if they did, white juries refused to render guilty verdicts. In some up-country counties, such as Spartanburg, state Republican officials estimated that practically all of the white adult male population belonged to the Klan or sympathized with it.

The Ku Klux Klan was of very recent origins in 1871 but had spread quickly throughout the former Confederate states. It was founded in 1867 by a group of Confederate veterans in Pulaski, Tennessee, who initially intended for it to be nothing more than a social club, similar in purpose and organization to the Freemasons and other secret fraternal orders popular with American males in the nineteenth century. Like the Freemasons, early Klan members created their own ritual, costume, and hierarchy from a mishmash of precedents in ancient mythology: the name "Ku Klux" was derived from the Greek word *kuklos*, meaning circle, and one of the titles in the organization was "Grand Cyclops," after the Greek mythological figure. As the Klan spread, however, it acquired a different purpose. In Tennessee and the Carolinas in 1868, local "dens" of the Klan began acting as vigilantes, calling themselves "regulators" or "night riders" who enforced law and order according to local custom rather than the dictates of the postwar state governments created by Congress and the Republican Party. Never a centralized organization to begin with, local Klansmen operated autonomously and rarely cooperated with one another beyond the county level. Regardless of that fragmentation, the primary targets of their terrorism remained the same: any blacks who challenged white supremacy by daring to vote, teach, or acquire land, and "carpetbaggers," white Northerners who came to the South after the war to seek their fortunes or to assume office in the Reconstruction state governments.

The violence and intimidation the Klan visited upon freedmen and -women and white Republicans seriously challenged the federal government's plans for the postwar South. After passing the Civil Rights Act of 1866, congressional Republicans had pegged their hopes for Reconstruction on enfranchising the former slaves as full and equal U.S. citizens. In this manner, the freedmen would become a core constituency for the Republican Party in the South and prevent the defeated Confederates from reassuming control of government and society there. The ratification of the Fourteenth Amendment in 1868 made this plan part of the Constitution by granting the freedmen and -women U.S. citizenship and guaranteeing them equal protection under the law. When some Southern states failed to extend their franchise to the freedmen, Republicans in Congress responded with the Fifteenth Amendment, which prohibited states from denying the right to vote to any citizen because of "race, color, or previous condition of servitude."

Republicans had great success in passing their legislative agenda for Reconstruction in Washington, D.C., but the enforcement of those laws in the South

Figure 1.1 Racial Violence in the Reconstruction South *The political cartoonist Thomas Nast condemns the Ku Klux Klan and other perpetrators of racial violence in this illustration from the magazine* Harper's Weekly. *At the center, a black couple kneeling under the words "Worse Than Slavery" cradles their dead child, while a schoolhouse burns and a lynched figure hangs in the background. A hooded Klansman and "White League" supporter clasp hands over their work. The federal government intervened by passing the Ku Klux Klan Act and launching a congressional investigation of racial violence in the South. Source:* Library of Cogress.

remained very much in question. The 20,000 federal troops stationed in the South in 1867 were not nearly enough to pacify regions such as the Carolina up-country, where the Klan was at its greatest strength. Furthermore, military officers were reluctant to assume control over matters of law enforcement without specific requests from civilian authorities to do so, lest they alienate the defeated Southern white population even further. As news of the Klan's expansion and pervasive influence in the South made its way to the nation's capital, Republican leaders agreed that further legislation to counteract it was necessary.

In a special message to Congress in December 1870, President Ulysses S. Grant noted that the Klan and similar organizations were using violence to prevent citizens from voting in the Southern states. Acting on a request he had received from the governor of North Carolina for assistance, he asked Congress to investigate the matter. Congress formed a committee to review affairs in North Carolina, and then in April 1871, it created another, much larger committee to expand the investigation into other states. This group, titled the Joint Select Committee to Inquire into the Condition of Affairs in the Late Insurrectionary States, was composed of seven senators and fourteen representatives, thirteen of whom were Republicans and eight of whom were Democrats.

At approximately the same time that it formed the Joint Select Committee to investigate the Klan, Congress also passed the Ku Klux Klan Act. This law gave the president the power to use federal troops and courts to protect the lives, property, and rights of U.S. citizens in the South. For the first time, crimes committed by private persons against other citizens became eligible for prosecution under federal rather than state law. Provisions included in the Ku Klux Klan Act effectively gave the president the ability to declare martial law in any state or region he deemed under Klan influence. The most controversial of these provisions concerned suspension of the writ of habeas corpus, a cornerstone of American civil liberties. The writ of habeas corpus protects citizens from unlawful imprisonment by requiring that any person placed under arrest be charged with a specific crime and placed on trial. By allowing the president to suspend it, Congress made it possible for suspected Klansmen to be jailed indefinitely. Many congressmen, even some Republicans, questioned the constitutionality of this provision and of the Ku Klux Klan Act in general, but the majority who supported the law believed the Klan could not be defeated without such a powerful weapon.

Congressmen formulated and debated this legislation in Washington while freedmen and -women in the South confronted the Klan face to face. Casting a ballot or even expressing an interest in voting could put a former slave's life in jeopardy. Those who joined militias, held office, or tried to improve their economic circumstances faced similar reprisals, while the promise of assistance from Washington must have seemed far off indeed. In 1871, a showdown was brewing between the Ku Klux Klan and the federal government that placed people like Elias Thomson squarely in the middle of the battle to determine Reconstruction's fate in the postwar South.

Using the Source: Congressional Hearings and Reports

The Joint Select Committee undertook one of the most far-reaching congressional investigations ever conducted up to that time. During the summer and fall of 1871, it heard testimony from witnesses in Washington, D.C., and sent subcommittees to interview witnesses throughout the South. Most of its work was concentrated on North Carolina and South Carolina, where the activities and impact of the Klan were reported to be most severe, but committee members also visited Alabama, Florida, Georgia, Mississippi, and Tennessee, compiling a record of testimony that numbered in the thousands of pages. In February 1872, the Joint Select Committee submitted this testimony and its reports to Congress. The majority report, signed by every Republican on the committee, endorsed the Ku Klux Klan Act of 1871 and recommended continuing the president's powers to combat the Klan through the use of federal troops, courts, and suspension of the writ of habeas corpus. The minority report, signed by every Democrat on the committee, did not deny the existence of Klan-related violence but blamed it on misguided federal Reconstruction policy, which had left the Southern states in the hands of carpetbaggers and former slaves.

What Can Congressional Hearings and Reports Tell Us?

Since its publication in 1872, historians have found the thirteen volumes of the Joint Select Committee's report a remarkably detailed and comprehensive source for studying Reconstruction in the South. One of its chief advantages as a source is its sheer size. The committee conducted its work thoroughly, and the hundreds of witnesses who testified before it represented a broad spectrum of Southern society: white and black, rich and poor, male and female, Republican and Democrat. One historian has called their testimony "the richest single source" for understanding Southern society during the Reconstruction era. In the case of freedmen and -women, testimony before the committee provides invaluable first-person narratives of what the transition from bondage to freedom was like.

Another advantage of working with this source has to do with the methods by which the Joint Select Committee collected its evidence. Its procedures resembled legal hearings: oaths were administered to witnesses, and witnesses were subjected to cross-examination, all in meetings open to the public. No witnesses appeared anonymously or gave secret testimony. While those procedures may have prevented many from testifying for fear of reprisals, they nevertheless lent an air of authenticity to the witnesses' descriptions of the Klan that was not necessarily accorded to rumors or sensationalistic stories reported in the press. The Klan conducted its terrorism under cover of night and in disguise. By its very nature, it did not submit willingly to public scrutiny. For the most part, however, the witnesses who appeared before the committee in Southern towns and counties were eyewitnesses to the Klan's activities, making their testimony the most complete and reliable account of this secret organization's operations during Reconstruction.

The disadvantages associated with using the Joint Select Committee's report stem mostly from its inherent political biases. The Republicans who dominated the Joint Select Committee by a two-to-one margin were most interested in finding evidence that the Klan was a conspiratorial organization bent on depriving black and white Republicans of their civil and political liberties. Such evidence could be used to justify imposing martial law in those regions affected by the Klan. Democrats accused the Republicans of using the committee to drum up stories of Klan brutality and lawlessness that could be publicized to Republican advantage in the upcoming election of 1872. While the Democrats on the committee could not deny the violence of the Klan, they used their questioning of witnesses to cast doubt on its political motives, depicting Klansmen instead as isolated, ill-advised characters pushed to extremes by desperation and offended honor. It is important to remember that Congress had already passed the Ku Klux Klan Act when the Joint Select Committee conducted its work. Given that the committee's majority was made up of the same Republicans who had passed that piece of legislation, how likely was it that the committee's findings would challenge its enforcement? By passing the Ku Klux Klan Act *before* its investigation of the Klan, Congress clearly anticipated the outcome of the Joint Select Committee's work.

As you read the testimony, you will quickly realize that neither the Republicans nor the Democrats on the Joint Select Committee resembled neutral fact finders. Each side brought an agenda to the proceedings that influenced the nature of the testimony before the committee. Consider, for example, these excerpts from the testimony of D. H. Chamberlain, the Republican attorney general of South Carolina, given before the committee in Washington, D.C., on June 10, 1871. A good historian quickly learns to read between the lines of such evidence, looking carefully at the questions as well as the answers to determine what biases and ulterior motives shaped the construction of this source.

An oath to tell the truth similar to that given in a court of law	D. H. Chamberlain, sworn and examined.
	By the Chairman:
Republican senator John Scott of Pennsylvania chaired the committee and typically initiated the questioning	*Question:* How long have you been a resident of the State?
	Answer: I have been a resident there since December, 1865.
	Question: Please go on and state to the committee the knowledge you have acquired, from your official position, as to the efficiency with which the laws are executed throughout the State of South Carolina, and the protection afforded to life and property in the State. Make your statement in general terms.
	Answer: The enforcement of the law has, from time to time, been very much interrupted and disturbed from special causes; lately by what are popularly known as Ku-Klux operations. . . .

Invites Chamberlain to speak freely about law enforcement

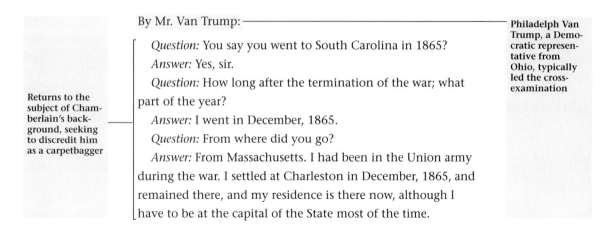

By Mr. Van Trump: ——————————————————————

Philadelph Van Trump, a Democratic representative from Ohio, typically led the cross-examination

Returns to the subject of Chamberlain's background, seeking to discredit him as a carpetbagger

> *Question:* You say you went to South Carolina in 1865?
>
> *Answer:* Yes, sir.
>
> *Question:* How long after the termination of the war; what part of the year?
>
> *Answer:* I went in December, 1865.
>
> *Question:* From where did you go?
>
> *Answer:* From Massachusetts. I had been in the Union army during the war. I settled at Charleston in December, 1865, and remained there, and my residence is there now, although I have to be at the capital of the State most of the time.

One other disadvantage to bear in mind about the Joint Select Committee's report is that while the committee's hearings had the appearance of legal proceedings, they did not work with the same standards of evidence as a court of law. In particular, the Republican majority of the committee was willing to accept hearsay, what someone had heard but not personally witnessed, as evidence. Democrats on the committee objected mightily to this, likening it to accepting rumors and gossip as facts. They equated the two-dollars-a-day allowance the committee paid to witnesses with bribery and accused the local Republican officials of coaching witnesses as well. In the thousands of pages of testimony in the Joint Select Committee's report, some witnesses do appear more reliable than others.

Questions to Ask

Several questions should immediately come to mind as you read the testimony provided to the Joint Select Committee. First, who were the witnesses? Where did they come from, and why were they testifying? Second, what information did the witnesses provide about the Klan's purposes and operations? Third, how reliable was that information? Was their testimony based on firsthand experience, personal opinion, or hearsay and rumor? After analyzing the testimony, you can then try to determine what influence it had on the Joint Select Committee's recommendations to Congress.

- Who were the people testifying before the Joint Select Committee?
- What did they say about the Klan's motives and operations?
- How reliable was their testimony?
- How did the committee use their testimony?

Source Analysis Table

Source	Personal Information	Description of the Klan's Activities and Motives	Reliability of Evidence Provided
WITNESS TESTIMONY			
1. Samuel T. Poinier			
2. D. H. Chamberlain			
3. Elias Thomson			
4. Lucy McMillan			
5. Mervin Givens			

Source	Description of the Klan	Assessment of Federal Response to the Klan
COMMITTEE REPORTS		
6. Majority Report		
7. Minority Report		

To download and print this table, visit the book companion site at **bedfordstmartins.com/brownshannon**.

The Source: Testimony and Reports from the Joint Select Committee to Inquire into the Condition of Affairs in the Late Insurrectionary States

All of the testimony that follows is taken from the Joint Select Committee's investigation of the Ku Klux Klan in South Carolina. Sources 1 and 2 come from testimony heard in Washington, D.C., while Sources 3, 4, and 5 are from testimony heard in Spartanburg, South Carolina. Sources 6 and 7 are excerpts from the committee's majority and minority reports, which were completed after the investigation was over.

1 *Testimony of Samuel T. Poinier,* Washington, D.C., June 7, 1871

Poinier was a Republican newspaper editor and a federal tax collector in South Carolina at the time of his testimony.

Samuel T. Poinier sworn and examined.

By the Chairman:[1]

Question: Please state in what part of South Carolina you reside.

Answer: In Spartanburg County, the most northern county in the State.

Question: How long have you resided there?

Answer: Since February, 1866; a little over five years.

Question: From what part of the United States did you go to South Carolina?

Answer: I went there from Louisville, Kentucky. . . . I went there in 1866 with no intention whatever of remaining. I went entirely for social reasons, to marry, and I was persuaded to stay there. My wife was a native of Charleston, and I found her up in Spartanburg after the war, where a large number of Charleston people went during the bombardment of the city. . . .

Question: Were you in the Union Army?

Answer: Yes, sir: I went out from Kentucky.

Question: Proceed with your statement.

[1] Republican senator John Scott from Pennsylvania.

Source: United States Congress, *Report of the Joint Select Committee to Inquire into the Condition of Affairs in the Late Insurrectionary States,* vol. 2, *South Carolina, Part I* (Washington, D.C.: Government Printing Office, 1872), 25–28, 33–34.

Answer: Just before our last campaign,[2] it was May a year ago, I . . . identi-fied myself publicly with the republican party. I made my paper a republican paper. I did everything I could in the last State election for the reelection of Governor Scott[3] and our other State officers. From that time I have been in very deep water. . . . I was ordered away last fall, immediately after our last election, in November. It was soon after the first appearance of this Ku-Klux organiza-tion, or whatever it is. Soon after these outrages occurred in our county I re-ceived a note ordering me away from there, stating that I must leave the county; that all the soldiers of the United States Army could not enable me to live in Spartanburg. . . . Two days prior to our election, a party of disguised men went, at night, and took out two white men and three negroes, one of them a colored woman, and whipped them most brutally. Two of them were managers of the box[4] at that election; and the men told them that if they dared to hold an election at that box they would return and kill them. That was the first ap-pearance of any trouble in the State. . . .

Question: Were those people of whom you spoke in disguise?

Answer: They were all in disguise. One of the colored men who were whipped swore positively as to the identity of some of them, and the parties were arrested, but nothing could ever be done with them; they proved an *alibi*, and some of them have since gone to Texas. . . .

Question: Go on and state any similar occurrences in that county since that time. . . .

Answer: Since that time outrages of that nature have occurred every week. Parties of disguised men have ridden through the county almost nightly. They go to a colored man's house, take him out and whip him. They tell him that he must not give any information that he has been whipped. They tell him, more-over, that he must make a public renunciation of his republican principles or they will return and kill him. . . .

Question: Do the facts that have transpired and the manner in which they have occurred satisfy you of the existence of the organization in that portion of South Carolina?

Answer: Yes, sir; I have no doubt of it in the world. I have received anony-mous communications signed by the order of "K.K.K.," directing me to leave the county, stating that I could not live there; that I was a carpet-bagger. But personally I have never met with any trouble.

By Mr. Van Trump:[5]

Question: You have a connection with the partisan press there?

Answer: Yes, sir. I am editing a republican paper.

Question: Do you advocate the cause of the negro in your paper?

[2] The election of 1870.

[3] Robert K. Scott was the Republican governor of South Carolina.

[4] Ballot box.

[5] Democratic representative Philadelph Van Trump from Ohio.

Answer: Not the negro especially. I advocate the general principles of republicanism.

Question: You support the whole republican doctrine in your paper?

Answer: So far as general principles go, I do. I do not approve or uphold the State government in many of its acts; but, so far as the general principles of republicanism are concerned, I uphold it very strongly. I advocate the right of the colored people to vote and to exercise their civil and political privileges. . . .

Question: These men who assert that their object is to put down the negro and get possession of the Government are prominent men, are they not?

Answer: Yes, sir.

Question: Can you name a single man?

Answer: Well, I cannot name anybody specially who has made such a remark, but I hear it in the hotels.

Question: Have you yourself heard them make the remark?

Answer: I have heard the remark made; it is a common thing.

Question: Is it not rather an uncommon remark?

Answer: It is not, there.

Question: You cannot recollect the name of a single person who has made that declaration?

Answer: No sir, I cannot recall any now.

2   *Testimony of D. H. Chamberlain,* Washington, D.C., June 10, 1871

Chamberlain was a Republican and the attorney general of South Carolina.

D. H. Chamberlain, sworn and examined.

By the Chairman:

Question: How long have you been a resident of the State?

Answer: I have been a resident there since December, 1865.

Question: Please go on and state to the committee the knowledge you have acquired, from your official position, as to the efficiency with which the laws are executed throughout the State of South Carolina, and the protection afforded to life and property in the State. Make your statement in general terms.

Answer: The enforcement of the law has, from time to time, been very much interrupted and disturbed from special causes; lately by what are popularly known as Ku-Klux operations. There have been a great many outrages committed, and a great many homicides, and a great many whippings. I speak

Source: *Report of the Joint Select Committee,* vol. 2, *South Carolina, Part I,* 48–51.

now, of course, of what I have heard; I have never seen any outrages committed myself; I am simply stating what I believe to be fact. . . .

Question: In what part of the State are these offenses committed which you attribute to the influence of this organization?

Answer: Notably in Spartanburg, Newberry, Union, and York Counties; those are the principal counties that have been the scenes of these disturbances. But they have extended into Laurens, Chester, and Lancaster Counties.[1] . . .

Question: Have there been any convictions for these offenses in the State, so far as your information goes; offenses committed by these organized bands?

Answer: No sir, no convictions, and no arrests, except in the case of this wounded Ku-Klux.[2] . . .

By Mr. Van Trump:

Question: You say you went to South Carolina in 1865?
Answer: Yes, sir.
Question: How long after the termination of the war; what part of the year?
Answer: I went in December, 1865.
Question: From where did you go?
Answer: From Massachusetts. I had been in the Union army during the war. I settled at Charleston in December, 1865, and remained there, and my residence is there now, although I have to be at the capital of the State most of the time.

By Mr. Stevenson:[3]

Question: When did it first come to your knowledge that this organization existed in the State of South Carolina?

Answer: It would be difficult to say. My conviction that there is such an organization has grown up very gradually. . . . I cannot fix the date exactly.

Question: Had you any knowledge of the fact that there were acts of violence and disorders in that State about the time of the election in 1868?

Answer: Yes, sir.

Question: Had you any information of the sending of arms at that time into that State?

Answer: O, I remember that a great many arms were purchased by private individuals, if you refer to that. I know that at the time, during the canvass,[4] there was considerable excitement when it was understood that the democrats,

---

[1] All seven of these counties were in the piedmont, or up-country, region of South Carolina, where the black and white populations were roughly equal.

[2] Chamberlain is referring to a Klansman wounded during a raid on the Newberry County Courthouse. He was jailed and then released on bail and subsequently either died while in the care of a friend or was spirited away by friends to avoid prosecution.

[3] Republican representative Job Stevenson from Ohio.

[4] Campaigning for votes.

as we call them, were arming themselves with Winchester and Henry rifles, or something of the kind.

Question: Repeating rifles?

Answer: Yes, sir. . . .

By Mr. Blair:[5]

Question: Did you have any actual knowledge of the fact that the democrats were then arming?

Answer: No, sir.

Question: Then you make this statement as a rumor merely?

Answer: Well, yes, sir; I should use, perhaps, a little stronger term than rumor. I had heard it so often that it came to be a belief with me, but it was hearsay. . . .

Question: Was it a common report that those arms all went into the hands of democrats?

Answer: As I heard it, it was understood that those arms were imported into the State upon order of individuals. I do not know but a republican might have had his order filled, but the belief was that they were generally ordered by democrats.

By Mr. Stevenson:

Question: You have no knowledge of any general arming among the republicans at that time?

Answer: No, sir.

Question: You were a republican, then, were you not?

Answer: Yes, sir.

By Mr. Blair:

Question: Did not the republicans have arms?

Answer: O, yes.

By Mr. Van Trump:

Question: Did not the negroes have arms?

Answer: Yes, sir; it is very common for people to have their shot-guns, to have some kind of arms. I suppose that in this instance people thought that there was an unusually large number brought in at a particular time, and that they were not for sporting purposes. They were repeating rifles.

Question: Have you been a politician for any part of your life?

Answer: No, sir; I do not think I have ever been a politician.

Question: Have you never heard a thousand rumors during an election that had no foundation in fact?

Answer: Yes, sir; many of them.

Question: Got up for excitement merely?

Answer: Yes, sir.

---

[5] Democratic senator Frank Blair from Missouri.

3   *Testimony of Elias Thomson,*
Spartanburg, South Carolina, July 7, 1871

Elias Thomson (colored) sworn and examined.

By the Chairman:

> *Question:* Where do you live?
> *Answer:* Up on Tiger River, on Mrs. Vernon's plantation.[1]
> *Question:* What do you follow?
> *Answer:* Farming.
> *Question:* Do you live on rented land?
> *Answer:* Yes, sir.
> *Question:* How much have you rented?
> *Answer:* I think about fifty acres.
> *Question:* How long have you been living there?
> *Answer:* Ever since the surrender; I never left home.
> *Question:* Have you ever been disturbed any up there?
> *Answer:* Yes, sir.
> *Question:* How?
> *Answer:* There came a parcel of gentlemen to my house one night—or men. They went up to the door and ran against it. My wife was sick. I was lying on a pallet, with my feet to the door. They ran against it and hallooed to me, "Open the door, quick, quick, quick." I threw the door open immediately, right wide open. Two little children were lying with me. I said, "Come in gentlemen." One of them says, "Do we look like gentlemen?" I says, "You look like men of some description; walk in." One says, "Come out here; are you ready to die?" I told him I was not prepared to die. "Well," said he, "Your time is short; commence praying." I told him I was not a praying man much, and hardly ever prayed; only a very few times; never did pray much. He says, "You ought to pray; your time is short, and now commence to pray." I told him I was not a praying man. One of them held a pistol to my head and said, "Get down and pray." I was on the steps, with one foot on the ground. They led me off to a pine tree. There was three or four of them behind me, it appeared, and one on each side, and one in front. The gentleman who questioned me was the only one I could see. All the time I could not see the others. Every time I could get a look around, they would touch me on the side of the head with a pistol, so I had to keep my head square in front. The next question was, "Who did you vote for?" I told him I voted for Mr. Turner—Claudius Turner, a gentleman in the neighborhood. They said, "What did you vote for him for?" I said, "I thought a good deal of him; he was my neighbor." I told them I disremembered who was on the ticket besides, but they had several, and I voted the ticket. "What did you do that for?" they said. Says I, "because I thought it was right."

---

[1] The Vernons were Thomson's former masters.

Source: Report of the Joint Select Committee, vol. 2, *South Carolina, Part I*, 410–15.

They said, "You thought it was right? It was right wrong." I said, "I never do anything hardly if I think it is wrong; if it was wrong, I did not know it. That was my opinion at the time and I thought every man ought to vote according to his notions." He said, "If you had taken the advice of your friends you would have been better off." I told him I had. Says I, "You may be a friend to me, but I can't tell who you are." Says he, "Can't you recognize anybody here?" I told him I could not. "In the condition you are in now, I can't tell who you are." One of them had a very large set of teeth; I suppose they were three-quarters of an inch long; they came right straight down. He came up to me and sort of nodded. He had on speckled horns and calico stuff, and had a face on. He said, "Have you got a chisel here I could get?" I told him I hadn't, but I reckoned I could knock one out, and I sort of laughed. He said, "What in hell are you laughing at? It is no laughing time." I told him it sort of tickled me, and I thought I would laugh. I did not say anything then for a good while. "Old man," says one, "have you got a rope here, or a plow-line, or something of the sort?" I told him, "Yes; I had one hanging on the crib." He said, "Let us have it." One of them says, "String him up to this pine tree, and we will get all out of him. Get up, one of you, and let us pull him up, and he will tell the truth." I says, "I can't tell you anything more than I have told. There is nothing that I can tell you but what I have told you and you have asked me." One man questioned me all this time. One would come up and say, "Let's hang him a while, and he will tell us the truth"; and another then came up and said, "Old man, we are just from hell; some of us have been dead ever since the revolutionary war." . . . I was not scared, and said, "You have been through a right smart experience." "Yes," he says, "we have been through a considerable experience." One of them says, "we have just come from hell." I said, "If I had been there, I would not want to go back." . . . Then they hit me thirteen of the hardest cuts I ever got. I never had such cuts. They hit me right around my waist and by my hip, and cut a piece about as wide as my two fingers in one place. I did not say a word while they were whipping, only sort of grunted a little. As quick as they got through they said, "Go to your bed. We will have this country right before we get through; go to your bed," and they started away. . . .

Question: Who is Claudius Turner?

Answer: He is a gentleman that run for the legislature here. He was on the ticket with Mr. Scott.

Question: The republican ticket?

Answer: Yes, sir; the radical[2] ticket. . . .

By Mr. Van Trump:

Question: Explain to me, if you can, if the object of this Ku-Klux organization is to intimidate the colored people, why they were so particular as to make you promise, under penalty of death, that you would never disclose the fact that you had been visited; do you understand why that is?

---

[2] Radical Republicans were known for their support of black suffrage and the disenfranchisement of former Confederate military and civilian officers.

Answer: I can explain this fact this far: You know when they said to me to not say anything about this matter, I asked them what I must say, and when I asked, "What must I say? I will have to say something," they said, "What are you going to say?" I said, "What must I say?" He said, "Are you going to tell it?" I told them, "I have to say something, of course, and what must I say; what can I say?" Then they said, looking straight at me—

Question: Why is it that so often in giving your testimony you have to get up and make gesticulations like an orator? Have you been an orator?

Answer: No, sir, but I was showing the way they did me, and what they said to me. They said, "You just let me hear of this thing again, and we will not leave a piece of you when we come back."

Question: To whom have you talked lately about this case, or consulted here in town?

Answer: I have not consulted much about it.

Question: How long have you been waiting to be examined?

Answer: Since Tuesday about 10 o'clock.

Question: Have any white republicans been to see you?

Answer: No, sir; nobody at all.

Question: Did you see them?

Answer: I don't know who the republicans are here. I may have seen some.

Question: Do you pretend to say that since Tuesday you have not talked with any white about your case?

Answer: With none about the Ku-Klux matter.

4   *Testimony of Lucy McMillan,*
Spartanburg, South Carolina, July 10, 1871

Lucy McMillan (colored) sworn and examined.

By the Chairman:

Question: Where do you live?

Answer: Up in the country. I live on McMillan's place, right at the foot of the road.

Question: How far is it?

Answer: Twelve miles.

Question: Are you married?

Answer: I am not married. I am single now. I was married. My husband was taken away from me and carried off twelve years ago.

Question: He was carried off before the war?

Answer: Yes, sir; the year before the war; twelve years ago this November coming.

Source: Report of the Joint Select Committee, vol. 3, *South Carolina, Part 2,* 604–7.

Question: How old are you now?

Answer: I am called forty-six. I am forty-five or -six.

Question: Did the Ku-Klux come where you live at any time?

Answer: They came there once before they burned my house down. The way it happened was this: John Hunter's wife came to my house on Saturday morning, and told they were going to whip me. I was afraid of them; there was so much talk of Ku-Klux drowning people, and whipping people, and killing them. My house was only a little piece from the river, so I laid out at night in the woods. The Sunday evening after Isham McCrary[1] was whipped I went up, and a white man, John McMillan, came along and says to me, "Lucy, you had better stay at home, for they will whip you anyhow." I said if they have to, they might whip me in the woods, for I am afraid to stay there. Monday night they came in and burned my house down; I dodged out alongside of the road not far off and saw them. I was sitting right not far off, and as they came along the river I knew some of them. I knew John McMillan, and Kennedy McMillan, and Billy Bush, and John Hunter. They were all together. I was not far off, and I saw them. They went right on to my house. When they passed me I run further up on the hill to get out of the way of them. They went there and knocked down and beat my house a right smart while. And then they all got still, and directly I saw the fire rise.

Question: How many of these men were there?

Answer: A good many; I couldn't tell how many, but these I knew. The others I didn't. . . .

Question: What was the reason given for burning your house?

Answer: There was speaking down there last year and I came to it. They all kept at me to go. I went home and they quizzed me to hear what was said, and I told them as far as my senses allowed me.

Question: Where was this speaking?

Answer: Here in this town. I went on and told them, and then they all said I was making laws; or going to have the land, and the Ku-Klux were going to beat me for bragging that I would have land. John Hunter told them on me, I suppose, that I said I was going to have land. . . .

Question: Was that the only reason you know for your house being burned?

Answer: That is all the reason. All the Ku-Klux said all that they had against me was that I was bragging and boasting that I wanted the land. . . .

By Mr. Van Trump:

Question: Do you mean to say that they said they burned the house for that reason?

Answer: No sir; they burned the house because they could not catch me. I don't know any other reason. . . .

Question: Who was John Hunter?

Answer: He is a colored man. I worked for him all last summer. I worked with him hoeing his cotton and corn.

---

[1] Another freedman who testified before the committee in Spartanburg.

Question: What was he doing with these Ku-Klux?

Answer: I don't know. He was with them. . . .

Question: How did you come to be named Lucy McMillan?

Answer: I was a slave of Robert McMillan. I always belonged to him.

Question: You helped raise Kennedy and John?[2]

Answer: Not John, but Kennedy I did. When he was a little boy I was with him.

Question: Did he always like you?

Answer: Yes, sir. They always pretended to like us.

Question: That is while you were a slave?

Answer: Yes, sir, while I was a slave, but never afterward. They didn't care for us then.

---

[2] Sons of Robert McMillan.

5 *Testimony of Mervin Givens,*
Spartanburg, South Carolina, July 12, 1871

Mervin Givens (colored) sworn and examined.

By Mr. Stevenson:

Question: Your name in old times was Mery Moss?

Answer: Yes, sir; but since freedom I don't go by my master's name. My name now is Givens.

Question: What is your age?

Answer: About forty I expect. . . .

Question: Have you ever been visited by the Ku-Klux?

Answer: Yes, sir.

Question: When?

Answer: About the last of April.

Question: Tell what they said and did.

Answer: I was asleep when they came to my house, and did not know anything about them until they broke in on me.

Question: What time of night was it?

Answer: About twelve o'clock at night. They broke in on me and frightened me right smart, being asleep. They ordered me to get up and make a light. As quick as I could gather my senses I bounced up and made a light, but not quick enough. They jumped at me and struck me with a pistol, and made a knot[1] that you can see there now. By the time I made the light I catched the voice of them, and as soon as I could see by the light, I looked around and saw by the

---

[1] Bump.

Source: Report of the Joint Select Committee, vol. 2, South Carolina, Part 2, 698–700.

size of the men and voice so that I could judge right off who it was. By that time they jerked the case off the pillow and jerked it over my head and ordered me out of doors. That was all I saw in the house. After they carried me out of doors I saw nothing more. They pulled the pillow-slip over my head and told me if I took off they would shoot me. They carried me out and whipped me powerful.

Question: With what?

Answer: With sticks and hickories. They whipped me powerful.

Question: How many lashes?

Answer: I can't tell. I have no knowledge at all about it. May be a hundred or two. Two men whipped me and both at once.

Question: Did they say anything to you?

Answer: They cursed me and told me I had voted the radical ticket, and they intended to beat me so I would not vote it again.

Question: Did you know any of them?

Answer: Yes, sir; I think I know them.

Question: What were their names?

Answer: One was named John Thomson and the other was John Zimmerman. Those are the two men I think it was.

Question: How many were there in all?

Answer: I didn't see but two. After they took me out, I was blindfolded; but I could judge from the horse tracks that there were more than two horses there. Some were horses and some were mules. It was a wet, rainy night; they whipped me stark naked. I had a brown undershirt on and they tore it clean off. . . .

By Mr. Van Trump:

Question: There were, then, two men who came to your house?

Answer: Yes, sir; that was all I could see.

Question: Were they disguised?

Answer: Yes, sir.

Question: How?

Answer: They had on some sort of gray-looking clothes, and much the same sort of thing over their face. One of them had a sort of high hat with tassel and sort of horns.

Question: How far did John Thomson live from there?

Answer: I think it is two or three miles.

Question: Were you acquainted with him?

Answer: Yes, sir.

Question: Where?

Answer: At my house. My wife did a good deal of washing for them both. I was very well-acquainted with their size and their voices. They were boys I was raised with. . . .

Question: Did you tell anybody else it was John Thomson?

Answer: I have never named it.

Question: Why?

Answer: I was afraid to.

Question: Are you afraid now?

Answer: I am not afraid to own the truth as nigh[2] as I can.

Question: Is there any difference in owning to the truth on the 12th of July and on the 1st of April?

Answer: The black people have injured themselves very much by talking, and I was afraid.

Question: Are you not afraid now?

Answer: No, sir; because I hope there will be a stop put to it. . . .

Question: Do you think we three gentlemen can stop it?

Answer: No, sir; but I think you can get some help.

Question: Has anybody been telling you that?

Answer: No, sir; nobody told me that. . . .

Question: Why did you not commence a prosecution against Thomson and Zimmerman?

Answer: I am like the rest, I reckon; I am too cowardly.

Question: Why do you not do it now; you are not cowardly now?

Answer: I shouldn't have done it now.

Question: I am talking about bringing suit for that abuse on that night. Why do you not have them arrested?

Answer: It ought to be done.

Question: Why do you not do it?

Answer: For fear they would shoot me. If I were to bring them up here and could not prove the thing exactly on them, and they were to get out of it, I would not expect to live much longer.

[2] Near.

6

Majority Report of the Joint Select Committee to Inquire into the Condition of Affairs in the Late Insurrectionary States, February 19, 1872, Submitted by Luke P. Poland

Poland was a Republican representative from Vermont.

The proceedings and debates in Congress show that, whatever other causes were assigned for disorders in the late insurrectionary States, the execution of the laws and the security of life and property were alleged to be most seriously

Source: Report of the Joint Select Committee, vol. 1, *Reports of the Committee,* 2–3, 98–99.

threatened by the existence and acts of organized bands of armed and disguised men, known as Ku-Klux. . . .

The evidence is equally decisive that redress cannot be obtained against those who commit crimes in disguise and at night. The reasons assigned are that identification is difficult, almost impossible; that when this is attempted, the combinations and oaths of the order come in and release the culprit by perjury either upon the witness-stand or in the jury-box; and that the terror inspired by their acts, as well as the public sentiment in their favor in many localities, paralyzes the arm of civil power. . . .

The race so recently emancipated, against which banishment or serfdom is thus decreed, but which has been clothed by the Government with the rights and responsibilities of citizenship, ought not to be, and we feel assured will not be left hereafter without protection against the hostilities and sufferings it has endured in the past, as long as the legal and constitutional powers of the Government are adequate to afford it. Communities suffering such evils and influenced by such extreme feelings may be slow to learn that relief can come only from a ready obedience to and support of constituted authority, looking to the modes provided by law for redress of all grievances. That Southern communities do not seem to yield this ready obedience at once should not deter the friends of good government in both sections from hoping and working for that end. . . .

The law of 1871[1] has been effective in suppressing for the present, to a great extent, the operations of masked and disguised men in North and South Carolina. . . . The apparent cessation of operations should not lead to a conclusion that community would be safe if protective measures were withdrawn. These should be continued until there remains no further doubt of the actual suppression and disarming of this wide-spread and dangerous conspiracy.

The results of suspending the writ of *habeas corpus* in South Carolina show that where the membership, mysteries, and power of the organization have been kept concealed this is the most and perhaps only effective remedy for its suppression; and in review of its cessation and resumption of hostilities at different times, of its extent and power, and that in several of the States where it exists the courts have not yet held terms at which the cases can be tried, we recommend that the power conferred on the President by the fourth section of that act[2] be extended until the end of the next session of Congress.

For the Senate:	For the House of Representatives:
JOHN SCOTT, Chairman	LUKE P. POLAND, Chairman
Z. CHANDLER[3]	HORACE MAYNARD[4]

---

[1] The Ku Klux Klan Act.

[2] To suspend the writ of habeas corpus.

[3] Republican senator from Michigan.

[4] Republican representative from Tennessee.

BENJ. F. RICE[5]	GLENNI W. SCOFIELD[6]
JOHN POOL[7]	JOHN F. FARNSWORTH[8]
DANIEL D. PRATT[9]	JOHN COBURN[10]
	JOB E. STEVENSON
	BENJ. F. BUTLER[11]
	WILLIAM E. LANSING[12]

[5] Republican senator from Arkansas.
[6] Republican representative from Pennsylvania.
[7] Republican senator from North Carolina.
[8] Republican representative from Illinois.
[9] Republican senator from Indiana.
[10] Republican representative from Indiana.
[11] Republican representative from Massachusetts.
[12] Republican representative from New York.

---

7   *Minority Report of the Joint Select Committee to Inquire into the Condition of Affairs in the Late Insurrectionary States,* February 19, 1872, Submitted by James B. Beck

Beck was a Democratic representative from Kentucky.

The atrocious measures by which millions of white people have been put at the mercy of the semi-barbarous negroes of the South, and the vilest of the white people, both from the North and South, who have been constituted the leaders of this black horde, are now sought to be justified and defended by defaming the people upon whom this unspeakable outrage had been committed. . . .

There is no doubt about the fact that great outrages were committed by bands of disguised men during those years of lawlessness and oppression. The natural tendency of all such organizations is to violence and crime. . . . It is so everywhere; like causes produce like results. Sporadic cases of outrages occur in every community. . . . But, as a rule, the worst governments produce the most disorders. South Carolina is confessedly in the worst condition of any of the States. Why? Because her government is the worst, or what makes it still worse,

Source: Report of the Joint Select Committee, vol. 1, *Reports of the Committee,* 289, 463–64, 514–16, 588.

her people see no hope in the future. . . . There never was a Ku-Klux in Virginia, nobody pretends there ever was. Why? Because Virginia escaped carpet-bag rule. . . .

The Constitution was trampled under foot in the passage of what is known as the Ku-Klux law; a power was delegated to the President which could be exercised by the legislative authority alone; whole communities of innocent people were put under the ban of executive vengeance by the suspension of the writ of *habeas corpus* at the mere whim and caprice of the President; and all for what? For the apprehension and conviction of a few poor, deluded, ignorant, and unhappy wretches, goaded to desperation by the insolence of the negroes, and who could, had the radical authorities of South Carolina done their duty, just as easily have been prosecuted in the State courts, and much more promptly and cheaply, than by all this imposing machinery of Federal power, through military and judicial departments. . . .

. . . The antagonism, therefore, which exists between these two classes of the population of South Carolina does not spring from any political cause, in the ordinary party sense of the term; but it grows out of that instinctive and irrepressible repugnance to compulsory affiliation with another race, planted by the God of nature in the breast of the white man, perhaps more strongly manifested in the uneducated portion of the people, and aggravated and intensified by the fact that the Negro has been placed as a *ruler* over him. . . .

We feel it would be a dereliction of duty on our part if, after what we have witnessed in South Carolina, we did not admonish the American people that the present condition of things in the South cannot last. It was an oft-quoted political apothegm, long prior to the war, that no government could exist "half slave and half free." The paraphrase of that proposition is equally true, that no government can long exist "half black and half white." If the republican party, or its all-powerful leaders in the North, cannot see this, if they are so absorbed in the idea of this newly discovered political divinity in the negro, that they cannot comprehend its social repugnance or its political dangers; or, knowing it, have the wanton, wicked, and criminal purpose of disregarding its consequences, whether in the present or in the future, and the great mass of American white citizens should still be so mad as to sustain them in their heedless career of forcing negro supremacy over white men, why then "farewell, a long farewell," to constitutional liberty on this continent, and the glorious form of government bequeathed to us by our fathers. . . .

The foregoing is a hurried, but, as we believe, a truthful statement of the political, moral, and financial condition of the State of South Carolina, under the joint rule of the Negro and the "reconstructive" policy of Congress.

FRANK BLAIR

T. F. BAYARD[1]

S. S. COX[2]

---

[1] Democratic senator from Delaware.

[2] Democratic representative from New York.

JAMES B. BECK

P. VAN TRUMP

A. M. WADDELL[3]

J. C. ROBINSON[4]

J. M. HANKS[5]

[3] Democratic representative from North Carolina.
[4] Democratic representative from Illinois.
[5] Democratic representative from Arkansas.

Analyzing Congressional Hearings and Reports

1. How did the descriptions of the Ku Klux Klan differ between witnesses examined in Washington, D.C. (Sources 1 and 2), and those examined in South Carolina (Sources 3, 4, and 5)? How would you explain those differences?

2. Briefly compare the nature of evidence presented in the testimony: How did it differ between black and white witnesses? In what ways did the Klan's attacks on blacks differ from those on white Republicans? What do you think accounts for such differences?

3. What patterns did you find in the cross-examination of witnesses? How did Van Trump and other Democrats on the committee seek to discredit or shape the testimony they heard, and do you think they succeeded in any instances? Which witnesses do you think were most successful in answering their cross-examinations? Did any of the witnesses contradict themselves?

4. Consider whether the majority and minority reports (Sources 6 and 7) could have been written before the committee heard any witnesses. Using your notes from the second portion of the table on page 9, do you think any of the congressmen sitting on the committee had their minds changed about the Ku Klux Klan or the federal government's response to it by the testimony they heard? What specific examples or passages from the reports would you use to support your answer?

5. What does this source tell you about the limits of federal power during Reconstruction? According to the testimony and reports, what accounted for the breakdown of law and order in South Carolina, and how was it most likely to be restored? How did Republicans and Democrats differ in this regard?

6. Using the testimony you have read here, describe the social and economic conditions faced by the freedmen and -women of the South during Reconstruction. What evidence do Thomson, McMillan, and Givens (Sources 3, 4, and 5) provide of the ways in which African American men and women valued and acted on their freedom after 1865 and of the limits whites tried to impose on that freedom?

The Rest of the Story

As noted in the Joint Select Committee's majority report, the Ku Klux Klan Act of 1871 did succeed in suppressing the Klan's activities in those regions where it was enforced. In October 1871, while the Joint Select Committee was still at work, President Grant suspended the writ of habeas corpus in nine South Carolina counties, including Spartanburg, and sent in federal troops to arrest approximately 1,500 suspected Klansmen. Even more Klansmen fled the region to avoid prosecution. In a series of trials managed by U.S. Attorney General Amos Akerman in late 1871 and in 1872, about ninety Klansmen were sentenced to prison terms ranging from three months to ten years. Most of those given long sentences were released within a year or two, under amnesty offered by President Grant. Overall, very few Klansmen were ever brought to meaningful justice for their crimes, but by the election of 1872, reports of Klan terrorism had declined considerably, and the organization's ability to intimidate black voters appeared to have been broken.

During the 1920s, the Ku Klux Klan was revived by whites who felt threatened by Catholic and Jewish immigrants as well as by African Americans. At its peak, this version of the Klan included three million members and spilled beyond the South into western and northern states. After ebbing in the 1940s, the Klan surged again during the civil rights movement of the 1950s and 1960s. This incarnation was much smaller than its predecessor in the 1920s but more violent in its resistance to racial equality. Today a number of white supremacist organizations continue to call themselves the Ku Klux Klan, but they are poorly organized and constantly at odds with one another and with similar hate groups on the far right of American politics.

In the larger story of Reconstruction, it would seem that the Ku Klux Klan Act and the congressional investigation of the Klan were shining examples of how the federal government and the freedmen and -women of the South acted in partnership to advance the cause of racial justice and equality in the United States. Unfortunately, these successes were short-lived. During his second term, Grant reduced considerably the number of federal troops posted in the South, and the Republicans split between a liberal faction still committed to racial equality and a more conservative faction willing to jettison Reconstruction policies and black voters in return for political compromises with Democrats on other issues.

The third branch of the federal government did not help African Americans in their pursuit of equality either. In two cases from the 1870s, the Supreme Court interpreted the Fourteenth Amendment in such a way that it severely restricted the federal government's ability to intervene on behalf of private citizens when their civil and political rights were violated. In the *Slaughterhouse Cases* (1873), the Court ruled that the Fourteenth Amendment protected only those rights that were derived directly from the federal government, most of which dealt with matters of interstate or foreign travel or business; the civil rights of most concern to blacks in the South still fell under the jurisdiction of state courts and law enforcement. In *U.S. v. Cruikshank* (1876), the Court ruled that the Fourteenth Amendment empowered the federal government only to prosecute violations of civil rights by the states, not by individual persons (violations in that category still fell under state jurisdiction). The combined effect of these two decisions was to place responsibility for protecting the rights of the South's African American population under the authority of the state governments, while making any federal intervention on their behalf similar to that pursued under the Ku Klux Klan Act unconstitutional.

After the last of the former Confederate states had fallen back into Democratic hands in 1877, Southern whites found new ways to confine blacks to second-class citizenship that were far more subtle than the Klan's political terrorism. Insulated from federal intervention by the Supreme Court's decisions and congressional indifference, Southern states passed laws that disenfranchised blacks by imposing poll taxes and literacy tests. They also erected a system of social segregation known as Jim Crow laws that limited black access to education and economic opportunity. When blacks challenged this system, mobs and night riders responded with the same methods used by the Klan, most notably lynching and arson, to prevent any sustained resistance to white rule. Not until the civil rights movement of the 1950s would the federal government again embrace the cause of racial justice in the South with the same vigor it had shown during its battle against the Klan in 1871.

To Find Out More

Like all federal government reports, the Joint Select Committee's report was published by the Government Printing Office in Washington, D.C. In every state, libraries designated as federal repositories receive copies of such publications, and your college or university library may in fact be one. The full citation for the report is *Report of the Joint Select Committee to Inquire into the Condition of Affairs in the Late Insurrectionary States*, 13 volumes (Washington, D.C.: Government Printing Office, 1872). It can also be found under the title *Senate Reports*, 42d Congress, 2d sess., no. 41 (serial 1484–96) or *House Reports*, 42d Congress, 2d sess., no. 22 (serial 1529–41). Some libraries may also catalog it under the title printed on the spine of each volume, *The Ku Klux Conspiracy*. Volume 1 contains the majority and minority reports, and the subsequent volumes contain the verbatim testimony of witnesses before the committee.

For a more accessible selection of the testimony heard by the Joint Select Committee, see Albion W. Tourgée, *The Invisible Empire* (1880; repr., Baton Rouge: Louisiana State University Press, 1989). Tourgée was a disillusioned carpetbagger when he published his autobiographical novel about Reconstruction, *A Fool's Errand*, in 1879. A year later, he published *The Invisible Empire* as an exposé of the Ku Klux Klan.

The *Report of the Joint Select Committee* is not yet available in a digitized format, but several online resources address the experience of freedmen and -women during Reconstruction. The Freedmen's Bureau Online, at **freedmensbureau.com**, is an excellent starting point for conducting Web-based research on the Reconstruction era. It features transcriptions of documents from the National Archives, including a section on "Records Relating to Murders and Outrages" in the Reconstruction South. The Freedmen and Southern Society Project, at **history.umd.edu/Freedmen**, includes primary sources on the experience of emancipation. America's Reconstruction: People and Politics after the Civil War, at **digitalhistory.uh.edu/reconstruction/section4/ section4_presrecon.html**, is an online exhibit on Reconstruction that includes some useful images and primary sources.

For the definitive modern study of the Ku Klux Klan during Reconstruction, see Allen W. Trelease, *White Terror: The Ku Klux Klan Conspiracy and Southern Reconstruction* (New York: Harper and Row, Publishers, 1971). The Klan's place in the wider current of political violence in the Reconstruction-era South is explained in George C. Rable, *But There Was No Peace: The Role of Violence in the Politics of Reconstruction* (Athens: University of Georgia Press, 1984). The best comprehensive history of Reconstruction, Eric Foner's *Reconstruction: America's Unfinished Revolution, 1863–1877* (New York: Harper and Row, Publishers, 1988), also provides a good summary of the Klan's origins and role in Reconstruction. The African American response to the Klan and other forms of political intimidation is addressed in Steven Hahn, *A Nation under Our Feet: Black Political Struggles in the Rural South from Slavery to the Great Migration* (Cambridge, Mass.: Belknap Press, 2003). The film *Birth of a Nation* (1915), directed by D. W. Griffith and based on Thomas Dixon's popular novel *The Clansman* (1905), is a stunning example of how the Klan was mythologized during the Jim Crow era as an organization that defended white Southerners against the depredations of Northern carpetbaggers and black Republicans during Reconstruction.

Picturing a Western Myth

Photography and the Blackfeet Indians

I n 1996, Elouise Cobell, a member of the Blackfeet tribe of Native Americans and founder of the Blackfeet National Bank, filed a federal lawsuit on behalf of her tribe to force the U.S. Department of Interior to provide a full accounting of its century-long oversight of native lands. Cobell, a trained accountant and director of the Blackfeet Reservation Development Fund Inc., took this drastic action because she "got fed up" with the federal government's chaotic bookkeeping and evasive answers to questions she asked about the workings of the Indian Trust Fund, which was created in the late nineteenth century to manage Native Americans' land.

This lawsuit, still in the courts as of 2006, points to both failures and successes in Native American history. The U.S. government failed to honor the autonomy of native tribes and failed to negotiate an honest economic settlement with them, but tribes and their members succeeded in surviving U.S. government encroachments onto their lands and into their cultures, and tribes such as the Blackfeet continue to challenge federal control of their communities.

At the end of the nineteenth century, few Americans, white or native, would have predicted any success for the nation's tribal people. Early in 1890, the U.S. Census Bureau declared white settlements so pervasive across the continent that there was no longer a defined American "frontier." That same year, U.S. troopers at Wounded Knee, South Dakota, shot 146 Sioux men, women, and children in a preemptive strike that effectively suppressed the native insurgency sparked by a resurrection ritual known as the "Ghost Dance." Following the massacre at Wounded Knee, it seemed improbable that the surviving

250,000 Native Americans in the United States would grow to a total population of four million by 2000. In the late nineteenth century, Native Americans' friends and foes shared the belief that the nation's indigenous population was a "vanishing" people, destined to become extinct or to abandon their tribal cultures, adopt modern modes of life, and assimilate — as individuals, not as tribal members — into white society. Indeed, the policy of the U.S. government was to teach — or force — Native Americans to give up their tribal identities and follow the government's dictate to "walk the white man's road."

Thus, when Glacier National Park in northwestern Montana opened in the summer of 1911, its advertising promised tourists a "wilderness experience," including glimpses of the "vanishing" Blackfeet Indian whose tribe once controlled the area that became Glacier Park. Countless brochures, calendars, postcards, and magazine layouts featured photographs of the Blackfeet, described as "specimens of a Great Race soon to disappear." The publicity campaign was so successful that the image of the Blackfeet, with their feathered headdresses and buffalo-hide tipis, became the standard image of all American Indians, despite great variations in dress and housing among Native Americans. Equally standard was the notion that Native American cultures were automatically doomed by modernity. If natives adjusted to modern life, then they were no longer Indians; they had, in effect, "vanished."

The belief that Native Americans were destined to simply disappear into the culture and commerce of modern Anglo society ignored the policy decisions made by European Americans that actually prevented tribes' assimilation into Anglo society. Belief in the "vanishing Indian" also ignored the creative capacity of people like the Blackfeet to survive, as a tribe, through economic and cultural adaptation. In fact, the story of the Blackfeet and Glacier National Park is a powerful illustration of the methods that Native Americans used to survive in the face of Anglo expansion. At Glacier, the Blackfeet carved out a very modern market niche: they sold back to white Americans who were seeking a "wilderness experience" the mythic image of a "vanished people."

Blackfeet accommodation to the demands of white society represents a larger struggle over the meaning of assimilation and the resources needed to achieve assimilation. A core feature of American identity has always been economic independence and the personal autonomy to use earnings and profits to support your own ethnic community or cultural institutions. However, between 1855 to 1895, treaties with the Blackfeet denied the tribe and its members this economic autonomy. In those decades, the Blackfeet signed treaties allowing the U.S. government to build roads, telegraph lines, military posts, missions, schools, and "government agencies" throughout their territory; the tribe also granted access to minerals, water, and, of course, acreage. In exchange, the U.S. government agreed to provide "useful goods and services" and to create programs promoting the "civilization and Christianization" of the Blackfeet. In sharp contrast to all other "civilized" business deals of the day, the government did not pay the Blackfeet in actual cash funds that tribal members could bank and invest. So while the government said it wanted the Blackfeet to "walk the white man's road," it refused to make the cash payments necessary for the Blackfeet to take that journey in a truly American way: on their own cultural terms, with their own independent resources. Not only were all government payments made in goods, services, and programs that the government deemed appropriate for civilizing and Christianizing the tribe, but all such payments were also made according to the U.S. government's timetable and sometimes withheld if the government had other priorities. As a result, treaties with the United States did not give the Blackfeet independent access to the economic resources that would have allowed them to create their own style of assimilation.

Compare this with the experience of immigrants to the United States in the nineteenth century. Although the immigrants struggled economically, they were not denied control over their own wages or business profits. As a result, they were able to direct their earnings toward building independent ethnic communities from which they could influence the timing and terms of their accommodation to modern American society. But U.S. policy did not allow native tribes such as the Blackfeet to create a similar economic base.

In the four decades between 1870 and 1910, between the close of the Civil War era and the opening of Glacier National Park, the problems with federal Indian policy became clear to the Blackfeet. In these decades, the buffalo disappeared from the northern Montana grasslands, partly because whites overhunted the buffalo for sport and partly because the only economic activity left to the Blackfeet lay in supplying buffalo meat to the tribe and selling buffalo hides to whites. So they, too, overhunted. At the same time, more than 20,000 land-hungry white settlers poured into the Montana territory, occasionally meeting with violent resistance from the Blackfeet and fighting off that resistance with the help of the U.S. Army. Military reprisals against Blackfeet resistance were so harsh in these years that a *New York Times* editorial denounced the killing of women and children as a tactic for pacifying the Blackfeet.

The combination of food shortages, smallpox, and conflict with whites reduced the Blackfeet population from 8,000 in 1855 to 2,500 in 1880. Another 20 percent died of starvation in the winter of 1884 when the federal government failed to deliver food allotments owed in exchange for land. The starving remainder of the Blackfeet nation negotiated two major land sales to the government in 1887 and 1895. By the turn of the century, the 2,000 surviving residents of the Blackfeet reservation still owned 1.5 million acres of grazing land, but they had relinquished ownership of the western mountains, lakes, and streams that had been a vital source of the tribe's spiritual and dietary nourishment. In each of the two major land sales, the Blackfeet received $1.5 million—half of what they asked for. Again, payment never came as a direct infusion of capital that the tribe could control and invest; it was always in the form of goods and services controlled and distributed by the Bureau of Indian Affairs, by then a famously corrupt arm of the federal government.

As white ranchers, farmers, and miners were moving onto Blackfeet lands, an emerging lobby of white conservationists was increasingly alarmed that

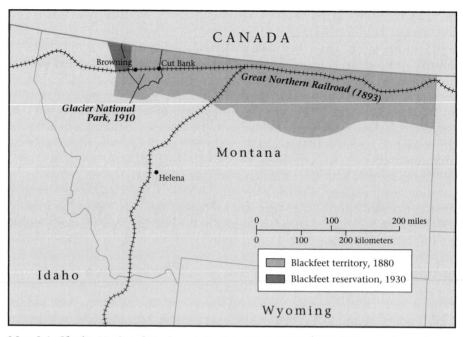

Map 2.1 Glacier National Park and the Blackfeet, 1880–1930 *This map shows the reach of the Great Northern Railway and its connecting lines by 1909, on the eve of congressional approval for Glacier National Park. With the railway lines already built, advocates for the national park could argue that tourists would have easy access to the park's natural beauty and manufactured luxuries. As the map indicates, the Blackfeet had given up millions of acres of land by 1909, and they would give up even more after the park was built.*

uncontrolled development would destroy the West's natural beauty and resources. The conservationists realized that they could protect pockets of the region by appealing to Americans' nostalgia for the vanishing wilderness. In 1910, conservationists joined with the Great Northern Railway Company, which stood to profit from tourism trade in Montana. Together, they won congressional approval for Glacier National Park, 1,600 square miles of alpine beauty that had once formed the "backbone" of the Blackfeet's world (see Map 2.1). The Great Northern financed the construction of roads and trails, two magnificent hotels, and a series of smaller "chalets" and tourist-friendly camps around the park. In less than a decade, aggressive marketing increased tourism to Glacier National Park from 4,000 visitors in the summer of 1911 to almost 20,000 in the summer of 1920.

The Blackfeet tribe survived this modern development by adapting to its demands. Every summer, members of the tribe relocated from the reservation, just outside Glacier National Park, to live in designated areas within the park. The Great Northern Railroad paid these tribal members to occupy traditional tipis and wear costumes that twentieth-century whites thought of as authentic. Although publicity stills occasionally depicted a Blackfeet male spearing a fish or holding his bow and arrows, the rules governing national parks actually denied Blackfeet their treaty rights to hunt and fish in their old territory.

For those Blackfeet who profited from their summertime performances as historical artifacts in a living museum, this pragmatic use of their culture was layered with irony. Glacier Park's marketing myth of the "vanishing" Indian was reinforced by government policy on the Blackfeet reservation, where federal agents spent the money owed to the tribe on programs to dissolve tribal identity and transform Blackfeet hunters into the individualized American family farmer.

As part of the government's effort to put Native Americans "on the white man's road," the Dawes Severalty Act of 1887 had made it U.S. policy to encourage all natives to divide tribally held lands into individually held, 160-acre plots and to farm independently from the tribe. The government promised to hold each plot of land in trust for twenty-five years and then grant the land as well as citizenship to the former tribal member who had individually farmed that land. The Dawes Act established the Indian Trust Fund, whose accounting procedures the Blackfeet are today challenging in court. Back in 1887, the act was hailed as a reform that would save Native Americans by making them individual American citizens rather than tribal members. But the Dawes Act failed to acknowledge economic realities, much less tribal loyalties. For the Blackfeet, the family plot ideal was unsuited to Montana's harsh environment. White farmers at this time realized that western agriculture demanded vast grain acreage supported by substantial investment in irrigation, planting, and harvesting technology. But in implementing the Dawes Act, Indian agents insisted that the Blackfeet could survive and assimilate by farming small plots of oats, barley, and vegetables.

Reports by the U.S. Commissioner of Indian Affairs indicate that the Blackfeet adopted some features of the government's assimilation program and resisted others. For example, the commissioner reported in 1900 that the number of reservation Blackfeet who wore "citizens' dress" — the clothing style of whites—had increased to 2,085 from only 40 in 1886. There were similar increases in the Blackfeet's use of "citizens'" household wares, wagons, and foodstuffs simply because they were paid for their land with all manner of modern, American goods. But in that same 1900 report, the commissioner admitted that only 500 acres on the Blackfeet reservation were under farm cultivation. Denied the independent authority to invest tribal funds in livestock ranching (a more viable option for their climate and culture), native men resisted federal efforts to turn them into vegetable gardeners in a grassland climate of hot, dry summers and long, cold winters. Indeed, the most prosperous Blackfeet were mixed-bloods whose white fathers had profited by bringing their livestock to graze for free on their Blackfeet mothers' tribal grasslands.

In the first three decades of the twentieth century, as the Great Northern Railroad was eulogizing the passing of a "Great Race," the Blackfeet were not in fact vanishing, but nor were they strictly adhering to the government's assimilation plan. Instead, they were striving to create an alternative method of survival that retained tribal integrity while utilizing the opportunities presented by the surrounding white society. An excellent example of the Blackfeet's creativity in this regard is their adaptation of the Sun Dance. Although the dance was not as threatening to white power as the "Ghost Dance," Christian missionaries and federal agents regarded it as a blatant display of "heathen worship" that had to be exterminated if the Blackfeet were ever to assimilate. But other whites, including, eventually, those at Glacier National Park, were fascinated by the Blackfeet's elaborate ritual of sacred vows to the holy sun. By the turn of the century, the Blackfeet had rescheduled the Sun Dance to coincide with the Fourth of July, thereby turning it into a patriotic celebration that became a major tourist event that the church and the government dared not oppose. In this way, as well as other ways, the Blackfeet preserved their tribal traditions while adapting to the demands of modern life.

Using the Source: Photographs

The Great Northern Railroad used photographs to sell its images of the "vanishing" Blackfeet to the American public. In fact, the belief that Native Americans were on the verge of extinction inspired a great many nineteenth-century photographers to pile their bulky cameras, tripods, glass plates, developing chemicals, and darkroom tents onto the backs of horses and venture out west. Thus, a modern technology was used to document the existence of those thought to be threatened by modernity. The photographs that have survived as tangible documents can help us appreciate the complex blend of old and new that resulted in survival for tribes like the Blackfeet.

Photographs are one of the most modern types of documents available. For centuries, people have consulted written texts, paintings, sculpture, music, and all sorts of manufactured artifacts to reconstruct human life in the past. But it was only in the 1840s that technological invention made it possible to capture and preserve an image of a physical object. Photographs revolutionized human access to the past, giving every viewer a unique window on people and places long gone.

Native Americans became the subjects of photographs as early as the 1850s, when Indian delegations to Washington, D.C., were regularly photographed as part of the official record of treaty negotiations. Joseph Henry, the first secretary of the Smithsonian Institution, tried to raise government funds in 1867 to build a complete photographic record of the "principal tribes of the U.S." by arguing that "the Indians are passing away so rapidly that but few years remain within which this can be done, and the loss will be irretrievable . . . when they are gone."

Henry was not granted his funds, so photography of Indians proceeded in a haphazard way, driven by technology and influenced by commercial, cultural, and personal motives. Native warriors went to portrait studios in the 1860s, where they sat motionless for the eighty seconds required to capture an image on a glass plate. Professional photographers out west, burdened by early technology's requirement that they develop every photo within ten minutes of taking it, still managed to capture images of people in their native environments.

Thanks to the introduction of George Eastman's handheld "box" camera in 1888, photography became the pastime of amateurs as well as the business of professionals, and the "vanishing" Indian continued to be a favorite photographic subject into the twentieth century. Today, there are more than 90,000 photographs at the National Museum of the American Indian (NMAI) at the Smithsonian Institution in Washington, D.C. And the NMAI is just one of dozens of photographic archives in the United States that serve, according to one historian, as "a collective witness to Indian transitions."

What Can Photographs Tell Us?

Photographs are a valuable historical source for an obvious reason: they give us visual access to a wealth of information on the natural world, material culture, social life, and human emotion. Photographs allow us to gather subtle details about life in the past that cannot be gathered from any other source; the camera, as we all know, doesn't lie. But we also know that every camera has an angle. More precisely, every camera has a photographer operating it, a person who brings some mix of cultural attitudes, personal emotions, economic motives, and artistic assumptions to the picture-taking process. When reading a photograph for evidence of the past, we cannot afford to regard the camera as a neutral technology or the photograph as a purely "objective" witness. We must regard every photograph as the creative product of a photographer's point of view and must put each photograph into the context in which it was taken.

Imagine, for example, how distorted our view of Blackfeet life in the early twentieth century would be if the only surviving photographs were the publicity shots commissioned for Glacier National Park. The highly skilled, world-famous photographers, such as Edward S. Curtis and Roland Reed, who created these photographs for companies like the Great Northern Railway often manipulated the scene by dressing tribal people in anachronistic costumes, blocking out signs of modern life, and posing natives in a wistful or stoic stance. Thanks to the development of the easy-to-use "box" camera in the 1890s, we also have access to somewhat more candid images of the Blackfeet on their own reservation, outside the gates of Glacier Park. These amateur photographs, probably taken by store merchants or U.S. Indian agents, did not block out modern life or the Blackfeet's accommodation to that life.

Consider this detail from an amateur photograph taken around 1930 at a traditional tribal dance on the reservation, where the audience included tourists from Glacier Park. On the one hand, it provides a wealth of evidence on the blending of native culture with modern American culture. On the other hand, it raises a host of unanswererable questions about the thoughts and feelings of those who appear in the photo.

Consider the meaning of the American flags

What is the significance of farm machinery next to a tipi?

Important clue for dating the photo

Note the use of sunglasses

While this photograph offers valuable information on the Blackfeet's incorporation of American products into daily tribal life, it cannot tell us the relationship between the material objects and the tribal women. Does the automobile signify the natives' own prosperity, or is it a sign of white wealth derived from Blackfeet land? Do the American flags denote the Blackfeet's deference to governmental power or a calculated use of white icons in tribal rituals? Might the flags simply testify to Blackfeet patriotism? Such questions remind us that photographs alone cannot reveal all we want to know about the objects in front of the camera.

Questions to Ask

The selection of images included in this chapter allows you to compare commercial photographs with amateur photographs and consider what conclusions you can, and cannot, draw from each set. We know the economic motives of the commercial photographers, the economic purpose of their photos, and the economic reasons that the Blackfeet posed for those photos. But we are left to guess at the motives of the amateur photographers standing behind the camera on the reservation and at the attitudes of the Blackfeet whose images, shorn of mythic romance, were recorded for posterity.

- How do the commercial photographs place the Blackfeet in a mythic past?
- How do the commercial photos argue for the Blackfeet's cooperation with modern life?
- What do the amateur photographs reveal about the Blackfeet's accommodation to modernity?
- What conclusions, if any, can you draw from the photos about Blackfeet attitudes toward white society?
- Is one set of photographs more "true" to the past than the other?

Source Analysis Table

The photographs you will be examining include commercial photographs used for publicity by the Great Northern Railway Company and shots taken by amateur photographers on the Blackfeet reservation outside Glacier National Park. By comparing them, you can consider the ways in which traditional Blackfeet culture became a marketing tool for whites, the ways in which traditional native culture continued to have meaning for the Blackfeet, as well as the ways in which the Blackfeet adapted to modern market society.

	Signs of Traditional Culture	Signs of Modern Society
COMMERCIAL GLACIER PARK PHOTOS		
1. Greetings from Glacier National Park		
2. Great Northern Railway Calendar		
3. Blackfeet and Park Golfers		
4. Spearfishing in Glacier National Park		
5. Two Guns White Calf Reading		

	Signs of Traditional Culture	Signs of Modern Society
AMATEUR RESERVATION PHOTOS		
6. Old Ration Place		
7. Blackfeet Performance		
8. Family at Sun Dance Encampment		
9. Students with Their Harvest		
10. Mad Plume Family Harvest		
11. Blackfeet Girl at Glacier National Park Switchboard		
12. Sewing Class at the Cut Bank Boarding School		

To download and print this table, visit the book companion site at **bedfordstmartins.com/brownshannon**.

The Source: Photographs of the Blackfeet at Glacier National Park and on the Reservation, 1890–1930

COMMERCIAL PHOTOGRAPHS FROM GLACIER NATIONAL PARK

1 *Greetings from Glacier National Park,* c. 1920

The following photo was used in a wide variety of Glacier National Park publicity materials throughout the 1920s. This photo appeared at the top of park stationery and on the front of specialized brochures sent to convention participants. It was often accompanied by the words "Ki-tuk-a, Stum-ik-Us-tsi-kai-yi" and "Ok-yi! Ik-so-ka-pi," along with the translation: "Us Indians will be glad to see you at Glacier Park this summer and next summer too" and "We shake hands with you!" Typically the photo's caption promised that the men in the photo would be at the Glacier Park train station to greet conventioneers when they arrived.

Source: Great Northern Railway Collection, Glacier Park Views, Minnesota State Historical Society. Photographer unknown.

2   *Great Northern Railway Calendar*, 1923

The Great Northern Railway Company made extensive use of commercial photographs of the Blackfeet in this popular form of advertising.

Source: Great Northern Railway Collection, Glacier Park Views, Minnesota State Historical Society. Photographer unknown.

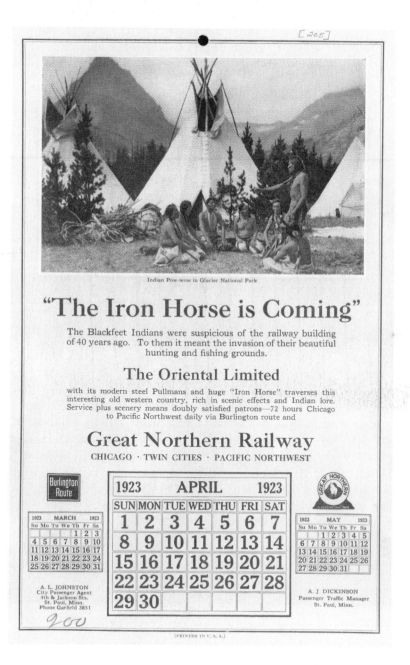

3   *Blackfeet and Park Golfers, c.* 1930

Blackfeet sometimes served as caddies for Glacier Park golfers, but this undated publicity photo does not depict the natives in that role.

Source: Great Northern Railway Collection, Glacier Park Views, Minnesota State Historical Society. Photographer unknown.

4 | *Spearfishing in Glacier National Park,* date unknown

Though it made for an impressive publicity shot, the Blackfeet art of spearfishing could not actually be pursued in Glacier National Park.

Source: Great Northern Railway Collection, Glacier Park Views, Minnesota State Historical Society. Tomer J. Hileman, photographer.

5   *Two Guns White Calf Reading,* date unknown

Two Guns White Calf often appeared in Glacier Park publicity shots. Here, Tomer Hileman posed him reading a book by Zane Grey, a famous writer of western stories.

Source: Great Northern Railway Collection, Glacier Park Views, Minnesota State Historical Society. Tomer J. Hileman, photographer.

AMATEUR PHOTOGRAPHS TAKEN ON BLACKFEET RESERVATION IN MONTANA

6   *Old Ration Place,* date unknown

Blackfeet sale of tribal lands to the U.S. government was paid for in food rations. After the buffalo disappeared, Blackfeet gathered each week for the one and a half pounds of beef, half pound of flour, and small amounts of beans, bacon, salt, soda, and coffee allocated to each man, woman, and child.

Source: Montana Historical Society.

7

Blackfeet Performance, c. 1930

This photo from the Great Northern Railway's photo archives does not appear to have been used for Glacier Park publicity. It suggests that park visitors in the 1930s took day trips to the reservation to view Blackfeet performances. This may have been a combined celebration of the Blackfeet's Sun Dance and the Fourth of July.

Source: Great Northern Railway Collection, Glacier Park Views, Minnesota State Historical Society. Photographer unknown.

8   *Family at Sun Dance Encampment,* 1908

Blackfeet traveled to a central location on the reservation for the annual Sun Dance. This 1908 photo, taken at that year's Sun Dance encampment, shows one family's display of finery and prized possessions.

Source: Photo by Thomas Magee.

9   *Students with Their Harvest,* 1912 (p. 48 top)

Source: Photo by E. L. Chase.

10   *Mad Plume Family Harvest,* c. 1920 (p. 48 bottom)

Source: Photo courtesy of Mae Vallance.

These two photos reflect the government's effort to encourage Blackfeet vegetable farming in the decades following the 1887 Dawes Act. The students shown in Source 9 attended the Cut Bank Boarding School, where sailor suits were the regulation uniform. Albert and Susan Mad Plume and members of their family display their harvest for a photographer in Source 10. They were among the full-blooded Blackfeet who supported the government's plans for agricultural self-sufficiency.

11 | *Blackfeet Girl at Glacier National Park Switchboard,* c. 1920

This photo, probably taken in the 1920s, is from the Great Northern Railway's photo archive but was not used for publicity. It suggests that some Blackfeet were hired into jobs at Glacier Park that gave them training in marketable skills.

Source: Great Northern Railway Collection, Glacier Park Views, Minnesota State Historical Society. Photographer unknown.

12 | *Sewing Class at the Cut Bank Boarding School,* 1907

At government-sponsored boarding schools, Blackfeet were taught to use modern technology and encouraged to assimilate into American culture. Native recollections of these schooling experiences vary widely; some former students have very positive memories, while others report being made to feel inferior.

Source: Courtesy of the Sherburne Collection, University of Montana Archives.

Analyzing Photographs

1. What are the differences in the ways that tradition and modernity are depicted in the commercial photographs taken in Glacier Park and in the amateur photographs taken on the reservation? How do you explain those differences?

2. What do the amateur photographs taken on the reservation tell us about the Blackfeet tribe's incorporation of modern material goods into their daily lives?

3. If the publicity photos taken at Glacier National Park are inauthentic representations of Blackfeet life, how can they contribute to our historical knowledge about Native Americans?

4. If the Blackfeet wanted to preserve their tribal independence and cultural integrity, why did they cooperate with Glacier National Park officials instead of rising up against tribal reliance on government "rations"?

5. Imagine finding a box of old and completely unidentified family photographs in the attic of the house you just moved into. What steps would you take to figure out who was in the photos, when the photos were taken, and who took them?

6. Every photograph calls up a variety of stories in our minds. Write two different "stories" to describe what might be going on in the photographs in Source 3 and Source 9. What additional evidence would you seek to test the validity of your stories?

The Rest of the Story

A visit to the Indian Trust Web site makes clear that Elouise Cobell's lawsuit against the U.S. Department of Interior is still being aggressively pursued by the Blackfeet, in alliance with other native tribes, and is still being resisted by the U.S. government. At the center of the suit is the 1887 Dawes Act, whose allocation of 160 acres of reservation land to individual Indian families was insufficient to produce a livelihood in western regions like Montana. The act denied outright ownership of the 160 acres. Instead, the government held that land "in trust" for twenty-five years. In addition, the "surplus" reservation land that was not broken up for family plots was leased to white ranchers, farmers, and mining companies. When Indian families were unable to survive on their 160-acre plots (and prevented from selling the land outright), the government stepped in and leased those lands to whites who had the resources to extract the water and minerals and to buy grazing herds. Elouise Cobell's lawsuit asks: What has the Department of Interior done with all the money from more than a century of leasing and selling off Indian lands? Can the government produce accounts proving that Native Americans were properly recompensed for their lands?

In 2003, the Blackfeet tribe awarded Cobell the status of "warrior," a unique honor for a woman. But even as she pursues this legal battle, Cobell insists that the lawsuit does not seek reparations for all the injustices that Native Americans have suffered since Europeans first came to the North American continent. It is narrowly focused on the matter of accounting and payment for the lands under the control of the Indian Trust Fund. In response, the government insists that it cannot possibly account for all the monies extracted from Indian lands because, it openly admits, there has been a long history of mismanagement and theft, and documents have been routinely destroyed. Back in 1929, the General Accounting Office reported that "numerous expenditures [have been] made from these funds" that did not go to Indian landowners and conceded that the trust fund's accounting methods were so poor that it was impossible to certify that "the Indian received the full measure of benefit to which he was entitled." More than sixty years later, a 1992 congressional report again confirmed a history of inadequate accounting and payment practices in a report titled "Misplaced Trust: The Bureau of Indian Affairs' Mismanagement of the Indian Trust Fund."

In 1999, Judge Royce C. Lamberth, the U.S. district judge then charged with overseeing this case, indicated his skepticism about the government's reliability by transferring jurisdiction over the Indian Trust from the Department of Interior to the U.S. district court. Frustrated with the government's obstruction tactics in the case, Lamberth ruled that the Interior Department's "degenerate tenure as Trustee-Delegate for the Indian Trust . . . is shot through with bureaucratic blunders, flubs, goofs and foul-ups, and peppered with scandals, deception, dirty tricks and outright villainy, the end of which is nowhere in sight." In 2006, the U.S. Court of Appeals removed Judge Lamberth from the case.

Despite the government's continued efforts to appeal every court judgment against the Department of Interior, Elouise Cobell remains optimistic that there will ultimately be a settlement of the case. It won't amount to the $176 billion that Cobell estimates the government owes to individual Native American landowners; it likely won't even amount to the $27.5 billion that has been proposed. But Cobell and her allies are not retreating, and their legal campaign proves that Native Americans have not vanished; they are quite alive and quite capable of using modern methods to promote tribal prosperity.

To Find Out More

The commercial photographs of the Blackfeet used in this chapter can be found in the archives of the Great Northern Railway Company at the Minnesota State Historical Society in St. Paul, Minnesota. The reservation photographs of the Blackfeet were taken from William E. Farr, *The Reservation Blackfeet, 1882–1945: A Photographic History of Cultural Survival* (Seattle: University of Washington Press, 1984). This chapter was inspired by original research conducted at the

Newberry Library in Chicago and the Minnesota State Historical Society by Amy E. Scott in 1996, when she was an undergraduate at Grinnell College.

Collections of Native American photographs are open for public viewing at the National Museum of the American Indian in Washington, D.C., and in archives in various state and local historical societies. The NMAI, which is part of the Smithsonian Institution, also has a Web site that presents "Online Exhibitions" of photographs on different native tribes and topics (see "Exhibitions" at **nmai.si.edu**). Two excellent published collections of Native American photographs are *Spirit Capture: Photographs from the National Museum of the American Indian,* edited by Tim Johnson (Washington, D.C.: Smithsonian Institution Press, 1998), and *The Photograph and the American Indian* (Princeton, NJ: Princeton University Press, 1994), edited by Alfred L. Bush and Lee Clark Mitchell.

The NMAI offers a useful Web site (**si.edu/resource/faq/nmai/start.htm**) that lists resources and readings on Native American history and contemporary life. The NativeWeb site (**nativeweb.org**) also provides links and articles about Indians in the past and present. The Bureau of Indian Affairs Web site, at **doi.gov/bureau-indian-affairs.html**, includes historical and contemporary documents on Native Americans, along with an index to relevant government and other Web sites.

Among the many studies of the encounter between Native American and European American cultures, two of the most useful are Brian W. Dippie, *The Vanishing American: White Attitudes and U.S. Indian Policy* (Middletown, Conn.: Wesleyan University Press, 1982), and Mark David Spence, *Dispossessing the Wilderness: Indian Removal and the Making of the National Parks* (New York: Oxford University Press, 1999). For information on Native American history and modern life, see *The Native American Almanac: A Portrait of Native America Today,* edited by Arlen Hirschfelder and Martha Kreipe de Montano (New York: Prentice Hall, 1993).

More specific historical background on the Blackfeet Indians is available in John C. Ewers, *The Blackfeet: Raiders on the Northwestern Plains* (Norman: University of Oklahoma Press, 1967); Howard L. Harrod, *Mission among the Blackfeet* (Norman: University of Oklahoma Press, 1971); and Paul Rosier, *Rebirth of the Blackfeet Nation, 1912–1954* (Lincoln: University of Nebraska Press, 2001). James Welch's highly praised novel, *Fools Crow* (New York: Viking Press, 1986), tells the story of the Blackfeet tribe through the eyes of a young male tribe member coming of age in the decades after the Civil War.

For information on the Blackfeet tribe today, go to **blackfeetnation.com**. Elouise Cobell maintains a Web site about the lawsuit against the Indian Trust at **indiantrust.com**. Recent population data on Native Americans is available under "The American Indian and Alaskan Native Population: 2000" at **factfinder.census.gov/home/aian/index.html**.

CHAPTER 3

Reading the 1894 Pullman Strike

Chicago's Daily Papers Report the News

Victor Harding was working as a reporter for the *Chicago Times* in the summer of 1894 when the Pullman labor strike tied up rail lines from Lake Michigan to the Pacific Ocean. On the night of July 5, when federal troops had marched into Chicago to break the strike at its center, Harding mounted a horse and rode up and down the city's miles of railway track to witness the uprising of thousands of unemployed workers. He saw twenty railcars overturned at Forty-third Street, saw gangs of boys with iron pipes destroy a railway switching mechanism, and watched the smoke billow up from railcars set afire. Harding noted that few of the rioters were railroad workers and even fewer police were taking action to stop the rebellion. Chicago seemed headed for a conflagration, and the unions, the railway companies, the police, and the army seemed unable to stop it.

The Pullman strike had begun in May 1894 as a peaceful labor protest against a single Chicago employer. On its face, there was nothing remarkable about this particular local strike against the Pullman Palace Car Company. Although all labor strikes were illegal in the United States in this industrializing era, that fact did not silence the thousands of workers' protests staged in the three decades following the Civil War. The Pullman strike might have erupted and been put down like countless others. But uniquely combustible conditions in the early summer of 1894 ignited the local Pullman strike, causing it to explode first into a national labor boycott of more than twenty railroads and then into a violent confrontation between the federal government, the railroad companies, and American workers. A singular mix of employer intransigence, government aggression, worker bitterness, and general economic desperation transformed the Pullman strike into a pivotal event, galvanizing debates over the rights of employers and workers in an industrialized democracy and over the role of government in labor disputes.

Long before the strike, the Pullman Palace Car Company and its president, George Pullman, were famous. Pullman had perfected the passenger railcar, providing comfortable seats and sleeper cars to the traveling public in the 1870s and 1880s. Pullman's cars were so popular and his business dealings so shrewd that by 1890 three-quarters of the nation's railroads were under contract to carry only Pullman company passenger cars, and the brand name "Pullman" had become synonymous with "passenger car." In addition to the fame of his product, George Pullman was well known for creating the "model" industrial town of Pullman, Illinois, just fifteen miles south of Chicago.

Some observers admired Pullman town's array of 1,400 redbrick rental units, which ranged from boardinghouses and two-bedroom tenements to four-bedroom homes. Others praised its modern system of water, gas, and sewage. Still others, however, criticized the town George Pullman built because it lacked any elected government and the company exercised paternalistic control over the company-owned schoolhouse, shopping arcade, library (where borrowers had to pay a member's fee), and hotel—the fanciest building in town and the only place where alcoholic beverages could be sold. Still others complained that George Pullman owned the only church building in town and set the rent too high for working-class congregations. But he was firm on the subject of rent in Pullman town: this real estate endeavor was no charity. Investors in the Pullman Land Association were assured of a steady 5 percent return on their shares in the town's rental properties.

Pullman workers experienced both boom and bust in the year before their strike. The World's Columbian Exposition, held in Chicago in 1893 to celebrate American industrial progress, momentarily stimulated full employment and high wages in Pullman town. But the New York stock market crash that same year led to the bankruptcy of 16,000 businesses nationwide—including hundreds of railroads. The depression of 1894 was the worst the United States had ever suffered in its tumultuous economic history, and the worst it would suffer until 1929.

In the town of Pullman itself, the depression caused layoffs, wage cuts, and increased resentment over the company's housing policies. During the Exposition's boom time, less than 40 percent of the 4,500 Pullman workers had chosen to live in the company town. Most chose to live in neighboring towns, with lower rents, greater independence, and the opportunity to buy their own homes. When the depression began, the Pullman company laid off workers, cut wages by as much as 40 percent, and then gave rehiring preference to those workers who agreed to take up residence in Pullman town, where the rents were not reduced at all. Bitterness over these practices grew because management salaries did not decline during the depression and because those who owned stock in the Pullman Palace Car Company were still receiving their guaranteed annual dividends of 8 percent. Angry that they were bearing more than their fair share of the economic depression, Pullman workers joined the American Railway Union (ARU) early in 1894 and voted to strike in May, after

Figure 3.1 Pullman Workers Head for Home This photo shows Pullman workers on a regular workday, headed toward their homes just south across Florence Boulevard, which was named for Pullman's daughter. These factory buildings have been demolished, but the brick houses that workers rented have become valued properties in today's housing market. *Source:* Historic Pullman Foundation.

George Pullman and his managers refused to negotiate with the union over wages or rents.

The minute Pullman workers affiliated with the ARU, their local labor conflict became part of a national struggle within the railway industry, the most important arm of transport and travel in the United States. It was no accident that this conflict was centered in the midwestern city of Chicago, which had become a transportation nexus by 1894. On one side of the struggle, the railroad owners belonged to voluntary collectives like the General Managers' Association (GMA), which represented the twenty-four railroads with terminals in Chicago. GMA members secretly set wage scales and work rules for its member railway lines and negotiated with a few highly skilled workers in small craft unions while blacklisting all workers who tried to form industry-wide unions. On the other side of the struggle was the ARU, a brand-new, national, "industrial" union in which skilled, semiskilled, and unskilled railroad workers joined together in one industry-wide association. Railway owners feared the potential power of the ARU, which first appeared in 1893 and claimed 150,000 members by 1894. Just weeks before the Pullman strike began, the ARU reached a favorable settlement in a strike against the Great Northern Railroad, and the members of the GMA understood that this new union was the player to beat.

The ARU, led by its charismatic president, Eugene V. Debs, gathered for its national convention in Chicago in late June 1894. The local Pullman strike had been under way for six weeks, and the company had refused all invitations to arbitrate the dispute. At that moment, public sympathy lay with the workers, who appeared to be battling a stubborn, paternalistic employer. Debs and the ARU hoped for a great victory by refusing to handle any Pullman cars on the railway lines, thereby forcing George Pullman to the negotiating table. But the railway owners who belonged to the GMA knew that any ARU victory would encourage railway workers' general unionizing efforts. For that reason, the members of the GMA adopted a strategy of solidarity with the Pullman Company and insisted that their railways were contract-bound to carry Pullman cars, so if workers refused to attach Pullman cars to their trains, then the railways would be forced to cease all service, not just Pullman car service. In taking this rigid position the GMA was betting that public sympathy would turn against the ARU if the boycott of Pullman cars halted not only passenger cars but all vital arteries of trade, travel, and mail service.

The resulting chaos on the railroad lines lasted from June 26 to July 10, but those two weeks brought a bloody end to both the national boycott and the local Pullman strike. During the first week of the showdown, nearly 100,000 railway workers refused to handle Pullman cars, and the GMA's twenty-four railway companies refused to run trains without Pullman cars. Even Eugene Debs was stunned by the strength and speed of the strike, which revealed railway workers' anger at their own employers as much as it showed support for Pullman workers. The standoff between the ARU and the GMA tied up lines across the country. During that first week, vital trade arteries in twenty-seven states were stalled and snarled, which meant delays and disruptions for travelers, manufactured goods, fuel, livestock, produce, and—most important—the U.S. mail. During the second week of the standoff, control of events shifted from the railway workers to the federal government, which used court injunctions and federal troops to force an end to the ARU's boycott of Pullman cars.

In the summer of 1894, officials in President Grover Cleveland's administration were in no mood to negotiate with workers. In the wake of the stock market crash, the gross national product was down by almost 10 percent, national unemployment was climbing above 15 percent, and the United Mine Workers had just rallied 125,000 miners to a nationwide coal strike. Moreover, the highest officials in the administration had worked as lawyers for railway companies and shared railway owners' philosophical belief that labor unions infringed on employers' property rights. Even if administration officials had been more sympathetic to labor unions, the federal government in 1894 had no formal mechanism for mediating disputes between labor and management. For all of these reasons, no one in the White House viewed arbitration of the strike as an option. Instead, on July 2, a federal judge issued sweeping injunctions forbidding the ARU from interfering with rail service, from interrupting U.S. mail service, or from inducing railway workers to withhold their labor. Working in cooperation with the GMA, the U.S. attorney general's office effectively declared all ARU activity to be illegal. It then dispatched more than 16,000 federal troops to enforce the court orders.

The injunctions and the appearance of troops in various cities sparked the strike's first violence, including street protests, attacks on railway property, fires in rail yards, and violent confrontations between prolabor demonstrators and authorities. Armed but ill-trained federal marshals scuffled with those who had been left unemployed and disaffected by the nationwide economic depression. No one in the government, the GMA, or the ARU could control the outcome. Fifty-one people died, and more than 500 were arrested in street skirmishes. In the end, none of the violence occurred in Pullman town, and only a handful of those arrested were ARU members, but on July 10 seventy-one union leaders—including Eugene Debs—were arrested and charged with violating the federal injunctions. With its leaders in jail and troops on the streets, ARU members could not sustain their boycott, and Pullman workers could not sustain their strike. By July 19, the trains were running, and the Pullman Palace Car Company was ready to hire anyone who pledged not to join a union.

Using the Source: Newspaper Articles

The old saying that "newspapers are the day books of history" certainly holds true in the case of public events such as the Pullman strike. While there exists an array of primary sources on the strike, including court proceedings, judicial rulings, government testimonies, speeches, pamphlets, and even novels, it is the daily newspaper articles on the strike that allow us to watch events as they unfolded and to feel the passions of the moment. When incidents like the Pullman strike occur in today's world, we all gather around the television set and tune to the station we trust for news coverage. In 1894, people gathered around the pages of their favorite newspaper, in which reactions were both chronicled and shaped. It is because of newspapers' central role in recording events and reflecting attitudes that historians so often include newspapers among their sources.

By the time of the Pullman strike, urban newspapers had become a vital part of American public life. In the thirty years following the Civil War, the number of U.S. cities with populations over 50,000 had increased from sixteen to fifty-eight; by 1890, 19 percent of Americans lived in these sizable urban communities. Chicago's population alone had grown from almost 300,000 in 1870 to more than one million in 1890. In this expanding sea of strangers, newspapers offered not only a basis for common knowledge about civic affairs and influential people but also a means by which city dwellers could identify with (or against) strangers across town.

At the same time, urban newspapers in late nineteenth-century America had become big businesses that competed for readers by charging one or two cents for a ten-page daily. In Chicago in 1890, there were twenty-six daily newspapers, with circulation rates between 10,000 and 230,000. Nine of those newspapers provided general news in English, ten offered the news in a foreign language, and the rest provided financial or neighborhood news. Then, as now, information was the commodity that these newspapers sold, although late nineteenth-century newspapers were much less subtle than today's newspapers when inserting editorial opinion into news stories. After all, in a city like Chicago, where the competition was fierce, a newspaper's editorial opinion was as important as its information in winning readers' loyalty.

What Can Newspaper Articles Tell Us?

The best way to appreciate the value of newspapers as a historical source is to think about how difficult it would be to reconstruct an event in the past without the benefit of newspapers. In that situation, even the most basic information is hard to establish. If we relied solely on recollections from individuals with no duty to "cover" an event, we would be hard-pressed to determine with any accuracy when or where an event occurred or who, exactly, was present. Thus, in tracing events that took place before there was televised news footage, newspapers serve as the most immediate eyewitnesses to unfolding stories. In the case of the Pullman strike, for example, newspapers were competing to provide the most extensive coverage of daily developments throughout the city and the country. The result is a printed record of local skirmishes, fires, and arrests, along with the names and affiliations of otherwise-anonymous individuals. By gathering the bits and pieces of data from various newspaper articles, we can trace patterns and make connections that reporters were too close to see and not paid to analyze.

The immediacy of daily newspapers provides an excellent gauge of the public climate at the time an event was actually occurring. Newspapers cannot tell us what readers were thinking, but they can tell us what information and opinions readers were being exposed to, and circulation figures can give us a sense of the popularity of different editorial positions on an event. In Chicago, eight of the city's nine daily English-language newspapers opposed the ARU's use of the railway boycott to aid the Pullman strikers. Only one newspaper, the *Chicago Times*, supported the ARU. Although the *Times* lost most of its commercial advertising during the strike, its circulation rose from just 40,000 to over 100,000 in the heat of the boycott, suggesting that its editorial stance temporarily won over new readers.

The advantages of newspapers—providing local details, reflecting the immediate climate, and appealing to a particular readership—are the very reasons why we must also be cautious in using newspapers as sources of information and must never rely on a single story to reconstruct events. The key disadvantage of newspapers as a source is the fact that reporters are "on deadline" and do not always have time to check and recheck their facts. Information gathered in the heat of the moment may be incomplete. The second disadvantage of newspapers as a historical source is that newspapers offer editorial positions as well as the news. When we read newspapers from the past, we have to be alert to the possibility that a newspaper's editorial position shaped its presentation of news events; we must watch for the ways in which legitimate opinion on the editorial page became slanted reporting on the news page.

In the case of the Pullman strike, the connection between editorial position and news reporting is not difficult to detect. The 1894 strike coincided with the infamous period of "yellow journalism," when competitive newspapers violated their own boastful claims to accuracy by inflating, exaggerating, and even fabricating "facts" to increase circulation. It was often a newspaper's editorial stance that dictated the direction in which a story would lean. To appreciate the role of editorial bias in shaping news reporting during the Pullman strike, consider these excerpts from the *Chicago Tribune* and the *Chicago Times* on June 30, 1894 — four days after the national railway boycott began and three days before U.S. troops were called up. Note the ways in which each reporter's language, as well as his choice of content, served to shape each story:

CHICAGO TRIBUNE, JUNE 30, 1894

"Law is Trampled On"

With the coming of darkness last night Dictator Debs' strikers threw off the mask of law and order and began the commission of acts of lawlessness and violence. A Pan Handle train carrying seven sleeper cars was flagged at Riverdale, and the engineer and fireman, under threat of being killed if they moved, were forced to hold the train while a mob of 800 men detached the Pullmans. . . . The mob grew in numbers and resisted efforts of the train men to recoup the Pullmans.

CHICAGO TIMES, JUNE 30, 1894

"Mail Trains Must Move"

At noon today United States Marshall Byington received telegraphic instructions . . . to move all mail trains that were being detained in this city on account of the Pullman boycott. He . . . notified the . . . American Railway Union . . . giving them until 2 p.m. to decide whether or not they would offer any interference. A committee of strikers called on [Byington] an hour later and informed him that the trains would be allowed to proceed. . . . Passenger trains on the Ohio & Mobile roads were allowed to go out this morning without sleepers.

It is easy to tell from these two paragraphs that the *Chicago Tribune* was opposed to the ARU boycott and the *Chicago Times* supported it. The more difficult task is to piece together a single, plausible version of events from such varying and possibly inflated stories. We cannot assume that the version that appeared in the majority of papers is the most accurate, nor can we assume that the story whose editorial bias we agree with is the most accurate. Newspapers can alert us to obscure events, but we often have to consult other sources, such as police reports or sworn testimony, to determine the validity of news reports.

While we have to sift through the biased language of a news article to figure out what actually happened on a particular day, we can also make good use of that biased language to grasp the level of emotion surrounding an event. Passionate prose about the "Dictator Debs" acting in the "darkness" of night may not accurately depict the ARU's president during the Pullman strike, but it does suggest the heightened tempers in Chicago, and we must consider the strong possibility that such hot language further intensified the climate. Just the fact that Chicago newspapers covered their front pages with strike stories in late June and early July constitutes historical evidence. The sheer quantity of coverage, and the size of the headlines, conveyed a sense of crisis. And the more frightening the boycott appeared, the more likely people were to turn against the ARU and support the federal troops. So while sensational coverage in newspapers has to be corroborated, it also serves as its own kind of historical evidence.

The newspaper stories you will be examining in this chapter are a seven-day sample from the sixty-six-day Pullman strike, representing coverage in the *Chicago Tribune* and the *Chicago Times*. The *Tribune* was a staunchly Republican newspaper and a strong opponent of the ARU boycott. It was the city's oldest newspaper in 1894, and its daily circulation of 75,000 made it the third-most popular paper in the city. The *Chicago Times*, a boycott supporter, was the second-oldest newspaper in Chicago and had been a Republican newspaper until it was purchased by a Democratic politician in 1893. The *Times*'s prolabor stance therefore represented a recent effort to improve its anemic circulation of 40,000 by reaching out to a new, more working-class audience. In using these newspapers to trace events and emotions in the Pullman strike, you may want to take this background information into consideration.

Questions to Ask

As you read through this sample of newspaper reports on the Pullman strike, you will want to keep track of two different things: (1) factual claims about specific events that could be verified by checking other newspapers or other types of sources and (2) the language and slant in the news stories that reveal each newspaper's editorial bias.

- Which stories make you feel that you are learning what actually happened that day?

- Which stories contribute more to your sense of the emotional climate in Chicago in the summer of 1894 than to your knowledge of events?
- What specific differences do you see in the two newspapers' reports day by day?
- How does the language in the headlines convey each newspaper's editorial stance?
- Who does the *Tribune* cast as the leading villain and the leading hero in the boycott drama? Who is the hero and who is the villain in the pages of the *Times*? What part does George Pullman play in either paper?

Source Analysis Table

The fourteen news stories you will be examining from the *Chicago Tribune* and the *Chicago Times* differ in both factual claims and editorial bias. Factual claims are statements of names, dates, and events that you could verify by consulting other sources, such as police records, sworn testimony, or other news stories. Editorial bias becomes apparent in the newspaper's choice of words or omission of some information and its emphasis on other information that is intended to encourage the reader to sympathize with one side in the boycott and to dislike the other side. The accompanying table gives you space to note examples of factual claims from each news article and examples of editorial bias.

Date and Source	Factual Claims	Editorial Bias
May 12, 1894 *1. Chicago Tribune*		
2. Chicago Times		
May 15, 1894 *3. Chicago Tribune*		
4. Chicago Times		
June 26, 1894 *5. Chicago Tribune*		
6. Chicago Times		
June 28, 1894 *7. Chicago Tribune*		
8. Chicago Times		

(continued)

Date and Source	Factual Claims	Editorial Bias
July 1, 1894 9. *Chicago Tribune*		
10. *Chicago Times*		
July 7, 1894 11. *Chicago Tribune*		
12. *Chicago Times*		
July 15, 1894 13. *Chicago Tribune*		
14. *Chicago Times*		

To download and print this table, visit the book companion site at **bedfordstmartins.com/brownshannon**.

The Source: Chicago Newspaper Articles on the Pullman Strike, May 12, 1894–July 15, 1894

FIRST FULL DAY OF THE LOCAL PULLMAN STRIKE

| 1 | *Chicago Tribune*, May 12, 1894, page one |

PULLMAN MEN OUT

DISCHARGES THE CAUSE

Committeemen Laid Off and Their Comrades Act.

Two thousand employees in the Pullman car works struck yesterday, leaving 800 others at their posts. This was not enough to keep the works going, so a notice was posted on the big gates at 6 o'clock . . . saying: "These shops closed until further notice."

Mr. Pullman said last night he could not tell when work would be resumed.

The American Railway Union, which has been proselyting for a week among the workmen, announces that it will support the strikers. Just exactly how, Vice-President Howard would not say. He intimated, however, that the trainmen on the railways on which are organized branches of the union might refuse to handle any of the Pullman rolling stock. It is not believed, however, that such action will be taken and it is equally impossible to see how the union can otherwise aid the strikers.

The walk-out was a complete surprise to the officials. . . . Mr. Pullman had offered to allow the men the privilege of examining the books of the company to verify his statement that the works were running at a loss. When the men quit work at 6 o'clock Thursday evening none of them had any idea of striking. . . . But the Grievance Committee of Forty-six held a session at the Dewdrop Saloon in Kensington which lasted until 4:30 o'clock in the morning. At that time a ballot was taken which resulted: 42 to 4 in favor of a strike. A second ballot was unanimous. So a messenger was sent to the freight car builders to order them to stop, and all seventy-five walked out of the big gate. One department at a time, the men went out so that by 10 o'clock 1500 men were out. Thirteen hundred and fifty men kept at work until noon, but only 800 came back after lunch. . . .

Included among the strikers were 400 girls from the laundry, sewing-rooms, and other departments. In the afternoon, everyone—men, women, and children—put on their best clothes and assembled on the ball grounds. They stood in groups or rolled around in the grass, making no demonstration and acting in a subdued manner.

2   *Chicago Times,* May 12, 1894, page one

PULLMAN MEN OUT

Nearly 4,000 Throw Down Their Tools and Quit

Refuse to Strike Another Link Till Wrongs Are Righted

Firing Three Men Starts It

Almost the entire force of men employed in the Pullman shops went out on strike yesterday. Out of the 4,800 men and women employed in the various departments there were probably not over 800 at work at 6 o'clock last evening. The immediate cause of the strike was the discharge or laying off of three men in the iron machine shop. The real but remote cause is the question of wages over which the men have long been dissatisfied and on account of which they had practically resolved to strike a month ago.

The strike of yesterday was ordered by a committee of forty-six representing every department at the Pullman works. This committee was in session all night Thursday night, and finally came to the conclusion to order a strike 4:30 o'clock yesterday morning. The vote stood 42 in favor of a strike and 4 against.

The terms upon which the men insist before returning to work are the restoration of the wage scale of 1893, time and one-half for overtime, and no discrimination against any of those who have taken a prominent part in the strike.

The position of the company is that no increase in wages is possible under the present conditions. . . . The position of the men is that they are receiving less than a living wage, to which they are entitled. . . . President George M. Pullman told the committee that the company was doing business at a loss even at the reduced wages paid the men and offered to show his books in support of his assertion.

FOURTH DAY OF THE LOCAL PULLMAN STRIKE

3   *Chicago Tribune,* May 15, 1894, page eight

THEY MAY GO HUNGRY

Grocers Threaten to Cut Off Credit for Pullman Strikers

It will soon be a question of how to get food with the Pullman strikers if the strike continues much longer. A committee of the Kensington grocerymen, who furnish supplies for the men, told the Grievance Committee yesterday they were in a peculiar position. To extend credit to men on an indefinite strike meant ruin, while to refuse credit probably would mean a boycott when the men resumed work and began to earn money. So the grocers wanted to know how long the strike was going to last. . . . The strikers' committeemen said they had no means of knowing, so there the matter rests. The Arcade Mercantile Company [in Pullman], which ran a strictly cash concern in the market and a credit place in the Arcade, closed up the credit branch. . . . Eugene V. Debs, President of the American Railway Union, is certain that the strikers will win. He said so several times yesterday but absolutely refused to give reasons for his supreme confidence. He still hints darkly at what will happen if the union should refuse to handle Pullman cars.

"Why," he said, "the boys all over the country are clamoring to tie up the Pullman cars. They are in an inflammable mood and longing for a chance to take part in this affair. . . . The whole country is in an inflammable condition. . . . When a man gets $2 a day he can live and is therefore a coward—afraid to try to get more—but when he gets cut down to $1.40 or $1 he gets desperate. The difference between that and nothing is so slight he feels he has almost nothing to lose and everything to gain by a strike. . . ."

The strikers are following the advice of their leaders to stay at home and let whiskey alone. Morning, noon, and night the streets in Pullman and Kensington are as quiet and deserted as of a Sunday. There are no groups at the street corners; no loafers in the saloons. Even at the headquarters the crowd rarely exceeds 200 men, and these sometimes become bored and go home, leaving the hall empty. . . . John S. Runnells, general counsel for the Pullman company, said yesterday: "The statement made in some of the newspapers that after a while there would be a great number of evictions at Pullman and consequent scenes of excitement is entirely untrue."

4   *Chicago Times,* May 15, 1894, page one

SKIMS OFF THE FAT

Pullman Company Declares a Dividend Today

Quarterly 2 Per Cent Thrives at the Men's Expense

Full Pockets Swallow $600,000 While Honest Labor Is Starving

Today the Pullman company will declare a quarterly dividend of 2 per cent on its capital stock of $30,000,000 and President George M. Pullman is authority for the statement that his company owes no man a cent. This despite the assertion of Mr. Pullman that the works have been run at a loss for eight months. Six hundred thousand dollars to shareholders, while starvation threatens the workman.

H. J. Pingrey, vestibule builder at the Pullman shops, has worked or reported daily for work since Jan. 1, till the strike, and during that time has been able to put in eighty days, for which he received $100. During that time he paid back to the company $40 for house rent and still owes $10 on that account.

The Rev. Mr. Oggel, who preaches in the beautiful green stone church on Watt Avenue, hard by the Pullman shops, marveled greatly in his sermon of Sunday night that Pingrey and his fellow workmen should have been so foolish as to go on a strike. The Rev. Mr. Oggel draws about $40 a week salary paid by Pullman workmen, and house rent free, to expound the gospel of Christ. . . .

Another matter which caused a ripple of excitement among the men was the announcement made by a committee representing the merchants . . . that under the existing circumstances . . . they could not give further credit to the strikers for goods. . . . Mr. Heathcoate [ARU local president] told the committee that . . . no individual merchant need hope to avert the certain boycott which would follow his refusal to give his customers credit. . . . "These are the merchants who have made a living out of the working men here for years and now when our time of trouble comes, they abandon us almost before we have a chance to ask for accommodation; we are not asking them for charity."

FIRST DAY OF THE NATIONAL ARU BOYCOTT OF PULLMAN CARS

5	*Chicago Tribune,* June 26, 1894, page eight

BOYCOTT IS ON TODAY

American Railway Union Begins its Fight on Pullman

The American Railway Union at noon today will begin a test of its strength with railways using the Pullman Palace Car company's sleeping and dining-room cars. At that hour the boycott of Pullman cars ordered by the union will go into effect. Though its purpose is to force the Pullman company to consent to an arbitration of the Pullman strike, its manifestation will be nothing more or less than a fight with the railways in which the Pullman company will take no part.

The railway lines have already been told through the press that they must haul no Pullman cars in their trains. They have accepted the implied challenge and yesterday their representatives in joint meeting voted to stand together as one and resist the union's demand. Their contracts with the Pullman company. . . impose a penalty for failure to haul the Pullman cars and they will certainly haul them, say the managers. Representative men among them declare the boycott will amount to but little. . . . George M. Pullman yesterday made a statement of his company's position. It contained no offer to arbitrate the strike.

6   *Chicago Times,* June 26, 1894, page one

UNITED TO FIGHT

Railway Managers Arrayed against the A.R.U.

In the big fight which will open between the Pullman Palace Car company and the American Railway union at noon today, Mr. Pullman will have the concerted aid of all the railroad companies which use his cars. At a meeting of the board of general managers of the railroads running into Chicago, the following resolutions were adopted:

"... That it is the sense of this meeting that the said proposed boycott, being confessedly not in the interest of any employees of said railroad companies, or on account of any grievance between said railroad companies and said employees, is unjustifiable and unwarranted. ... That we hereby declare it to be the lawful right and duty of the said railway companies to protest against said proposed boycott; to resist the same in the interest of their existing contracts and for the benefit of the traveling public, and that we will act unitedly toward that end."

THIRD DAY OF THE NATIONAL RAILWAY BOYCOTT

7   *Chicago Tribune,* June 28, 1894, page one

DEBS IS A DICTATOR

His Warfare on the Railroads Is Waged Effectively

The American Railway Union became aggressive yesterday in its efforts to force a settlement between Mr. Pullman and his striking employees. By calling out their switchmen, it threw down the gauntlet to the Erie, Grand Trunk, Monon, Eastern Illinois, Northern Pacific, Wisconsin Central, Chicago Great Western, Baltimore and Ohio, Pan-Handle, and Santa Fe railroads. It continued the warfare commenced the night before against the Illinois Central and continued it so successfully that the road had to abandon its suburban service at 9 o'clock. Its freight service was at a standstill all day and the same is practically true of other roads. In no case, however, did the strikers prevent the departure of any regular passenger trains from Chicago. ...

Debs' master stroke, however, occurred at midnight, when every employee on the Santa Fe belonging to the American Railway Union was ordered out. ... Whether the men will obey the mandate will be learned today. ...

So far no marked violence has been attempted. Two hundred policemen put in the day in various railroad yards, but their services were not needed.

Chief Brennan says he has 2,000 men who can be massed at any point inside of an hour.

8   *Chicago Times,* June 28, 1894, page one

NOT A WHEEL TURNS IN THE WEST

Complete Shutdown of All Roads in the Territory beyond the Missouri River

Chicago Center of Eastern Trouble

It May Be the Biggest Tie-Up in All History

All the western half of the United States has begun to feel the paralysis of the American Railway Union's boycott of Pullman. From the Missouri River to the Pacific Coast, from the Canadian to the Mexican line, there is scarcely a railway that has not been gripped by the boycott. At every important division point in the west, southwest, and northwest, there are trains blockaded because the American Railway Union men will not run them with Pullman cars attached and the railway managers will not allow them to run otherwise. Some roads are absolutely and utterly blockaded, others feel the embargo slightly yet, but it grows in strength with every hour. It is spreading eastward from Chicago, too. No man can tell what the end will be. . . . This is the end of the second day. This, when so far the American Railway Union has done little beyond ordering the withdrawal of switching crews, switch tenders, and towermen. By tomorrow, they promise that all conductors, engineers and firemen on freight and passenger trains will join in the strike and then, well, nobody can tell.

General Manager Ainsley of the Wisconsin Central notified his men that unless they go to work today he will supply their places with nonunion men. Then there may be trouble. . . .

The six o'clock train on the Great Western started out with two Pullman sleepers and one Pullman diner. It ran about two car lengths. The conductor rang the bell, the train stopped, the whole crew got down and cut off those three cars. This with a squad of policemen standing by and the company's officials looking on. The train pulled out without the Pullmans. It was the most decisive thing the boycotters have done yet.

SIXTH DAY OF THE NATIONAL RAILWAY BOYCOTT

9   *Chicago Tribune*, July 1, 1894, page one

MOBS BENT ON RUIN

Debs' Strikers Begin a Work of Destruction

Men Who Attempt to Work Are Terrorized and Beaten

Dictator after the Managers

Continued and menacing lawlessness marked the progress yesterday of Dictator Debs and those who obey his orders in their efforts at coercing the railroads of the country into obeying the mandates of the American Railway Union. The Rock Island was the chief sufferer from the mob spirit which broke loose the moment its men struck. It was as much as a man's life was worth to endeavor to operate a train on that road to transact the business of the company, and at 6:20 o'clock the culmination was reached by the deliberate wrecking of a passenger train at Blue Island.[1] A striker named Murvin rushed to a switch over which an officer was standing guard, pushed him aside, threw the switch, and derailed the train. Strange to say, he was arrested. Fortunately, none of the passengers was hurt, but unfortunately for the road the cars were thrown across the track in such positions that they effectively blocked traffic. At 10 o'clock the officials threw up their hands and discontinued service for the night. At Blue Island, anarchy reigned. The Mayor and police force of that town could do nothing to repress the riotous strikers and they did their own sweet will. . . .

On the Illinois Central it was the same old story of destruction of the company's property without interference from the police. . . . Dictator Debs was as blatant as ever yesterday. He asserted . . . that the fight against Pullman was now a thing of the past. He is waging his warfare against the General Managers, who had committed the sin of combining against him.

[1] Blue Island was a close-knit community sixteen miles southwest of downtown Chicago. Many of the town's residents worked in local railway freight yards.

10 | *Chicago Times,* July 1, 1894, page one

ONE IS DERAILED

Rock Island Engine Runs Off at Blue Island

It Almost Brings on a Riot

Rock Island train No. 19 for Kansas City and St. Paul was partly derailed at Blue Island at 6:30 o'clock last night. The switch was thrown by James Mervin,[1] a switchman, and the heavy engine and tender left the rails and stuck fast in the mud, completely blocking the track. The train fortunately did not go over the embankment. It was well filled with passengers. . . .

Mervin was arrested by Deputy Sheriff Leibrandt and will be brought to Chicago for examination.

The train was a mixed train and was composed of three Pullmans . . . and ran along without interference until it reached the crossover switch at the west end of the Blue Island yard. There were some fifty strikers standing in the pouring rain on the right of the track just at the switch. The front wheels passed over them, there was a lurch, and the powerful engine careened to the left. . . . Several passengers who were standing on the platform were violently thrown to the ground, and some of them bruised besides being bespattered with mud. The wildest consternation ensued among them. . . . For a few minutes it looked as if a bloody conflict would follow. All was excitement, but added to the demand of the deputies for the crowd to stand back came a similar demand from several of the American Railway Union to let the law take its course. . . .

Mayor John Zacharias rushed down . . . in the drenching rain in his shirt sleeves. The prisoner shook him by the hand, and it was not until then that anyone seemed to know who the prisoner was. His name is James Mervin, aged 32 years, a switchman, and has been employed in the Rock Island yards at Blue Island. Mervin seemed to have hosts of friends [who] demanded bail, and the mayor fixed it at $5,000. . . . Scores of Mervin's friends proffered the small fortunes for the bond, but up to the latest hour they had not been able to subscribe the requisite amount. Mervin . . . denies, and his friends who were standing by him deny, that he touched the switch.

[1] The *Tribune* spelled the arrested man's name "Murvin"; the *Times* spelled it "Mervin."

**FEDERAL TROOPS HAD BEEN IN CHICAGO
FOR THREE DAYS**

11   *Chicago Tribune,* July 7, 1894, page one

YARDS FIRE SWEPT

Hundreds of Freight Cars, Loaded and Empty, Burn

Rioters Prevent Firemen from Saving the Property.

From Brighton Park to Sixty-first street the yards of the Pan-Handle road were last night put to the torch by the rioters. Between 600 and 700 freight cars have been destroyed, many of them loaded. Miles and miles of costly track are in a snarled tangle of heat-twisted rails. Not less than $750,000—possibly a whole $1,000,000 of property—has been sacrificed to the caprice of a mob of drunken Anarchists and rebels. That is the record of the night's work by the Debs strikers in the Stock-Yards District.

They started early in the afternoon. . . . They were done by 10 o'clock; at that hour they had a roaring wall of fire down the tracks. . . . The flames of their kindling reddened the southwestern sky so that the whole city could know they were at work.

This work the rioters did calmly and systematically. They seemed to work with a deliberate plan. There was none of the wild howlings and ravings that marked their work of the night before.

12   *Chicago Times,* July 7, 1894, page one

MEN NOT AWED BY SOLDIERS

Most of the Roads at a Standstill

Railway Union Is Confident of Winning against Armed Capital

Despite the presence of United States troops and the mobilization of five regiments of state militia, despite threats of martial law and total extermination of the strikers by bullet and bayonet, the great strike inaugurated by the American Railway Union holds three-fourths of the roads running out of Chicago in its strong fetters, and last night traffic was more fully paralyzed than at any time since the inception of the tie-up. . . . With the exception of an occasional car or two moved by the aid of the military, not a wheel is turning. . . .

In the southwest section of the city all railroad property is considered fair game for the attack of the mob. Apparently the police of this district think so, too, for they stand by and appear indifferent to the annihilation of property. Wholesale destruction by incendiarism yesterday succeeded to the train wrecking of the day previous. . . . Nothing pertaining to the railroads seems sacred to the crowd. A splendid new towerhouse, which operates the Pan-Handle's intricate interlocking switches . . . was only spared yesterday through the efforts of a party of striking tower operators of the railroad. . . . The strikers saw there was danger of the fire spreading from a burning toolhouse nearby, a plank walk connecting the two. They tore this sidewalk up and thus saved the towerhouse. . . .

If the soldiers are sent to this district, bloodshed and perhaps death will follow today, for this is the most lawless element in the city, as is shown by their riotous work yesterday. . . . But the perpetrators are not American Railway Union men. The people engaged in this outrageous work of destruction are not strikers, most of them are not even grown men. The persons who set the fires yesterday on the authority of the firemen and police are young hoodlums. . . . The setting fire to the cars yesterday was done openly where anyone could see it and when the slightest effort would have resulted in the apprehension of the guilty ones, but no such effort was made. The firemen were overwhelmed with the work of attending to a dozen different fires and could not, and the police on the scene apparently didn't care to or would not make arrests. . . . At six o'clock, the police had not a single prisoner.

THE STRIKE DRAWS TO A CLOSE

On July 10, Debs and other ARU officers had been arrested for violating the federal court injunction of July 2 constraining ARU activity. They were held for several hours until posting $10,000 bail.

13   *Chicago Tribune*, July 15, 1894, page one

WITH A DULL THUD

The Strike Collapses with Wonderful Rapidity

DEBS' WILD ASSERTIONS

He Is Still Defiant While His "Union" Crumbles about Him

Like the last flicker of a candle that is almost burned out is the "war to the knife" defiance hurled yesterday by Eugene V. Debs in the face of the railroad managers of Chicago. Deserted by the men who answered his first calls for help, denounced by many who followed his banner of revolt only to lose their positions . . . with the very fabric of the American Railway Union falling upon his head and the support on which he stood slipping rapidly from under his feet, he declared that the strike was "on and would be fought to a successful issue."

The value of Mr. Debs' utterances at this stage of the game are shown conclusively by comparing threats and assertions he made yesterday . . . with the condition of affairs last night. . . . "The Northwestern will not be turning a wheel tonight," said Mr. Debs. At midnight not a wheel on the Northwestern had failed to turn. The Northwestern people are inclined to look upon Mr. Debs' declaration as a huge joke. . . . And so it was on the Chicago, Milwaukee and St. Paul, which, according to Debs, was to suffer the same fate as the Northwestern. The officials of the road regard his threats with derision.

14 *Chicago Times,* July 15, 1894, page one

DEBS SURE HE CAN WIN

Says the Battle Is But Begun

More than 1,000 railroad men held an enthusiastic meeting at Uhlich's hall yesterday afternoon, the speakers being President Debs and Vice-President Howard.

President Debs then told the men that the situation was more favorable than it had been at any time since the men were called out. He said that telegrams from twenty-five points west of the Mississippi showed that the roads were completely tied up. . . . "I cannot stop now that defiance has been flung in our teeth by the General Managers' Association. I propose to work harder than ever and teach a lesson to those bigoted idiots. . . . The managers refuse to treat for peace. They say war to the end, and yet the law does not send them to jail. The law seems to be against us . . . but if the law makes it a crime to advise your men against the encroachments of capital by all the gods united I will rot in jail. . . .

"There are men who have returned to their work, but they are traitors. . . . We are better without them. Let them range themselves on the other side and we can then close up ranks and see where we stand. We must unite as strong as iron, but let us be peaceable in this contest. Bloodshed is unwarranted and will not win. It is not by blood that we want to win."

Analyzing Newspaper Articles

1. In noting factual claims in each newspaper's story, where did you find conflicting statements about the same event or the use of entirely different types of facts?

2. How did the two papers differ in their reports on violent incidents?

3. What differences did you find in the way the two newspapers depicted Eugene V. Debs, George Pullman, the General Managers' Association, the Pullman workers, and the members of the ARU?

4. Based on the news stories in this chapter, how would you describe the philosophical differences separating the two newspapers? How do those differences reflect the larger national conflicts between workers and employers that were at the root of the Pullman strike?

5. There is an air of crisis in the Pullman strike coverage in both newspapers. Given the context of the strike—rapid urbanization and industrialization as well as sudden economic depression—what deep fears did the *Tribune* convey to its readers? What fears did the *Times* transmit? How might the expression of these fears have influenced the course of the strike?

6. Write your own news article, dated July 7, 1894, in which you use information from both the *Times* and the *Tribune* to tell a story that you regard as factually reliable even if you cannot be complete.

The Rest of the Story

In the aftermath of the Pullman strike, the *Times* and the *Tribune* offered predictably different coverage of the single most surprising outcome of the whole event: the report issued by the U.S. Strike Commission in mid-November 1894, just four months after the strike collapsed. The commission, which had been appointed by President Grover Cleveland, was composed of three well-respected men of America's ruling elite. Their detailed report was read with shock by both supporters and opponents of the strike because it was far more favorable to labor and far more critical of employers than anyone had expected.

Over the course of three hot weeks in August 1894, the commission took sworn testimony from 111 witnesses, including Pullman workers; representatives of the ARU, the GMA, and the Pullman company; newspaper reporters; police and politicians from Chicago; members of the U.S. Army; and various other interested parties. After listening to testimony that came to over 650 pages, the three commissioners criticized the ARU for tying up the nation's rail system over a local factory dispute, but their report basically blamed the strike on George Pullman's stubborn refusal to negotiate with his workers. The report then praised the Pullman workers for their "dignified, manly and conservative conduct" throughout the strike. Finally, and most unexpectedly, the commissioners harshly condemned the General Managers' Association for its "arrogant and absurd" claim to the right to collectively set wages and working conditions across the railway industry while denying workers the right to organize as a competitive body.

The headline for the *Chicago Times*'s November 13 story on the commission report read "All in Labor's Favor." That same day, the *Tribune* declared,

"Report Is a Roast." The *Times* characterized the report as a "stroke on behalf of justice" and reprinted the report's argument that Pullman should have cut salaries, rents, and profits more—and wages less—in order to more fairly distribute the pain of the depression. The *Times* skipped over the commissioners' critique of the ARU for getting involved in the strike in the first place and focused instead on their finding that the union was not responsible for the "disgraceful" violence in July. Not surprisingly, the *Times* applauded the commission's "bitter condemnation" of the "all-powerful" GMA.

In its editorial on the U.S. Strike Commission report, the *Tribune* called the report's dismissal of ARU responsibility for violence a "wild assertion." Focusing on George Pullman as one bad apple in the capitalist bin, the *Tribune* scoffed at the commission's "caustic view" of the GMA. So while the paper endorsed the commission's criticism of Pullman's stubbornness, it did not comment on the commission's more threatening notions that the employer should have distributed depression profits differently or that the GMA should allow unions. Instead, the *Tribune* chose to reprint an article from *Harper's Weekly* that fumed over the commissioners' "astonishing" radicalism and asked, "what is the state of mind of men who sign such a report?"

The U.S. Strike Commission's most historically significant recommendations were that unions be legitimized by government policy and that the government set up a system for labor arbitration in order to avoid "barbarous" and costly strikes in the future. The *Times* claimed that such ideas "may serve organized labor for a charter and a creed," but the *Tribune* was curiously quiet on the subject of these far-reaching policy recommendations. *Tribune* readers were left with only the reprint of the *Harper's Weekly* article, which warned that the commissioners' views were "the first stage in a socialistic revolution" and represented the end of "civilized society."

Six months later, the *Tribune* took solace in the Supreme Court's judgment that Eugene Debs was guilty of violating a legitimate federal injunction, and the newspaper expressed pleasure that "Dictator Debs" would be spending six months in jail. As it turned out, however, Debs's sentence was less predictive of labor's future than the commission report. It would take forty years, until the New Deal, before the government fully implemented the report's recommendations for labor arbitration. But the Pullman strike—and the report that emanated from it—marked a significant shift in public support for government as a strike mediator, not a strike breaker.

To Find Out More

The 1894 issues of the *Chicago Tribune* and *Chicago Times* used for this chapter were accessed on reels of microfilm, which must be read on a microfilm "reader." We would all prefer to read old newspapers on a computer, of course, but digitizing newspapers from the past would be an enormously expensive project. For that reason, the National Endowment for the Humanities, in cooperation with state archives, is funding two tax-supported projects to preserve newspapers. The United States Newspaper Program (USNP) is supposed to "locate, catalog, and preserve *on microfilm* all newspapers published in the U.S. from the eighteenth century to the present." At the same time, the National Digital Newspaper Program (NDNP) will digitize "historically significant" newspapers from around the United States published between 1836 and 1922. When completed, this digital project will be maintained by the Library of Congress and freely accessible on the Web.

The USNP and the NDNP testify to the importance that researchers and librarians attach to newspapers as a record of American society. Thanks to these projects, a future researcher seeking a particular newspaper from a particular day will not be told that the paper source has disintegrated into the dustbin of history. For more information on these programs, see **neh.gov/projects/ usnp.html** and **neh.gov/projects/ndnp.html**. Many public and university libraries own microfilm of past issues of local newspapers or will borrow reels of newspaper microfilm for you through interlibrary loan.

There are two classic works on the Pullman strike: Almont Lindsey's *The Pullman Strike: The Story of a Unique Experiment and a Great Labor Upheaval* (Chicago: University of Chicago Press, 1942) is an informative, but very partisan, defense of the Pullman workers and the American Railway Union, while Stanley Buder's *Pullman: An Experiment in Industrial Order and Community Planning, 1880–1930* (New York: Oxford University Press, 1967) is less lively but more balanced. More recent perspectives on the strike are available in *The Pullman Strike and the Crisis of the 1890s* (Urbana: University of Illinois, 1999), a collection of essays edited by Richard Schneirov and others. Connections between the Pullman strike and popular urban culture in the 1890s are traced in Carl Smith's *Urban Disorder and the Shape of Belief* (Chicago: University of Chicago, 1995) and James Gilbert's *Perfect Cities* (Chicago: University of Chicago, 1991). David Ray Papke reviews the legal aspects of the event in *The Pullman Case: The Clash of Labor and Capital in Industrial America* (Lawrence: University Press of Kansas, 1999).

A half dozen significant documents can be found by searching "Pullman Strike" at the History Matters Web site: **historymatters.gmu.edu**. An explanation of the link between the Pullman strike and Labor Day appears at **pbs.org/newshour/bb/business/september96/labor_day_9-2.html**, and the Eugene V. Debs Foundation's Web site (**eugenevdebs.com**) offers additional information.

The history of newspapers includes very general and very particular studies. Among the general studies, Michael Schudson's *Discovering the News: A Social History of American Newspapers* (New York: Basic Books, 1978) offers an interesting discussion of "objectivity" in news reporting. For the newspapers and events related to the Pullman strike, see David Paul Nord, *Newspapers and New Politics: Midwestern Municipal Reform, 1890–1900* (Ann Arbor: University of Michigan, 1979) and *Communities of Journalism: A History of American Newspapers and Their Readers* (Urbana: University of Illinois, 2001).

CHAPTER 4

Immigrant to the Promised Land

Memory and Autobiography

When Hilda Satt thought back on her childhood in Wloclawek, Poland, she remembered Sabbath dinners in the family dining room, golden noodle soups, apple puddings, aromatic spices, holiday wines, copper pots, silver trays, and shiny brass candlesticks. Alongside those sweet memories lay Hilda's bitter recollections of persecution by the Russian officials who controlled Wloclawek, a city of some 50,000 people located about ninety miles northwest of Warsaw. Wloclawek lay within the sizable territory between the Baltic Sea and the Black Sea known as the "Pale of Settlement." There, the ruling Russian government confined all of Russia's five million Jews and enforced a system of discrimination that fueled Christian residents' superstitions about Jewish life and faith.

It was not personal poverty but fear of Russian oppression that caused Hilda's father, Louis Satt, to decide to emigrate to the United States in 1891. Since 1881, new legal restrictions on Jews' religious and economic life, coupled with violent military attacks (known as pogroms), destabilized and sometimes terrorized Jewish communities within the Pale. The Satt family was not as impoverished by these attacks as others because Louis was a tombstone carver, which meant that his skilled craft was always in demand. The Satts owned a relatively spacious home and workshop in Wloclawek, and Louis's wife, Dena, employed a cook and a nursemaid to help with their six children. Louis drew on these economic resources to establish a new home in America. Connections with a *Landsmann* (fellow countryman) took him to Chicago, where a population of almost 50,000 eastern European Jews created a demand for tombstones with Hebrew, Yiddish, Polish, Russian, and German inscriptions. Within a year of his arrival in Chicago, Louis Satt was able to open his own shop, to finance his family's ocean voyage to America, and to furnish a six-room apartment in the heart of Chicago's Russian Jewish neighborhood. Hilda and her siblings were enrolled in the Jewish Training School nearby, and even though Dena no longer had household servants, the Satts' future looked prosperous.

That picture changed overnight in 1894 when Hilda's father died. Dena moved the family into cheaper housing and tried to support her six children by working as a street peddler. Hilda later looked back on her widowed mother's fear "of hunger and cold, not so much for herself as for the rest of us. Food, coal, clothing, and shelter had become her only interests in life." Before Hilda reached the legal working age of fourteen, she left school and went to work with her older sister in a knitting factory. Four years later, she moved to a factory that manufactured ladies' "shirtwaist" dresses,[1] where she was paid by the number of cuffs she could sew while sitting at a machine from eight in the morning until six at night. Until she discovered the evening classes and social clubs at the Hull-House settlement, a community center in her neighborhood, Hilda had little to break the "deadly monotony" of "a life that offered only food and warmth and shelter" (Hilda Satt Polacheck, *I Came a Stranger: The Story of a Hull-House Girl,* ed. Dena Polacheck Epstein [Urbana: University of Illinois Press, 1989], 60).

The hardships that Hilda Satt faced as an immigrant to the United States in the 1890s have a familiar ring to them. The popular version of the immigrant experience in America is captured in the Statue of Liberty's poetic plea:

> Give me your tired, your poor,
>
> your huddled masses, yearning to breathe free,
>
> The wretched refuse of your teeming shore.
>
> Send these, the homeless, the tempest-tost to me

But this well-intentioned picture of human misery, crafted by the immigrant poet Emma Lazarus in 1903, obscures the fact that most immigrants to America have not been the poor, wretched refuse of the world. They have often been people like the Satts, who possessed the resources needed to relocate and made careful, rational calculations about improving the family's opportunities by moving to the United States. For example, in 1891, the year Louis Satt arrived, there were rumors of impending new persecutions of Jews, and, in response, the emigration of eastern European Jews to America doubled. Just three years later, however, when an economic depression made jobs scarce in the United States, the emigration of Jews from the still-oppressive Pale of Settlement sharply declined. This tells us that Europe's "teeming masses" did not rush blindly to the United States in the late nineteenth century; they came when the balance of political and economic factors pushing them out of their homelands and pulling them to the United States made emigration a sensible,

---

[1] A shirtwaist was a women's blouse with pleats in the front to resemble a man's dress shirt and with buttons in the back. A shirtwaist dress combined that blouse style with a long, dark skirt. This style became popular as young women moved into sales and office jobs.

Figure 4.1 Hilda Satt as a Young Girl This undated photo shows Hilda Satt as a young girl in Chicago. A studio portrait such as this would have been a luxury in the 1890s, suggesting that it was taken before her father died when Hilda was a comfortably well-dressed daughter in a middle-class immigrant family. Because we know that Hilda was twelve when her father died, we can estimate that this photo was taken when she was between ten and twelve. By the age of fifteen, Hilda was working in a knitting factory.

Source: Special Collections, Richard J. Daley Library, University of Illinois at Chicago.

if risky, venture. We need not deny the harsh economic and political pressures that immigrants faced in their homelands in order to grasp that the individuals who responded to those pressures by moving across the ocean to a strange, new country often had some resources, skills, or family backing.

Immigrants were free to make their own calculations about immigration because, until 1924, the United States did not restrict immigration. Racial prejudice had led Congress to pass the Chinese Exclusion Act in 1882, but no other nationality was excluded by U.S. law. American employers resisted the demands for immigration restriction put forth by nativists (those who feared that foreigners would corrupt American life) and argued that a steady influx of immigrant workers into the nation's growing industries was strengthening the American economy and therefore American life. Social reformers argued that immigrants brought cultural diversity, which enriched American culture. Employers' calls for open immigration did not mean, however, that they advocated good wages and safe working conditions for the foreigners who came. Many of the 23.5 million immigrants who entered the United States between 1880 and 1920 lived and worked under harsh conditions. Even those immigrants who arrived with some resources often struggled to survive, and they often allied with social reformers to improve conditions.

Hilda Satt's experience in Chicago illustrates significant features of life for urban, working-class, immigrant families at the beginning of the twentieth century. Her father's death produced the economic adversity common to many households in which parents, especially widows, could not earn enough for survival, and adolescents—even children—had to take low-paying, back-breaking factory jobs. Hilda's story is also a reminder that immigrants had to do more than merely survive the journey, the oppressive labor, the dirty streets, the crowded housing, the strange language, the new laws, the alien neighbors, and the unfamiliar shopkeepers. Hilda Satt, like every immigrant, had to shape a new identity that reconciled her homeland culture with her American experience. Some immigrants achieved this by joining labor unions, some by affiliating closely with ethnic societies or ethnic churches, and still others by focusing on business or politics. Hilda's way of forging an American identity out of her roots as a middle-class Polish Jew was through education, a route she was able to pursue because of Hull-House, the settlement house in her Chicago neighborhood.

Hull-House, which opened its doors in 1889, was the second settlement house established in the United States. By 1900, there would be 400 of these privately funded community centers in American cities. Hull-House was staffed by native-born, middle-class, volunteer "residents" who lived at the settlement and dedicated themselves to providing education and recreation for their immigrant, working-class "neighbors." Hull-House was unique among settlements in the breadth and depth of its offerings; in its commitment to democratic reform on behalf of the poor, immigrants, and workers; and in its firm but delicate guidance under the hand of Jane Addams, the settlement's "head resident."

Hilda Satt Polacheck subtitled her memoir "The Story of a Hull-House Girl" because her decade there as a student, club member, and teacher shaped her future life in America. In fact, Hull-House influenced the lives of thousands of immigrant and working-class families in its neighborhood around Halsted and Polk streets on Chicago's industrial west side. By the time Hilda was a regular at Hull-House, the settlement had expanded far beyond its original old wood mansion to include a dozen brick buildings circling an entire square block, with a playground in the center. It appealed to those neighbors who sought secular activities and wanted to learn English, read history and literature, or argue about politics. It also attracted those looking for music lessons, dance classes, dramatic productions, a pottery workshop, a sewing machine, a basketball court, a day-care center—or just a hot bath. Every week at Hull-House, young Hilda Satt encountered literally thousands of her neighbors who went to the settlement for a class or a game, a debate or a rehearsal, a club or a dance.

Satt's memoir is one of the few surviving ethnic testimonies on life at Hull-House. Her voice supports the claims made by volunteers that Hull-House offered immigrants an alternative to the disdain and exploitation they met elsewhere in Chicago. Her stories suggest that the settlement respected the status that she and other immigrants had enjoyed back home, offered the sort of welcome they had expected from America, and provided them with the practical tools they needed to achieve their economic, political, and cultural goals.

Using the Source: Autobiographies

"Autobiography" and "memoir" are twin terms referring to life stories written by the people who lived them. For readers who want their history up close and personal, there is something very attractive about memoirs. They seem unfiltered, untouched by an expert, unmediated by authorities. Whether discovered as yellowed sheets of paper in a box hidden in the attic or cleanly bound between covers in a library, memoirs often appear to be the most authentic and transparent form of history.

Hilda Satt Polacheck's 170-page memoir, *I Came a Stranger: The Story of a Hull-House Girl*, is just the sort of engaging life story that readers turn to for an immediate sense of history. It is also a text that invites some consideration of the challenges autobiography poses as a historical source.

What Can Autobiographies Tell Us?

It is easy to understand why we are drawn to autobiographies. Life stories offer us unique access to the "feel" of a place and a time; they provide sounds, smells, tastes, attitudes, and emotions that only eyewitnesses can recall, and they often testify to the quality of relationships that we can only infer from a distance. For example, historians have long debated about whether the native-born, middle-class residents of Hull-House were patronizing toward their immigrant, working-class neighbors. Polacheck's eyewitness testimony does not end this debate, but the publication of her memoir in 1989 offers support to those who argue that Hull-House was more egalitarian than patronizing. After all, Polacheck was there, and her memoir testifies that the settlement residents treated their neighbors with dignity and respect.

If we want to draw on *I Came a Stranger* as a primary source of information about interactions at Hull-House, however, we have to keep three basic principles in mind: first, human memory is a complex tool for retrieval, so we cannot presume that an individual's life stories provide an unfiltered image of the past; second, the overall emotional message conveyed by a memoir is often more reliable than the specific events recounted; and third, independent information about a memoirist's life is valuable for corroborating autobiographical claims.

Cognitive psychologists tell us that our memories are not stored in our minds like neat reels of film. Instead, our minds hold, lose, regain, and reshape pieces to the incomplete puzzle that is our past. Typically, autobiographers arrange the puzzle pieces of their memory (and imagine the missing pieces) according to their current beliefs about what happened in the past. Those beliefs, and the stories that arise from them, have been shaped by intervening experiences and by the philosophical message that the autobiographer wishes to convey to the reader. Every autobiographer writes to convey some message, and that aim—not pure, unadulterated memory—shapes the memoir.

Hilda Satt Polacheck wrote her autobiography in the 1950s, when she was a widow in her early seventies. It was based "principally on her memory" because, as her daughter Dena Epstein explains, Polacheck "had no diary" (Polacheck, 179). While some memoirists conduct their own historical research and consult piles of scrapbooks, letters, and personal artifacts to buttress their recollections, most, like Hilda Satt Polacheck, rely solely on memory. Anyone wishing to draw on Polacheck's autobiography as evidence of life at Hull-House would have to treat it as a product of memory, not as a reel of documentary film. Her words on the page testify to the fact that Polacheck, in her seventies, had a powerful memory of being treated with unconditional positive regard at Hull-House. Her written memories, however, cannot prove the accuracy of every story she tells to illustrate this positive treatment, nor do these memories count as evidence of every settlement neighbor's experience. But the overall message in her memoir can be used as evidence that it was quite possible for a Jewish immigrant girl to have encounters at Hull-House that were so rewarding that she retained positive feelings for more than half a century.

Beyond that, we can seek out independent information on Polacheck's life to corroborate or put into historical context her sunny depiction of interactions at Hull-House. For example, we can independently verify that Hilda Polacheck was a democratic socialist throughout her life and can infer from that fact that she did not bow down to the rich and powerful. We might use this information to conclude that Polacheck's happy memories of egalitarian treatment at Hull-House must be accurate since her socialism would have made her critical of settlement workers who acted superior to the neighbors. But we also know that her Hull-House contacts paved the way for her to marry well and live a good life. Might she have filtered out of her memory or deliberately omitted from her memoir any undemocratic interactions at Hull-House simply because the settlement, for her, meant opportunities?

The many questions we can raise about a memoir do not invalidate memoirs as valuable sources of historical knowledge; such questions simply remind us to be cautious about what we conclude from memoirs, and encourage us to do as much independent research as possible to corroborate and contextualize them.

In the case of Hilda Polacheck, the historian who conducted the independent research was her daughter, Dena Polacheck Epstein. Years after Hilda died in 1967, Epstein retrieved eight different, incomplete, handwritten versions of her mother's life story and set about trying to compile the most accurate version. Epstein sought independent documentation for every story in the memoir by checking old city directories, Chicago newspapers, Hull-House records, school records, and letters between Hilda and her husband, William Polacheck. She had to do detective work just to determine her mother's birth date; some of Hilda's recollections indicated she was born in 1887, others pointed to 1888, and still others to 1889. It was the letters, combined with her mother's enrollment records at the Jewish Training School and the University of Chicago, that convinced Epstein that Hilda Satt was actually born in 1882.

So what? How does a trivial fact like her birth date contribute to our understanding of the memoir? Knowing that Hilda was born in 1882 tells us that she was fifteen years old in early 1898, and we know from her memoir and additional records that she had left school by that age and gone to work in the knitting factory. That independent knowledge casts a curious light on this passage from the memoir, in which Hilda recalls the Spanish-American War:

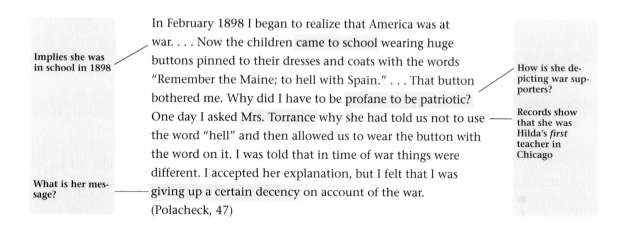

Implies she was in school in 1898

How is she depicting war supporters?

Records show that she was Hilda's *first* teacher in Chicago

What is her message?

In February 1898 I began to realize that America was at war. . . . Now the children came to school wearing huge buttons pinned to their dresses and coats with the words "Remember the Maine; to hell with Spain." . . . That button bothered me. Why did I have to be profane to be patriotic? One day I asked Mrs. Torrance why she had told us not to use the word "hell" and then allowed us to wear the button with the word on it. I was told that in time of war things were different. I accepted her explanation, but I felt that I was giving up a certain decency on account of the war. (Polacheck, 47)

Since we know that Hilda Satt was, in fact, too old to have been a schoolchild in Mrs. Torrance's class in 1898, and since Epstein tells us that her detective work turned up very few inaccuracies in Hilda's story, we could simply dismiss this bit of autobiographical fiction as a bizarre fluke. But most historians would want to combine this tale about the Spanish-American War with existing knowledge of Polacheck's life to strengthen our understanding of her motives in writing her memoir, because inaccuracies in a memoir often reveal larger truths about the author and the author's purpose.

Consider the fact that Polacheck concocted this uncharacteristically false story on a particular subject: war. Combine that with the fact that throughout her autobiography Polacheck explicitly aligned herself with Jane Addams's philosophy of antimilitarism and that throughout her adult life Polacheck was active in the Women's International League for Peace and Freedom, the organization Addams founded in protest against World War I. By taking into account Polacheck's peace activism, we can see her phony Spanish-American War story as quite "true" to the memoir's political purpose, if not Polacheck's actual childhood experience. Remembering, too, that she wrote this memoir in the early 1950s, during the military buildup of the cold war, we can appreciate her sly invention of an innocent schoolgirl's voice to express antiwar views. This was just the sort of disarming rhetorical strategy that she might have learned from her mentor, Jane Addams, at Hull-House.

Questions to Ask

As you read through these excerpts from *I Came a Stranger: The Story of a Hull-House Girl,* keep in mind that memoirs are not transparent, unfiltered accounts of the past; they are complex constructions of memory and meaning. They can be enormously useful in re-creating the past, but we must handle them with care.

- What aspects of this story are "true" in the sense that they can be verified with independent, objective sources of information?
- What aspects of this story are "true" in the sense that they convey the values that Hilda Satt Polacheck, in her seventies, wanted to affirm as her own?
- The fatherless Satt family struggled against poverty in Chicago. Does it make any difference that the family had been middle class back in Poland?
- Does Hilda seem to identify primarily by her ethnic group, her religion, her gender, or her economic class?
- What does Hilda love about America? In her memoir, how does she tie her love of America to her experiences at Hull-House?

Source Analysis Table

The excerpts from Hilda Polacheck's memoir included here focus on her encounters with Hull-House when she was a teenager and a young woman. The following table can help you compare examples of stories that you regard as factual and verifiable with examples of unverifiable stories that you see as conveying Polacheck's beliefs and values.

Excerpt from Autobiography	Stories That Can Be Verified	Unverifiable Stories That Convey Core Values
1. I Discover Hull-House		
2. The Oasis in the Desert		
3. "The Ghetto Market"		
4. The University		
5. New Horizons		

To download and print this table, visit the book companion site at **bedfordstmartins.com/brownshannon**.

The Source: *I Came a Stranger: The Story of a Hull-House Girl* by Hilda Satt Polacheck

1   *I Discover Hull-House*

Several days before Christmas 1896 one of my Irish playmates suggested that I go with her to a Christmas party at Hull-House. I told her that I never went to Christmas parties.

"Why not?" she asked.

"I do not go anywhere on Christmas Day," I said.

"But this party will not be on Christmas Day. It will be the Sunday before Christmas Day," she said.

I repeated that I could not go and she persisted in wanting to know why. Before I could think, I blurted out the words: "I might get killed."

"Get killed!" She stared at me. "I go to Hull-House Christmas parties every year, and no one was ever killed."

I then asked her if there would be any Jewish children at the party. She assured me that there had been Jewish children at the parties every year and that no one was ever hurt.

The thought began to percolate through my head that things might be different in America. In Poland it had not been safe for Jewish children to be on the streets on Christmas. I struggled with my conscience and finally decided to accompany my friend to the Hull-House Christmas party. . . .

My friend and I arrived at Hull-House and went to the coffee shop where the party was being held. There were many children and their parents seated when we arrived. It was the first time that I had sat in a room where there was a Christmas tree. In fact, there were two trees in the room: one on each side of the high brick fireplace. The trees looked as if they had just been brought in from a heavy snowstorm. The glistening glass icicles and asbestos snow looked very real. The trees were lighted with white candles and on each side stood a man with a pail of water and a mop, ready to put out any accidental fire.

People called to each other across the room. Then I noticed that I could not understand what they were saying. It dawned on me that the people in this room had come from other countries. Yet there was no tension. Everybody seemed to be having a good time. There were children and parents at this party from Russia, Poland, Italy, Germany, Ireland, England, and many other lands, but no one seemed to care where they had come from, or what religion they professed, or what clothes they wore, or what they thought. As I sat there, I am sure I felt myself being freed from a variety of century-old superstitions and inhibitions. There seemed to be nothing to be afraid of.

Source: Hilda Satt Polacheck, *I Came a Stranger: The Story of a Hull-House Girl,* edited by Dena Polacheck Epstein (Urbana: University of Illinois Press, 1989).

Then Jane Addams came into the room! It was the first time that I looked into those kind, understanding eyes. There was a gleam of welcome in them that made me feel I was wanted. She told us that she was glad we had come. Her voice was warm and I knew she meant what she said. . . .

The children of the Hull-House Music School then sang some songs, that I later found out were called "Christmas carols." I shall never forget the caressing sweetness of those childish voices. All feelings of religious intolerance and bigotry faded. I could not connect this beautiful party with any hatred or superstition that existed among the people of Poland.

As I look back, I know that I became a staunch American at this party. I was with children who had been brought here from all over the world. The fathers and mothers, like my father and mother, had come in search of a free and happy life. And we were all having a good time at a party, as the guests of an American, Jane Addams.

We were all poor. Some of us were underfed. Some of us had holes in our shoes. But we were not afraid of each other. What greater service can a human being give to her country than to banish fear from the heart of a child? Jane Addams did that for me at that party. . . .

2 | *The Oasis in the Desert*

Four years passed before Hilda returned to Hull-House because once she began factory work, she was too tired in the evenings to go out. When she was seventeen, Hilda could no longer stand a life confined to sewing cuffs during the day and reading romance novels at night.

One evening in 1900, after a particularly boring day at the factory, I decided to walk over to Hull-House three blocks from where I lived. I had not been there since that eventful Christmas party.

This event marked the beginning of a new life for me. . . .

After a span of fifty years, I look back and realize how much of my leisure time was spent at Hull-House and how my life was molded by the influence of Jane Addams. I was not only hungry for books, music, and all the arts and crafts offered at Hull-House, but I was starved for the social stimulus of people my own age. All this was to be found at the house on Halsted and Polk streets. . . .

Hull-House was in the Nineteenth Ward of Chicago. The people of Hull-House were astounded to find that while the ward had 1/36th of the population of the city, it registered 1/6th of the deaths from typhoid fever. Miss Addams and Dr. Alice Hamilton launched an investigation that has become history in the health conditions of Chicago.

. . . Many of the pipes supplying drinking water were found to be defective, so the polluted sewage would seep into the drinking water, spreading the germs of typhoid fever. . . .

The bathing problem in the neighborhood was no small matter. I still recall the huge kettles of water being heated on the stove and the washtub being dragged into the kitchen for our weekly baths. But we did get scrubbed once a week. There were, however, many people in the neighborhood who did not have the stamina for carrying kettles of hot water. This led to a discussion of public baths, one day. One of our German neighbors was telling my mother that in Germany she would go to a public bath whenever she wanted a bath. By this time I had the feeling that Hull-House was a place from which "all blessings flow," and I asked somebody if there were any public baths there. I was told where the public bath was. I found out later that it was through the efforts of Jane Addams that this public bath had been established. . . .

Yes, Hull-House was an oasis in a desert of disease and monotony. And monotony can become a disease. The work at the factory, the making of cuffs, and more and more cuffs, had a dulling effect on all my senses. The only variation in this deadly monotony was that some days the cuffs would be blue and other days they would be green or pink or yellow. But the thought of going to Hull-House in the evening made the day's work bearable.

And then there was the possibility of seeing Jane Addams in action, a woman with that supreme faith that the world could be made into a better place for the whole human race. One evil condition after another was brought to the attention of city authorities, in a patient, simple, but resolute manner. The problems of the immigrants, who were to play a significant part in the pattern of American life, were brought to the surface, waking the conscience of Chicago. . . .

Jane Addams was never condescending to anyone. She never made one feel that she was a "lady bountiful." She never made one feel that she was doling out charity. When she did something for you, you felt she owed it to you or that she was making a loan that you could pay back. . . .

I remember Miss Addams stopping me one day and asking me if I had joined the dancing class. She thought I worked too hard and needed some fun. So I joined the dancing class and learned the waltz, two-step, and schottische.[1] By this time I was able to pay the dollar that paid for ten lessons.

. . . We danced once a week in this carefree class, all winter. In June, the class closed for the summer with a gay cotillion, every bit as gay, if not as elaborate, as the ones staged today to introduce debutantes to society. No matter where the members of the dancing class came from, dingy hovels, overcrowded tenements, for that one night we were all living in a fairland.

My sister and I next joined the gymnasium. We managed to scrape together enough money to buy the regulation gymnasium suit—wide bloomers and blouse—though if anyone could not afford the suit, she could attend anyway. Miss Rose Gyles was the teacher, and she put us through the paces once a week.

---

[1] The schottische is a round dance resembling a slow polka.

The gymnasium was like an oasis in a desert on Halsted Street. Hundreds of boys, who had no other means of recreation, could go to the gymnasium and play basketball till they were so worn out that they could only go home and go to bed.

One evening, as I entered the reception room, Miss Addams called me into the residents' sitting room and asked me to join a class in English composition. The class was just being organized and the instructor was to be Henry Porter Chandler, of the University of Chicago. Not many students had applied, and Miss Addams asked me to register for the class as she did not want Mr. Chandler to feel that people were not interested in such a class.

I told Miss Addams that I had never written anything. But she insisted, and so I went into the dining room where four or five people were gathered. She introduced me to Mr. Chandler. Mr. Chandler outlined a course of work. He asked us if we had ever written anything. Most of us had not. He then told us that there were certain kinds of writing, such as book reviews, short stories, arguments, criticisms, and some others. He asked each of us to write anything that we wanted and to bring it to the class the following week. He then dismissed the class.

Mr. Chandler was the secretary to William Rainey Harper, the first president of the University of Chicago, and an instructor in English composition.

I could not sleep that night. Why was it that he did not tell us how to write? How could a person just write? Then the thought came to me that if you had something to say, perhaps you could write it down on paper. I kept thinking, Have I something to say?

3   *"The Ghetto Market"*

Hilda's first essay, "The Ghetto Market," described the filth she saw at the open market in her neighborhood. Precisely because she was an immigrant with actual experience in "the old world," she did not romanticize the market as a charming example of old-world customs. In the essay's first and last paragraphs, Hilda echoed many Hull-House attitudes.

During that week, I did not attend any classes at Hull-House. Every evening, as soon as I reached home from work, I would hurry through with supper and helping with the dishes and then would sit at the kitchen table and write. I still have that "masterpiece." Here it is:

"THE GHETTO MARKET"
Sociologists who are studying and seeking to remedy conditions among the wretchedly poor have done vast good. The poor may now be clothed; they receive medical attention and surgical care which none but the very rich could afford to pay for. They need not be ignorant, for schools are free and there are

many devoted women in the social settlements who are laboring night and day to make up for whatever deficiency may exist in the capacity of the city institutions. But there is one injustice untouched; one wrong which is crying for immediate remedy. This is the unsanitary, filthy food which the poor in certain quarters are forced to eat. Not until the city takes the matter in hand and orders all vegetables, meat and fish to be sold only in adequate and sanitary rooms will this condition be entirely overcome; for as long as the old market of the Ghetto district exists, so long will the inhabitants of the district patronize it. . . .

Is this question not well worthy of consideration? Cannot the poultry shop, fish stall and cake stand be kept off the street, free from the dust and the flies? Why should this class of people who work harder than any other be compelled to eat inferior food when they might be supplied with good food for the same money? Are there not plenty of men employed in building houses, ice boxes and various appliances for keeping provisions? Yet these people eat food sold on the street under the filthiest conditions.

The next time the class met, I brought the masterpiece, over which I had sweated five nights and a whole day Sunday, to Mr. Chandler. Each member of the class had brought a composition. Mr. Chandler did not look at the papers. He told us he would let us know the following week what he thought of our efforts.

4   *The University*

After a miserable day at the factory, when everything seemed to happen, my machine had broken down and I had lost several hours of work, I arrived at Hull-House. The composition class was to meet that night. What would Mr. Chandler think of my composition? Would he pay any attention to it? He had probably thrown it into the wastebasket. It couldn't possibly be worth anything, I kept telling myself.

The class assembled and Mr. Chandler opened his briefcase and pulled out a mass of papers. He handed them to the various authors, without any comment.

My heart missed several beats.

Then he handed me my paper and said: "Very good." I do not remember anything else that he said that night. But as the class was being dismissed, Miss Addams came into the room and said that she wanted to talk to me, that I was to wait for her. She talked for a few minutes with Mr. Chandler, then she took me into the octagon[1] and said these magic words: "How would you like to go to the University of Chicago?" She was very calm, as if she had asked me to have a cup of tea.

[1] The "octagon" was a small, eight-sided room in Hull-House that Jane Addams used as her more public office space.

She did not realize that she had just asked me whether I wanted to live. I just sat there looking at her.

"Did you say the University of Chicago?" I finally gasped.

"Yes," she said. "Mr. Chandler told me that your paper shows promise, and he will make all the arrangements."

"But that is impossible," I said.

"Nothing is impossible," said Jane Addams.

For some time I could not talk. I kept thinking, I did not graduate from grammar school. How could I hope to go to the great university?

Miss Addams, with her infinite patience, sat there holding my hand. I know she was living through my thoughts.

If this could happen, then all sorts of miracles could happen. But then, did not miracles happen in Hull-House all the time?

"But what about a high school diploma?" I asked. "I heard that no one can go to college without a high school diploma."

"Mr. Chandler said that you could come as an unclassified student," she said.

"But what about money?" I was beginning to lose hope.

"You will be granted a scholarship," she said. "It will cost you nothing."

"But I must contribute to the support of the family," I said. "My wages are needed at home."

"Well, I thought of that, too," she said smiling. "We will make you a loan of the amount that you would earn, and whenever you are able, you can pay it back."

By this time tears were running down my cheeks. What had I done to deserve all this? She took my hand and said: "I know how you feel, my dear. I want you to go home and talk this over with your mother, and let me know what you want to do. But I want you to go, remember that."

I went home and found Mother and my sister sitting at the kitchen table, drinking tea. I sat down without removing my coat. My sister looked at me.

"What's happened to you?" she said.

I just sat there staring—then I blurted out: "Miss Addams wants me to go to the University of Chicago."

"But how can you?" my sister asked.

Then I poured out my soul. I told them what Miss Addams had said about a loan, how my tuition would be free, how my life would be changed.

"This can happen only in America," Mother said.

"Yes," I said, "because in America there is a Jane Addams and Hull-House."

The exciting events of the night before did not keep me from going to work the next day. I sewed cuffs all day. As soon as I had finished eating supper, I dashed off to Hull-House. I waited for Miss Addams to come out of the dining room.

She saw me at once and took me into the octagon. The walls were covered with the photographs of the great humanitarians of the world: Leo Tolstoy, Abraham Lincoln, Henry Demarest Lloyd, John Peter Altgeld, Susan B. Anthony, Peter Kropotkin, Eugene V. Debs, and a host of others. And while these faces were looking down at us, I told Miss Addams that my mother and sister had consented to my going.

It was with a great deal of satisfaction that I told the foreman of the shirt-waist factory that I was leaving.

Memories keep coming back. It must have been the winter term when I matriculated at the University of Chicago. I remember that it was very cold traveling to the university early in the morning.

I was told to go to Mr. Chandler's office. He took me to the registration office and I registered for three classes. I was to take English literature with Mr. Percy Boynton, German with Mr. Goettsch, and composition with Mr. Chandler.

. . . Since I did not have to worry about grades, being an unclassified student, I could drink in all the fabulous information that came from Mr. Boynton's mouth. And reading the assigned books became a tonic to my soul. I soon came to know Ben Jonson, Alexander Pope, Beaumont and Fletcher, Keats, Shelley, and Shakespeare.

In 1904 there were separate classes for men and women. Most of my classes met in Lexington Hall. It was a poorly constructed building and was drafty and often very cold. In the composition class, when we were told to write about anything, I became bold, and perhaps a little impudent, and wrote a paper on why women students were assigned to cold, drafty buildings while the men were in more solid ones.

I think I got a high mark on that paper, but Mr. Chandler made no comment.

The subject of the next assignment was a debate on "Woman Suffrage." We were asked to hand in an outline as to which side we would take. I don't know why, but I chose to be against woman suffrage. The next day Mr. Chandler asked me to stay for an interview and in short order he convinced me that I was not against woman suffrage and that there was no point in writing something that I did not believe. I am sure that he still remembered my previous paper on the discrimination shown to women students and he was not going to allow me to contradict myself as to woman's rights. He proved to be right.

When the university closed for the summer, I evaluated my work. The English literature course had opened all sorts of vistas to me. But I think I did not pass. The jump from the fifth grade in the grammar school to Chaucer was a little too much for me. But the course gave me an everlasting desire to read and study, so it was not a loss. I did pass in German and I think I fared well in the composition class.

That term at the University of Chicago opened a new life to me. And I have never stopped being grateful for having been given the opportunity to explore the treasures to be found in books.

I often wonder what sort of a life I would have lived if I did not have that short term in the university made possible by Jane Addams.

After the short but eventful term at the University of Chicago, I must confess I was at loose ends. I was determined not to go back to the factory to sew cuffs. But I knew that I had to earn my living and help support the family.

I now felt prepared to do more interesting and stimulating work. The question was, What could I do?

The answer came sooner than I dared hope. Miss Addams was preparing to go to Bar Harbor for the summer and she suggested that I take the job of answering the doorbell and the telephone. . . .

Most of the classes were discontinued during the hot summer months. But there had been a great demand for English classes for adult foreigners. A delegation of the students called on Miss Addams and asked her to allow the classes to continue during the summer. Miss Addams agreed to try one class if a teacher could be found. I volunteered.

As I look back on that momentous event, I realize how presumptuous it was of me to offer to teach a class at Hull-House, where the standards were very high. I had no training in teaching. But English had fascinated me from the start; I had worked very hard to learn it, so why could I not teach the immigrants what I had learned? . . .

Here my training at the Jewish Training School became a blessing. Mrs. Torrance[2] had been very meticulous about pronunciation, and I used her method that summer with surprising and satisfactory results. Most of my students learned to speak without an accent. The great value of not having an accent, in those days, was that you could get a better job. And that was rewarding.

But the great reward came that fall, when Miss Addams told me that I could continue to teach the class for the winter. The day I picked up the *Hull-House Bulletin* and saw my name listed as a teacher of an English class equaled only the day when I was told that I could go to the University of Chicago.

[2] Mrs. Anna Torrance had been Hilda's teacher when she began school in Chicago.

5   *New Horizons*

Being allowed to teach English to immigrants at Hull-House did more for me than anything that I imparted to my students. It gave me a feeling of security that I so sorely needed. What added to my confidence in the future was that my class was always crowded and the people seemed to make good progress. From time to time Jane Addams would visit the class to see what I was doing, and she always left with that rare smile on her face; she seemed to be pleased.

There were no textbooks for adult beginners in English at that time. It soon became evident that it would be a waste of time to talk about cat, rat, mat, fat, sat to people who probably had been to high school in a foreign country.

This situation was emphasized for me one evening when Miss Addams brought a Greek professor to my class. He had come to America for the express purpose of learning English and had come to Chicago because he wanted to see relatives who were living near Hull-House. These relatives had suggested that he find out what Hull-House was doing about teaching English to adults. Miss Addams told me that the professor would stay one or two nights in my class to see what was being done. The crowning glory of my teaching was when he decided to join the class and attended all winter.

But to come back to the subject of textbooks, since there were none, I decided to use the Declaration of Independence as a text. It was a distinct success. The students did not find the words difficult; so in addition to learning English, we all learned the principles of Americanism.

I next introduced the manual on naturalization and the class learned English while studying how to become a citizen. It was all very exciting and stimulating.

My students were now beginning to confide in me. Classes at Hull-House were never just classes where people came to learn a specific subject. There was a human element of friendliness among us. Life was not soft or easy for any of them. They worked hard all day in shops and factories and made this valiant effort to learn the language of their adopted country. . . .

Hull-House had a unique arrangement for getting work done. No teachers or attendants were paid. It was all volunteer work. The residents of Hull-House were occupied with outside work during the day, and each gave a certain number of evenings to teaching and directing clubs. The only people who were paid were those who devoted their full time to the house.

So in the fall, when volunteers returned, I decided to look for a job. I had learned to use a typewriter, so I decided to look for more "genteel" work. I still shuddered when I thought of those cuffs.

[Hilda took a new job operating a billing machine at a large mail-order house. — Eds.]

. . . I was taken to a large room that was filled with long tables on which the billing machines had been placed. There were about three feet between the machines. I was assigned to a machine and an instructor came to show me how the work was done. She also told me the rules of the office. I was told that no talking was permitted during working hours. . . .

. . . About the third day my mother noticed that my voice was husky. . . . I suddenly realized that I had not been using my vocal cords for three days and that my voice was beginning to show the lack of exercise. I suddenly realized that "genteel" work can be as deadly monotonous as factory work.

I made a feeble protest. I saw no reason why I could not speak to the girl next to me once in a while. The next day I was told that I was "too smart" for the job, and I was fired. . . .

I was again looking for a job. Miss Addams suggested that I might try A. C. McClurg & Co., a publishing house and at the time the largest bookstore in Chicago. With a letter of introduction from Jane Addams, I was given a very friendly interview and got the job.

Working among books was almost as good as taking a course in literature. It gave me the opportunity of knowing what books were being published. I was keenly interested in what books people were reading. And I had the great privilege of working at McClurg's when *The Quest of the Silver Fleece* was published. It was the first time that I came across the name of W. E. B. Du Bois. This book aroused a keen interest in the growth of cotton in the South and the part that the Negro played in the industry.

I still spent my evenings at Hull-House, and one evening Miss Addams asked me to help organize a social and literary club for young men and women about my age. We all needed an outlet for recreation. About thirty young people joined the club, which was named the Ariadne Club. . . .

I now had the opportunity to come into contact with young men. The club met once a week, and how I looked forward to those meetings. . . . Since this was a social and literary club, one week was devoted to dancing and the next to study. For the more serious evening, a member was usually assigned to write a paper and to read it before the club. This was followed by a discussion.

And what subjects we discussed.

Papers were written on the collection of garbage, grand opera, clean streets, single tax, trade unionism, and many others. I think our subjects were influenced by what was going on at Hull-House. . . .

It was about this time that I found a copy of *Uncle Tom's Cabin*. I was deeply moved by the misery of the slaves. For the first time I read about slavery. For the first time I found out that people could be bought and sold on the auction block; that children could be taken from parents; that fathers could be sold, never to see their families again. . . .

Most of the club members had no contact with Negroes. We even found that some of the members had never seen a Negro. Dr. James Britton, who was the club leader, told us that most of the Negroes had lived longer in America than any of us present and were fully entitled to anything and everything that the country offered. I thought of all the racial hatreds in Poland, Germany, and Russia, and I was thankful that I was being cured of this disease of intolerance.

In this connection, I recall that shortly after I had arrived in Chicago, one of my playmates told me that I must cross the street when I approached the Chinese laundry on Halsted Street. When I wanted to know why, she told me that if you pass the laundry, the "Chinaman" will come out with a long knife and kill you. I realize now that my playmate must have been told this fantastic tale by someone. Until I found out that the Chinese man who operated this laundry was the soul of kindness, I was afraid to pass the laundry.

We also had music in the Ariadne Club. The members who could play an instrument, or sing, would perform; we heard some very good concerts. Many of the members who worked all day would study music at night. I recall when a piano lesson could be had for twenty-five cents. Some of the members attended the Hull-House Music School, and I venture to say that not a few became successful musicians.

The Ariadne Club also produced plays. I recall taking part in *David Garrick,* in which I played a fussy and obnoxious old maid.

My interest in the theater was a direct outgrowth of the dramatics at Hull-House. It was a preparation for life.

Analyzing Autobiographies

1. Which items on your list of "stories that can be verified" (p. 87) are useful for understanding how Hull-House operated? Which items are important for understanding Hilda Polacheck's individual experience?

2. If you were not able to verify the stories, could you still use them to create a factual history of Hull-House? Why or why not? Could you use uncorroborated stories to write a profile of Hilda Polacheck? Why or why not?

3. Dena Polacheck Epstein said that her mother's "uncritical picture of Jane Addams was a sincere expression of her feelings toward the woman who substantially changed her life." How useful is such an affectionate portrait for our understanding of Addams and Hull-House?

4. How do you think Hilda's life in Poland as a child from a relatively educated, middle-class family influenced her reaction and her mother's reaction to Hull-House? Why would you assume the accuracy of Hilda's report that her mother approved of her attending the University of Chicago?

5. Does Polacheck seem to be depicting herself primarily as a foreign immigrant, a Jew, a female, or a member of the working class? If she has all of these identities, how do you explain her choice to emphasize one identity over the others?

6. Hilda Polacheck professed her love of America throughout this memoir, which she wrote in the 1950s. Using your list of "unverifiable stories that convey core values" (p. 87), describe the qualities of American life that Polacheck chose to praise in her memoir, and explain why you either trust or doubt that these comments are reliable evidence of her beliefs in the 1950s.

The Rest of the Story

In 1912, at the age of thirty, Hilda Satt married William Polacheck, an American-born German Jew from Milwaukee who prospered in the lighting-fixture business. Hilda did not work for pay once she married, but she did continue to support her mother. In fact, Hilda's own life resembled her mother's life back in Poland: she had a comfortable home, nice belongings, and servants to help with the four healthy children she bore in ten years.

Like many educated, socially conscious American women of her day, Hilda used her middle-class privilege to engage in social and political reform work. William shared the political views that Hilda had acquired at Hull-House, and they both engaged in the sort of prosocialist, prolabor, proreform activities that were still quite respectable in the years before World War I and the Bolshevik Revolution. The lasting connection to Hull-House proved important when Hilda's life again mirrored her mother's, and she suddenly became a widow at age forty-five, with four children between the ages of four and thirteen to support. Unlike her mother, however, Hilda had some financial resources to draw on and was comforted by the thought that she was

> better prepared to meet hardship than my mother had been. The years I had spent at Hull-House, under the influence of Jane Addams, were now my strength and support. I had been taught to think clearly and meet events with courage. I kept thinking of the many tragedies enacted day after day in the reception room at Hull-House. The immediate task before me was to earn enough money to care for the children.

Hilda met her responsibilities during the Depression by working. In her first job, she was manager of a large apartment building back in Chicago, a position she gained through Hull-House friends. Later, she was hired as a "reporter" for the Illinois branch of the Federal Writers' Project, a New Deal program to employ writers. During World War II, she ran a sewing room for Russian war relief. She had joined Jane Addams's peace organization, the Women's International League for Peace and Freedom, as a protest against World War I and remained active in the league during the cold war and the early years of the Vietnam War. In the last twenty years of her life, Hilda was cared for by her children. She died in 1967 at the age of eighty-five, leaving her unpublished memoir in a pile of "loose sheets and revisions."

When Hilda wrote her memoir in the early 1950s, she was out of sync with the times. In those very conservative cold war years, when many Americans feared communist subversion by foreigners and political leftists, Hilda wrote an immigrant memoir that proclaimed loyalty to both the Declaration of Independence and socialist ideals. At a time when many regarded Jane Addams and Franklin Delano Roosevelt as past collaborators with the leftist enemy, Hilda described them as patriots who had instilled loyalty to American principles in the hearts of immigrants and workers. And in an era when women's capacities were disdained, Hilda documented women's accomplishments. Her memoir, like so many others, is a philosophical testament as much as it is a life story. Little wonder that publishers in the cold war years told Hilda that readers were not interested in the life of an "obscure" Jewish woman. It was the social movements in the last forty years of the twentieth century that created new interest in immigrants, women, and social activists and thus made it possible for the University of Illinois Press to publish *I Came a Stranger: The Story of a Hull-House Girl* as part of its series on Women in American History. Once again, history shaped Polacheck's memoir.

To Find Out More

I Came a Stranger: The Story of a Hull-House Girl is readily available in your library or through interlibrary loan. You can find many similar, published memoirs that are documented in the way Dena Epstein documented her mother's, with explanatory endnotes that tell you if events reported are consistent with other historical sources. One very accessible, well-documented collection of American immigrant autobiographies is *Immigrant Voices: New Lives in America, 1773–1986*, edited by Thomas Dublin (Urbana: University of Illinois Press, 1993).

If you have a particular topic area in which you would like to find an individual's life story told in the first person, you can do a subject search in your library's electronic catalog; for example, you might use keywords such as "Asian Americans—autobiography." Libraries are more likely to catalog books as autobiographies than as memoirs. If you want to read an unpublished, undocumented autobiography, the librarian at your local historical society or a university's archives can probably assist you. Or you can visit the Library of Congress Web site at **memory.loc.gov** to sample any one of that site's 400 autobiographies, some as short as 5 pages and others as long as 500 pages.

To read more about Jane Addams and Hull-House, visit the Web site Urban Experience in Chicago: Hull-House and Its Neighborhoods, 1889–1963, at **uic.edu/jaddams/hull/urbanexp/contents.htm**, or see Jane Addams, *Twenty Years at Hull-House*, edited by Victoria Bissell Brown (Boston: Bedford Books, 1999), and Mina J. Carson, *Settlement Folk: Social Thought and the American Settlement Movement, 1885–1930* (Chicago: University of Chicago Press, 1990).

Among the many fine books available on American immigration are John Bodnar's *The Transplanted: A History of Immigrants in Urban America* (Bloomington: Indiana University Press, 1985) and David Roediger's *Working toward Whiteness: How America's Immigrants Become White: The Strange Journey from Ellis Island to the Suburbs* (New York: Basic Books, 2005). You can view an interactive "scrapbook" about Ellis Island, the New York point of entry for immigrants between 1892 and 1924, at **historychannel.com/ellisisland/index2.html**. At **tenement.org**, you can take a virtual tour of the New York tenements occupied by immigrants in that same era. Two excellent Web sites for collections of written documents and photographs on American immigrants are operated by the Library of Congress (**memory.loc.gov/learn/features/immig/alt/introduction.html**) and the University of Minnesota's Immigration History Research Center (**ihrc.umn.edu**).

CHAPTER 5

Selling Respectability

Advertisements in the African American Press, 1910–1913

I n 1910, eighty black American citizens were lynched—hanged by a white mob without benefit of trial—in the United States. That figure was lower than it had been in 1901, when 108 blacks were lynched, and it was higher than it would be in 1915, when 53 blacks were lynched. But the lynching rate in 1910 was consistent with the pattern of lynchings in the years between 1889 and 1918, when white Americans typically lynched eighty-four black citizens every year. The year 1910 was notable, however, because in that year a coalition of African Americans and progressive whites formed the National Association for the Advancement of Colored People (NAACP). The NAACP's purpose was to combat this sort of physical violence against black citizens as well as to challenge the whole system of white supremacy that governed political, economic, and social life in these years. The organization's stated aim was "to make 11,000,000 Americans physically free from peonage, mentally free from ignorance, politically free from disenfranchisement, and socially free from insult."

The NAACP had its work cut out for it. In the three decades since the end of Reconstruction, white racists had successfully reversed the legal, political, and economic gains made by blacks in the 1870s and 1880s. Blacks who were children when slavery ended in 1863 had come of age in an optimistic moment: black men could vote and hold elective office, blacks and whites shared the same public facilities, and more than thirty black colleges were opened. The 1870s and 1880s were not easy decades for African Americans, but young black men and women in those years could believe that progress was possible. By the time that generation of blacks reached middle age in the 1890s and early

1900s, however, they had experienced a brutal cancellation of their rights as citizens and their dignity as human beings.

The founders of the NAACP had witnessed the disenfranchisement of black men in every southern state, starting with Florida in 1889 and ending with Georgia in 1908, through the use of stratagems such as the poll tax, the literacy test, and the grandfather clause. They had also seen the introduction of laws throughout the South mandating the strict segregation of blacks from whites in all public facilities, from railway cars to drinking fountains. The men and women, black and white, who launched the NAACP fully intended to challenge the legality of segregation, even though the U.S. Supreme Court had already ruled segregation constitutional. In the 1896 case *Plessy v. Ferguson,* the Supreme Court declared that public facilities could be separate as long as they were equal. Such endorsement from the federal government was a reminder that white supremacy was not confined to the South. Northern states had not passed formal segregation laws, but informal customs presumed black inferiority: blacks found it difficult to obtain housing or professional work in integrated settings, uncomfortable to shop or recreate in white areas, and unpleasant, if not dangerous, to challenge racial barriers.

In 1910, racial prejudice permeated every region of the United States. National culture was suffused with religious and scientific claims that all nonwhites were by nature inferior to all whites. Some racists said nonwhites were cursed by God, while others said blacks were retarded in their biological evolution. Either way, the justification for formal and informal segregation was that black people were less intelligent than white people—and less moral.

The assumption of blacks' intellectual inferiority justified the racial segregation of schools and low investment in black schools. It also justified racists' dismissal of black political arguments, black scholarship, and black artistic endeavors as the flawed products of under-evolved minds. Of equal importance in this racist campaign was the charge of blacks' moral inferiority. By defining all African Americans as childlike creatures with weak moral fiber, racists could blame black poverty on blacks' inherent laziness and dissipation. At the same time, the charge of moral inferiority allowed racists to depict all African American men and women as sexual beasts who posed a direct threat to respectable, civilized white society. So while white men in these years were never charged when they raped black women, white riots against black communities, as well as white lynchings of black citizens, were often ignited by the cry that a black man had raped a white woman. Even in the absence of such violence, the widely accepted image of the black American as a stupid, lazy, sexual predator worked powerfully to deny African Americans their claims to equality.

It was in this racialized context that African Americans at the turn of the twentieth century tried to build respectable homes and stable communities. For guidance in this risky endeavor, they could draw from two very different racial strategies. One approach, articulated by Booker T. Washington, counseled blacks to accept the fact that they had to begin "at the bottom" and earn their way up. Washington, the principal of Tuskegee Industrial Institute, discouraged blacks from seeking college degrees or pursuing professions, arguing instead for vocational training and employment as domestic servants, farmers, artisans, shopkeepers, and industrial laborers. Washington believed that if blacks made a solid contribution in the marketplace, working hard and earning a steady living, buying homes and starting small businesses, they would eventually be granted legal equality. Washington favored this economic strategy over black agitation for voting rights or challenges to segregation.

An alternative racial strategy was articulated by Dr. W. E. B. DuBois, who claimed that blacks would never make economic progress without the vote, access to all public facilities, collegiate as well as vocational education, and blunt renunciation of all racist theories. DuBois did not oppose vocational training or dismiss the value of hard, daily labor, but he held that all such efforts were futile if not coupled with political agitation for the rights that the Constitution promised to all its citizens. He also insisted that black progress required leadership by a "talented tenth" of educated race leaders who could guide the masses out of the lowly status to which racism had consigned them.

In the 1890s, many blacks optimistically embraced Washington's economic approach on its practical merits. His accommodationist approach had, after all, garnered substantial funding from liberal whites for both educational and entrepreneurial efforts. But doubts about Washington's approach arose in the early 1900s as it became evident that black progress in the marketplace did not earn blacks the respect promised. On the contrary, black economic success increased racists' hatred because it fundamentally challenged their belief in black laziness and stupidity. Well-dressed blacks were more vulnerable to verbal and physical abuse than those in humble clothing; blacks who owned their own businesses were often the targets of lynch mobs; and white rioters typically attacked black stores and rampaged through neighborhoods where blacks were homeowners.

The formation of the NAACP was in fact a response to the bloody Springfield, Illinois, riot of 1908, in which the false cry of rape sent an angry white mob into the city's black neighborhood, leaving eight dead, dozens injured, and thousands of dollars' worth of damage to black homes and businesses. The eruption of such racial violence in a northern city galvanized progressive whites and blacks, including W. E. B. DuBois, into establishing an assertive, interracial organization that would challenge Washington's policy of accommodation. DuBois resigned his professorship at Atlanta University in order to become the NAACP's director of publicity and research, even though the fledgling organization could not guarantee his salary. It was from his new post that DuBois launched the monthly magazine *The Crisis: A Record of the Darker Races,* which was to serve as the official organ of the NAACP.

The Crisis was a hard-hitting political journal that ran sharp editorial critiques of racist policies and detailed reports on specific cases of racial discrimination alongside proud stories of African Americans' triumphs in defiance of racism. The magazine thus reflected DuBois's rejection of any sort of accommodation to white supremacy and defined the NAACP in contrast to Booker T. Washington. But *The Crisis* also reflected attitudes that DuBois shared with many of Washington's followers, in particular the belief that black citizens must counter negative stereotypes by being especially ambitious, hardworking, moral, upright, well read, well groomed, and well spoken—in short, respectable.

Figure 5.1 W. E. B DuBois and the Publications Staff of **The Crisis** *W. E. B. DuBois is seated here in the light, airy editorial offices of* The Crisis *at 70 Fifth Avenue in New York City. DuBois had begun the magazine in two small offices of the New York* Evening Post *building, but he relocated it in 1913 after a political dispute with Oswald Garrison Villard, the* Post's *editor and a cofounder of the NAACP. DuBois dictated all magazine copy onto the reusable wax cylinders of a Dictaphone, an early sound recording device invented by Thomas Edison, and then staff members typed up his words. Source:* Photographs and Prints Division, Schomburg Center for Research in Black Culture, The New York Public Library, Astor, Lennox, and Tilden Foundations.

This set of prescriptions for black respectability can be viewed in several ways: as a daring resistance to racist images of bestial blacks, as blind obedience to the notion that blacks must earn their rights through good behavior, as a realistic strategy for making political and economic progress, and as a way for upwardly mobile blacks to set themselves above their more impoverished brothers and sisters. In fact, historians have employed every one of those interpretations when analyzing the attitudes evident in *The Crisis*. Such an array of arguments about blacks' values and motives is not a reflection of historians' confusion. It is a testament to the complicated mix of resistance and accommodation that African Americans needed to survive in the early decades of the twentieth century.

Using the Source: Magazine Advertisements

In examining notions of respectability in the African American community, you will find advertisements to be particularly useful. The products, services, and opportunities that people sell and buy reveal a great deal about their values and aspirations. The ads in *The Crisis* were addressed directly to the black community, which makes this magazine a valuable site for exploring the marketplace that blacks operated among themselves and how that marketplace served the magazine's main goal: to advance the status and dignity of African Americans.

From the first issue of *The Crisis* in November 1910, advertising was included in its pages. "It is our purpose," explained Editor DuBois, "to make the advertising a means of real service to our readers as well as a source of income to us." The matter of income was not inconsequential. The NAACP had no reserve of funds for subsidizing the magazine. DuBois had to make this controversial political publication a financial success in its own right, and he had to do so despite the opposition of Booker T. Washington, who had the power to tell many black businesses not to advertise in the defiant new journal. So when *The Crisis* first began, a business owner's decision to take out an ad in the new magazine was as much a political statement as a commercial one. The advertiser both endorsed the NAACP's policies and calculated that there was a healthy market among the magazine's readers.

Confidence among the magazine's first advertisers was well rewarded. *The Crisis* was an immediate—and, to DuBois, "phenomenal"—success. He had cautiously printed only 1,000 copies of the first issue, and it sold out at ten cents per copy. In January 1911, *The Crisis* sold 3,000 copies; in February, 4,000; in March, 6,000. By 1913, the magazine had a circulation of 30,000 while membership in the NAACP was only 3,000. With those kinds of figures, DuBois gained an independence within the organization that made it impossible for NAACP officers to rein in his rhetoric, even when they feared he might offend potential white supporters.

The circulation figures also meant that *The Crisis* was an attractive place to advertise if your target audience was Americans who agreed with DuBois's editorial stance on race. Analysis of the magazine's advertisements can help determine who made up the early target audience for *The Crisis*. It seems logical to expect that the audience was comprised of the elite, that "talented tenth" of American blacks who had the education, self-esteem, ambition, and professional status that DuBois thought necessary to demand racial equality. But in 1913, there were only a few thousand African Americans with college degrees, fewer than 3,000 black physicians, and not even 1,000 black lawyers. The 30,000 readers of *The Crisis* could not all have been members of the black elite. The audience must have extended beyond DuBois's "talented tenth," but in what direction? If we look at the advertisements that ran in *The Crisis*, we will find clues about the makeup of the magazine's readership.

What Can Magazine Advertisements Tell Us?

When trying to determine a community's values and aspirations—what a group of people cares about and hopes to become—we often turn to advertisements because the whole purpose of advertising is to appeal to the needs and values of its target audience. We can read ads to determine what products were available to consumers seeking to feed, clothe, and house themselves and to learn how advertisers defined those basic needs. Advertising also tells us what luxury products were on the market and what hopes and dreams advertisers appealed to when persuading consumers to spend money on luxuries.

There are some very particular advantages to using advertisements from a narrowly targeted publication such as *The Crisis*. Correspondence and records from the NAACP tell us that DuBois exercised a strong editorial hand in accepting ads for the magazine; his involvement makes it more valid to argue that the attitudes conveyed in the advertising are consistent with the political position of *The Crisis*. The magazine certainly ran no ads for Cream of Wheat cereal or Aunt Jemima pancake mix, both produced by white-owned companies whose trademark images were African American figures in smiling, servile roles. But it is unlikely that those companies even tried to advertise in *The Crisis*. None of the era's popular, widely advertised products such as Ivory Soap, Gold Medal Flour, Pabst's Blue Ribbon Beer, or Coca-Cola ever appeared on the advertising pages of *The Crisis*. Those national, white-owned companies could reach black consumers through the pages of white-owned publications. They did not contribute advertising revenue to black daily newspapers and certainly not to a journal as outspoken as *The Crisis*.

The absence of such national advertising—and its revenue—in black publications is in itself evidence of economic segregation in the United States early in the twentieth century. Advertisements in *The Crisis* reveal the dimensions of the separate black economy and can be analyzed for signs of the strengths and the weaknesses in that economy. DuBois agreed with Washington that blacks must pursue economic independence and prosperity. The ads in *The Crisis* provide information on how African Americans were pursuing that goal. They offer us a taste of the variety of black economic pursuits and remind us that blacks could be found all along the class spectrum, from poor to working class to middle class to wealthy. By analyzing these advertisements, we can also explore the subtle ways in which black Americans asserted their economic and moral respectability in a segregated country.

Because we live in an advertising-drenched society and as consumers we "analyze" ads every day, we often find it easier to examine ads from the past than other sorts of historical documents. However, that familiarity can be a disadvantage because it may lead us to exaggerate just how much ads can tell us. We can correct for this by remembering that we don't buy every product we see advertised; we don't even "buy" all the claims advertisers make about the products we do purchase. Therefore, we do not want to jump to the conclusion that readers of *The Crisis* literally or figuratively bought everything in the magazine's ads. Advertising cannot tell us what people actually did buy; for that, we would need to see every company's sales figures. Because it is virtually impossible to ever find such figures, especially for small, black businesses, we can rely on ads only as *indirect* evidence of economic activity.

The biggest mistake we can make in using advertisements as historical evidence is to pull one or two particularly funny or startling ads out of context and use them to represent the attitudes of an entire population of consumers. If all advertising is an indirect measure of a community's beliefs and behavior, then certainly no single ad can be used to represent an entire community's values. To guard against overgeneralization, historians analyze whole sets of ads over a period of time, looking at the ordinary alongside the unique, before making any claims about the target audience. To understand the need for caution when analyzing a single ad, consider this example from the December 1912 issue of *The Crisis*. In most respects, it is typical of the magazine's ads, but in one respect it is very unusual.

This ad, like many in *The Crisis*, was not selling a product; it was selling a job, an opportunity to make money. In the straightforward fashion that was typical of *Crisis* ads, it listed the ostensible virtues of the product, gave the price and profit, and described the potential market. In the sample of advertisements included in this chapter, you will find several ads similar to this one and can use them to theorize about the magazine's audience. However, you will seldom find references to skin whitening in ads from the early years of *The Crisis*. Other press outlets for black advertisers carried many skin-whitening (and hair-straightening) products, but *The Crisis* did not; the Sphinx Hansope ad is quite unusual in that regard. This reminds us that DuBois's political views shaped the magazine's advertising. It also reminds us that it would be a mistake to use this one, atypical ad to argue that *Crisis* readers aspired to whiter skin, just as it would be a mistake to base any generalization on a single ad.

Questions to Ask

The ads included in this chapter are a representative sample of ads that appeared in *The Crisis* between 1910 and 1913. Because the magazine grouped most of the advertisements together at the back, in a six-page section called "The Advertiser," readers not seeking jobs, products, or services could simply skip the advertisements. You may want to consider that fact in your analysis, along with other questions about African Americans' needs and values at a time when white racists sought to deny to blacks any measure of independence or respectability.

- What do these ads tell us about racial segregation in the United States in these years?

- What can we tell from these ads about the experiences and values of the black middle class?
- What can we tell from these ads about the economic opportunities available to those blacks who sought to better their circumstances?
- How do these advertisements endorse *The Crisis*'s editorial demand for racial equality and black dignity?
- Where do you find evidence that *The Crisis* asserted black respectability through its use of traditional gender roles?

Source Analysis Table

To aid your work, these advertisements have been arranged by descriptive categories: housing, economic opportunities, education and race pride, beauty and fashion. The following table allows you to categorize the ads in alternative ways for the purposes of historical analysis. As you peruse the ads, keep track of examples that illustrate these analytical categories, which move us beyond static description and toward detecting social patterns.

Analytical Categories	Examples in the Ads
The separate black economy resulting from segregation	
***The Crisis* readers' access to economic opportunity and upward mobility**	
The use of religion, education, and gender to affirm black equality and respectability	

To download and print this table, visit the book companion site at **bedfordstmartins.com/brownshannon**.

The Source: Advertisements from *The Crisis*, November 1910–March 1913

HOUSING

1   *Philip A. Payton, Jr., Company*
     The Crisis, Volume 1, January 1911, p. 35

2

White Rose Working Girls' Home
The Crisis, Volume 1, March 1911, p. 4

'Phone 2877 Lenox

WHITE ROSE WORKING GIRLS' HOME
217 East 86th Street

Bet. Second and Third Avenues
Pleasant temporary lodgings for working girls, with privileges, at reasonable rates. The Home solicits orders for working dresses, aprons, etc.

Address:
MRS. FRANCES R. KEYSER, Supt.

3

Hotel Dale
The Crisis, Volume 2, July 1911, p. 127

NEW JERSEY

HOTEL DALE
CAPE MAY, NEW JERSEY

This magnificent four-story structure, with every modern convenience, has just been completed at a cost of $50,000.

It is, without exception, the finest and most complete hostelry in the United States for the accommodation of our race.

The view from the hotel is magnificent: on the front, overlooking the celebrated golf links, the vista stretches away to take in the beautiful driveways and farm of the inland section of the Cape. The rear commands an extensive view of the harbor and sea. The invigorating ocean breezes reach every section of the hotel.

The Hotel Dale contains one hundred light, airy and luxuriously furnished rooms with every modern convenience. Electric lights throughout the entire house. Suites with bath and long distance telephone connections.

The open-air amusements available to the guests are numerous. The lawn of the hotel contains both croquet and tennis courts.

The sea bathing at Cape May is unsurpassed on the Atlantic Ocean. It is remarkable for its fine surf and is perfectly safe at all times for women and children. The hotel has its own private bath houses.

The sailing and fishing in the harbor and adjacent sounds are always attractive and boats may be had at all times.

The hotel is under the personal management of the owner, E. W. Dale, one of the most progressive and successful business men of our race. His experience as a hotel man has enabled him to use his very thorough knowledge of details in bringing the equipment of his hotel to perfection.

E. W. DALE, Owner and Proprietor

Mention THE CRISIS.

ECONOMIC OPPORTUNITIES

4   *Bussing-Wheaton Kitchen Supplies*
The Crisis, Volume 4, April 1912, p. 266

Agents—Big Money

Selling our seven-piece combination kitchen set, made up of articles absolutely needed in every household. They sell on sight. Mr. Jarvis sold fifty sets in one day. Send $1 for sample. Sent prepaid to any address in United States or Canada. Also our improved Slidewell Casters for chairs, which sell to everybody everywhere. Set of four sent postpaid for 15 cents.

BUSSING-WHEATON CO.
23 PARK ROW   DEPT. A   NEW YORK

5   *Jackson Specialty Company*
The Crisis, Volume 5, November 1912, p. 46

Don't Slave for Wages

Be your own boss. We show you how.
Particulars free.

JACKSON SPECIALTY CO.
Box 22A   East Lynn, Mass.

6 *N.Y. & N.J.*
Industrial Exchange
The Crisis, Volume 1,
November 1910, p. 19

7 *International Realty*
Corporation
The Crisis, Volume 2,
October 1911, p. 262

Do You Want a Position?

Best Places
Best Families

The New York and New Jersey Industrial Exchange, through its Employment Agency Department, furnishes more Colored Help to the leading families in the city and in the suburban towns than any other medium in New York.

It is located in the acknowledged best section of the city, being in the Henry Phipps' Model Tenements for Colored Families. No other Exchange is so well patronized by the foremost families, many of whom have never employed Colored Help before.

Our demand for competent Southern Help exceeds the supply many times over. Call and register. No charge. Bring your references. We can place you in a good position. If inconvenient to pay our required office fee, you are at liberty to take advantage of our Credit System. This new feature has proven extremely beneficial to many worthy persons seeking employment.

N.Y. & N. J. Industrial Exchange
237-239 West 63d Street
Telephones 5016-4546 Columbus

If you are honest, ambitious and determined to succeed in business—a business absolutely your own—we can help you. We will teach you by mail the secrets of Real Estate, Brokerage and Insurance business, list properties and propositions with and for you to handle so you can make money from the very start.

We Teach You All the Secrets of Real Estate, Brokerage and Insurance Business

We Instruct You In
Salesmanship.
Advertising.
Office System.
Real Estate Titles.
Conveyancing.
How to List Properties.
How to Judge Values.
How to Option Properties.
How to Find Prospective Customers.
How to Close Deals.
How to Secure Loans.
How to Get Insurance Business.
How to Organize and Finance Corporations. In fact, all the essential secrets known to and practiced by the successful broker and promoter.

We also give you a thorough *Commercial Law Course*, enabling you to meet for yourself and overcome difficulties that may arise. In short, we start you on the road to *success*.

Success and Independence

Mr. Gates says: "I started into this business without capital and have built up one of the most successful agencies in Vermont." Mr. Dunbar of Kansas says: "I have cleared up for myself during the year (his first year) over $9,000." Mr. Reynaud of Texas says: "I have done remarkably well for a beginner, having made over $6,500 in commissions since I started, nine months ago."

Our 64-page book, sent free, tells you how to start—a postal card will bring it—write today.
INTERNATIONAL REALTY CORP.,
519 Manhattan Bldg., Chicago, Ill.

8 *Cottman & Cottman Shipping*
The Crisis, Volume 1, December 1910, p. 32

The Firm for the Negro Farmers and Shippers to Deal With

Try Us Before Shipping Elsewhere.

FRUITS AND VEGETABLES   OYSTERS AND GAME   POULTRY AND EGGS

COTTMAN & COTTMAN

WHOLESALE COMMISSION MERCHANTS.   107 Pine Street. Philadelphia, Pa.

Reference: The People's Savings Bank   Bell 'Phone Connection: Lombard 4035

---

9 *Nyanza Drug Co. & Pharmacy*
The Crisis, Volume 1, December 1910, p. 32

NYANZA DRUG CO.
(Incorporated.)

35 W. 135th ST.,   NEW YORK CITY

CAPITAL STOCK, $15,000

Shares $5.00

Write for information. The best paying investment ever offered our people.

NYANZA PHARMACY

is the only colored Drug Store in New York City, and the purpose of the Corporation is to establish chains of stores, carrying Drugs and everything incidental to the Drug business. It is really the indisputable duty of every self-respecting member of the race to give it his support.

AGENTS WANTED EVERYWHERE

---

10 *Blackdom, New Mexico*
The Crisis, Volume 3,
February 1912, p. 170

WANTED

500 Negro families (farmers preferred) to settle on FREE Government Lands in Chaves County, New Mexico. Blackdom is a Negro colony. Fertile soil, ideal climate. No "Jim Crow" Laws. For information write

JAS. HAROLD COLEMAN

Blackdom - - - - - New Mexico

EDUCATION AND RACE PRIDE

11   *Wilberforce University,* The Crisis, Volume 2, May 1911, p. 43

FORWARD!

March Your Son Off to Wilberforce.

The only school for Negro Youth which has a Military Department equipped by the National Government and commanded by a detailed United States Army Officer.

DEPARTMENTS:

**MILITARY   CLASSICAL   THEOLOGICAL
NORMAL   SCIENTIFIC   MUSICAL
BUSINESS   TECHNICAL   PREPARATORY**

Banking taught by the actual operations in the Students' Savings Bank. Twelve Industries, 180 acres of beautiful campus, Ten Buildings. Healthful surroundings, exceptional community. Maintained in part by the State of Ohio.

W. S. SCARBOROUGH, President.
WM. A. JOINER, Superintendent, C. N. & I.

---

12   *Daytona Educational and Industrial School for Negro Girls*
The Crisis, Volume 4, September 1912, p. 213

The Daytona School became Bethune Cookman College in 1923. Mary McLeod Bethune founded the National Council of Negro Women in the 1930s and was a close advisor to First Lady Eleanor Roosevelt.

Daytona Educational and Industrial School for Negro Girls

Daytona, Florida

It reaches, by reason of its location, a large territory of Negro children deprived of educational privileges.

Its comfortable home life and Christian influences insure a certain individual attention and superior training impossible in larger institutions of its kind.

Mrs. Frances R. Keyser, formerly in charge of the White Rose Home for Working Girls, in New York City, has been elected Principal of the Academic Department. Write for catalog and detailed information.

MARY McLEOD BETHUNE
Founder and Principal

13   *Knoxville College*
The Crisis, Volume 2,
June 1911, p. 85

Knoxville College

Beautiful Situation, Healthful Location
The Best Moral and Spiritual Environment
A Splendid Intellectual Atmosphere
Noted for Honest and Thorough Work
Offers full courses in the following de-
partments: College, Normal, High School,
Grammar School and Industrial.
Good water, steam heat, electric lights,
good drainage. Expenses very reasonable.
Opportunity for Self-help.
Fall Term Opened Sept. 27, 1911.
For information address

President R. W. McGranahan
KNOXVILLE, TENN.

14   *Provident
Hospital and
Training
School for
Colored Nurses*
The Crisis, Volume
5, March 1913,
p. 260

Provident Hospital and Training School for Colored Nurses

Aim: To keep its technic equal to the best

Founded 1891

The first training school for colored
nurses in this country, Freedman's
excepted.

Comprises a training school for
nurses, hospital, dispensary, and
thoroughly equipped children's department; when funds are ample, post-
graduate work may be undertaken.

The hospital is open to all. The
races co-operate in the board of
trustees, in the medical staff and in
administration; the institution is the
only one of its kind in which a colored
man may act as interne.

Cost of buildings and equipment,
$100,000; free from debt. Endowment,
$50,000, contributed mostly by wills
made by colored men. Additional
endowment needed, $50,000.

The nurses' course covers three
years; training and instruction given
by both races, according to the highest
modern standards.

| 15 | *Self-Published Books on the Race Question*
The Crisis, Volume 2,
March 1911, p. 32 |

| 16 | *Mary White Ovington on the Race Question*
The Crisis, Volume 2, July 1911, p. 132 |

Mary White Ovington was one of the white founders of the NAACP and was the organization's executive secretary for more than thirty years.

17   *National Negro Doll Company*
The Crisis, Volume 2, July 1911, p. 131

Give the Child a Doll

The Most Beautiful of All the Toys on the Market Are the
NEGRO DOLLS

❡ YOUR child would be happy if it had a Negro doll such as are sent out by the National Negro Doll Company, Nashville, Tennessee. Every race is trying to teach their children an object lesson by giving them toys that will lead to higher intellectual heights. The Negro doll is calculated to help in the Christian development of our race. All dolls are sent by express, charges paid.

DOLLS FOR THE SEASON 1911-1912 NOW READY

Prices from **50c.** up to **$8.50**

For Illustrated Booklets, Prices and Other Information, Send Five Cents to the
National Negro Doll Company
519 Second Avenue N., Nashville, Tenn.

R. H. BOYD, President   H. A. BOYD, Manager

BEAUTY AND FASHION

18   *Solomon Garrett, Tonsorial Artist*
The Crisis, Volume 1, December 1910, p. 33

SOLOMON GARRETT
Tonsorial Artist

782 Fulton Street, near Adelphi Street
BROOKLYN, N. Y.

All Kinds of Workmanship
Cigars and Tobacco for Sale
Daily and Weekly Papers and Magazines

Brooklyn Agents for THE CRISIS

19   *Madame C. J. Walker Manufacturing Company*
The Crisis, Volume 4, January 1912, p. 130

Madame C. J. Walker was an enormously successful black entrepreneur who developed treatments for women's hair. She did not market those treatments as hair straighteners. She donated large sums of money to the NAACP's antilynching campaign and to Mary McLeod Bethune's school (see Source 12 on p. 115).

20 · The Dunbar Company: Face Powder
The Crisis, Volume 5, December 1912, p. 104

It Has Come at Last

It had to come and it was for us to introduce it.

A Face Powder for Colored Women

CRISIS-MAID
Perfect Face Powder

Whether the complexion is cream, olive or brown, we have a tint to match it.

It is *scientifically perfect*, embodying certain ingredients soothing to the most sensitive skin, while a soft breath of Oriental perfume enhances its cosmetic value.

It is the final touch to milady's toilette; adding a certain inexpressible charm to her appearance, which evokes words of admiration from friends and passersby.

Its quality is unsurpassed.

Miss Clough says:

"Its quality equals that of the most expensive imported powders."

Price 50c. postpaid
Send 2c. stamp for sample

Address:

The Dunbar Company

EXCLUSIVE DISTRIBUTORS

**26 Vesey Street
New York**

MISS INEZ H. CLOUGH
Formerly of the Williams and Walker Company; now playing the "Big Circuit" in vaudeville.

Mention THE CRISIS.

Analyzing Magazine Advertisements

1. What evidence of economic segregation do you find in the ads?

2. Within that segregated economy, what sorts of job opportunities and business ventures were available to African Americans in the pages of *The Crisis*?

3. What can you infer about the magazine's readership based on the advertisements? Do these advertisements suggest that only an elite, "talented tenth" of the black population was reading *The Crisis*? Who do you imagine turned to these ads at the back of the magazine?

4. Did *The Crisis* advertisements conform to traditional notions of morality, gender roles, and beauty? Did they radically challenge racist stereotypes? Could they do both at the same time?

5. African American history for the years between 1900 and 1915 typically focuses on the differences between the "prove yourself" strategy of Booker T. Washington and the "demand your rights" approach of W. E. B. DuBois. How can these ads be used to argue that readers of *The Crisis* drew on one or both of these strategies in their daily lives?

6. In the face of racist segregation, African Americans advocated for integration while creating separate institutions, services, and businesses. Now that you have perused these advertisements, write an editorial for *The Crisis* in which you argue for either economic integration or racial separatism as the best pathway to African American rights and respectability.

The Rest of the Story

W. E. B. DuBois served continuously as editor of *The Crisis* from 1910 until he resigned in 1934 in a heated and somewhat ironic disagreement with the NAACP board of directors over the issue of segregation. DuBois had begun his political career fiercely opposed to any black cooperation with white-imposed, legally coded racial segregation. During the 1920s, however, he became persuaded that black nationalism, rooted in strong, separate black communities, was the key to black advancement. He came to regard the NAACP's legal campaigns for racial integration as futile and threatening to black autonomy, and he increasingly looked for socialist solutions to America's economic inequalities.

DuBois's belief in socialistic black nationalism foreshadowed the radical black politics of the late 1960s and early 1970s, but for young African Americans in the 1920s, DuBois seemed hopelessly out of date. Despite his enthusiasm for black pride and autonomy, he was too intellectual and too traditional in his gender attitudes to fully embrace the cultural experiments of the Harlem Renaissance. He was also too elitist to approve of Marcus Garvey's mass movement to rally working-class blacks in support of black nationalism. In fact, the advertising in *The Crisis* during the 1920s and early 1930s became more elitist as early promotions for get-rich-quick sales opportunities disappeared, along with many of the ads for small businesses. Those ads were replaced by more ads for schools and colleges, beauty products, and books about famous African Americans. DuBois's independent stance, combined with the economic depression that began in 1929, caused the circulation of *The Crisis* to decline considerably by 1934. At that point, the NAACP board asserted its authority, insisting that the magazine's editorial policy conform to the organization's integrationist goals, and so DuBois quit—at age sixty-six.

For the next twenty-nine years, until his death at age ninety-five, DuBois continued to evolve intellectually and politically; he produced several major scholarly works that are still read and admired today. During the anticommunist era of the 1950s, DuBois was arrested and tried as a foreign agent but was acquitted. Nonetheless, the federal government deprived him of his passport and freedom to travel for several years. In 1960, when he was finally allowed to leave the United States, DuBois moved to the west African nation of Ghana and began work on the *Encyclopedia Africana*. He died in Ghana on August 27, 1963. News of DuBois's death that day was announced from the speakers' platform at the March on Washington, D.C., where Martin Luther King Jr. delivered his "I Have a Dream" speech.

Throughout the twentieth century, the NAACP persisted in challenging the "separate but equal" principle that the Supreme Court had endorsed in 1896. The organization funded lawsuit after lawsuit and was finally victorious when the Supreme Court ruled against racial segregation in the 1954 *Brown v. Board of Education* case. In the decades since, the NAACP has continued to work against racial discrimination in legal, political, cultural, and educational arenas. *The Crisis* continues to be the official publication of the NAACP and today has a circulation of 250,000. The "statement of purpose" on the magazine's Web site (**www.thecrisismagazine.com**) announces that *The Crisis* is "dedicated to the indefatigable pursuit of racial equality." In this regard, it is still operating very much as a legacy of W. E. B. DuBois.

To Find Out More

All of the advertisements in this chapter were taken from issues of *The Crisis* published between November 1910 and March 1913. Bound volumes containing past issues of *The Crisis* are available in many libraries and through interlibrary loan. The history of the NAACP has recently been chronicled in *The Ticket to Freedom: The NAACP and the Struggle for Black Political Integration* by Manfred Berg and John David Smith (Gainesville: University Press of Florida, 2005). For current information on the NAACP and *The Crisis,* see **naacp.org** and **thecrisismagazine.com**. Additional background on black activism in the early twentieth century can be found in John Hope Franklin and August Meier, *Black Leaders of the Twentieth Century* (Urbana: University of Illinois, 1982);

Kevin K. Gaines, *Uplifting the Race: Black Leadership, Politics, and Culture in the Twentieth Century* (Chapel Hill: University of North Carolina Press, 1996); and Deborah Gray White, *Too Heavy a Load: Black Women in Defense of Themselves* (New York: W.W. Norton, 1999).

For histories of American advertising, see James D. Norris, *Advertising and the Transformation of American Society, 1865–1920* (New York: Greenwood Press, 1990); Roland Marchand, *Advertising the American Dream: Making Way for Modernity, 1920–1940* (Berkeley: University of California Press, 1985); and Juliann Sivulka, *Soap, Sex, and Cigarettes: A Cultural History of American Advertising* (Belmont, Calif.: Wadsworth Publishing, 1997). For specific studies of race in American advertising, see Marilyn Kern-Foxworth, *Aunt Jemima, Uncle Ben, and Rastus: Blacks in Advertising, Yesterday, Today, and Tomorrow* (Westport, Conn.: Praeger, 1994), and M. M. Manring, *Slave in a Box: The Strange Career of Aunt Jemima* (Charlottesville: University of Virginia Press, 1998). Further discussion of how to use advertisements as historical evidence and links to Web sites that feature ads from the past can be found at the History Matters Web site (**historymatters.gmu.edu/mse/Ads/online.html**).

CHAPTER 6

Living under Fire

World War I Soldiers' Diaries

Sergeant Elmer Straub was sound asleep in his tent on the northeastern edge of the western front at 3:30 A.M. on November 1, 1918. Suddenly, "one of the fiercest barrages that I have ever heard in my life started off. The machine guns in the rear of us started to chatter and above all of the big guns they could be heard spitting their indirect fire over the German lines." According to the entry that Straub made in his diary the next morning, "Our tent is only twenty feet directly in front of the third piece[1] and every time it shoots we rise about two inches from the jar of it all. The night had turned into day from the light of the guns firing. . . . I got up and gave the scene the once over and then I crawled under my blankets and went to sleep." Straub then thought to add, "Probably it seems impossible to one not knowing the conditions to believe that one could sleep during such a time, but in a few minutes I was asleep, and there I stayed until 6:30 this morning."

Elmer Straub, a college-student-turned-artillery-man from Indianapolis, Indiana, had managed to sleep through the opening shots of the last great Allied offensive that would, in just over a week, put an end to World War I. By the time he wrote this entry in his daily war-front diary, Straub was quite familiar with "the conditions" because he had been in France for more than a year, so he was among the most experienced U.S. soldiers at the battlefront that day. As an enlisted member of the 150th Field Artillery battalion of the Forty-second "Rainbow" Division[2] of the American Expeditionary Force (AEF) in

[1] "Piece" was a term for a piece of artillery, likely a three-inch, French-made "75."

[2] The Forty-second "Rainbow" Division was comprised of National Guard units from all over the United States.

France, Straub had already been in several major battles and witnessed the dramatic expansion of U.S. forces throughout the summer. By August, 10,000 raw American recruits were arriving daily by transport ship; by September, there were three million Americans in country; and by the end of that month, more than a million of them were amassed between the Argonne Forest and the Meuse River in northeastern France, ready to join with their French and British allies for a final, all-out offensive against the German army.

World War I raged in Europe for four years, from 1914 to 1918. Treaties had drawn the Allied Powers (Britain, France, and Russia) into a war alongside Serbia against the Central Powers (Austria, Germany, and Turkey). The United States under President Woodrow Wilson stayed out of this war between imperial powers until 1917, when political and economic interests dictated U.S. entry on the Allied side. But American reluctance to join the fray meant that the U. S. military was not a decisive player in the European action until the last six months of the war. What exactly did the American forces contribute in those six months to help bring an end to this seemingly endless war? And what survival strategies did men at the front adopt to do the jobs they were assigned, get through the day—and sleep through the night?

What the Americans contributed was men: 3.9 million of them were mobilized for the fight overseas; 2.6 million actually served in combat. Those men coped with the war's intense battle conditions by focusing on the immediate, the everyday, the small details of life that they could control. The war sped up in its closing months, and its momentum overwhelmed any U.S. effort to create a smooth-running, well-oiled military machine. So the men at the front focused on finding food any way they could, getting sleep any way they could, hoping for a relief order that would move them away from the front lines and the incessant pounding of the artillery, and figuring out how, each day, they could possibly transport themselves, their guns, their gear, and their wounded from one location to another. At the same battle and on the same day when Sergeant Straub wrote about sleeping through the artillery barrage, Corporal Eugene Kennedy noted in his diary that, given only fifteen minutes to "strike tents, roll packs and march," he managed to grab "a loaf of bread and shove it in the breast of my overcoat." And Captain John Trible, writing in his diary on that same day in the same battle, noted that his medical unit had moved to a "pretty civilized" village, had "secured a billet" with a local family, and "slept in beds for the first time in two months." These were small victories over tangible problems. The solutions offered quick doses of instant gratification and could block out the larger, more terrifying questions of whether they would live or die and whether the Allies would win or lose.

Immediately upon entering the war in April 1917, the United States faced a logistical nightmare. In the spring of 1917, America had a standing army of just 128,000 and only 164,000 National Guard reserves. Our exhausted allies were calling for a quick infusion of four million fresh soldiers to turn the tide against Germany. To meet that need, the federal government instituted a draft. For the first time in U.S. history, the vast majority of the American men who served in the wartime military were conscripts, not volunteers; since being drafted was the norm, conscripts were not accused of any cowardly reluctance to serve. Sergeant Straub volunteered after spring classes ended at Indiana University, but both Corporal Kennedy and Captain Trible waited to be called up.

Sergeant Straub's first night in the army at Fort Benjamin Harrison in Indiana illustrated the U.S. military's growing pains: Straub had no cot to sleep on. So he got a pass, walked into town, and bought his own cot. The slow-moving, bureaucracy-bound, tradition-heavy peacetime U.S. Army had to shift into high gear in order to recruit, house, feed, train, supply, and then ship a whole new fighting force across the Atlantic Ocean. Once trained and deployed, each division of 28,000 men would need twenty tons of food, ammunition, and other supplies every single day. Much of that material, along with the men, had to be carried in British ships because the U.S. shipbuilding effort was inadequate. In fact, even though America had been supplying manufactured goods, including rifles and ammunition, to the Allies throughout the war, the U.S. military remained utterly dependent on French and British artillery, airplanes, ships, and tanks once it joined the war. In the nineteen months between declaring war and celebrating the armistice, the United States never manufactured more than 20 percent of the artillery and aircraft that it used in France.

At the start of 1918, when the United States was still organizing its army back home, Europe was stuck in a two-year stalemate that had mired millions of European soldiers in muddy trenches running from Belgium to Switzerland. French and British military leaders arguing for efficiency, wanted to integrate the U.S. recruits into the existing Allied army, under European generals. But General John J. Pershing, U.S. commander of the AEF in Europe, believed that only an energetic, independent American army fighting out in the open on its own terms could break the European stalemate, and the general assumed he had until 1919 to build such an army.

So Pershing was surprised in March 1918 when Germany broke the stalemate with a powerful offensive that brought the German line to within thirty miles of Paris. A separate peace treaty signed with the new Soviet government in Moscow in December 1917 had freed the Germans to shift all their resources to the western front, and they hoped an early spring campaign would destroy the war-weary Allies at a moment when there were only 300,000 U.S. soldiers in France.

The Germans did not win the war that spring, but they did shape the Allies' timetable. Speed was now essential. Fresh, eager, and wholly inexperienced American troops began to pour into France and joined the French and British in bloody summertime battles that pushed the Germans back along the River Marne, where Sergeant Straub manned artillery posts and Captain Trible, a physician attached to the Medical Corps of the Third Infantry Division, patched up a never-ending stream of wounded men. Even as they were winning battles, U.S. soldiers were mowed down by German machine guns alongside their French and British comrades. By mid-July, the Allies had the Germans on the defensive, but the pace of this reignited war outran U.S. efforts to coordinate troop numbers with supplies and transport. Tons of food rotted on the

Figure 6.1 Mired in the Mud, 1918 More than a million American soldiers moved toward the Argonne Forest and the war's final battle in September 1918, and congestion along the supply lines continued to plague the military's strategy. Here we see a wartime traffic jam in the French village of Esnes, which had been devastated in the Battle of Verdun two years earlier. Muddy roads meant that men, trucks, and horses crawled along at a pace of two miles per hour. *Source:* Library of Congress.

docks in the French port of Calais because there were not enough trucks to move it to the front and the trucks that were available sank in the mud on roads too narrow and bombed out to carry the battle traffic.

By September, the European Allied Command was certain that a concerted offensive in the Meuse-Argonne region could win the war. General Pershing negotiated for an independent American command in the Argonne sector of the battle, starting on September 26. But first he wanted to fight an independent battle that he had been planning for a year: he wanted to strike at St. Mihiel, where earlier French losses had given the Germans control over a bulge in the western front. So on September 11, just two weeks before Pershing was supposed to amass 1.2 million Americans in the Argonne Forest, he was sixty miles south with 600,000 of those men—including Straub, Trible, and Kennedy—staging an independent American assault on the Germans at St. Mihiel. As it

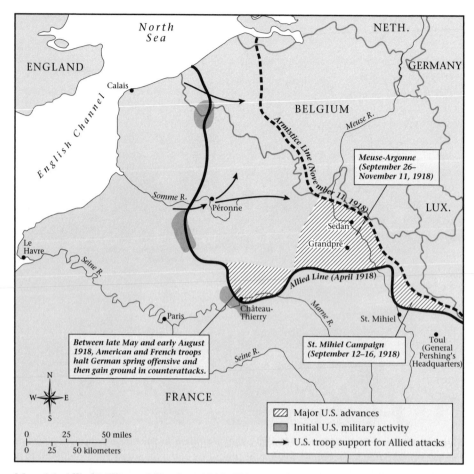

Map 6.1 Allied Military Offensive, 1918 *This map shows the locations of the battle at the St. Mihiel bulge in September 1918 and the Meuse-Argonne campaign, which raged from late September until the armistice on November 11, 1918. Note the distance that the Allied troops covered as they pressed northeast from April 1918 until the end of the war seven months later.*

turned out, the Germans were already retreating from the St. Mihiel bulge, so the American victory was quick and comparatively painless, incurring only 7,000 casualties in a war that had already claimed millions of lives on both sides. More a psychological than a strategic victory, the St. Mihiel battle secured the Germans'—and the Allies'—respect for Americans' fighting energy and increased Americans' confidence on the eve of their biggest challenge (see Map 6.1).

The coordinated Allied offensive that began in the Meuse-Argonne region on September 26, 1918, was neither quick nor painless. For forty-seven days, an exhausted German army resisted the unremitting Allied advance over land once lost and now regained with the aid of fresh, often inexperienced

American recruits, who died at a rate of 550 per day. The logistical woes that had plagued the United States since entering the war were magnified in this huge battle over uneven terrain that was made more impassable by persistent rain, narrow, bomb-rutted roads, and acres of muddy trenches and barbed-wire entanglements. Trucks stuck in battlefield traffic jams could not bring food in or evacuate the wounded. At one point, General Pershing could not even get his vehicle to the front of the line—and he certainly could not protect his men from hunger, cold, mud, rain, bugs, blood, death, or fear. His gallant visions of open warfare were frustrated by the realities on the ground, but still Pershing's young men faced the horrors of battle with a straightforward, can-do spirit that impressed allies and enemies alike. There was nothing particularly elegant or clever about the American contribution to the final six months of World War I; the AEF simply threw itself against the front line every day, grabbing as much food and sleep as it could along the way.

Using the Source: Wartime Diaries

"Diaries are forbidden to be kept near the front," wrote Major General James G. Harbord in *his* diary on September 4, 1918. "They are likely to fall into hostile hands," claimed Harbord, "as diaries by German soldiers are found to be one of the prolific sources of information obtained from prisoners of war. Every Boche[3] seems to keep one."

Not every American soldier kept a war-front diary, but many did ignore the ban on diaries at the front. Some of those diaries may have informed the Germans about supplies and morale in the AEF, though it is unlikely the musings of a lowly soldier revealed any secrets about troop movements or battle strategies.

World War I diaries do not lay out the grand panorama of "the Great War." Daily entries from sergeants and corporals do not serve us if we want to grasp the debates over strategy between General Pershing and his European counterparts, nor do they help us grasp the worldwide impact of the war's economic and political outcome. But diaries are a superb source if we want to understand how it felt, on the ground, to be a small actor in this momentous historical event.

What Can Wartime Diaries Tell Us?

The most obvious advantage to wartime diaries as a source is that, unlike letters, they were not subject to the scrutiny of the military censor. Soldiers could write things in diaries that they could not, or perhaps would not, tell the folks back home. Wartime diaries often have a quality of casual immediacy and

---

[3] Harbord was using a derogatory French term for "German." In French, *alboche* means simply "German," while *caboche* means "blockhead" or "head of a small nail."

private candor that cannot always be found in letters from the front. In addition, a diary offers the historian a running record over a period of time, whereas letters are episodic, offering only snapshots of an unfolding story that the diary tracks from day to day. Indeed, one of the striking features of the three diaries excerpted here is that the diarists made entries—some very brief, others quite detailed—virtually every day while they were overseas in the AEF, no matter how difficult the battlefield circumstances. Their regular entries give us a unique picture of daily life in wartime and reveal the surreal mix of danger, duty, and daily needs that confronted every enlisted man in World War I. Corporal Eugene Kennedy's diary entry from the Argonne Forest on October 17 reminds us of the risks a soldier faced when foraging for food or building a bridge at the western front:

Hungry soldiers at the Meuse-Argonne front were not about to hand over a lucky catch to the mess sergeant

An explosion due to a mine planted by the "bosche" had blown 2 men (French), two horses and a wagon into fragments. [The wagon] was full of grub. We each loaded a burlap bag with cans of condensed milk, peas, lobster, salmon and bread. I started back . . . but was nabbed by a "Frenchy" and had to give up the chow. Quinn was behind me when suddenly another mine exploded. The biggest I ever saw. Rocks and dirt few sky high. Quinn was hit in knee and had to go to hospital. . . . At 6:00 P.M. each of our four platoons left camp in units to go up front and throw . . . an artillery bridge across the Aire River. . . . We were heavily shelled and gassed causing much confusion.

This "Frenchy" must have outranked Kennedy, but it is the man's nationality, not his rank, that Kennedy chooses to record

We get a sense of the speed required when Kennedy writes that he had to "throw" a bridge across a river

Danger lurked in the most mundane places

It is quite possible that wartime diarists were writing for a particular reader and not simply for themselves. Perhaps a soldier wanted his parents or his wife to know what the experience was like but thought it best not to share the details until after the war was over and his fate known. Thus we cannot presume that wartime diaries were written unself-consciously, with no audience in mind. Though rich in daily details, they may not reveal a soldier's innermost thoughts and fears.

Moreover, the diary that was written at the front may not be the version that we read in archives or in published form. All three of the diaries excerpted here, for example, have been copied from their original versions. Were they altered at the same time?

Corporal Eugene Kennedy's diary was painstakingly transcribed in a precise hand onto engineers' graph paper. Corporal Kennedy probably made the copy himself. Did he edit out some remarks? We know he added a few. For example, in his November 1 entry, he wrote, "this date marked the opening of the last big drive." While that is a historically accurate statement, it is not something Corporal Kennedy could possibly have known on November 1, 1918.

After typing up his wartime diary in 1920, Dr. John Trible spoke directly to his imagined reader, explaining that the original diary was "written on any available piece of paper and tied together" and that the entries were "copied exactly as they were written." Rather than eliminate comments, Trible added pages of very frank annotations to his typically brief wartime entries, making his 219-page document part diary and part memoir.

When Elmer Straub allowed the Indiana Historical Commission to publish his diary in 1922, he included an introductory paragraph assuring his reader that "in recopying this diary I have tried to keep, throughout the whole work, just what was in the original." Straub apologized for misspellings and inconsistent verb tenses by explaining that "I had no special set time each day when I could sit down and write what was going on. I wrote . . . sometimes under very trying conditions, when it took all I had to keep from throwing it away." Did Straub, the university student, keep his diary out of a sense of duty to record history? Can that account for his unusual aside to the reader on November 1, 1918, that someone "not knowing the conditions" might find it "impossible . . . to believe that one could sleep during" an artillery barrage? Or did he add this note later, for the published version?

The stories behind each of these documents bring to mind yet another cautionary note about wartime diaries as evidence of soldiers' experiences: those who kept diaries during World War I were probably not representative members of the AEF. All three diarists included here were white, native-born, and educated. Moreover, none were in the infantry that marched directly onto the field with rifles and bayonets during a battle; Straub manned artillery from whatever heights he could find, Kennedy built roads and bridges, and Trible provided medical care. These men were culturally equipped and militarily situated to be able to keep diaries. By contrast, the vast majority of the white men who served in the AEF were rifle-carrying infantrymen, 18 percent were foreign-born, and almost one-quarter were functionally illiterate. Occasional racist remarks in these diaries indicate that these three men shared the disdain that many whites had for the 520,000 blacks who made up 13 percent of the AEF. African Americans always served in segregated units and typically as supply-carrying laborers, not rifle-bearing soldiers. Almost half of the AEF's black recruits were illiterate, and fewer than 700 were allowed to serve as officers, so they were unlikely to have had the skills or the time to keep a diary.

Although the soldiers who kept diaries came from the more comfortable, educated ranks of U.S. society, their reports of hunger, cold, bugs, mud, and ever-present danger offer good evidence that the war was a great leveler and few were spared the harsh conditions at the front.

Questions to Ask

The diary excerpts included here were selected from entries written during the St. Mihiel offensive in mid-September 1918 and during the Meuse-Argonne offensive in October and November, as well as from entries at the time of the armistice. The overlap of dates allows you to compare their daily experiences in the closing weeks of the war.

- How informed were these soldiers about the overall progress of the war?
- What seems to have been the impact of the rain, the mud, the roads, and the traffic on the actual conduct of the war?
- None of the three diarists carried rifles and bayonets into battle. What were their combat experiences? What dangers did they face?
- If one of these diaries had fallen into German hands, how could the Germans have made use of the information contained in these entries?
- Do these diarists appear to be writing to themselves or to some imagined reader who was not in the war?

Source Analysis Table

Use the following table to keep track of each diarist's attention to immediate and more distant concerns. You may track the frequency of comments on each topic by using tally marks or page numbers, or you may add notes on the date and tone of each comment to help you compare the diaries.

Source	Food and Sleep	Rain and Mud	Roads and Transport	Combat and Danger	Germans	Politics of War and Peace
1. Kennedy						
2. Trible						
3. Straub						

To download and print this table, please visit the book companion site at **bedfordstmartins.com/brownshannon.**

The Source: World War I Diaries from the St. Mihiel and Meuse-Argonne Battles, September 17, 1918–November 11, 1918

The selection of daily entries from the Kennedy, Trible, and Straud diaries were all taken from two moments at the end of the war: the St. Mihiel offensive in September 1918 and the Meuse-Argonne offensive in October and November 1918. In these entries, the soldiers talk about their daily experience at the front, what matters occupy their attention, and how men manage the normal business of life (eating, sleeping, staying clean, and keeping dry and warm) while also fighting a war.

1 *Corporal Eugene Kennedy, Company "E," 303rd Engineers, Seventy-eighth Division, AEF*

Corporal Kennedy lived in upstate New York and turned thirty-one years old, the top age limit for military draft eligibility, in February 1918. Two months later, he received his draft notice, and by June 1918 he was serving in Europe.

Thur., Sept. 12, 1918 Hiked through dark woods. No lights allowed, guided by holding on the pack of the man ahead. Stumbled through underbrush for about half mile into an open field where we waited in soaking rain until about 10:00 P.M. We then started on our hike to the St. Mihiel front, arriving on the crest of a hill at 1:00 A.M. I saw a sight which I shall never forget. It was the zero hour and in one instant the entire front as far as the eye could reach in either direction was a sheet of flame, while the heavy artillery made the earth quake. . . . We waded through pools and mud across open lots into woods on a hill and had to pitch tents in mud. Blankets all wet and we are soaked to the skin. Have carried full pack from 10 P.M. to 2 A.M. without a rest and I wouldn't mind a "blighty."[1] Despite the cannonading I slept until 8:00 A.M. and awoke to find every discharge of 14″ artillery shaking our tent like a leaf. Remarkable how we could sleep. No breakfast. . . . Cautioned to be ready to move at a moment's notice. Firing is incessant so is rain. See an air battle just before turning in.

[1] A "full pack" contained the items needed for daily life and weighed close to ninety pounds; a "blighty" was a military leave to England.

Source: Corporal Eugene Kennedy, untitled diary, June 5, 1917–June 19, 1919, Hoover Institution on War, Revolution, and Peace archives, Stanford University.

Fri., Sept. 13, 1918 Called at 3:00 A.M. Struck tents and started to hike at 5:00 A.M. with full packs and a pick. Put gas mask at alert position and hiked about 5 miles to St. Jean. . . . Passed several batteries and saw many dead horses who gave out at start of push. Our doughboys are still shoving and "Jerry"[2] is dropping so many shells on road into no man's land that we stayed back in field and made no effort to repair shell-torn road. Plenty of German prisoners being brought back. . . . Pitched tent in shrubbery. At last a night's rest. Guns booming all the time.

Sat., Sept. 14, 1918 Hiked up to same road again with rifle, belt, helmet, gas mask and pick. Shells are not falling fast today. We are just in rear of support lines. First time under shell fire. Major Judge's horse killed. R.G. Gibbs has a finger knocked off each hand while burying some of our men killed in opening drive. Clothing, bandages, equipment of all sorts, dead horses and every kind of debris strewn all over. . . . Big pit fall in road about 50′ across and 30′ deep. Worked hard all day. Terribly congested traffic.

Mon., Sept. 16, 1918 Nice day. Worked on road. Jerry drops shells over occasionally. Saw three of our doughboys dead along side of road. Traffic in good shape now. . . . Never saw such litter. Reports coming back that our division is being badly cut up.

Tue., Sept. 17, 1918 Worked near town that is reduced to a heap of stone (Regneville).[3] Trenches are 20′ deep and in some places 15′ across. The wire entanglement is beyond description.[4] Several traps left by Germans. Man in our division had his arm blown off picking up a crucifix. . . . Wonder how it was possible to advance over such ground. . . . Camped in woods just vacated by Germans.

Thur., Sept. 19, 1918 More rain. Camp in awful shape. Taking stone from Regneville homes to repair road. . . . Hard work. . . . More gas alarms at night. Many dead soldiers in woods, half mile up road.

Sun., Sept. 22, 1918 Worked all day on road. They are in good shape now. Germans shell our area. . . . Never saw such mud.

Mon., Sept. 23, 1918 Rain and cold. Worked on road. . . . Pres. Poincare[5] and wife visit restored territory.

---

[2] British slang for a German.

[3] The cemetery near Regneville has graves of 4,153 of the Americans killed in the St. Mihiel offensive. In all, 7,000 American casualties, both killed and wounded, resulted from this four-day battle.

[4] Wire entanglements were elaborate fences of wood and barbed wire that troops on both sides erected in fields to make it difficult for opponents to advance in either direction.

[5] Raymond Poincaré (1860–1934), president of the Republic of France (1913–1920).

[On October 3, Kennedy's division moved sixty miles northwest to join the Meuse-Argonne offensive, which had begun on September 26.—Eds.]

Mon., Oct. 7, 1918 Hiked until 3 A.M. Raining. Pitched tent in mud. Got up in time to eat. Very cold. Laid around 'till 5:30 P.M. Loaded on lorries. 18 men to an auto, 8 would fit. Raining hard. Rode about 3 hrs. Unloaded near Clermont. . . . Hiked four miles and pitched tents in Argonne forest.

Tues., Oct. 8, 1918 Nothing to eat. Detailed in evening to go after rations. Hike 4 miles each way. Nearly frozen. Greene brought jam from commissary so we had hard tack[6] and jam before going to bed. Some feast.

Wed., Oct. 9, 1918 Detailed again to go after rations. Tough trip but got half a loaf of bread from Negro in box car.

Sun., Oct. 13, 1918 Found a fine German garden. Onions, carrots, cabbage, celery, and potatoes. Got some bread from a "froggy"[7] for a pack of Bull Durham.[8] Good feed. Territory all plowed up with shells. Germans had a fine home here and abandoned a lot of supplies.

Wed., Oct. 16, 1918 Took bath at Apremont in a tent. Freezing weather but bath feels fine. First in 7 weeks.

Thur., Oct. 17, 1918 Struck tents at 8:00 A.M. and moved about 4 miles to Chatel. Pitched tents on a side hill so steep that we had to cut steps to ascend. . . . An explosion due to a mine planted by the "bosche" had blown 2 men (French), two horses and a wagon into fragments. [The wagon] was full of grub. We each loaded a burlap bag with cans of condensed milk, peas, lobster, salmon and bread. I started back . . . but was nabbed by a "Frenchy" and had to give up the chow. Quinn was behind me when suddenly another mine exploded. The biggest I ever saw. Rocks and dirt flew sky high. Quinn was hit in knee and had to go to hospital. . . . At 6:00 P.M. each of our four platoons left camp in units to go up front and throw . . . an artillery bridge across the Aire River.[9] . . . We were heavily shelled and gassed causing much confusion. . . . I went back and collected platoon, took some quick flops,[10] and ducked some close ones. We put a bridge across 75' span, constructed entirely from old blown bridge. Job finished and back at camp at 11:30 P.M. No casualties. . . . The toughest job we had so far.

[6] Hard, saltless biscuit that did not get stale too fast.

[7] Slang for a Frenchman.

[8] A U.S. brand of cigarette.

[9] As an "engineer" assigned to building roads and bridges, Kennedy was often exposed to combat. In this case, his job was to quickly construct a bridge on which artillery could perch.

[10] Kennedy and his men had to flop on the ground to avoid getting shot.

Fri., Oct. 18, 1918   Nothing doing all day, waiting for night to work under cover of darkness. Started up front at 6:00 P.M. . . . Put bridge in highway that had been blown out. Worked one half hour when "Jerry" shelled us so strong that we had to leave job. We could hear snipers' bullets sing past us and had to make our way back carefully along R.R. track bank, dodging shells every few steps. Gas so thick that masks had to be kept on, adding to the burden of carrying a rifle, pick, shovel, and hand saw. Had to run from one dug-out to another until it let up somewhat when we made a break for road and hiked to camp about 3 kilos. Gas masks on most of the way, shells bursting both sides of road. Arriving in camp Mac had hot coffee for us.

Fri., Nov. 1, 1918   Started out at 4:00 P.M. The drive is on.[11] Fritz is coming back at us. Machine guns cracking . . . artillery from both sides. A real war and we are walking right into the zone. Ducking shells all the way. The artillery is nerve racking and we don't know from which angle "Jerry" will fire next. Halted behind shelter of R.R. track just outside of Grandpre after being forced back off main road by shell fire. Jerry is shelling Grandpre all the time. Trees splintered like toothpicks. Machine gunners on top of R.R. bank. Breakfast served to us in a protected gully along road. Pushed into Grandpre at 10:00 A.M. to clear streets for the artillery to advance. . . . Sniper's bullets . . . wounded Sgt. Adams, Louderback, Harrison, Koerner, and Greaetehouse.

Sun., Nov. 3, 1918   Plenty of evidence of Hun[12] evacuation. All culverts and innumerable spots in R.R. blown out. . . . Many dead Germans along the road. One heap on a manure pile. Started to fill in shell holes when I was selected with Bill Harvey, Frank Gilberg and Jos Ewell to make reconnaissance of roads in vicinity. Interesting job. Devastation everywhere. Our barrage had rooted up the entire territory like a ploughed field. Dead horses galore, many of them have a hind quarter cut off. The Huns need food. Dead men here and there. The sight I enjoy better than a dead German is to see heaps of them.

Sat., Nov. 9, 1918   Moved out with full packs at 8 A.M. Hiked to Les Islettes about 20 kilos. Hard tack and "corn willie"[13] for lunch. YMCA, K of C,[14] Salvation Army here and we picked up "beaucoup" eats, especially chocolate.[15] Bunked in a fine big chateau.

---

[11] Slang for a German.

[12] A derogatory term for a German, implying that he was like the barbarous warriors who served under Attila in the fifth century C.E.

[13] Soldiers' slang term for canned corned beef, which they were served regularly and complained about regularly.

[14] Knights of Columbus is a Catholic mens service organization.

[15] In French, *beaucoup* means "many," "much," or "in abundance." Chocolate was Kennedy's favorite food; earlier diary entries indicate that while other men scouted for liquor, Kennedy always sought chocolate.

Sun., Nov. 10, 1918   First day off in over two months. Went to church where an American chaplain read Mass and an American soldier choir sang. Seemed good. Co. took at bath and we were issued new underwear but the "cooties"[16] got there first. . . . The papers show a picture of the Kaiser entitled "William the Lost" and say that he had abdicated. Had a good dinner. Rumor at night that armistice was signed. Some fellows discharged their arms in the courtyard but most of us were too well pleased with dry bunk to get up.

[16] Slang for lice.

2

Captain John M. Trible, Medical Corps, Sanitary Train, Third Infantry Division, AEF

Captain Trible was drafted to serve as a lieutenant in the infantry, but he applied to serve as an officer in the Medical Corps instead and was appointed to that branch of the service in July 1917. He went to France in February 1918. At the time he entered the service, Trible was thirty-three years old, married, the father of a young son, and working as a physician in Cuero, Texas.

Thur., Sept. 12, 1918   Left Uruffe at 8 P.M. last night, arrived in woods north of Borcq at 7 A.M. in the morning after a fierce night of rain and mud and inky darkness. It has rained all day and eight of us are in a tent resting up. Information as to the action in front of us is mighty good. Hun prisoners are passing here now. We are in front of the St. Mihiel salient or spur,[1] and not far from Metz in Germany. *Post-war annotation: During this night we passed one truck train that was all lighted up, which was very unusual to say the least, and we learned afterwards that these trucks were loaded with German prisoners, carrying them to the rear, for it made no difference to the French if the lights on this train should attract hun shells, for that would mean just so many less German prisoners to feed and care for. The drivers on all of these trucks were Indo-Chinamen, who did not value their lives any more than did the French.*

Tues., Sept. 17, 1918   Another moonlit night with the usual bombardment. Some of our Division is moving this morning, and we expect to follow during the day. *Post-war annotation: The St. Mihiel drive was over and our Division*

[1] The bulge in the battlefront that made St. Mihiel vulnerable from three sides.
Source: The Diary of John Trible, Captain M.C., U.S. Army, February 26, 1918–May 18, 1919, Tulane University Manuscripts Division, Joseph Merrick Jones Hall Tulane University Libraries, 1–219.

*was being withdrawn, after having so few casualties that it had not been necessary
for any of our four hospitals to even unpack their equipment. . . . Our casualties did not
number over three men killed and seven or eight wounded. . . . When the infantry units
went over the top after the barrage, they met with little or no resistance to speak of.*

[Captain Trible and his medical unit began making their way northwest toward the
Meuse-Argonne front as soon as the St. Mihiel battle was over. But he had duties
along the way. — Eds.]

Wed., Sept. 18, 1918   Had a most miserable night last night. Left Borcq at
2 P.M. and traveled in a long truck train that stopped every ten minutes,
reached Julvecourt at 2 P.M. today, nothing to eat, nor no water to drink while
en route.

Fri., Sept. 20, 1918   Rained most of the day. Went to Julvecourt and interviewed the prisoner I had been appointed to defend.[2]

Sat., Sept. 21, 1918   Trial of the attempted rape case in which I am to act as
counsel for the defendant was deferred on account of difficulty getting witnesses. Very chilly and cold and rained all morning.

Mon., Sept. 23, 1918   The country hereabouts is packed with American
troops. It is cold, damp, and gloomy. We anticipate that there will be a big fight
on in a few days.

Tues., Sept. 24, 1918   The sun came out and it is drying up a little and is
also a little warmer. . . . Had a successful courtmartial case this afternoon as my
client . . . won out and was acquitted. ***Post-war annotation:*** *I secured his acquittal with considerable difficulty as Midgely [the prosecuting officer] was determined he should be convicted, which probably was what should have happened.
Midgely was sore at me about the management of the case for some time for I won
his acquittal on technicalities.*

Wed., Sept. 25, 1918   Rec'd ten letters from my girl today; they had some
very clear pictures of the man crying and on a donkey hitched to a cart.[3] . . .
This morning before daybreak, a barrage north of us started, and we believe the
American offensive has been launched, though no one knows.

Thurs., Sept. 26, 1918   Left the woods where we were at two A.M. this
day and came north of Verdun. The real American attack—battle of the
Argonne—started at eleven o'clock last night, the barrage was fierce. We slept

---

[2] With lawyers in short supply at the front, any professionally trained officer could be asked
to serve as a soldier's legal counsel.

[3] Trible's "girl" is his wife, Ottie Belle Trible; "the man" is his four-year-old son, John Bowles
Trible.

all morning in the woods and have been watching prisoners being brought in. All reports are favorable for this, the apparently greatest of all battles.

Mon., Sept. 30, 1918   We understand that we are to relieve the 79th Division on the line at once, but the congested roads will make it slow going. We understand that the huns are vigorously counterattacking our troops, it is said with no other results than heavy loss of life. ***Post-war annotation:*** *It is probable that we owed the length of our stay here to the bad roads and the terrible congestion on them, for in a way we were shut off from the world and couldn't get out. . . . Through the firing and the heavy traffic worked thousands of men of the Engineers with picks and shovels, and little sacks filled with rocks from shell holes. They were literally building up the road under our feet. . . . There was no living thing in all this sector but soldiers. All vegetation was dead, most of the trees were shattered, and the others had been killed with gas.*

Sun., Oct. 6, 1918   Had an awful day of it as we have been flooded with wounded, many of whom died on our hands and the others were desperately wounded. There has been terrific artillery action today. . . . I am about all in as my nerves are shot to pieces. It is very damp and chilly. ***Post-war annotation:*** *These desperately wounded were a wonderful bunch, they did not whimper or complain, all they wanted was something to smoke, and we had plenty of tobacco for all of them, also we had a generous supply of morphine, which we used freely. . . . We also had plenty of whiskey which we also used freely to get them warmed up.*

Sat., Oct. 12, 1918   Many wounded again during the night. . . . Our evacuation service is absolutely rotten, many men thus lose their only chance of life. Today is quieter. . . . Still we know very little of what is happening, except that it seems to be favorable, though at a high cost. We have many wounded in our ward.

Thurs., Oct. 17, 1918   This is our sixth anniversary. May the next be spent with her whom I love. . . . Very few patients and very poor evacuation. Only lost six men yesterday. We are being relieved today by the 90th Division.

Fri., Oct. 18, 1918   There seems to be a doubt as to whether our division is being relieved or not.

Sun., Oct. 20, 1918   Rec'd orders last night to move at daybreak this morning to a point near Septsarges, 8 kilometers north of here. . . . We are acting as a shock hospital and are located on a road on the top of a high hill. It has simply poured all day and is very cold. We had to pitch and equip our tents in a sea of mud and water. My hands are so cold that it is with difficulty that I write this.

Sat., Oct. 26, 1918   We have now been in for twenty-seven days without rest or relief.

[Trible's division was finally relieved of duty on October 28, and Trible was ordered to Velaines, Belgium, to serve in a hospital there.—Eds.]

Thurs., Nov. 7, 1918   From the news of today the huns are on the run everywhere, as all armies have made big advances. . . . The usual rumors are afloat that peace has been declared. We are hopeful but not assured.

Sun., Nov. 10, 1918   Was in luck today . . . letters from my girl. . . . The news therein is not good for it is as I feared, both she and J.B. were sick with the influenza, but they have a good doctor, Dr. Peck of Dallas, and apparently both are doing well. Everything is rumor and everyone has at least one story to tell. . . . Retribution is now coming very rapidly to [the Germans] to pay them for their violation of international law and the laws of humanity. It has been quite cold today. I wrote and thanked Dr. Peck for his great kindness to my loved ones.

Mon., Nov. 11, 1918   Eleven in the morning—orders cancelled—the French flag appears on passing cars and there is great enthusiasm, for it is announced that the armistice was signed at five this morning, to take effect at eleven A.M. on the eleventh day of the eleventh month of the year 1918. . . . Everywhere the Huns are retreating in great disorder, leaving supplies and guns. This surely is one of the great days in history.

---

3   *Sergeant Elmer F. Straub, 150th Field Artillery, Forty-second "Rainbow" Division*

Elmer Straub had been a student at Indiana University before the war. He registered for the draft but must have been a member of the National Guard because his Forty-second "Rainbow" Division was comprised of National Guard units. Upon enlisting in late July 1917, Straub joined an artillery unit.

Sat., Sept. 7, 1918   It is just one year today since we left Indianapolis.

Sun., Sept. 8, 1918   In an old half-shot-down building near here, in this village of Mandres, there is a branch of the Salvation Army and this morning nearly all of the boys slipped away and got two pancakes, syrup and a cup of coffee for nothing; they certainly treat the boys right. The commissaries and the Red Cross also gave out raincoats, underwear, sox and towels but the Y.M.C.A. are regular robbers. . . . We will be spending our time peering over 'No Man's Land' in the St. Mihiel sector. For noon mess we had fried potatoes, hard

Source: Sergeant Elmer Straub, *A Sergeant's Diary in the World War,* volume 3, Indiana World War Records (Indianapolis: Indiana Historical Commission, 1923), 11–343.

tack and coffee and we are expected to keep alive on that, for I suppose we will get nothing but that from now on until we get off the front. . . . Swell food for men who get as little sleep and do as much work as we do! After mess Hoover and I went over to the Salvation Army where we bought some soap and safety razor blades and then the old man in charge gave us some great big California grapes and they surely went good. . . . At 8:00 we took the horses out to graze as they do not get half the food they ought to.

Mon., Sept. 9, 1918   We got up to the O.P. [observation post] about 9:45 A.M. . . . It is right in the front lines and about four kilometers in front of our guns. There is more artillery stationed between our guns and the O.P. than I have ever seen before. The 'big party' is to start sometime between the 15th and the 20th of this month and the first day's objective is the village of Pannes. We can see the lay out of both the American and German infantries; the Americans are in the valley directly in front of our O.P. and the Germans are on the high ground just beyond. During the morning we located about fifteen villages that are now in German hands and also got the terrain pretty well in mind. . . . During the afternoon . . . I went out in the big woods right in back of the O.P. and picked several hats of great big blackberries.

Thurs., Sept. 12, 1918   At 1:05 A.M. the party started off; only the heavy artillery started the thing and according to all dope it was a big surprise to the Germans. There was so little retaliation fire that they used only about half the artillery they had up here. . . . At 10 A.M. [we] started forward . . . into Pannes. The road was certainly a sight, there were three columns of troops going forward on this one narrow little road. The road itself was in an awful condition, full of shell holes, bridges out and all torn up. The Engineers were working on the bridges and filling up the shell holes, wounded were being brought back this way. . . . We could overlook the whole valley that not twelve hours before was 'No Man's Land' and now it is crowded with human bodies, both dead and alive. . . . The Germans . . . left everything behind in their hurry to get out, and considering all of it, American casualties were very small. . . . In the villages that we passed through we saw many, many French civilians who had lived in their old homes under German military rule ever since the start of the war. When our officers would pass them they would all come to attention showing that the Germans had made them live and regard them as "THE RULERS" of the land, and when our men and officers treated them well they would do anything for our convenience.

[At 4:30 A.M. on Friday, October 4, Straub and his artillery regiment, with horses, trucks, and wagons, began their sixty-mile march northwest to the Argonne sector.—Eds.]

Mon., Oct. 7, 1918   This morning . . . when we got to the edge of Montfaucon, the Colonel stopped and we all dismounted. . . . The Colonel showed us a big valley where he said we could put our gun positions. . . . This is the Argonne Woods.

Tues., Oct. 15, 1918   Maxwell had been out last night stealing food and when he got up this morning we started to eat again. We made three batches of fudge and had toast, butter, pancakes, fried potatoes and sugar. . . . We found out that our doughboys gained their objective but had to drop back. . . . [They] have had about 1500 casualties since they have been up here and they are in pretty bad shape.

Wed., Oct. 16, 1918   The battery is lower now on horses than it ever has been, we have only 131 left and my single mount looks like a real skeleton because of lack of food.

Fri., Oct. 18, 1918   We went . . . on up toward the front. We saw very, very many American and German dead lying around and the whole country is terribly devastated. Mud is no name for it. . . . I hope and pray that all of our horses fall dead or something happens to prevent us from taking up our new gun position; our first piece will be put 100 feet from 12 German dead and more than twenty dead horses. . . . This life is certainly one h--- and I surely hope that something very unusual happens to break the spell of mud, rain, work, monotony, and dissatisfaction that we are under.

Sat., Oct. 19, 1918   The country around is practically the same as that we saw a few days ago, all torn up, full of shell holes, dead lying wherever one looks and the whole country dead except for the American soldiers. We tied our horses at the base of a very steep hill and then took our instruments and climbed to the top, where we could see all over the surrounding country, our lines and the German lines. We immediately . . . put on the phone and then Lieut. Knaff started to adjust the battery on a German O.P. that was located in the top of a tree near the edge of the woods. . . . It took about 40 rounds and the tree was no more. . . . All thru this valley one can see American dead lying about and it seems as if the first aid men who are supposed to litter these men off do not do their work properly because . . . it is certainly a gruesome looking place. On our way back I took a short cut and got into some sneezing gas. I was afraid to run my horse as he is so poor that I thought he would drop dead; I have been sneezing ever since.

Sat., Oct. 26, 1918   This morning while I was eating, Lieut. Knaff told me that the position we had located was not far enough in advance. . . . By the time I arrived at the [new] position it was clear and there was a deal of aerial activity. . . . About 2:00 the Germans began to . . . fire both H.E. and shrapnel;[1] each H.E. shell contains a little mustard gas so I inhaled weak gas all the rest of the day. . . . While the gun squads were putting the guns in place I tried to help Coleman and some of our detail boys with our instrument wagon which had gotten stuck in a shell hole on account of a balky horse they had pulling it. Shells were coming thick and fast, both H.E. and gas, so all of the work was very

---

[1] High explosives (H.E.) destroy property, while shrapnel and mustard gas kill people.

slow. . . . It was 12:30 before the pieces were in place and laid ready to fire, and then when I looked the place over I found that the third piece was in a ditch.

Mon., Oct. 28, 1918   This morning we all got up happy as there had been no one killed during the night. . . . The gas was very strong during the night. . . . Two of our horses had been killed during the night and one of our men was sent to the hospital with gas. . . . After I had finished my breakfast and watered and fed my horse, I again started to work on our hole—making it deeper . . . and now I think we are pretty safe.

Fri., Nov. 1, 1918   After I had taken my shave this A.M. . . . I decided I ought to have a few trinkets so I started out to meet one of the columns of prisoners. . . . I asked one fellow whether he had a watch and he said yes; so I made him give it to me and then I went to one of the others who gave me another watch, and the third gave me a knife, so I figured that I had enough. I did not like the idea of taking their things from them but some one else would have, so I suppose it was all right. There were many wounded being brought in, both German and American; the German prisoners who were not injured always carried the wounded men in, whether German or American. Three German medics were captured and they were put to work taking care of wounded. . . . They were certainly good workers and did the work right. . . . The nerve that the boys display when they come in wounded is certainly remarkable. They don't even whimper. . . . I held one American "Doughboy's" hand as he died. . . . It was sure a mess of blood at the first aid station and it finally 'got to' Perry and me, so we stopped and went to tend our horses. . . . I talked to many of [the German prisoners] and they were all anxious to go to America and were overly glad that they were thru with the whole thing. . . . The Germans certainly praise the Americans and say that they have never seen such wonderful artillery work. As I was talking to one he looked at my name . . . and he asked me whether or not I was German. I told him that I was, and then he told me that he lived beside an old shoemaker named Straub in Strassburg. Before I could say much more to him he was rushed on and I lost him in the crowd, everything was one big, mad whirl. We are now firing at a range that requires a number 00 charge, the heaviest charge we have. . . . As a whole the day has been rather exciting and I have smoked so many cigarettes that my tongue burns like fire. I have just taken the cotton out of my ears.

Sat., Nov. 2, 1918   I could not go to sleep immediately so I sat up until 11:30 and read until I got sleepy. One would at least think that one would have a few unpleasant dreams after a day such as the one yesterday, but after I got to sleep, I slept thru until 8:00 this morning without a whimper. After breakfast . . . we started forward to locate a new gun position.

Wed., Nov. 6, 1918   There is an awful lot of "snow" going around about peace talk and the latest dope we have is that the "doughboys" are about 30 kilometers in front of us and are still going toward the rear. Things are quiet and they say the war is over for them.

Thurs., Nov. 7, 1918 Well the night was about as quiet as we have had for the past four or five months. . . . This morning I saw an American Y.W.C.A. girl. . . . She is the first woman I have seen for about four months.

Fri., Nov., 8, 1918 During the night I had an awful coughing spell and short breath and I think it is the effects of the gas that we were in there. . . . We hear that peace is practically at hand.

Mon., Nov. 11, 1918 Of course all morning the boys were waiting for news of peace. Battery had their wireless up and at 9:30 received word that Germany had accepted our peace terms and that at 11:45 there would be no more firing on any of the fronts. Of course the fellows had a smile on their faces but there was not any rejoicing to amount to anything. . . . The "snow" is already out as to what we are going to do next, and I'll say that it is not very pleasing news. We are either to go to Austria or Germany for M.P. duty.

Analyzing Wartime Diaries

1. How often did these men mention food in their diaries? Were there differences in how often Kennedy, Straub, and Trible talked about wanting, finding, or stealing food? What do you think might account for any differences you find?

2. Why were the roads so bad along the western front? If you had been deployed there in 1918, would you have wanted to have a horse or a truck?

3. Of all the discomforts these diarists mentioned—inadequate food, rain, cold, mud, "cooties," unmarked mines, dead bodies lying around, constant artillery sounds—which, for you, would be the most difficult to cope with? Which seems the most troublesome to each diarist?

4. What differences do you find in how the three diarists spoke about, and seem to feel about, the German soldiers? How do you explain these differences?

5. Compare Captain Trible's comments on the armistice on November 10 and 11 with Corporal Kennedy's on November 10 and Sergeant Straub's on November 11. Why do you think the reactions of the young soldiers from New York and Indiana were different from those of the thirty-four-year-old physician from Texas?

The Rest of the Story

Sergeant Elmer Straub's prediction that he would be sent to Germany after the war proved accurate. He and his artillery battery were stationed in Bad Neuenahr, near the Rhine River, from December 1918 through March 1919. Straub's thirty pages of diary entries from this period do not say much about the nature of his duties, apart from taking care of his horses and serving as a military presence, but the entries are thick with descriptions of the good food, comfortable beds, hours of sleep, and friendly German people. Straub then spent four months at the University of Edinburgh, under U.S. Army auspices, before he was discharged on August 5, 1919. He walked into his parents' home in Indianapolis at 7:30 A.M. on August 7.

After the war, Corporal Eugene Kennedy stayed in France, where his engineering company worked on reconnaissance maps. His fifty pages of post-armistice entries, like Straub's, said more about his meals (including his "first ice cream in fourteen months") and his sightseeing trips around France than about his military work. But, like Straub, Kennedy continued to keep the daily diary until he reached his home near Albany, New York, in June 1919. His final entry stated, "Peg and I . . . ordered announcement cards. We then called on Father Looney and made arrangements to be married July 9th."

Captain Trible continued to serve as an army physician for six months after the war. He wrote in his diary about his post-armistice duty caring for American soldiers, in both France and Germany, who were suffering from influenza. Entries in November and December made frequent mention of the hundreds of flu cases he was treating and the number of men dying each day.

Neither Trible, Straub, nor Kennedy wrote about the flu before the war ended, but this pandemic, which killed twenty million individuals worldwide in 1918–1919, was taking its toll on the U.S. military in the last weeks of the war. Indeed, the crowded conditions in training camps and troop ships in the summer of 1918 encouraged the spread of the deadly epidemic. Between September and November, 23,000 enlisted men in training in the United States died of flu-induced pneumonia; another 9,000 soldiers died of the flu in France. Overall, an estimated one-quarter of the U.S. Army suffered from the flu during the war, and in the unrelenting final weeks of battle, almost 100,000 members of the AEF (including General Pershing) suffered from it. Of the 126,000 American soldiers who died in the war, 66,000 soldiers died from the flu.

All historians of World War I acknowledge the contributions and sacrifices of American soldiers during the war, but no one pretends that their sacrifices can compare to those made by the Allied forces with whom the United States fought. The 60,000 Americans who died in combat represent a small fraction of the five million Allied deaths and the three million deaths on the German side. The U.S. casualty rate—dead and wounded combined—was about 206,000, or 8 percent of the 2.6 million Americans who served in combat, whereas the British casualty rate was 35 percent, the French casualty rate was 76 percent, and the Austro-Hungarian casualty rate was a staggering 90 percent.

All three of the diarists profiled in this chapter survived the war, making them quite representative of the American soldiers who served. Thousands came home without a limb, without their sight, without their sanity. But the vast majority, including Kennedy, Trible, and Straub, returned home and resumed their lives as workers and family members in their communities. In the coming decades, the American veterans of World War I would become a forceful lobby for government benefits to those who had served the nation under fire. After World War II, political leaders who had been World War I veterans, including President Harry Truman, helped enact the GI Bill, providing returning soldiers with aid that had not been available after World War I.

To Find Out More

Corporal Eugene Kennedy's entire diary is available at the Hoover Institution on War, Revolution, and Peace at Stanford University, Palo Alto, California. Captain John Trible's entire diary, with annotations, is available in the Special Collections division of the Howard-Tilton Memorial Library at Tulane University, New Orleans. Sergeant Elmer Straub's diary was published as *A Sergeant's Diary in the World War* as volume 3 of the Indiana World War Records (Indianapolis: Indiana Historical Commission, 1923).

There are surprisingly few published diaries by World War I soldiers. Two that were recently published are *The Great War at Home and Abroad: The World War I Diaries and Letters of W. Stull Holt* (Manhattan, Kans.: Sunflower University Press, 1998) and *All for Heaven, Hell, or Hoboken: The World War I Diary and Letters of Clair F. Pfennig, Flash Ranger, Company D, 29 Engineers, A.E.F.* (St. Louis: Crimson Shamrock Press, 1999). Some published volumes, such as Chester E. Baker's *A Doughboy's Diary* (Shippensburg, Pa.: Burd Street Press, 1998), are actually memoirs written after the war was over. Despite its title, *War Birds: Diary of an Unknown Aviator* (New York: George H. Doran Company, 1926) is actually a novel by Elliot White Springs, but it does not announce itself as fiction.

The best collections of unpublished wartime diaries are located at the U.S. Army Military History Institute at Carlisle Barracks in Carlisle, Pennsylvania, and in the collection assembled by the Virginia War History Commission at the Virginia State Archives in Richmond, Virginia. Other World War I diaries can be found online at The Veterans History Project, run by the Library of Congress at **www.loc.gov/vets/**, which links to the World War I Docu-ment Archive at **www.loc.gov/vets/stories/ex-war-wwi.html**. Another valuable site for World War I memoirs and diaries is the Great War Society at **www.worldwar1.com .tgws/**.

A library search under "World War 1914 1918 personal narratives" will produce an array of memoirs by U.S. veterans. There are also a number of interesting collections of wartime letters, including Josiah P. Rowe Jr., *Letters from a World War I Aviator* (Boston: Sinclaire Press, 1986); *A Yankee Ace in the RAF: The World War I Letters of Captain Bogart Rogers* (Lawrence: University Press of Kansas, 1996); and *Out Here at the Front: The World War I Letters of Nora Saltonstall* (Boston: Northeastern University Press, 2004), which offers the viewpoint of an army nurse in a mobile unit at the western front.

For recent overviews of the entire war, from its start in 1914 through the armistice, see John Keegan, *The First World War* (New York: Alfred A. Knopf,

1999), and Martin Gilbert, *The First World War: A Complete History* (New York: Owl Books, 2004). For an excellent overview of the U.S. war experience, both at home and abroad, see Robert H. Zieger, *America's Great War: World War I and the American Experience* (New York: Rowman and Littlefield, 2000). Frank Freidel's engaging narrative of the war, *Over There: The Story of America's First Great Overseas Crusade* (Boston: Little, Brown and Company, 1965), uses many excerpts from diaries and letters as well as splendid photographs.

For an interesting study of soldiers' experiences in the war, see Jennifer Keene, *Doughboys, the Great War, and the Remaking of Modern America* (Baltimore: Johns Hopkins University Press, 2001). She has also written an overview of the wartime experiences of soldiers and civilians as part of the Daily Life through History Series: *World War I* (Westport, Conn.: Greenwood Press, 2006). See, too, Carol Byerly, *Fever of War: The Influenza Epidemic in the U.S. Army during World War I* (New York: NYU Press, 2005); Arthur E. Barbeau and Henri Florette, *The Unknown Soldier: African-American Troops in World War I* (Philadelphia: Temple University Press, 1974); and Nancy Gentile Ford, *Americans All!: Foreign-Born Soldiers in World War I* (College Station: Texas A&M University Press, 2001). *The Great War: 1918* is a one-hour film documentary, including interviews with World War I veterans, that effectively captures the doughboys' experiences.

CHAPTER 7

Flappers in the Barrio

A Chapter from a Historian's Book

The 1920s are one of the most notoriously misrepresented eras in American popular culture. Our image of the "roaring" decade is dominated by "the flapper," a young woman wearing a knee-high chemise, smoking a cigarette, dancing the Charleston, and swinging her long beads. That image embodies our collective sense that the Twenties were a time of bold change; the war was over, the Victorian era was past, and modern life had begun. In fact, the era was a time of serious struggle between modernizing forces for change, conservative forces that wanted to maintain Victorian social customs, and reactionary forces that wanted to turn the clock back on the democratic gains of the Progressive era. Rather than a decade of unbridled experimentation, the Twenties were a time of intense negotiations between a world we view as "traditional" and a world we recognize as "modern." Two cultures that made their mark on the 1920s, the youth culture and the Mexican American culture, offer insight into the subtleties of these negotiations.

The mere existence of an identifiable, self-conscious youth culture was evidence of change. Adolescence in American society had, historically, been a time of apprenticeship in adult culture, either in paid jobs where youth were surrounded by and supervised by adults, or in family roles on the farm, in the shop, or in the kitchen. Between 1920 and 1930, however, the share of adolescents spending their days clustered together in high schools increased from 23 percent to 38 percent, and the privileged slice of youth who could attend colleges for four years increased sharply from 8 percent in 1920 to 12 percent in 1930. This concentration of young people served as a critical mass of trendsetters and consumers who defined a separate youth culture. The females among these students, and their wage-earning cohort, announced their generational identity by discarding corsets in favor of looser, shorter dresses, bobbing their hair short, wearing makeup, smoking cigarettes, drinking prohibited liquor, and dancing to jazz music.

Advocates for these trends used such superficial behaviors as proof that the passage of woman suffrage in 1920 had ushered in a new day of sexual equality. Reactionaries were appalled that their just-enacted prohibition on alcohol was being scorned by youth who, though apolitical in every other way, seemed to define themselves in joyful opposition to this particular law. Traditionalists, especially women who had fought for woman suffrage, worried that young women were trading in a cultural legacy of female moral authority, women's sole claim to power in American society, in exchange for the freedom to play with men by men's rules.

In all of the anxious commentary about wanton youth, few noticed how little had actually changed. Across class, race, and ethnicity, young people in the 1920s still assumed that men were destined to be income-earning husbands and fathers and that women were still meant to be at home as wives and mothers. The number of women who chose to live independent of marriage actually decreased in the 1920s; 90 percent of women workers continued to be segregated into just ten occupational categories (including clerical work, domestic service, sales, schoolteaching, and nursing); and women's wages continued to be two-thirds that of men's. The overall number of wives working for pay increased in this decade, but this was a response to inadequate pay for working-class men rather than a sign of female liberation. Despite appearances to the contrary, the fundamentals of family structure and gender roles were unchanged in the "Roaring Twenties."

The styles introduced by 1920s youth culture mostly affected people's experiences before marriage. Traditional "courtship" with the person you intended to marry was replaced with "dating" a variety of people before committing to marriage, and the very private sexual overtures of betrothed Victorian couples gave way to more casual "necking" and "petting" with a series of partners. This modern form of sexual expression sometimes occurred in that new and dangerous dating machine, the chaperone-free automobile. But necking just as often took place in party settings, which guaranteed that free expression would not go far enough to turn into scandal. After all, contraception was still technically illegal and largely inaccessible for single women, and unwed mothers were still stigmatized and economically stranded. Elders' fears for young women's sexual safety were not, therefore, baseless; when playing by men's rules, unprotected women always took a bigger risk for higher stakes. The evidence from the 1920s suggests, however, that most young people understood this. So while they drank, danced, kissed, and caressed with greater abandon than their parents, they also established their own customs that preserved the traditional family system they would inherit.

Just as discussions of youth culture in the 1920s have typically exaggerated change, so have popular portrayals of Mexican American culture in this era often overstated the homogenizing threat of mass media. The assumption has been too easily made that Mexican ethnic identity survived only in rigid isolation from modernity, and that movies, magazines, radios, phonographs, and advertising spelled the loss of that identity. But here again, as with youth culture, the evidence suggests negotiation and accommodation between the old and the new.

Exclusionary laws passed in the 1920s put quotas on the number of southern and eastern European immigrants allowed into the United States, but powerful western farmers in need of field labor insisted that there be no limit on immigrants from Mexico or Latin America. The demand for Mexican labor combined with the disruptions to village life caused by the 1910 Mexican revolution and expanded rail service between Mexico and the United States meant that the Mexican population in California increased from 90,000 to nearly 360,000 in the 1920s, more than four times the overall growth rate for the state.

The largely working-class population of Mexican Americans in the United States in the 1920s contended with poverty and racism. Very few from Mexico enjoyed a comfortable place among that 40 percent of Americans who earned more than half of the nation's total income in the twenties; none were included in the elite 5 percent of Americans who took in about 30 percent of the nation's income. Mexicans Americans, like most U.S. workers, were in that bottom 55 percent that lived on 20 percent of the nation's income, typically earning below the $2,000 poverty line for a family of four. Racial prejudices compounded Mexican Americans' economic problems. Those nativists who viewed Mexicans as a "menace" to U.S. civilization and wanted them barred from immigrating drew on existing attitudes toward blacks and Native Americans to bolster their arguments. Mexicans, they said, were as intellectually "low-powered as the Negro" and as morally corrupt as the average "Amerind." One writer claimed that Mexican fathers commonly earned money by prostituting their daughters, concluding that the Mexican man's attitude toward women was like "that of an Indian buck toward his squaw."

In the face of these hostile elements, Mexican American parents struggled to sustain a strong, moral family life and to create a Mexican American culture that combined Mexican traditions with U.S. opportunities. The expansion of national consumer brands, mass marketing, and chain stores in the 1920s did not immediately eliminate local ethnic businesses in cities like Los Angeles. Nor did the rise of a mass media in film, radio, and the recording industry dictate Anglo cultural homogeneity. During the 1920s, one-third of Mexican families owned radios, which were tuned to local, Spanish-language radio broadcasts. When U.S. law forbade the import of Mexican-made records, a Mexican American recording business emerged in Los Angeles marketing urban *corridos*, a genre of storytelling folk song that proved eminently adaptable for singing about modern city life. Ninety percent of Mexican families went to local movie houses in the 1920s, spending as much as $22 a year for shows that combined Mexican American vaudeville acts with silent pictures that posed no language barrier. To take advantage of this burgeoning market, Hollywood made some movies explicitly for Mexican American audiences with such stars as Ramon Navarro and Delores del Rio.

Figure 7.1 Mexican American Singer Luisa Espinel, 1921 This photo of the Mexican American singer Luisa Espinel shows off a stylish blend of 1920s evening dress and a traditional Latin hair comb. In the 1920s and 1930s, Espinel was an internationally known interpreter of Spanish songs, which she had learned from her father, Fred Ronstadt, while growing up in Tucson, Arizona. Espinel's niece, Linda Ronstadt, has been a Grammy-award-winning singer of mainstream pop songs since the 1970s while also recording popular albums of traditional Mexican music.
Source: Courtesy of Arizona Historical Society/Tucson, AHS#69493.

To a Mexican traditionalist, such embrace of modern media products looked like corruption of an old and dignified culture. To the U.S. nativist, Mexican participation in the creation of modern media looked like degradation of Anglo-American culture. But for those immigrant parents from Mexico working to raise children who could make the most of U.S. opportunities while retaining a Mexican identity, the cultural process was a fluid, daily mix of ethnic traditions and new circumstances. Like Anglo-American parents, Mexican American parents had a clear goal: family formation and family cohesion within a culture that fit the modern marketplace. Whatever their ethnicity, parents in the 1920s sought to protect that goal against the new demands that work, school, and a consumer culture made on their children, especially their daughters. Modern forces tended to emphasize individual achievement, individual identity, and individual choice, all of which could disrupt family cohesion. Parents' success in the 1920s at containing modern impulses within the traditional family system is a study in cultural accommo-dation.

Using the Source: Secondary Sources

In every other chapter of this book, you are examining different sorts of "pri-mary" sources. These are the original documents that historians examine and interpret in order to create the books and articles that we often think of as "his-tory" but which are technically called "secondary sources." In this chapter, you have the opportunity to observe how a practicing historian, Dr. Vicki L. Ruiz of the University of California, Irvine, integrates primary sources from the 1920s and oral interviews with Mexican American women to create a new perspective on both the era's youth culture and ethnic family life. By examining an excerpt from Ruiz's book, *From Out of the Shadows: Mexican Women in Twentieth-Century America*, you can consider the different parts and processes that go into con-structing a secondary source out of primary sources.

In the field of history, there are two basic types of secondary sources: books and articles. Ideally, both books and articles do the same things: they tell a story about the past, they provide an interpretation of that story, and they re-late their story and their interpretation to other historians' stories and inter-pretations. Once you become alert to these three operations, you increase your command of both books and articles. In this sense, reading secondary works of history is rather like using computers: you can more fully exploit their poten-tial if you understand their operating features and grasp the logic driving the basic system.

In the opening pages of "The Flapper and the Chaperone," which is chap-ter 3 of her book, Ruiz performs the operations that are central to any second-ary work of history. She conveys the story by opening with the scene in the barrio hall and immediately identifying tension between young women and their chaperones. In the second paragraph, Ruiz makes three arguments about the evidence she is going to present on generational conflict in the 1920s and 1930s, or "between the wars." Next, she describes the oral histories she will be drawing on because they are the primary source that makes her study special. And along the way, she introduces you to other historians—immigration his-torians, consumer culture historians, Chicano historians, 1920s historians—whom she will be drawing into her discussion. By the end of the first two and a half pages, Ruiz has acquainted you with her story, her arguments, some of her primary sources, and the other types of historians she has learned from. If you are aware that these are standard features in a secondary history, and that they typically appear early in the text, you will be alert to them as you read.

The key feature to identify in any secondary source is the historian's main argument. This means figuring out what the historian, not the reader, would say is the most important conclusion to be drawn from the evidence. One trick to identifying a historian's thesis lies in remembering that a thesis must be an argument, so a thesis statement must be arguable and open to debate. Look at Ruiz's second paragraph:

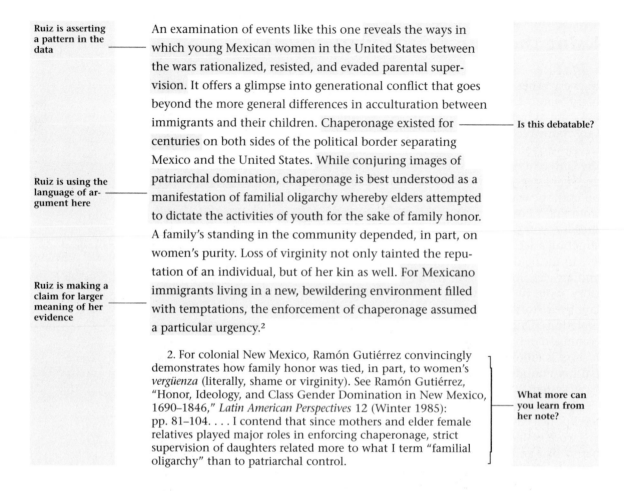

Ruiz is asserting a pattern in the data

An examination of events like this one reveals the ways in which young Mexican women in the United States between the wars rationalized, resisted, and evaded parental supervision. It offers a glimpse into generational conflict that goes beyond the more general differences in acculturation between immigrants and their children. Chaperonage existed for centuries on both sides of the political border separating Mexico and the United States. While conjuring images of patriarchal domination, chaperonage is best understood as a manifestation of familial oligarchy whereby elders attempted to dictate the activities of youth for the sake of family honor. A family's standing in the community depended, in part, on women's purity. Loss of virginity not only tainted the reputation of an individual, but of her kin as well. For Mexicano immigrants living in a new, bewildering environment filled with temptations, the enforcement of chaperonage assumed a particular urgency.[2]

Is this debatable?

Ruiz is using the language of argument here

Ruiz is making a claim for larger meaning of her evidence

2. For colonial New Mexico, Ramón Gutiérrez convincingly demonstrates how family honor was tied, in part, to women's *vergüenza* (literally, shame or virginity). See Ramón Gutiérrez, "Honor, Ideology, and Class Gender Domination in New Mexico, 1690–1846," *Latin American Perspectives* 12 (Winter 1985): pp. 81–104. . . . I contend that since mothers and elder female relatives played major roles in enforcing chaperonage, strict supervision of daughters related more to what I term "familial oligarchy" than to patriarchal control.

What more can you learn from her note?

This paragraph, coming very early in the chapter, alerts the reader to three positions Ruiz is going to take: first, that young Mexican women in the United States "rationalized, resisted, and evaded parental supervision"; second, that parental supervision was an expression of "familial oligarchy," not patriarchy; and third, that chaperonage took on new significance in the United States. We can figure that these are arguments—in contrast to a factual statement like "chaperonage existed for centuries"—because they are open to debate. Ruiz's description of the young women's three types of reactions to parental supervision represents her own characterization of their behavior; another historian might describe the behavior differently. Her claim that chaperonage "assumed a particular urgency" challenges a popular assumption that immigrants are forced to drop their cultural traditions in the United States. And Ruiz's assertion that "chaperonage is best understood" as a function of "familial oligarchy" even "while conjuring images" of patriarchy conveys through language choice that she is taking an argumentative stance. When a historian tells a reader that a behavior is "best understood" a certain way, he or she is arguing against other ways of interpreting that behavior. When a historian uses words with strong connotations, such as "conjuring" and "images," that historian is saying that other interpreters have been misled by appearances. By noticing such language, readers can sense that Ruiz is carving out a particular position on a scholarly argument about oligarchy (government by a few) and patriarchy (government by elder males). Notice that endnote 2 confirms that suspicion. When Ruiz writes "I contend," she is making clear that this is her own position.

So which is the central thesis of Ruiz's chapter on "The Flapper and the Chaperone"? Is it that young women adopted one of three reactions to parental supervision? That chaperonage was an expression of "familial oligarchy"? Or that chaperonage had a particular "urgency" in the U.S. context? Ruiz's second paragraph alerts us to these related arguments but does not tell us which one represents the main point she plans to draw from the evidence. By noticing these early arguments, we can keep track of which arguments the historian discusses the most fully, supports with the most evidence, or gives the most emphasis in the conclusion.

What Can Secondary Sources Tell Us?

For students of history, the distinct advantage of a secondary source is that it pulls together a massive amount of materials that may be scattered in archives and libraries from Beijing to Miami. The historians who examine and interpret such mounds of primary sources are doing a lot of work for the reader. These scholars add even more value to their product by explaining how the interpretive story they are telling with their sources compares to the interpretations other historians have made about similar sources and related stories. When historians inform their readers about the broader literature, known as the historiography, they are giving readers a window on a whole set of historical narratives and arguments, not just their own.

So, for example, Vicki Ruiz brings together in one chapter an array of sources about Mexican American daughters in the 1920s. She puts the quotes from her interviews into broader historical context, showing how individual women's experiences reflect patterns discernible in magazines and social science research, and she relates the interviews to one another, pointing out similarities and differences in her subjects' experiences.

The disadvantage of secondary sources is directly connected to their advantage: readers do not have immediate access to all of the primary and secondary sources that the historian used to construct the story and the argument, so it can be difficult for readers to check a historian's work. We are grateful to Vicki Ruiz for collecting, organizing, and interpreting an array of materials, but that gratitude rests on trust that she has been accurate and honest in presenting her evidence. Trusting a historian's honesty does not mean we believe that the historian's interpretation is "right." Trust in this case simply means we have confidence that the historian has not hidden or manufactured evidence. It is perfectly possible to trust a historian's presentation of evidence and still differ with his or her interpretation of that evidence.

The historical profession relies on two practical methods to guard against violation of readers' trust: documentation in endnotes, and peer review of books and articles. Nonhistorians often laugh, or sigh, over historians' extensive documentation in endnotes. Why, you might ask, are the few pages of Ruiz's book included here accompanied by thirty-eight endnotes? The answer is that those notes tell the reader where to find the primary and secondary sources that she used to support her argument. In Ruiz's endnote 2, for example, she supports her claim about the importance of unmarried daughters' virginity by referring to the work of Ramón Gutiérrez. It is not Ruiz's purpose to prove this claim; her aim is to build upon it. A reader who doubts this claim or wants to know more about it is invited to consult Gutiérrez. In this way, endnotes serve as a gathering place where readers can see how one historian has drawn from the work of other historians and can locate the work of those other historians. Equally important are endnotes that guide the reader to the precise location of the primary documents or, as you will see in Ruiz's notes, provide information on the people she interviewed.

Along with the use of endnotes, the custom of peer review is the historical profession's way of detecting fraudulent work. Peer review is a process by which a historian's work is reviewed by other historians, sometimes anonymously and commonly by historians in the same field. Reviewers often disagree with a historian's argument, but they do not often charge fraud; evidence, after all, can be used honestly and accurately and still be subject to different interpretations. Reviewers raise alarms of fraud only if they find that the primary sources cited do not exist or do not contain the evidence the endnotes say they contain, or if whole sentences and paragraphs appear to have been lifted, without quotation marks or citation, from another historian's writing. As cumbersome as peer reviews and endnotes may appear, they are the profession's way of making sure that historians are honest with one another and with their audience.

Documentation and peer review are particularly useful when historians want to introduce new topics into the study of history. As the title of her book indicates, Vicki Ruiz was literally bringing the story of Mexican American women "out of the shadows." Because she used extensive documentation and her methods were professionally scrutinized, this nontraditional topic could command attention and respect. Ruiz did not need to convince every reader that hers was the only correct interpretation of her evidence in order to have an impact. Her job was to stimulate new thinking about Mexican American families, connect her new evidence to existing evidence, raise significant questions about cultural accommodation and gender roles in immigrant family life, and establish in her text and endnotes that her argument is a well-supported one.

Questions to Ask

In this excerpted chapter from Ruiz's book on Mexican American women, you can consider the arguments she makes about young women's negotiation with their parents, the role of adult women alongside family patriarchs in enforcing control over daughters, and the urgency Mexican families felt in the United States to preserve chaperonage.

- How did American consumer culture threaten Mexican gender traditions?
- How did American consumerism reinforce women's traditional role in Mexican culture?
- Why did Mexican American adults sponsor beauty pageants and dances when those activities might corrupt adolescent females?
- In a Mexican American family in the 1920s, what were the benefits and the costs of having a teenage daughter engage in wage work?
- Does Ruiz focus her attention on daughters' autonomous actions, the debate over familial oligarchy versus patriarchy, or the pressure to preserve chaperonage in the United States?

Source Analysis Table

In her second paragraph, Ruiz articulates three arguments. You can track those three arguments to determine her central thesis or the point she most wishes to make with the evidence. In reading through the chapter, use this table to follow Ruiz's development of those three arguments.

Argument	Evidence Provided, by Page Number
Argument #1: Young women responded to parental supervision in three ways.	
Argument #2: Parental supervision was an expression of "familial oligarchy," not patriarchy.	
Argument #3: Chaperonage "assumed a particular urgency" in the U.S. context.	

To download and print this table, please visit the book companion site at **bedfordstmartins.com/brownshannon**.

The Source: *From Out of the Shadows: Mexican Women in Twentieth-Century America* by Vicki L. Ruiz

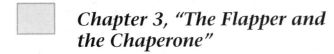

Chapter 3, "The Flapper and the Chaperone"

Imagine a gathering in a barrio hall, a group of young people dressed "to the nines" trying their best to replicate the dance steps of Fred Astaire and Ginger Rogers. This convivial heterosocial scene was a typical one in the lives of teenagers during the interwar period. But along the walls, a sharp difference was apparent in the barrios. Mothers, fathers, and older relatives chatted with one another as they kept one eye trained on the dance floor. They were the chaperones—the ubiquitous companions of unmarried Mexican American women. Chaperonage was a traditional instrument of social control. Indeed, the presence of *la dueña* was the prerequisite for attendance at a dance, a movie, or even church-related events. "When we would go to town, I would want to say something to a guy. I couldn't because my mother was always there," remembered María Ybarra. "She would always stick to us girls like glue. . . . She never let us out of her sight."[1]

An examination of events like this one reveals the ways in which young Mexican women in the United States between the wars rationalized, resisted, and evaded parental supervision. It offers a glimpse into generational conflict that goes beyond the more general differences in acculturation between immigrants and their children. Chaperonage existed for centuries on both sides of the political border separating Mexico and the United States. While conjuring images of patriarchal domination, chaperonage is best understood as a manifestation of familial oligarchy whereby elders attempted to dictate the activities of youth for the sake of family honor. A family's standing in the community depended, in part, on women's purity. Loss of virginity not only tainted the reputation of an individual, but of her kin as well. For Mexicano immigrants living in a new, bewildering environment filled with temptations, the enforcement of chaperonage assumed a particular urgency.[2]

Historians Donna Gabaccia and Sydney Stahl Weinberg have urged immigration historians to notice the subtle ways women shaped and reshaped their environments, especially within the family. In addition, pathbreaking works by Elizabeth Ewen, Andrew Heinze, and Susan Glenn examine the impact of U.S. consumer culture on European immigrants.[3] Indeed, while some Mexican American youth negotiated missionary idealizations of American life, other

Source: Vicki L. Ruiz, *From Out of the Shadows: Mexican Women in Twentieth-Century America* (New York: Oxford University Press, 1998), 12–26.

teenagers sought the American dream as promised in magazines, movies, and radio programs. . . .

For Mexican Americans, second-generation women as teenagers have received scant scholarly attention. Among Chicano historians and writers, there appears a fascination with the sons of immigrants, especially as *pachucos*.[4] Young women, however, may have experienced deeper generational tensions as they blended elements of Americanization with Mexican expectations and values. This chapter focuses on the shifting interplay of gender, cultures, class, ethnicity, and youth and the ways in which women negotiate across specific cultural contexts blending elements as diverse as celebrating Cinco de Mayo and applying Max Factor cosmetics.

In grappling with Mexican American women's consciousness and agency, oral history offers a venue for exploring teenage expectations and preserving a historical memory of attitudes and feelings. In addition to archival research, the recollections of seventeen women serve as the basis for my reconstruction of adolescent aspirations and experiences (or dreams and routines).[5] The women themselves are fairly homogeneous in terms of nativity, class, residence, and family structure. With two exceptions, they are U.S. citizens by birth and attended southwestern schools. All the interviewees were born between 1908 and 1926.[6] Although three came from families once considered middle class in Mexico, most can be considered working class in the United States. Their fathers' typical occupations included farm worker, miner, day laborer, and railroad hand. These women usually characterized their mothers as homemakers, although several remembered that their mothers took seasonal jobs in area factories and fields. . . .

Chicano social scientists have generally portrayed women as "the 'glue' that keeps the Chicano family together" as well as the guardians of traditional culture.[7] Whether one accepts this premise or not, within families, young women, perhaps more than their brothers, were expected to uphold certain standards. Parents, therefore, often assumed what they perceived as their unquestionable prerogative to regulate the actions and attitudes of their adolescent daughters. Teenagers, on the other hand, did not always acquiesce in the boundaries set down for them by their elders. Intergenerational tension flared along several fronts.

Like U.S. teenagers, in general, the first area of disagreement between an adolescent and her family would be over her personal appearance. As reflected in F. Scott Fitzgerald's "Bernice Bobs Her Hair," the length of a young woman's tresses was a hot issue spanning class, region, and ethnic lines. During the 1920s, a woman's decision "to bob or not bob" her hair assumed classic proportions within Mexican families. After considerable pleading, Belen Martínez Mason was permitted to cut her hair, though she soon regretted the decision. "Oh, I cried for a month."[8] Differing opinions over fashions often caused ill feelings. One Mexican American woman recalled that as a young girl, her mother dressed her "like a nun" and she could wear "no make-up, no cream, no nothing" on her face. Swimwear, bloomers, and short skirts also became sources of controversy. Some teenagers left home in one outfit and changed into another at school. Once María Fierro arrived home in her bloomers. Her father inquired, "Where have you been dressed like that, like a clown?" "I told him the truth," Fierro explained. "He whipped me anyway. . . . So from then on whenever I went to the track meet, I used to change my bloomers so that he wouldn't see that I had gone again."[9] . . .

The use of cosmetics cannot be blamed entirely on Madison Avenue ad campaigns. The innumerable barrio beauty pageants, sponsored by *mutualistas*,[10] patriotic societies, churches, the Mexican Chamber of Commerce, newspapers, and even progressive labor unions, encouraged young women to accentuate their physical attributes. Carefully chaperoned, many teenagers did participate in community contests from La Reina de Cinco de Mayo to Orange Queen. They modeled evening gowns, rode on parade floats, and sold raffle tickets.[11] Carmen Bernal Escobar remembered one incident where, as a contestant, she had to sell raffle tickets. Every ticket she sold counted as a vote for her in the pageant. Naturally the winner would be the woman who had accumulated the most votes. When her brother offered to buy $25 worth of votes [her mother would not think of letting her peddle the tickets at work or in the neighborhood], Escobar, on a pragmatic note, asked him to give her the money so that she could buy a coat she had spotted while window-shopping.[12]

The commercialization of personal grooming made additional inroads into the Mexican community with the appearance of barrio beauty parlors. Working as a beautician conferred a certain degree of status—"a nice, clean job"—in comparison to factory or domestic work. As one woman related:

> I always wanted to be a beauty operator. I loved makeup; I loved to dress up and fix up. I used to set my sisters' hair. So I had that in the back of my mind for a long time, and my mom pushed the fact that she wanted me to have a profession—seeing that I wasn't thinking of getting married.[13]

While further research is needed, one can speculate that neighborhood beauty shops reinforced women's networks and became places where they could relax, exchange *chisme* (gossip), and enjoy the company of other women.

During the 1920s, the ethic of consumption became inextricably linked to making it in America.[14] The message of affluence attainable through hard work and a bit of luck was reinforced in English and Spanish-language publications. Mexican barrios were not immune from the burgeoning consumer culture. The society pages of the influential Los Angeles–based *La Opinion*, for example, featured advice columns, horoscopes, and celebrity gossip. Advertisements for makeup, clothing, even feminine hygiene products reminded teenagers of an awaiting world of consumption.[15] One week after its inaugural issue in 1926, *La Opinion* featured a Spanish translation of Louella Parsons' nationally syndicated gossip column. Advertisements not only hawked products but offered instructions for behavior. As historian Roberto Treviño related in his recent study of Tejano newspapers, "The point remains that the Spanish-language press conveyed symbolic American norms and models to a potentially assimilable readership."[16]

Advertisements aimed at women promised status and affection if the proper bleaching cream, hair coloring, and cosmetics were purchased. Or, as one company boldly claimed, "Those with lighter, more healthy skin tones will become much more successful in business, love, and society."[17] A print ad [in English] for Camay Soap carried by *Hispano America* in 1932 reminded women readers that "Life Is a Beauty Contest."[18] Flapper fashions and celebrity testimonials further fused the connections between gendered identity and consumer culture. Another promotion encouraged readers to "SIGA LAS ESTRELLAS" (FOLLOW THE STARS) and use Max Factor cosmetics.[19] . . .

In her essay "City Lights: Immigrant Women and the Rise of the Movies," Elizabeth Ewen has argued that during the early decades of the twentieth century, "The social authority of the media of mass culture replaced older forms of family authority and behavior." Ewen further explained that the "authority of this new culture organized itself around the premise of freedom from customary bonds as a way of turning people's attention to the consumer market place as a source of self-definition."[20] Yet Mexican women had choices (though certainly circumscribed by economic considerations) about what elements to embrace and which to ignore. . . . Mexican American women teenagers positioned themselves within the cultural messages they gleaned from English and Spanish-language publications, afternoon matinees, and popular radio programs. Their shifting conceptions of acceptable heterosocial behavior, including their desire "to date," heightened existing generational tensions between parents and daughters.

Obviously, the most serious point of contention between an adolescent daughter and her Mexican parents regarded her behavior toward young men. In both cities and rural towns, close chaperonage was a way of life. Recalling the supervisory role played by her "old maid" aunt, María Fierro laughingly explained, "She'd check up on us all the time. I used to get so mad at her." Ruby Estrada recalled that in her small southern Arizona community, "all the mothers" escorted their daughters to the local dances. Estrada's mother was no exception when it came to chaperoning her daughters. "She went especially for us. She'd just sit there and take care of our coats and watch us."[21] . . .

Faced with this type of situation, young women had three options: they could accept the rules set down for them; they could rebel; or they could find ways to compromise or circumvent traditional standards. "I was *never* allowed to go out by myself in the evening; it just was not done," related Carmen Bernal Escobar. In rural communities, where restrictions were perhaps even more stringent, "nice" teenagers could not even swim with male peers. According to Ruby Estrada, "We were ladies and wouldn't go swimming out there with a bunch of boys." Yet many seemed to accept these limits with equanimity. Remembering her mother as her chaperone, Lucy Acosta insisted, "I could care less as long as I danced." "It wasn't devastating at all," echoed Ruby Estrada. "We took it in stride. We never thought of it as cruel or mean. . . . It was taken for granted that that's the way it was."[22] In Sonora, Arizona, like other small towns, relatives and neighbors kept close watch over adolescent women and quickly reported any suspected indiscretions. "They were always spying on you," Estrada remarked. Women in cities had a distinct advantage over their rural peers in that they could venture miles from their neighborhood into the anonymity of dance halls, amusement parks, and other forms of commercialized leisure. With carnival rides and the Cinderella Ballroom, the Nu-Pike amusement park of Long Beach proved a popular hangout for Mexican youth in Los Angeles.[23] It was more difficult to abide by traditional norms when excitement loomed just on the other side of the streetcar line.

Some women openly rebelled. They moved out of their family homes and into apartments. Considering themselves freewheeling single women, they could go out with men unsupervised as was the practice among their Anglo peers. Others challenged parental and cultural standards even further by living with their boyfriends. In his field notes, University of California economist Paul Taylor recorded an incident in which a young woman had moved in with her Anglo boyfriend after he had convinced her that such arrangements were common among Americans. "This terrible freedom in the United States," one Mexicana lamented. "I do not have to worry because I have no daughters, but the poor *señoras* with many girls, they worry."[24]

Those teenagers who did not wish to defy their parents openly would "sneak out" of the house to meet their dates or attend dances with female friends. Whether meeting someone at a drugstore, roller rink, or theater, this practice involved the invention of elaborate stories to mask traditionally inappropriate behavior.[25] In other words, they lied. In his study of Tucson's Mexican community, Thomas Sheridan related the following saga of Jacinta Pérez de Valdez:

> As she and her sisters grew older, they used to sneak out of the house to go to the Riverside Ball Room. One time a friend of their father saw them there and said, "Listen, Felipe, don't you know your daughters are hanging around the Riverside?" Furious, their father threw a coat over his longjohns and stormed into the dance hall, not even stopping to tie his shoes . . . Doña Jacinta recalled. "He entered by one door and we left by another. We had to walk back home along the railroad tracks in our high heels. I think we left those heels on the rails." She added that when their father returned, "We were all lying in bed like little angels."[26] . . .

The third alternative sometimes involved quite a bit of creativity on the part of young women as they sought to circumvent traditional chaperonage. Alicia Mendeola Shelit recalled that one of her older brothers would accompany her to dances ostensibly as a chaperone. "But then my oldest brother would always have a blind date for me." Carmen Bernal Escobar was permitted to entertain her boyfriends at home, but only under the supervision of her brother or mother. The practice of "going out with the girls," though not accepted until the 1940s, was fairly common. Several Mexican American women, often related, would escort one another to an event (such as a dance), socialize with the men in attendance, and then walk home together. In the sample of seventeen interviews, daughters negotiated their activities with their parents. Older siblings and extended kin appeared in the background as either chaperones or accomplices.[27] . . .

Of course, some young women did lead more adventurous lives. A male interviewer employed by Mexican anthropologist Manuel Gamio recalled his "relations" with a woman he met at a Los Angeles dance hall. . . . Elisa "Elsie" Morales . . . helped support her family by dancing with strangers. Even though she lived at home and her mother and brother attempted to monitor her actions, she managed to meet the interviewer at a "hot pillow" hotel. To prevent pregnancy, she relied on contraceptive douches provided by "an American doctor." Although Morales realized her mother would not approve of her behavior, she noted that "she [her mother] is from Mexico. . . . I am from there also but I was brought up in the United States, we think about things differently." Just as Morales rationalized her actions as "American," the interviewer perceived her within a similar, though certainly less favorable, definition of Americanization. "She seemed very coarse to me. That is, she dealt with one in the American way." Popular corridos, such as "El Enganchado" and "Las Pelonas," also touched on the theme of the corrupting influence of U.S. ways on Mexican women.[28] If there were rewards for women who escaped parental boundaries, there were also sanctions for those who crossed established lines.

Women who had children out of wedlock seemed to be treated by their parents in one of two ways—as pariahs or prodigal daughters. Erminia Ruiz recalled the experiences of two girlhood friends:

> It was a disgrace to the whole family. The whole family suffered and . . . her mother said she didn't want her home. She could not bring the baby home and she was not welcome at home. . . . She had no place to go. . . . And then I had another friend. She was also pregnant and the mother actually went to court to try to get him to marry her. . . . He hurried and married someone else but then he had to give child support.[29] . . .

Autonomy on the part of young women was hard to win in a world where pregnant, unmarried teenagers served as community "examples" of what might happen to you or your daughter if appropriate measures were not taken. As an elderly Mexicana remarked, "Your reputation was everything."[30] In this sense, the chaperone not only protected the young woman's position in the community, but that of the entire family.

Chaperonage thus exacerbated conflict not only between generations but within individuals as well. In gaily recounting tales of ditching the *dueña* or sneaking down the stairwell, the laughter of the interviewees fails to hide the painful memories of breaking away from familial expectations. Their words resonate with the dilemma of reconciling their search for autonomy with their desire for parental affirmation. It is important to note that every informant who challenged or circumvented chaperonage held a full-time job, as either a factory or service worker. In contrast, most women who accepted constant supervision did not work for wages. Perhaps because they labored for long hours, for little pay, and frequently under hazardous conditions, factory and service workers were determined to exercise some control over their leisure time. Indeed, Douglas Monroy has argued that outside employment "facilitated greater freedom of activity and more assertiveness in the family for Mexicanas."[31]

It may also be significant that none of the employed teenagers had attended high school. They entered the labor market directly after or even before the completion of the eighth grade. Like many female factory workers in the United States, most Mexican operatives were young, unmarried daughters whose wage labor was essential to the economic survival of their families. As members of a "family wage economy," they relinquished all or part of their wages to their elders. According to a 1933 University of California study, of the Mexican families surveyed with working children, the children's monetary contributions constituted 35 percent of total household income.[32] Cognizant of their earning power, they resented the lack of personal autonomy.

Delicate negotiations ensued as both parents and daughters struggled over questions of leisure activities and discretionary income. Could a young woman retain a portion of her wages for her own use? If elders demanded every penny, daughters might be more inclined to splurge on a new outfit or other personal item on their way home from work or, even more extreme, they might choose to move out, taking their paychecks with them. Recognizing their dependence on their children's income, some parents compromised. Their concessions, however, generally took the form of allocating spending money rather than relaxing traditional supervision.[33] . . .

Chaperonage triggered deep-seated tensions over autonomy and self-determination. "Whose life is it anyway?" was a recurring question with no satisfactory answer. Many women wanted their parents to consider them dutiful daughters, but they also desired degrees of freedom. While ethnographies provide scintillating tales of teenage rebellion, the voices of the interviewees do not. Their stories reflect the experiences of those adolescents who struggled with boundaries. How can one retain one's "good name" while experiencing the joys of youth? How can one be both a good daughter and an independent woman?

To complete the picture, we also have to consider the perspective of Mexican immigrant parents who encountered a youth culture very different from that of their generation. For them, courtship had occurred in the plaza; young women and men promenaded under the watchful eyes of town elders, an atmosphere in which an exchange of meaningful glances could well portend engagement. One can understand their consternation as they watched their daughters apply cosmetics and adopt the apparel advertised in fashion magazines. In other words, "If she dresses like a flapper, will she then act like one?" Seeds of suspicion reaffirmed the penchant for traditional supervision.

Parents could not completely cloister their children from the temptations of "modern" society, but chaperonage provided a way of monitoring their activities. It was an attempt to mold young women into sheltered young matrons. But one cannot regard the presence of *la dueña* as simply an old world tradition on a collision course with twentieth-century life. The regulation of daughters involved more than a conflict between peasant ways and modern ideas. Chaperonage was both an actual and symbolic assertion of familial oligarchy. A family's reputation was linked to the purity of women. As reiterated in a Catholic catechism, if a young woman became a "faded lily," she and her family would suffer dire consequences.[34] Since family honor rested, to some degree, on the preservation of female chastity (or *vergüenza*), women were to be controlled for the collective good, with older relatives assuming unquestioned responsibility in this regard. Mexican women coming of age during the 1920s and 1930s were not the first to challenge the authority of elders. Ramón Gutiérrez in his pathbreaking scholarship on colonial New Mexico uncovered numerous instances of women who tried to exercise some autonomy over their sexuality.[35] The Mexican American generation, however, had a potent ally unavailable to their foremothers—consumer culture. . . .

Even the Spanish-language press fanned youthful passions. On May 9, 1927, *La Opinion* ran an article entitled, "How do you kiss?" Informing readers that "el beso no es un arte sino una ciencia" [kissing is not an art but rather a science], this short piece outlined the three components of a kiss: quality, quantity, and topography. The modern kiss, furthermore, should last three minutes.[36] Though certainly shocking older Mexicanos, such titillating fare catered to a youth market. *La Opinion,* in many respects, reflected the coalescence of Mexican and American cultures. While promoting pride in Latino theater and music, its society pages also celebrated the icons of Americanization and mass consumption. . . .

United States consumerism did not bring about the disintegration of familial oligarchy, but it did serve as a catalyst for change. The ideology of control was shaken by consumer culture and the heterosocial world of urban youth. . . .

Mexican American women were not caught between two worlds. They navigated across multiple terrains at home, at work, and at play. They engaged in cultural coalescence. The Mexican American generation selected, retained, borrowed, and created their own cultural forms. Or as one woman informed anthropologist Ruth Tuck, "Fusion is what we want—the best of both ways."[37] These children of immigrants may have been captivated by consumerism, but few would attain its promises of affluence. Race and gender prejudice as well as socioeconomic segmentation constrained the possibilities of choice. . . .

In 1959, Margaret Clark asserted that the second-generation residents of Sal si Puedes [a northern California barrio] "dream and work toward the day when Mexican Americans will become fully integrated into American society at large."[38] Perhaps, as part of that faith, they rebelled against chaperonage.

Mexican American adolescents felt the lure of Hollywood and the threat of deportation, the barbs of discrimination, and the reins of constant supervision. In dealing with all the contradictions in their lives, many young women focused their attention on chaperonage, an area where they could make decisions. The inner conflicts expressed in the oral histories reveal that such decisions were not made impetuously.

Notes

1. Interview with María Ybarra, December 1, 1990, conducted by David Pérez.

2. For colonial New Mexico, Ramón Gutiérrez convincingly demonstrates how family honor was tied, in part, to women's *vergüenza* (literally, shame or virginity).

See Ramón Gutiérrez, "Honor, Ideology, and Class Gender Domination in New Mexico, 1690–1846," *Latin American Perspectives* 12 (Winter 1985): 81–104, and Ramón Gutiérrez, *When Jesus Came, the Corn Mothers Went Away: Power and Sexuality in New Mexico, 1500–1846* (Stanford: Stanford University Press, 1990). I contend that since mothers and elder female relatives played major roles in enforcing chaperonage, strict supervision of daughters related more to what I term "familial oligarchy" than to patriarchal control.

3. Donna R. Gabaccia, *From Sicily to Elizabeth Street* (Albany: SUNY Press, 1984); Sydney Stahl Weinberg, "The Treatment of Women in Immigration History: A Call for Change," in *Seeking Common Ground: Multidisciplinary Studies of Immigrant Women in the United States,* ed. Donna Gabaccia (Westport, Conn.: Greenwood Press, 1992), pp. 3–22; Stuart and Elizabeth Ewen, *Channels of Desire* (New York: McGraw-Hill, 1982); Elizabeth Ewen, *Immigrant Women in the Land of Dollars* (New York: Monthly Review Press, 1985); Andrew Heinze, *Adapting to Abundance* (New York: Columbia University Press, 1990); Susan A. Glenn, *Daughters of the Shtetl* (Ithaca: Cornell University Press, 1990).

4. Mauricio Mazón's *The Zoot Suit Riots* (Austin: University of Texas Press, 1984) and the Luis Valdez play and feature film *Zoot Suit* provide examples of the literature on *pachucos*. A doctoral student at Princeton University, Eduardo Pagán is completing a dissertation on pachucos and the politics of race during World War II.

[*Pachucos* were groups of young Mexican American men in the southwestern United States in the 1920s, 1930s, and 1940s who adopted a unique style of dress, including a long suit coat, and defied the efforts of American schools and police to force them to abandon their ethnic identity. — Ed.]

5. I would like to introduce these women by grouping them geographically. María Fierro, Rose Escheverria Mulligan, Adele Hernández Milligan, Beatrice Morales Clifton, Mary Luna, Alicia Mendeola Shelit, Carmen Bernal Escobar, Belen Martínez Mason, and Julia Luna Mount grew up in Los Angeles. Lucy Acosta and Alma Araiza García came of age in El Paso and Erminia Ruiz in Denver. Representing the rural experience are María Arredondo and Jesusita Torres (California), María Ybarra (Texas), and Ruby Estrada (Arizona). As a teenager, Eusebia Buriel moved with her family from Silvis, Illinois, to Riverside, California. *Note:* Of the seventeen full-blown life histories, nine are housed in university archives, seven as part of the *Rosie the Riveter* collection at California State University, Long Beach. I appreciate the generosity and longstanding support of Sherna Gluck who has given me permission to use excerpts from the *Rosie* interviews. This sample also does not include oral interviews found in published sources.

6. The age breakdowns for the seventeen interviewees are as follows: nine were born between 1908 and 1919 and eight between 1920 and 1926. This sample includes some who were chaperoned during the 1920s and others who were chaperoned during the thirties and forties. As a result, the sample does not represent a precise generational grouping, but instead gives a sense of the pervasiveness and persistence of unremitting supervision.

7. George J. Sánchez, "'Go After the Women': Americanization and the Mexican Immigrant Woman 1915–1929," in *Unequal Sisters: A Multicultural Reader in U.S. Women's History,* 2nd ed., eds. Vicki L. Ruiz and Ellen Carol DuBois (New York: Routledge, 1994), p. 285.

8. F. Scott Fitzgerald, *Flappers and Philosophers* (London: W. Collins Sons and Co., Ltd., 1922), pp. 209–46; Emory S. Bogardus, *The Mexican in the United States* (Los Angeles: University of Southern California Press, 1934), p. 741; Martínez

Mason interview, p. 44. During the 1920s, Mexican parents were not atypical in voicing their concerns over the attitudes and appearance of their "flapper adolescents." A general atmosphere of tension between youth and their elders existed — a generation gap that cut across class, race, ethnicity, and region. See Paula Fass, *The Damned and the Beautiful: American Youth in the 1920's* (New York: Oxford University Press, 1977).

9. Interview with Alicia Mendeola Shelit, Volume 37 of *Rosie the Riveter*, p. 18; Paul S. Taylor, *Mexican Labor in the United States, Volume II* (Berkeley: University of California Press, 1932), pp. 199–200; interview with María Fierro, Volume 12 of *Rosie the Riveter*, p. 10.

10. [*Mutualistas* were mutual aid societies, similar to those formed by other immigrant groups. These precursors to insurance companies in ethnic communities made it possible for members to pool their resources to pay for medical expenses, funerals, or other economic emergencies. — Ed.]

11. Rodolfo F. Acuña, *Community Under Siege: A Chronicle of Chicanos East of the Los Angeles River, 1945–1975* (Los Angeles: UCLA Chicano Studies Publications, 1984), pp. 278, 407–408, 413–14, 418, 422; *FTA News*, May 1, 1945; interview with Carmen Bernal Escobar, June 15, 1986, conducted by the author. For an example of the promotion of a beauty pageant, see issues of *La Opinion*, June–July 1927.

12. Escobar interview, 1986.

13. Sherna B. Gluck, *Rosie the Riveter Revisited: Women, The War and Social Change* (Boston: Twayne Publishers, 1987), pp. 81, 85.

14. The best elaboration of this phenomenon can be found in Roland Marchand, *Advertising the American Dream: Making Way for Modernity, 1920–1940* (Berkeley: University of California Press, 1985).

15. For examples, see *La Opinion*, September 26, 1926; May 14, 1927; June 5, 1927; September 9, 1929; January 15, 1933; January 29, 1938. Lorena Chambers is currently writing a dissertation focusing on the gendered representations of the body in Chicano cultural narratives. I thank her for our wonderful discussions.

16. Vicki L. Ruiz, "'Star Struck': Acculturation, Adolescence, and Mexican American Women, 1920–1940" in *Small Worlds: Children and Adolescents in America*, eds. Elliot West and Paula Petrik (Lawrence: University of Kansas Press, 1992): 61–80; Roberto R. Treviño, "*Prensa Y Patria:* The Spanish-Language Press and the Biculturation of the Tejano Middle Class, 1920–1940," *The Western Historical Quarterly*, Vol. 22 (November 1991): 460.

17. *La Opinion*, September 29, 1929.

18. *Hispano-America*, July 2, 1932. Gracias a Gabriela Arredondo for sharing this advertisement with me, one she included in her seminar paper, "'Equality' for All: Americanization of Mexican Immigrant Women in Los Angeles and San Francisco Through Newspaper Advertising, 1927–1935" (M.A. seminar paper, San Francisco State University, 1991).

19. *La Opinion*, June 5, 1927.

20. Stuart Ewen and Elizabeth Ewen, *Channels of Desire* (New York: McGraw-Hill, 1982), pp. 95–96.

21. Fierro interview; Estrada interview.

22. Escobar interview, 1986; Estrada interview, pp. 11, 13; interview no. 653 with Lucy Acosta conducted by Mario T. García, October 28, 1982 (on file at the Institute of Oral History, University of Texas, El Paso), p. 17. I wish to thank Rebecca Craver, coordinator of the Institute of Oral History, for permission to use excerpts from the Acosta interview.

23. Estrada interview, p. 12; Shelit interview, p. 9; Antonio Ríos-Bustamante and Pedro Castillo, *An Illustrated History of Mexican Los Angeles, 1781–1985* (Los Angeles: Chicano Studies Research Center, UCLA, 1986), p. 153.

24. Paul S. Taylor, "Women in Industry," field notes for his book, *Mexican Labor in the United States, 1927–1930*, Bancroft Library, University of California, 1 box; Richard G. Thurston, "Urbanization and Sociocultural Change in a Mexican-American Enclave" (Ph.D. dissertation, University of California, Los Angeles, 1957; rpt. R and E Research Associates, 1974), p. 118; Bogardus, *The Mexican*, pp. 28–29, 57–58. *Note:* Paul S. Taylor's two-volume study, *Mexican Labor in the United States*, is considered the classic ethnography on Mexican Americans during the interwar period. A synthesis of his field notes, "Women in Industry," has been published. See Taylor, "Mexican Women in Los Angeles Industry in 1928," *Aztlán*, 11 (Spring 1980): 99–131.

25. Interview with Belen Martínez Mason, Volume 23 of *Rosie the Riveter*, p. 30; interviews with Erminia Ruiz, July 30, 1990, and February 18, 1993, conducted by the author; Thomas Sheridan, *Los Tucsonenses* (Tucson: University of Arizona Press, 1986), pp. 131–32.

26. Sheridan, *Los Tucsonenses, loc. cit.*

27. Shelit interview, pp. 9, 24, 30; Ruiz interviews (1990, 1993); Escobar interview; García interview; Martínez Mason interview p. 30; Hernández Milligan interview, pp. 27–28; interview with María Arredondo, March 19, 1986, conducted by Carolyn Arredondo; Taylor notes.

28. "Elisa Morales," interview by Luis Recinos, April 16, 1927, Biographies and Case Histories II folder, Manuel Gamio Field Notes, Bancroft Library, University of California; Taylor, *Mexican Labor*, Vol. II, pp. vi–vii; Gamio, *Mexican Immigration*, p. 89. The corrido "El Enganchado" in Volume two of *Mexican Labor* offers an intriguing glimpse into attitudes toward women and Americanization.

29. Ruiz interview (1993).

30. Discussion following my presentation of "The Flapper and the Chaperone," May 28, 1995. Comment provided by B. V. Meyer.

31. Douglas Monroy, "An Essay on Understanding the Work Experiences of Mexicans in Southern California, 1900–1939," *Aztlán*, 12 (Spring 1981): 70. *Note:* Feminist historians have also documented this push for autonomy among the daughters of European immigrants. In particular, see Peiss, *Cheap Amusements*, Glenn, *Daughters of the Shtetl*, E. Ewen, *Immigrant Women;* and Alexander, "The Only Thing I Wanted Was Freedom." See also Meyerowitz, *Women Adrift*.

32. Heller Committee for Research in Social Economics of the University of California and Constantine Panuzio, *How Mexicans Earn and Live*, University of California Publications in Economics, XIII, No. 1, Cost of Living Studies V (Berkeley: University of California, 1933), pp. 11, 14, 17; Taylor notes; Luna Mount interview; Ruiz interviews (1990, 1993); Shelit interview, p. 9. For further delineation of the family wage economy, see Louise A. Tilly and Joan W. Scott, *Women, Work, and Family* (New York: Holt, Rinehart, and Winston, 1978).

33. These observations are drawn from my reading of the seventeen oral interviews and the literature on European immigrant women.

34. Rev. F. X. Lasance, *The Catholic Girl's Guide and Sunday Missal* (New York: Benziger Brothers, 1905), Esther Pérez Papers, Cassiano-Pérez Collection, Daughters of the Republic of Texas Library at the Alamo, San Antonio, Texas, pp. 279–80. I have a 1946 reprint edition passed down to me by my older sister who had received it from our mother.

35. Gutiérrez, "Honor, Ideology," pp. 88–93, 95–98.

36. *La Opinion,* May 9, 1927.

37. Ruth Tuck, *Not With the Fist: Mexican Americans in a Southwest City* (New York: Harcourt Brace, 1946), p. 134.

38. Margaret Clark, *Health in the Mexican American Culture* (Berkeley: University of California Press, 1959), p. 20.

Analyzing Secondary Sources

1. Which of the arguments in the second paragraph do you think Ruiz regards as her main point? Do you base your decision on the amount of space she devotes to each argument? The amount of evidence she provides? Her emphasis in the conclusion?

2. Endnotes tell a reader about the primary and secondary sources a historian consulted in developing an argument. Read Ruiz's first ten endnotes. What is the balance of primary sources to secondary sources in those endnotes? Are those two types of sources separated and noted differently in the endnotes? How can you distinguish between primary and secondary sources in the notes?

3. Historians often go to great effort to tell their stories using the "voices" of the people involved. Ruiz achieves this by using oral histories, including interviews conducted with her mother, Erminia Ruiz. Do you have as much confidence in oral histories as in other types of sources? Are they similar to memoirs? Do the benefits of oral histories outweigh the potential problems with them?

4. Vicki Ruiz argues that Mexican American daughters exercised some independence in regard to the tradition of chaperonage. Do you think her interpretation of the evidence exaggerates daughters' power in the family? Why must historians of women be especially careful to balance the agency of their subjects against the power others have over them?

5. If you were going to interview the daughter of an immigrant family today, what questions would you ask her to determine whether she is encountering conflict between her family's traditional culture and American culture?

The Rest of the Story

The stories of American youth culture and Mexican American culture in the 1920s offer similar echoes of the old notion that "the more things change, the more they stay the same." Despite all the worry over the sexual mores of youth or the assimilation of Mexican teens into American popular culture the fact remained that young men and women intended to follow the family traditions they had inherited, and Mexican American kids were not rejecting Mexican culture but rather were integrating it with American culture. As Ruiz observes in another section of her book, "in challenging chaperonage, Mexican American teenagers did not attack the foundation of familial oligarchy—only its more obvious manifestation."

When abrupt and severe change arrived in the form of the Great Depression of the 1930s, white, middle-class couples who had been teens in the 1920s were ill-prepared for the notion that the wife might need to work for pay outside the home. Young Mexican Americans, who had fashioned their own acculturation to the United States, were similarly ill-prepared when the U.S. government moved to remedy the unemployment of whites by forcing the repatriation of thousands of Mexicans. This meant that some young people, raised on American popular culture, found themselves exiled to their families' villages in remote parts of Mexico, where there were more chaperones than radios.

The population of Mexicans who remained in the United States in the wake of repatriation were largely American-born. Many of them demonstrated their commitment to building a Mexican American culture in the 1930s by utilizing New Deal opportunities to create strong labor unions that benefited from ethnic loyalty. The seventeen women that Ruiz interviewed for her chapter on "Flappers" all stayed in the United States. Seven of the women married Euro-American men, and all combined their household responsibilities as wives and mothers with wage work outside the home, in jobs ranging from airplane manufacture to retail sales. In most cases, their supervision of their daughters in the 1950s reflected a mixture of old and new: they did not require chaperones or harp as much on "family honor," but they made very clear the daughter's need to preserve her reputation by preserving her virginity.

In sketching these patterns, Vicki Ruiz herself engaged in the mixing of old and new that is expected of secondary works in history. She dug around in library shelves and research archives and unearthed the sorts of photographs, newspaper articles, advertisements, and social science research from the 1920s that typically comprise a historian's primary sources. She then expanded the available Mexican American women's "memoirs" by adding new oral histories to those that already existed. Ruiz read and interpreted these primary sources in the light of recent interpretations that have emerged from other studies of immigrant women's lives, youth culture and consumer culture in the 1920s, and Mexican American history. The result is a story of Mexican American women that adds much new information to our existing knowledge while affirming a collective, contemporary view among American historians that immigrants, youth, workers, consumers—in short, most women and men—are not passive in the face of traditional family controls or modern advertising. They actively and creatively combine the competing elements in their lives in ways that make economic, family, and cultural survival possible.

Ruiz's work is the first, not the last, book on Mexican American women's lives in the twentieth century. Like all who write works of secondary history, she consciously pointed to places where more research is needed and provided documentation that would allow future researchers to build on her work. Ruiz thereby entered into the ongoing collaboration among historians to build on one another's work in the creation of a richer story of the past.

To Find Out More

The secondary source excerpt for this chapter was taken from chapter 3, "The Flapper and the Chaperone," of Vicki L. Ruiz's *From Out of the Shadows: Mexican Women in Twentieth-Century America* (New York: Oxford University Press, 1998). This book is readily available in libraries and bookstores. As in most professional history books, Ruiz includes an acknowledgments section in which she lists the names of a dozen professional historians who read and commented on all or part of her manuscript before it was published. By reading a book's acknowledgments, preface, and introduction, you can often determine whether the work has been reviewed by other historians, either as anonymous judges or as helpful colleagues. In the case of history articles published in professional journals, you know that they have been prescreened, judged, and probably revised because they cannot achieve publication without that vetting process.

Useful companions to Vicki Ruiz's study are Douglas Monroy, *Rebirth: Mexican Los Angeles from the Great Migration to the Great Depression* (Berkeley: University of California Press, 1999); George J. Sanchez, *Becoming Mexican American: Ethnicity, Culture, and Identity in Chicano Los Angeles, 1900–1945* (New York: Oxford University Press, 1993); and Frances Esquibel Tywoniak and Mario T. Garcia, *Migrant Daughter: Coming of Age as a Mexican American Woman* (Berkeley: University of California Press, 2002).

For the interaction of modern consumer culture in the 1920s with youth, ethnic groups, and women, see Paula S. Fass, *The Damned and the Beautiful: American Youth in the 1920's* (New York: Oxford University Press, 1979); Lizabeth Cohen, *Making a New Deal: Industrial Workers in Chicago, 1919–1939* (New York: Cambridge University Press, 1990); and Kathy Peiss, *Hope in a Jar: The Making of America's Beauty Culture* (New York: Metropolitan Books, 1999).

CHAPTER 8

Painting a New Deal

U.S. Post Office Murals from the Great Depression

In the spring of 1941, Gustaf Dalstrom was hard at work painting a mural on the wall of the post office in St. Joseph, Missouri. On the eve of World War II, the federal government's New Deal was in its ninth year of struggle against economic depression, but recovery was elusive and unemployment still widespread. Dalstrom had a job thanks to one of the New Deal's public arts programs, and citizens of St. Joseph came to watch him work, equipped with lists of questions prepared by the local schools' art director. Dalstrom willingly paused in his labors to give brief talks about art in general and mural painting in particular.

As an artist employed by the U.S. government and engaged in conversation with local citizens about the imagery on their post office wall, Gustaf Dalstrom represented a "new deal" in the relationship among the government, the arts, and the American public. Amid the Great Depression of the 1930s, this artistic new deal was just one of the array of economic stimulus and reform programs that President Franklin Delano Roosevelt had created within his "New Deal" administration. Some of these programs were aimed at providing direct *relief* to the millions of Americans who were without any income in the 1930s. Other programs were intended to bring about *recovery* from the economic depression, while still others sought to institute *reforms* that would prevent future economic and social catastrophe on the scale of the Great Depression. Roosevelt did not view the arts as a luxury the nation could afford only in prosperous times. Instead, he and his allies regarded economic support for artists and public funding for the arts as a natural part of the New Deal's relief, recovery, and reform effort.

Before the New Deal, the federal government had played a very small role in sponsoring the visual arts in America. Tax funds were invested in the architecture of public buildings, but these were not a site for aesthetic innovation, and few officials at any level of government felt called to campaign for more public funding for the arts. Wealthy art patrons enjoyed the private control they exercised over the art world and the status that control signified; they had no desire to encourage public investment in the arts. Citizens who could not afford to purchase original artwork regarded it as an elite luxury; they did not demand that their taxes go to support the visual arts, and they did not often think of artists as fellow workers. Artists, meanwhile, debated whether public funding for the arts would enliven American art or invite government control over artistic expression.

The New Deal altered this history in three ways. Through its relief programs, it recognized artists as workers who, when faced with unemployment, deserved as much state assistance as any other category of workers. Through its recovery programs, the New Deal defined the arts as a vital tool for uplifting citizens' spirits, focusing them on their individual and collective capacities, and encouraging them to draw from good times in the past to plan for better times in the future. And through its reform programs, the New Deal created mechanisms for public funding of the arts that would allow for communication between federal officials and local citizens about what constituted "good" art for a particular community.

The New Deal's effort to provide relief to working artists is most famously evident in the Federal Arts Program (FAP). Men and women who could demonstrate that they had made a living from their artistic endeavors before the Depression were eligible for federal support of their work during the Depression. Between 1935 and 1943, the FAP subsidized 10,000 artists who, in exchange for a federal paycheck, produced tens of thousands of works of art—posters, sculpture, tapestries, murals—that were displayed in federal, state, county, and municipal buildings for decades to come. Members of Congress had questioned the wisdom of giving money to artists, who did not look, sound, or operate like typical American workers. But New Deal lobbyists argued that it made more economic sense to pay artists $1,200 a year to continue creating art, and then put that art in government buildings, than to hand out welfare checks to scruffy bohemians and get no product in return. Meanwhile, artists feared that an FAP relief check meant that the government would dictate what FAP artists produced. They had to be assured that the Roosevelt administration would not interfere with artistic freedom. While some FAP art was not approved for display in public buildings, no needy artists were denied FAP funds simply because the government disliked their artwork. Thus the Federal Arts Program, then, was both a direct relief effort for artists and a notable reform in which the government used tax monies to bring art to public places and, according to New Deal publicity, provide "art for the millions."

The arts figured into the New Deal's recovery and reform programs in other tangible and spiritual ways. As part of its effort to provide construction work for unemployed Americans, the Roosevelt administration built 1,100 new post office buildings in cities and towns across the nation. The Fine Arts Section of the U.S. Treasury Department then sponsored a series of competitions among artists to see whose proposals would win commissions to paint murals in each of the new post offices. These competitions launched an unprecedented public process that brought federal officials, artists, and local citizens together in sometimes heated debate over which proposals should be commissioned and how a commissioned artist's vision for the mural should be altered to suit local citizens' tastes.

For example, Gustaf Dalstrom won the commission to paint the mural in the St. Joseph, Missouri, post office because the federal and local officials who judged the competition liked his proposal to paint a scene titled *Negro River Music*. Dalstrom's vision was inspired by the music of Stephen Foster, a white American songwriter who idealized nineteenth-century African American life. When the local newspaper published news of Dalstrom's plan to depict a group of blacks happily gathered in song and dance, a delegation from St. Joseph's African American community met with the committee of civic leaders who had approved the design to complain that the mural would portray blacks as "lazy people with no other thoughts but singing, dancing, and clowning." This particular local protest by a group of African American citizens was not successful; Dalstrom's mural was painted as he designed it and as the local officials had approved it. But in other instances, especially in those communities where the mural critics had more power than the blacks of St. Joseph, Missouri, local protests were successful and led to alteration in the mural design.

The Treasury Department's post office mural project was both hailed and damned for its approach to recovery and reform. Supporters applauded the project for providing uplifting images to a citizenry in need of spiritual recovery from the hard times. Some of those images, such as Dalstrom's *Negro River Music*, harkened back to idealized moments of imagined ease and harmony, but those who led the Treasury's Fine Arts Section actually favored mural proposals that displayed Americans' capacity for hard work and extolled their ability to solve problems through cooperation and innovation. Advocates of the post office mural project believed that public art that conveyed a message of faith and confidence in the working people of America would energize the government's recovery efforts. They also believed that government efforts to organize and finance public discussions of art, which the competitions for post office murals certainly did, were a welcome expansion of the state's role as a sponsor of the arts in America.

Critics of the New Deal's post office murals saw the program as a disturbing case of state-sponsored political propaganda rather than as public sponsorship of the arts. Those critics who feared the size and power of the New Deal apparatus argued that government-commissioned and locally approved artwork might uplift the citizenry but also served to generate goodwill toward the federal government. An upbeat, colorful, mural-size reminder of the best in American life, painted on the wall of the local post office, could restore local confidence while at the same time persuading voters that a big, strong federal government provided valuable goods, including postal service and public art.

Figure 8.1 Post Office Mural, Silver Spring, Maryland *This post office mural celebrated the town of Silver Spring's "Old Tavern" from the Civil War era. Nicolai Cikovsky, the Russian immigrant who painted the mural, depicted Union soldiers reading their mail outside the Eagle Inn on Silver Spring's Georgia Avenue, where the new post office was built during the New Deal. The oil-on-canvas mural, measuring six by sixteen feet, was painted in Cikovsky's studio. Here it is being installed on the post office wall. Restored in 1997, the mural is on display at the Silver Spring Public Library.* Source: National Archives.

Other critics, who worried about artists' creative independence, criticized the post office murals project because the artists who won commissions in the mural competitions were not free to make their own aesthetic choices. Unlike the FAP, which allowed artists to produce whatever art they liked, the Treasury Department's Fine Arts Section exercised strong control over the style and content of the post office murals. In its effort to please the eye of the average American citizen standing in line at the post office, the government avoided abstract modern art, with its fractured forms and destabilized shapes. Instead, the Treasury-sponsored works reflected a particular movement in the artistic world known as American Scene painting, which shared the general public's disdain for abstract modern art. Like the New Deal itself, American Scene painting fostered a coalition between rural conservatives, represented by "Regionalists" in the art world, and urban radicals, who were the "Social Realists" among artists. Regionalists produced paintings that idealized traditional rural life, while Social Realists used gritty images to protest the social injustices of the urban, industrial world. Artists in both groups saw themselves as the creators of a uniquely American vision, and artists in both groups were by far the most successful at winning post office mural commissions.

Local committees typically approved of proposals for American Scene murals that celebrated everyday people engaged in familiar activities. Those committees included businessmen, club women, teachers, clergy, librarians, and the postmaster, and they were drawn to visual art that used an accessible style to celebrate local scenery and distinct regional histories. Some local citizens complained if a Social Realist went too far in showing the underside of American life, just as others complained when a sentimental Regionalist like Gustaf Dalstrom produced an image of "clowning" African Americans. But local responses were generally quite positive, producing just the sort of enthusiasm for accessible, community-approved public art that supporters praised and critics feared.

The persistence of unemployment in 1941, when Dalstrom was painting in Missouri, testifies to the weaknesses in Roosevelt's economic recovery efforts. But the popularity of the post office murals testifies to the New Deal's success at encouraging local communities to confront hard times with a mix of tradition, reform, and artistry.

Using the Source: Public Art

Most art historians today dismiss the New Deal's post office murals as mere "embellishments." In their eyes, the murals are not really "art" because the original vision of every artist was so altered, corrected, and revised by Treasury Department officials and local committees that the product does not qualify as an authentic artistic expression. Ironically, it is precisely this feature of post office mural art—the fact that it conformed to the aesthetic tastes of a broad swath of Americans—that makes it particularly useful for social and political historians who want to grasp the national mood of the 1930s and the Roosevelt administration's talent for harnessing that mood to its goals.

Visual images, like written texts, are best understood when we have a sense of the specific context in which the artist or author was working. When studying post office murals, for example, it is useful to remember that the supervising officials in the Fine Arts Section of the Treasury Department, along with the local committees approving the murals, preferred American Scene paintings over other styles. Artists who wished to win a commission for a "Section" mural quickly learned to "paint Section," which meant toning down tendencies toward modern, abstract imagery and emphasizing the positive qualities of common Americans. It is also useful to know that while the Treasury Department never stated its preference for the American Scene style, it did very explicitly state that the content of all post office mural art had to fit into one of three categories: either the history of the U.S. Postal Service itself, the history of the local community, or the community's everyday life. In the case of Detroit, Michigan, for example, a scene from everyday life in the 1930s meant the auto industry. William Gropper—who would go on to become a major figure in Social Realist art after World War II—won the commission for Detroit's Northwestern Branch Postal Station with his design for *Automobile Industry:*

Is labor individual or collective?

A strictly realistic rendering of an auto plant?

Significance of out-size bodies?

Scale of the men to their machines?

Gropper's blending of realism, romanticism, and abstraction in this mural can help us grasp the ways in which Americans in the 1930s, and especially supporters of the New Deal, mixed together their sense that workers were dwarfed by industrial capitalism with their belief that workers were the real engine that kept society progressing. The slight abstractions we see in this mural also illustrate the subtle ways in which modernism influenced popular culture in the 1930s, even among those who thought they were resisting modern abstraction.

What Can Public Art Tell Us?

Post office murals are not particularly useful to art historians who want to trace dramatic innovation or cutting-edge risks among the artistic visionaries of the 1930s. So predictable was the representational style of post office murals that emerging modern artists of the day, such as Jackson Pollock, refused to even submit sketches to the Treasury Department's "Section" competition. If we are interested in the history of popular culture and politics, however, the predominance of American Scene painting in the post office murals helps us understand how Americans in the 1930s combined their conservative attachment to the past amid hard times with their willingness to try on new identities and new methods in order to triumph over those hard times.

When we use visual art for insight into social attitudes, it does not matter whether the experts regard that visual art as "good" art. Popular art, whatever its quality, is valuable for revealing national moods and tastes. When we know that the popular American Scene school of painting rejected modern art on the grounds that it was a European expression ill-suited to capturing authentic American culture, we enrich our sense of America's proud isolation from Europe in the years preceding World War II. When we see how often and how delicately the post office murals balanced the Social Realists' tribute to industrial workers with the Regionalists' idealizing of rural life, we get a visual sense of the internal conflict that Americans faced when their modern economy collapsed under them: even as they cheered for factory workers, they longed for a simpler past on the farm. And when we remember that the post office murals were meant to inspire citizens to believe in their own productive capacities, and that community members influenced the murals' content, we can treat the murals as the common ground that artists, citizens, and government officials shared when defining American traditions and aspirations.

If we want to use visual images as evidence of broad social and political attitudes, we must keep in mind that broad context and not study the images within the narrow confines of art history. For example, the Social Realists who painted American Scene post office murals could be called "conservative" by art history standards because they rejected the innovations of abstract modernism. From the standpoint of political history, however, it was the Social Realists who were radical for making social and economic injustice their artistic subject at a time when abstract modernists seemed smugly unconcerned with the world's problems. Similarly, it is political history, not the murals themselves, that helps us explain why Roosevelt's New Deal administration wanted to combine sentimental Regionalism and defiant Social Realism under the patriotic tent of American Scene painting. The voter base for the Democratic Party's New Deal was a volatile coalition of urban, northern, unionizing workers and rural, southern white farmers and sharecroppers. Just as Roosevelt's speeches and public policies sought to appeal to each of those groups, so, too, the New Deal's public art tried to appeal to its competing constituencies. In this way, public art illustrates social and political trends and can serve as visualizations of the past.

Questions to Ask

The ten post office murals included in the next section all evoke the theme of work because that was such an important focus of the government's campaign to renew the depressed spirit of the American people. These murals come from different regions of the United States and from all three of the Treasury's thematic categories: postal history, local history, and everyday life. They give you an opportunity to examine images of industrial and agricultural workers that local citizens and the federal government found unifying and uplifting.

- How did mural artists combine traditional artistic realism with the new tool of modern abstraction to convey messages about American workers? What was the artists' purpose in distorting shapes and sizes?
- Does this sample of murals emphasize individual work or collective work? What message is conveyed by the depictions of the individual workers shown here?
- What can we learn from these murals about race and gender in the 1930s? How often, and in what settings, do nonwhite men or women appear as workers?
- Why did popular culture in the Depression place so much emphasis on the powerful, productive labor of the nation's white men?

Source Analysis Table

The post office murals included in this chapter represent many of the geographic regions, types of labor, and political messages that were depicted in the 111 post office murals sponsored by the New Deal. In regard to race and gender, however, this sample overstates the frequency with which nonwhite men and women appeared in the total set of post office murals. Although nonwhites comprised 10 percent of the workforce in 1930, and women comprised 22 percent, neither group appeared that often in the murals of workers. White men were overrepresented in the murals because of the era's social attitudes, particularly regarding paid labor. We made a special effort to select some murals that show women and nonwhite men so that you could consider how those workers were represented. The following table lets you keep track of the murals' depictions of gender and race as well as their artistic style and general view of workers.

Mural	Artistic Style: Social Realism or Regionalism?	Work Style: Individualistic or Collective?	Gender: Men's Jobs? Women's Jobs?	Race: White Jobs? Nonwhite Jobs?
1. *The Riveter*				
2. *Development of the Land*				
3. *Postman in a Storm*				
4. *Legend of James Edward Hamilton*				
5. *Tennessee Valley Authority*				
6. *Plowshare Manufacturing*				
7. *Assorting the Mail*				
8. *Mining*				
9. *Orange Picking*				
10. *Tobacco Industry*				

To download and print this table, visit the book companion site at **bedfordstmartins.com/brownshannon**.

The Source: Post Office Murals Depicting "Work" in Local Communities, 1936–1942

1

The Riveter *by Ben Shahn*

Bronx, New York, 1938

Shahn, a Lithuanian immigrant, was one of the best-known and most politically active artists to paint Section art. *The Riveter* was one of several panels that made up the mural *Resources of America,* which Shahn and his wife, Bernarda Bryson, painted for the Bronx post office.

Development of the Land *by Elsa Jemne*, Ladysmith, Wisconsin, 1938

Jemne, a native of St. Paul, Minnesota, had studied in Europe before World War I. She was criticized by both Treasury officials and the citizens of Ladysmith for inaccurately rendering the size and scale of the farmer and his corn in conveying her celebratory message.

3   Postman in a Storm *by Robert Tabor*
Independence, Iowa, 1938

Tabor was born in Independence, Iowa, and lived most of his life there. When he lost his traveling sales job during the Depression, he began to paint. He was funded by the Federal Arts Program before winning a Treasury Section commission for this mural.

| 4 | **Legend of James Edward Hamilton — Barefoot Mailman**
by *Stevan Dohanos,* West Palm Beach, Florida, 1940 |

Dohanos painted six scenes evoking the life of this Florida mailman, who died in 1887 "in the line of duty." Dohanos said in an interview in 1982 that "there is a difference of opinion as to whether sharks or alligators" caused Hamilton's demise.

5   Tennessee Valley Authority *by Xavier Gonzalez*
Huntsville, Alabama, 1937

President Roosevelt regarded creation of the Tennessee Valley Authority (TVA) in 1933 as one of the great achievements of the New Deal. Through the TVA, which covers more than 40,000 square miles, the federal government built dams that brought electricity to the rural Southeast, and it became actively involved in planning the region's resource conservation, agricultural, and industrial policies.

6 Plowshare Manufacturing *by Edward Millman*
Moline, Illinois, 1937

John Deere started building steel plows for prairie farming in Moline, Illinois, in 1837. Despite the Depression, the Deere Company celebrated its centennial as the leading employer in Moline with a record $100 million in gross sales.

7

Assorting the Mail *by Reginald Marsh,* Washington, D.C., 1936

There is no record of citizen complaints in Washington, D.C., about Marsh's nonliteral depiction of mailroom labor.

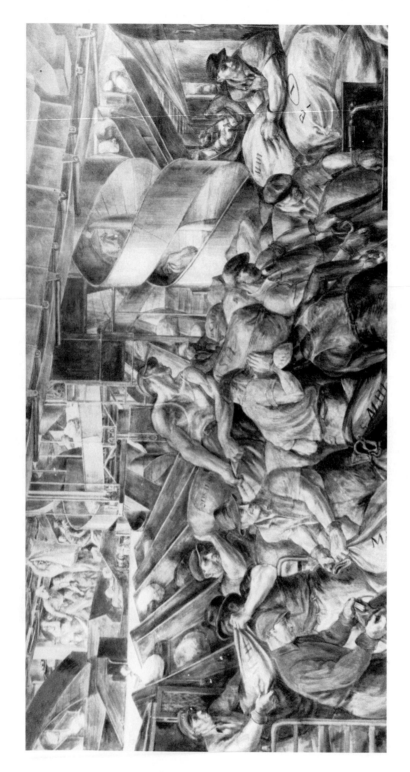

8

Mining *by Michael Lenson*, Mount Hope, West Virginia, 1942

The United Mine Workers of America (UMW) was founded in 1890, but the union struggled for legitimacy until the passage of the National Labor Relations Act of 1935 during the New Deal. The act established federal mechanisms for union formation and bargaining with employers. Mine workers in 1942 were led by John L. Lewis, the charismatic UMW president who gave his union a high profile on the national labor scene in the New Deal years.

9 Orange Picking *by Paul Hull Julian*
Fullerton, California, 1942

The "second gold rush" to California occurred in the early 1900s, when families from the Midwest moved westward in hope of making it rich in citrus farming. By 1942, family farming had largely been replaced by agribusiness, which hired migrant labor from Mexico.

10 Tobacco Industry *by Lee Gatch*
Mullins, South Carolina, 1940

For murals in southern post offices, the Treasury Section and its artists sought a balance between deference to the local power structure and a desire to depict African American life. So while supervisors were seldom depicted in industrial or agricultural murals outside the South, they were included in southern murals about work. At the same time, local southern committees asked that murals not show the poor whites who actually worked alongside blacks in the cotton and tobacco fields.

Analyzing Public Art

1. What key message do these New Deal murals convey about the virtues of the American worker? Which two murals would you select from this group to illustrate the government's message, and why did you choose them?

2. When comparing the industrial murals with the agricultural murals, do you find any difference in artistic style, work style, or composition of the workforce? How do you explain these differences?

3. How did an emphasis on the power of collective work serve to advance the New Deal's political agenda? How did depictions of individual workers foster citizens' confidence in the government?

4. As noted, this sample overrepresents the number of women and nonwhite men actually depicted in all 111 post office murals. What political and emotional purpose was served by emphasizing the productive role of white men in America in these Depression years?

5. Imagine that you are living back in 1942 and have just taken a tour to see these ten murals. Do you think this tour would make you feel optimistic about Americans' ability to prevail in the world war that the United States had recently entered? Would it give you confidence in the U.S. government? Why or why not?

6. The Treasury Department's Fine Arts Section sought to "stimulate the development of American art in general," but political critics and artists questioned the government's role in cultural life. Write your own commentary on the lessons you draw from the New Deal's arts programs about the appropriate role of government in fostering the arts in society.

The Rest of the Story

Many of the Treasury-sponsored murals painted during the New Deal still survive in post offices throughout the United States or in buildings that once were post offices. Some survive only in photographs because their buildings were torn down. Still others have not survived at all. What has most definitely survived is the debate over public funding for the arts that the New Deal ignited.

Federal spending on the arts dried up by 1942, when the U.S. government turned all of its resources toward fighting World War II. But in the years following the war, political debate over the role of the arts in society resumed. Many artists from the Social Realist school, such as William Gropper, became targets of the anticommunist McCarthy investigations in the 1950s because they criticized capitalism. At the same time, anticommunists also expressed hostility to the modern, abstract art movement, which now seemed to have subversive qualities of its own. One postwar newspaper editorial claimed, "Modern art is communistic because it is distorted and ugly. . . . Art which does not glorify our beautiful country in plain, simple terms that everyone can understand breeds dissatisfaction. . . . Those who create and promote it are our enemies."

World War II had changed America's place in the world, however, and many Americans embraced the modern art movement as a sign of this nation's closer ties to Europe and its more sophisticated status as a global power. In addition, cold warriors like President John F. Kennedy argued that America's modern, innovative art was a global advertisement for the authenticity of American freedom, and predicted that government support of artists' unshackled experimentation would prove that the United States, unlike the Soviet Union, was a free, truly civilized society. Like Franklin Delano Roosevelt, Kennedy combined genuine idealism about the uplifting power of art with a political opinion that government support of the arts was in the nation's self-interest.

In late 1965, two years after Kennedy's assassination, President Lyndon B. Johnson was able to turn Kennedy's dream into reality by incorporating the National Endowment for the Arts (NEA) into his Great Society program. In doing so, Johnson endorsed Kennedy's view that a truly great nation demonstrated its respect for freedom and civilization by generously funding artists' unpredictable search for self-expression. In their enthusiasm for this ideal, NEA supporters did not address the possibility that artists might use their public funding to create art that expressed unpopular criticisms of American life. No one set up mechanisms for resolving conflicts between government-funded artists and taxpayers who disagreed with those artists' views.

The NEA program to provide grants on the order of $5,000 to individual artists was only one of a variety of NEA programs operating between 1967 and 1995. During that time, thousands of young, experimental artists were selected to receive financial aid by a "peer panel" of artists who reviewed applications for NEA grants. At the same time, the NEA gave more substantial grants to local arts organizations, museums, and art schools. Coincident with, and likely related to, the creation of the NEA, arts flourished in the United States in these years, and artists found many more opportunities for creating, displaying, and selling their art than ever before.

The success of the arts in the United States intersected with the end of the cold war to produce a new kind of cultural collision. The political debate shifted away from freedom and communism and toward sexuality and race. In that context, many conservative activists combined their concerns over large government with their fears of artistic expression by homosexuals and non-whites who seemed to challenge traditional values. The debate came to a head in 1989, when news emerged that the NEA had given a $30,000 grant to the Institute of Contemporary Art in Philadelphia, which had in turn exhibited Robert Mapplethorpe's nude photos of multiracial sex acts within the sado-masochistic gay subculture. Conservatives were enraged at this use of taxpayer dollars. Mapplethorpe's death from AIDS that year only confirmed his status as a dangerous outsider whose work threatened, as one opponent put it, to "pollute" the body politic.

The ironic result of this incident was that Congress voted in 1995 to abolish all NEA grants to individual artists, even though funding for the Mapplethorpe exhibit had come through a grant to an organization. Today, the NEA funnels all of its now-reduced funds through local arts organizations, which are on notice not to support individual artists who might threaten the organization's future funding. The debate over whether taxpayer support for artistic freedom should require citizens to fund images they find repugnant has not ceased. But, as with the New Deal, the government's support for the NEA has stimulated lively public debate over the place of the arts in a democratic society.

To Find Out More

Alonzo Hamby explores the New Deal triad of relief, recovery, and reform in *Liberalism and Its Challengers: FDR to Reagan* (Oxford: Oxford University Press, 1985) and further examines the successes and failures of the New Deal in *For the Survival of Democracy: Franklin Roosevelt and the World Crisis of the 1930s* (New York: Free Press, 2004).

The most complete study of post office murals is Marlene Park and Gerald E. Markowitz, *Democratic Vistas: Post Office and Public Art in the New Deal* (Philadelphia: Temple University Press, 1984). Along with its lively history of the project, the book offers images of 162 murals along with a complete listing, by state, of most post office murals. Barbara Melosh's *Engendering Culture: Manhood and Womanhood in New Deal Public Art and Theater* (Washington, D.C.: Smithsonian Institution Press, 1991) includes many examples of post office murals in her larger study of the ways gender and race were depicted in New Deal art. In *Wall-to-Wall America: A Cultural History of Post Office Murals in the Great Depression* (Minneapolis: University of Minnesota Press, 1982), Karal Ann Marling tells the story of one Section-sponsored competition to make provocative arguments about the effect of the Depression on people's artistic tastes. For further discussions and examples of New Deal art, see Richard D. McKinzie, *The New Deal for Artists* (Princeton, NJ: Princeton University Press, 1973), and Belisario R. Contreras, *Tradition and Innovation in New Deal Art* (London: Associated University Presses, Inc., 1983). See, too, the federal government's online exhibit of New Deal–sponsored art at **archives.gov/exhibits/new_deal_for_the_arts/about_this_exhibit.html**.

Alan Howard Levy traces the history of federal government involvement in the arts in *Government and the Arts: Debates over Federal Support of the Arts in America from George Washington to Jesse Helms* (Lanham, Md.: University Press of America, 1997). See, too, Michael Brenson, *Visionaries and Outcasts: The NEA, Congress, and the Place of the Visual Artist in America* (New York: New Press, 2001). Current grants from the National Endowment for the Arts are listed on its Web site, at **arts.endow.gov**.

CHAPTER 9

Challenging Wartime Internment

Supreme Court Records from **Korematsu v. United States**

On Friday afternoon, May 30, 1942—almost six months after the bombing of Pearl Harbor—Fred Korematsu was arrested while standing outside a drugstore in San Leandro, California, smoking a cigarette and waiting for his girlfriend, Ida Boitano. The police charged Korematsu with violating a military order directed at residents of California, Oregon, and Washington who were "enemy aliens" born in Japan or U.S. citizens of Japanese descent. All were to report to an "assembly center," with just one suitcase in hand, prepared for evacuation from their homes and wartime "detention" in one of the ten "relocation centers," or internment camps that the government had constructed in isolated areas of eastern California, Idaho, Utah, Arizona, Wyoming, Colorado, and Arkansas. Fred Korematsu's Japanese-born parents and American-born brothers had reported, as ordered, to the Tanforan assembly center south of San Francisco by May 9. Indeed, virtually all who fell under the military order obeyed it. But Fred chose to disobey the order, and from that individual act arose one of the most famous Supreme Court cases in American history.

Fred Korematsu did not set out, at age twenty-two, to place his name at the center of the U.S. debate over civil liberties in wartime. He was a working-class Californian, a trained welder, a graduate of Castlemont High School in Oakland, and a registered voter, but not at all a political activist. He had tried to enlist in the army six months before Pearl Harbor. If gastric ulcers had not made Korematsu ineligible, he would have joined 5,000 other Americans of Japanese descent already serving in the U.S. armed forces. Once war broke out in December 1941, Korematsu's personal goal was to move to the Midwest with his white girlfriend and stay out of all the anti-Japanese trouble brewing on the West Coast in the wake of Japan's attack on Pearl Harbor. Nativists who had long opposed Japanese settlement in the United States used the occasion of war with Japan to stir up fears and hostilities. Because the bombing in Hawaii had left West Coast residents feeling vulnerable, and because 88 percent of the U.S. residents of Japanese descent lived on the West Coast, the anti-Japanese campaign was concentrated in that region.

For Japanese living in the United States, trouble began immediately after Pearl Harbor with implementation of a U.S. war plan to arrest all suspicious "enemy aliens" who might be involved in espionage. The Japanese attack had thrust America into a world war with European allies against Japan, Germany, and Italy. But German and Italian "enemy aliens" living in the United States were questioned only if they were affiliated with profascist organizations, and only half of the 10,000 questioned were interned during the war for their political beliefs. Government policy toward Japanese on the Pacific coast was entirely different. There, the U.S. government moved to evacuate all 40,000 immigrants born in Japan, who were known as issei. None of those immigrants were American citizens because the U.S. naturalization law in force since 1790 stipulated that an immigrant had to be "white" to be eligible for citizenship. Nativists convinced their allies in the military and Congress that resentment over this race-based rule, and the 1924 law excluding all future Japanese immigrants, would cause the issei to be loyal to Japan during the war.

In the two months following the attack on Pearl Harbor, key members of the army's command staff in San Francisco and key members of the California congressional delegation expanded the evacuation plan to include all nisei, the U.S.-born children of Japanese immigrants. The plan to evacuate these 72,000 Japanese American citizens was based on the belief that they too posed a security threat to the West Coast. Advocates of the plan argued, without proof, that Japanese espionage in Hawaii had facilitated the Pearl Harbor attack. Interestingly, no one ever proposed evacuating Hawaii's residents of Japanese descent, who constituted one-third of the Hawaiian population and were a vital part of the Hawaiian workforce. Evacuation of all West Coast Japanese, who constituted only 1 percent of the region's population, did not hurt the general economy but did help those associations of California growers that had for decades sought to eliminate direct competition from successful Japanese American farmers. Those with economic interests thus joined forces with anti-Japanese nativists during wartime to support the exclusion of all Japanese without regard for citizenship status and without individual questioning about political loyalties.

The debate within the government over treatment of Japanese Americans reflected a conflict between military necessity and constitutional rights. Advocates of military necessity won the debate by making three assertions: first, that Japanese Americans on the West Coast constituted an espionage threat because of their strategic location, their racial loyalty to Japan, and their bitterness over U.S. racism; second, that because "the Occidental"[1] eye cannot readily distinguish one Japanese resident from another," effective surveillance

---

[1] The "Occident" refers to Europe and America, as opposed to the "Orient" (Asia).

of suspicious individuals would be impossible; and third, that "their racial characteristics are such that we cannot understand or trust even the citizen Japanese." In other words, the fact of American racism was used to predict Japanese disloyalty and to explain why government officials could not distinguish loyal Japanese from the disloyal through the process of individual interrogation being used with German and Italian aliens in the United States.

On February 4, 1942, an 8:00 P.M. curfew was imposed on all people of Japanese ancestry living in the Pacific states. On February 19, President Franklin D. Roosevelt issued Executive Order 9066, which gave the U.S. military independent authority to designate sensitive areas during wartime, including the authority to determine which persons were to be excluded from those areas, and to provide transportation, food, and shelter for anyone evacuated. A month later, the U.S. Congress endorsed Roosevelt's action with Public Law 503. The very broad wording of both the executive order and the new law allowed Lieutenant General John DeWitt, commander of the western region of the United States, maximum latitude to take whatever protective measures he thought necessary in wartime. Aware of the bitter claims that lax security had been to blame for Pearl Harbor, and politically sympathetic to the anti-Japanese activists, DeWitt was determined that no sabotage or espionage would take place while the West Coast was under his command.

Like all Japanese Americans, Fred Korematsu paid close attention to the public debate over evacuation in the winter and spring of 1942. By the time the president issued Executive Order 9066, Fred had already been expelled from his local labor union for his Japanese heritage, and he was planning to take advantage of the government suggestion that Japanese Americans voluntarily relocate inland before any official evacuation proceedings began. But Fred, like many others, waited too long to relocate. On March 27, 1942, just four days after General DeWitt issued the first formal evacuation order, the government issued a "freeze" order, which meant that Japanese Americans could no longer voluntarily move inland. As a Japanese American, Fred could not leave the West Coast with his girlfriend. But when General DeWitt announced on March 30 that an evacuation "was in prospect for practically all Japanese," Fred knew that if he stayed on the West Coast, he would be evacuated to a camp. So he quickly underwent plastic surgery to disguise his ethnicity, and he acquired a fake ID, thinking he could evade the authorities and escape with his girlfriend. The ruse did not work; at the end of May, Fred was still identifiable as a Japanese American, and the San Leandro police picked him up—probably on a tip from his girlfriend.

The American Civil Liberties Union (ACLU), which was established during World War I to challenge government violations of the Bill of Rights during wartime, faced a serious dilemma in World War II. Members of the national board were closely aligned with President Roosevelt and hesitated to criticize his wartime policies, but ACLU activists on the West Coast were anxious to challenge the constitutionality of Japanese internment. Despite opposition from the ACLU leadership in Washington, D.C., ACLU lawyers in San Francisco and Seattle sought out Japanese American citizens who had been arrested for

Figure 9.1 Fred Korematsu with His Family *Fred Korematsu (third from the left) is shown here with his family in their Oakland, California, nursery. Fred refused to comply with the wartime internment orders and did not join his family when they were taken in 1942 to Tanforan, a former racetrack south of San Francisco. He later spent two years in an internment camp in Utah.* Source: Of Civil Wrongs and Rights: The Fred Korematsu Story.

violating military orders and tried to convince them to become a "test case." Fred Korematsu was one of only four Japanese Americans among the relatively few who violated orders in the first place to agree to challenge the order instead of paying the fine and quietly entering an internment camp. All four cases were complicated along the way by legalistic machinations, judicial technicalities, divisions within the ACLU and among the lawyers for the Japanese Americans, and serious disagreement between the War Department and the Justice Department over how to defend the government's internment policy.

It took two and a half years for Fred Korematsu's case to reach the Supreme Court. In those years, Fred was interned at a relocation camp in Topaz, Utah, where he witnessed the dry, dusty, and desolate conditions under which tens of thousands of Japanese Americans lived for up to three years. While in the camp, Fred met with some hostility from those issei and nisei who believed he was unwise to challenge the government's policies. Fred, like many other nisei, was allowed out of the camp on a work furlough, since his loyalty was never in question, so he worked in Salt Lake City and later in Detroit. Indeed, by the time Korematsu's case reached the Supreme Court in October 1944, tens of thousands of nisei were living in the Midwest and on the East Coast, away from the anti-Japanese hysteria in the Pacific states. They had been released from camps on work furloughs or to enroll in U.S. universities and colleges. Others were distinguishing themselves in wartime battle. The 442nd Regimental Combat Team, composed entirely of nisei from the internment camps, was the most decorated unit in the U.S. Army.

In the months before the *Korematsu* decision was handed down, members of the Roosevelt administration were arguing for the end of Japanese American internment, and the general who had replaced DeWitt on the West Coast had declared that evacuation was no longer a military necessity. But organized protests by some Japanese Americans in the internment camps had raised the hackles of anti-Asian activists, so Roosevelt postponed the end of the detention policy until after the November 1944 election. On December 17, 1944, the U.S. government announced that those Japanese Americans certified as loyal would not be detained or excluded from the West Coast after January 2, 1945. The next day, the Supreme Court announced its decision in the Fred Korematsu case: his conviction for violating the evacuation order was upheld; the military order itself was judged to be constitutional.

Using the Source: Supreme Court Records

The records of the Supreme Court in the *Korematsu* case can help us extend our understanding beyond the specifics of Japanese internment and grasp the larger legal precedents that were established by this wartime incident. The frenzy of war is short-lived, but Supreme Court judgments can last for decades. When we say that the Court's decisions set "precedent," we mean that each decision from the highest court in the land establishes a governing rule or principle that guides lower court rulings in future, related cases—until the Supreme Court chooses to look at the issue again and possibly overturn the established precedent. The records surrounding the Court's decision in the *Korematsu* case, therefore, reveal the wartime debate over internment while also showing the legal precedents that were articulated in this case and have not, to this day, been overturned.

The Supreme Court was not required to hear the *Korematsu* case. The Court is empowered to take any case it chooses from the 5,000 cases that petition for a hearing each year. The nine justices who sit on the Supreme Court actually consider only about 150 cases annually. The cases they choose are those that raise significant constitutional questions about the rights of the individual and the powers of the government; they are the cases that seem to demand a ruling precedent for the lower courts to follow.

At first glance, the Supreme Court's ruling in *Korematsu v. United States* appears to establish the principle that the federal government has the constitutional authority to select a group of citizens, based on their national origin, and evacuate them from their homes for the purpose of indefinite detention. However, when we read the actual records from the case, including the Supreme Court justices' opinions in the case, we find that the ruling defined the government's authority in very narrow terms. We also find that the most precedent-setting statement in the Court's ruling turned out to be the claim that "all legal restrictions which curtail the civil rights of a single racial group are immediately suspect. . . . Courts must subject them to the most rigid scrutiny." Even as it was allowing wartime violation of one group's civil rights in 1944, the Court was setting a broad, new legal rule for later courts to follow. Henceforth, all cases of racial discrimination in the United States would be judged according to this new principle, which came to be called "strict scrutiny."

What Can Supreme Court Records Tell Us?

The relative permanence of Supreme Court records is an obvious advantage in studying history; the precedents set down by the Court do not quickly shift with the winds of popular opinion. This means, however, that we cannot use the records from a case like *Korematsu v. United States* as a measure of popular opinion. The decisions rendered by the Supreme Court do not derive from a poll; they are not the result of a democratic election. For that reason, we must not presume that the arguments in the records represent the views of average Americans. Maybe they do; maybe they don't. The court records themselves cannot tell us. But the Constitution tells us that whether or not the majority of the American public agreed with the majority on the Supreme Court in a case like *Korematsu*, it was the Court's majority opinion that became the law of the land for the indeterminate future.

A great advantage to using Supreme Court records as a historical source is that they offer concise, generally well-written summaries of both the facts under dispute in the case and the constitutional principles and established precedents that shaped the justices' ruling on those facts. Indeed, the written arguments that the lawyers on both sides of the case present to the justices are called briefs because they are supposed to be concise statements of both the factual and legal issues in the case. In addition, justices' opinions can be quite brilliant summaries of both the facts in the case and the constitutional principles bearing on the case.

This virtue in Supreme Court briefs and opinions is also a disadvantage for those of us who are interested in history but have not studied the law. The court records are full of legal terminology and references to previous cases that the lawyers or justices use to support their positions. Another disadvantage of court records for those who simply want to know more about the history of a case is that lawyers and justices do not reveal all the background factors, emotional issues, political considerations, private relationships, and personal beliefs that informed a particular argument or decision. Despite these disadvantages, we can still get the gist of a legal argument without knowing the details of every reference, and a careful reading of the court records can give us clues about where to dig into the background of a case.

Consider these excerpts from an amicus curiae (friend of the court) brief filed by the attorneys general of the states of California, Oregon, and Washington in the *Korematsu* case. These particular friends were speaking on the side of the government, offering the Court their views on why the military evacuation of Japanese Americans was justified in wartime. Like most briefs, this one offered claims of fact, statements of opinion, constitutional principle, and legal precedent to support its position:

Factual claim to military necessity

Korematsu

Both the time required to examine this large group and the lack of an adequate test of loyalty and trained personnel, made treatment upon an individual basis impossible in the face of the emergency which required prompt action. The appellant, however, claims that the evacuation was the result of pressure brought by exclusion agitation groups and

Reference to legal precedent set in another wartime case the year before

Japanese baiters. . . . This charge was partly dissipated when this court held in *Hirabayashi v. United States* (320 U.S. 81 [1943]), that the curfew order . . . was issued for reasons of military necessity. . . . The exclusion of persons from critical areas in time of war, when required by military necessity, is within the scope of the joint war powers of the Congress and the President. . . . Of course, such an exercise of the war power must be reasonable under the circumstances that satisfy the "due process" requirements of the Fifth Amendment.

Use of constitutional principles

Hence, . . . the only substantial question here is whether or not . . . there existed a rational basis for the decisions of the military commander to evacuate and exclude all persons of

Do the facts justify placing military need over the Fifth Amendment?

Factual claims *and* legal precedent

Japanese ancestry from the Pacific coastal areas. . . . In holding that there was a reasonable basis for the application of curfew to all persons of Japanese ancestry, citizens and aliens alike . . . within the Western Defense Command, this court, in the *Hirabayashi* case, found that the following factors provided a reasonable basis.

So factual claims accepted by Supreme Court in prior case should be accepted in *Korematsu* case

Source: Landmark Briefs and Arguments of the Supreme Court of the United States: Constitutional Law, vol. 42, edited by Philip B. Kurland and Gerhard Casper (Washington, D.C.: University Publications of America, Inc., 1976), 537, 546, 549.

The amicus curiae brief then listed thirteen factors that supposedly made evacuation of Japanese Americans reasonable under the wartime circumstances. Among the reasons offered were the following: the attack on Pearl Harbor put the Pacific coast in danger; war production facilities on the Pacific coast were in danger; the majority of Japanese Americans lived on the Pacific coast; white hostility had increased Japanese solidarity; Japanese American children attended Japanese-language schools; in 1927, the vast majority of U.S.-born children of Japanese descent held dual citizenship; the Japanese consulate was influential with Japanese community elders in the United States. In the end, six of the Court's nine justices rendered a decision that the internment of West Coast residents of Japanese descent was constitutional. The other three justices dissented from the majority's opinion and wrote their own opinions on why the majority was wrong. The judicial opinions from *Korematsu* illuminate both the case-specific arguments heard in the courtroom and the larger constitutional issues debated among the justices themselves.

Questions to Ask

In the lawyers' briefs and justices' opinions that follow, you will see most of the points raised in the amicus curiae brief. In order to piece together the history of the case, you will want to keep track of the factual claims, the constitutional principles, and the legal precedents appearing in the briefs and in the justices' opinions.

- Did the majority of justices accept (or, to use court language, "take judicial notice of") the factual claims made in General DeWitt's *Final Report* about the security threat posed by Japanese Americans after Pearl Harbor?
- Where did the justices refer to legal precedent to support their opinions in this case?
- Korematsu was charged only with not obeying the "evacuation order" by not reporting to an "assembly" center. Why did the ACLU and justices disagree about the difference between evacuation and detention or between assembly centers and "relocation" centers?
- Why did the majority of Supreme Court justices choose to announce a bold, broad principle such as "strict scrutiny" in its ruling and then uphold Fred Korematsu's conviction?

Source Analysis Table

The records included here give you a sense of the arguments presented to the Supreme Court by the Justice Department, Fred Korematsu's lawyer, the American Civil Liberties Union, and the Japanese American Citizens' League (JACL). There are also excerpts from the majority and minority opinions issued by the Court at the conclusion of the case. The following table lets you keep track of the debates over factual claims, references to broad constitutional issues, claims to legal precedent, and statements of unsubstantiated opinion.

	Argument made by:	Argument for:	Argument against:
Factual claims about military necessity			
Constitutional issues of due process and war powers			
Legal claims to precedents in prior cases			
Statements of unsubstantiated opinion			

To download and print the table, visit the book companion site at **bedfordstmartins.com/brownshannon**.

The Source: Briefs and Supreme Court Opinions in *Korematsu v. United States,* October Term, 1944

1

Part Three of the Brief Submitted by the Solicitor General of the United States and the Department of Justice Supporting Korematsu's Conviction

In this section of its three-part brief, the Justice Department spoke directly to the question of "whether the evacuation from the local region of persons of Japanese ancestry . . . was a valid exercise of the war power under the circumstances." The footnotes in this section were part of the Justice Department's brief and constituted an important part of its claim to factual evidence.

The situation leading to the determination to exclude all persons of Japanese ancestry from Military Area No. 1 and the California portion of Military Area No. 2 was stated in detail in the Government's brief in this Court in *Hirabayashi v. United States. . . .* That statement need not be repeated here.[1] In brief, the facts which were generally known in the early months of 1942 or have since been disclosed indicate that there was ample ground to believe that imminent danger then existed of an attack by Japan upon the West Coast. This area contained a large concentration of war production and war facilities. Of the 126,947 persons of Japanese descent in the United States, 111,938 lived in Military Areas No. 1 and No. 2, of whom approximately two-thirds were United States citizens. Social, economic, and political conditions . . . were such that the assimilation of many of them by the white community had been prevented. There was evidence indicating the existence of media through which Japan could have attempted, and had attempted, to secure the attachment of many of these persons to the Japanese Government and to arouse their sympathy and enthusiasm for war aims. There was a basis for concluding that some persons of Japanese ancestry, although American citizens, had formed an at-

[1] The *Final Report* of General DeWitt (which is dated June 5, 1943, but which was not made public until January, 1944) . . . is relied on in this brief for statistics and other details concerning the actual evacuation. . . . We have specifically recited in this brief the facts relating to the justification for the evacuation, of which we ask the Court to take judicial notice, and we rely upon the *Final Report* only to the extent that it relates to such facts.

Source: Landmark Briefs and Arguments of the Supreme Court of the United States: Constitutional Law, vol. 42, edited by Philip B. Kurland and Gerhard Casper (Washington, D.C.: University Publications of America, 1976), 213–15.

tachment to, and sympathy and enthusiasm for, Japan.[2] It was also evident that it would be impossible quickly and accurately to distinguish these persons from other citizens of Japanese ancestry. The presence in the Military Areas Nos. 1 and 2 of persons who might aid Japan was peculiarly and particularly dangerous. . . . The persons affected were at first encouraged and assisted to migrate under their own arrangements, but this method of securing their removal . . . was terminated by Public Proclamation No. 4. . . . It was necessary to restrict and regulate the migration from the Area in order to insure the orderly evacuation and resettlement of the persons affected. . . . The rate of self-arranged migration was inadequate, partly because of growing indications that persons of Japanese ancestry were likely to meet with hostility and even violence.

[2] In addition to the authorities cited in the Hirabayashi brief, see Anonymous (An Intelligence Officer), "The Japanese in America, the Problem and the Solution," *Harper's Magazine*, October, 1942. . . . See also "Issei, Nisei, Kibei," *Fortune Magazine*, April, 1944.

2 — *Brief Submitted by Wayne M. Collins, Counsel for Appellant*

Mr. Collins's impassioned, ninety-eight-page (not so) brief made a variety of arguments against the military necessity for and constitutionality of evacuation and internment. The excerpts below, including the footnote, indicate the tone of Collins's brief and his arguments regarding General DeWitt's motives in interpreting Executive Order 9066 as an evacuation and internment order.

If [General DeWitt] really believed these people to be spies and saboteurs . . . why did he delay from December 7, 1941, to March 30, 1942, before removing the first contingent to assembly centers? . . . Was General DeWitt so blind that he didn't realize that in the interval between December 7, 1941, and the date of his unprecedented orders . . . boards of investigation could have examined the loyalty of each of the prospective deportees. . . . They could have been examined in less time than it took to build the shacks that were to house them.[1] The inconvenience and cost of examining would have been trifling. The cost

[1] The General issued several hundred individual civilian exclusion orders against "white" naturalized citizens of prior German and Italian allegiance whom he deemed dangerous. These were given individual hearings on the question of their loyalty. . . . If the General had time to provide examinations for these individuals can he be heard to deny he had time to examine Japanese descended citizens before evacuating them? His special treatment of these whites proves his bias against the native-born yellow citizen.

Source: Landmark Briefs and Arguments of the Supreme Court of the United States, 119, 152, 161, 163, 165, 196.

of housing, evacuation and administration of his program has cost this country many millions. . . . Why did he keep secret the reasons he insisted upon this frenzied evacuation? How could this nation abide the secret reasons he carried in his head when we had neither evidence nor ground to believe him to have been the wisest man in the nation? What are the facts upon which he would justify the outrage he perpetrated? . . .

What one day will be celebrated as a masterpiece of illogic . . . appears in General DeWitt's letter of February 14, 1942, one month before the evacuation commenced. (*Final Report,* p. 34). He characterizes all our Japanese as subversive. . . . He states . . . that "the Japanese race is an enemy race" and the native-born citizens are "Americanized" but their "racial strains are undiluted" and being "barred from assimilation by convention" may "turn against this nation." . . . The very fact that no sabotage has taken place to date is a disturbing and confirming indication that such action will be taken." . . .

Who is this DeWitt to say who is and who is not an American and who shall and who shall not enjoy the rights of citizenship? . . . General DeWitt let Terror out to plague these citizens but closed the lid on the Pandora's box and left Hope to smother. It is your duty to raise the lid and revive Hope for these, our people, who have suffered at the hands of one of our servants.

3 | *Amicus Curiae Briefs Submitted by the American Civil Liberties Union*

> Due to conflict within the ACLU, that organization was not Korematsu's attorney-of-record, but it did submit a "friend of the court" brief to persuade the Supreme Court to hear the *Korematsu* case and submitted another at the time of the hearing. These excerpts are taken from both briefs, as is footnote 2.

October 1943 Brief Asking the Supreme Court to Review the Judgment of the Ninth Circuit Court of Appeals

We believe that this case presents the question of the power of the military to detain citizens against whom no charges have been preferred. We contend that no such power has been granted by Congress, or could be constitutionally granted.

The issue is presented because the evacuation orders . . . made it quite plain that not evacuation only was required, but indefinite detention as well. . . . That the evacuation and detention were part of a single integrated program is made clear in a recently published report by the War Department. . . .

Source: Landmark Briefs and Arguments of the Supreme Court of the United States, 81–83, 302–4.

We submit that the Congress gave neither to the President nor to military authorities any power so far reaching, and that in the absence of legislation the President has no such power even in time of war. . . . It is only when martial law has been declared that executive authority may be exercised over citizens. . . . Finally, we submit that even the President and the Congress, acting together, may not detain citizens of the United States against whom no charges have been preferred. . . . The framers [of the Constitution] permitted the suspension of the writ of habeas corpus,[1] by which unlawful detention was normally challenged, but permitted such suspension only in time of invasion or insurrection . . . only at a time of direst immediate emergency, not at all as a precautionary measure.

October 1944 Brief Asking the Supreme Court to Overturn Fred Korematsu's Conviction

General DeWitt does try to show military necessity by reference to reported illegal radio signals which could not be located, lights on the shore, and the like. . . . The Government's brief . . . contains no reference . . . to illicit radio signals, signal lights . . . or to . . . hidden caches of contraband. . . . Moreover, in several respects the recital in the DeWitt Report is wholly inconsistent with the facts of public knowledge. It is well known, of course, that radio detection equipment is unbelievably accurate. . . . Secondly, the fact that no person of Japanese ancestry has been arraigned for any sabotage or espionage since December 7, 1941, certainly suggests, in view of the unquestionable efficiency of the F.B.I., that no such acts were committed. . . . Nowhere in [DeWitt's *Final Report*] is there a line, a word, about the reports of other security officers. General DeWitt does not tell us whether he consulted either the Director of the Federal Bureau of Investigation or the Director of the Office of Naval Intelligence. . . . Since no recommendation from either the Office of Naval Intelligence or the F.B.I. are referred to, one can only assume either that they were not sought or that they were opposed to mass evacuation.[2]

---

[1] [A writ of habeas corpus is an order that a prison official bring a prisoner before a court to show that the prisoner has been arrested and detained for actual legal cause. — Ed.]

[2] There is a fair indication that, whether or not its recommendations were asked, the Office of Naval Intelligence would have stated that mass evacuation was wholly unnecessary. In *Harper's Magazine* for October, 1942, there is an article by an anonymous officer . . . [which] is almost certainly from the Office of Naval Intelligence, which has always been understood as primarily concerned with Japanese intelligence work. The concluding paragraph states: "To sum up: the entire 'Japanese Problem' has been magnified out of its true proportion, largely because of the physical characteristics of the people. It should be handled on the basis of the *individual*, regardless of citizenship, and *not* on a racial basis."

4 · *Amicus Curiae Brief Submitted by the Japanese American Citizens' League on Behalf of Fred Korematsu*

The JACL submitted a 200-page "friend of the court" brief that emphasized Japanese American assimilation and loyalty to the U.S. government. In response to the charge that Japanese American loyalty was in doubt because many held dual citizenship, the JACL brief explained that, prior to 1924, Japanese law automatically conferred Japanese citizenship on any child born of Japanese parents anywhere in the world. After Japanese Americans persuaded the Japanese government to change that law, the percentage of U.S.-born children of Japanese descent holding dual citizenship plummeted by 85 percent.

It has been necessary to present the evidence concerning the assimilation, loyalty and contributions of Americans of Japanese ancestry because . . . [in] all the loose talk about "lack of assimilation" and "close-knit racial groups" there is no hint that the trained investigators who have pursued the subject for years were even consulted. . . . Dr. Robert E. Park, chairman of the Department of Sociology of the University of Chicago, directed a large-scale study of resident Orientals . . . [and] determined that the American of Japanese ancestry "born in America and educated in our western schools is culturally an Occidental, even though he be racially an Oriental." . . .

The civilians who, because they were influenced by Pearl Harbor sabotage rumors, became panic-stricken and requested evacuation . . . did not know the facts. Perhaps the politicians . . . too, were ignorant. But General DeWitt, who ordered the evacuation, certainly must have been aware of the truth and must have been cognizant of the grounds on which his fellow officer, General Delos C. Emmons, refused to order mass internment of the persons of Japanese descent in Hawaii.

Why then did General DeWitt, in spite of what he knew or could easily have learned, act upon the advice of racists and mean-spirited economic rivals? We contend that General DeWitt accepted the views of racists instead of the principles of democracy because he is himself a confessed racist. . . . On April 13, 1943, in testifying before the House Naval Affairs Committee in San Francisco, General DeWitt . . . said:

A Jap's a Jap. . . . I don't want any of them. We got them out. . . . They are a dangerous element, whether loyal or not. It makes no difference whether he is an American citizen. Theoretically, he is still a Japanese and you can't change him.

Source: Landmark Briefs and Arguments of the Supreme Court of the United States, 504–6, 527–28.

5

The Opinion of the Supreme Court,
Issued December 18, 1944

Justice Hugo L. Black issued the eight-page majority opinion of six of the Court's nine judges. Chief Justice Harlan Stone and Justices Stanley Reed, Felix Frankfurter, Wiley Rutledge, and William O. Douglas concurred. All of those justices, except for Chief Justice Stone, were appointed to the Supreme Court by President Franklin Delano Roosevelt.

It should be noted, to begin with, that all legal restrictions which curtail the civil rights of a single racial group are immediately suspect. That is not to say that all such restrictions are unconstitutional. It is to say that courts must subject them to the most rigid scrutiny. Pressing public necessity may sometime justify the existence of such restrictions; racial antagonism never can. . . . Executive Order 9066 . . . declared that "the successful prosecution of the war requires every possible protection against espionage and against sabotage." . . . In *Hirabayashi v. United States* . . . we sustained a conviction obtained for violation of the curfew order. . . . It was because we could not reject the finding of the military authorities that it was impossible to bring about an immediate segregation of the disloyal from the loyal that we sustained the validity of the curfew order as applying to the whole group. In the instant case, temporary exclusion of the entire group was rested by the military on the same ground. . . .

We uphold the exclusion order as of the time it was made and when the petitioner violated it. In doing so, we are not unmindful of the hardships imposed by it upon a large group of American citizens. But hardships are part of war, and war is an aggregation of hardships. . . . Citizenship has its responsibilities as well as its privileges, and in time of war the burden is always heavier. . . . The contention is that we must treat these separate orders [for exclusion and for detention] as one and inseparable; that, for this reason, if detention in an assembly or relocation center would have illegally deprived the petitioner of his liberty, the exclusion order and his conviction under it cannot stand. . . . We cannot say . . . that his presence in that [assembly] center would have resulted in his detention in a relocation center. . . . It is sufficient here to pass upon the [exclusion] order which petitioner violated. To do more would be to go beyond the issues raised, and to decide momentous questions not contained within the framework of the pleadings or the evidence in this case. . . . To cast this case in the outlines of racial prejudice, without reference to real military dangers which were presented, merely confuses the issue.

Source: United States Reports, vol. 323: Cases Adjudged in the Supreme Court at October Term, 1944, 214–24.

6 Justice Owen J. Roberts, Dissenting from the Majority

Justice Roberts was one of only two justices on the Supreme Court in 1944 who had not been appointed by President Roosevelt. In his five-page dissent, Justice Roberts criticized the majority's reliance on the Hirabayashi *precedent and its claim that it was valid to rule narrowly on evacuation and not address the question of detention without trial.*

The predicament in which the petitioner thus found himself was this: he was forbidden, by Military Order, to leave the zone in which he lived; he was forbidden, by Military Order, after a date fixed, to be found within that zone unless he were in an Assembly Center located in that zone. General DeWitt's report to the Secretary of War concerning the program of evacuation and relocation of Japanese makes it entirely clear . . . that an Assembly Center was a euphemism for a prison. No person within such a center was permitted to leave except by Military Order. . . . The civil authorities must often resort to the expedient of excluding citizens temporarily from a locality. . . . If the exclusion . . . were of that nature the *Hirabayashi* case would be an authority for sustaining it. But the facts above recited . . . show that the exclusion was part of an overall plan for forcible detention. . . . The two conflicting orders, one which commanded him to stay and the other which commanded him to go, were nothing but a cleverly devised trap to accomplish the real purpose of the military authority, which was to lock him up in a concentration camp. . . . We know that is the fact. Why should we set up a figmentary and artificial situation instead of addressing ourselves to the actualities of the case?

Source: United States Reports, vol. 323: Cases Adjudged in the Supreme Court at October Term, 1944, 225–30.

7 Justice Frank Murphy, Dissenting from the Majority

Justice Murphy had voted with all the other justices in the 1943 Hirabayashi *case, upholding a curfew for West Coast residents of Japanese descent. But his written opinion in the case stated that such a curfew for one ethnic group bore "a melancholy resemblance to the treatment accorded to members of the Jewish race in Germany" and "goes to the very brink of constitutional power." In his ten-page dissent from the majority's decision in the* Korematsu *case, Justice Murphy focused on balancing military necessity and citizens' constitutional rights.*

Source: United States Reports, vol. 323: Cases Adjudged in the Supreme Court at October Term, 1944, 233–42.

In dealing with matters relating to the prosecution and progress of a war, we must accord great respect and consideration to the judgements of the military authorities. . . . Their judgements ought not to be overruled lightly by those whose training and duties ill-equip them to deal intelligently with matters so vital to the security of the nation. At the same time, however, it is essential that there be definite limits to military discretion, especially where martial law has not been declared. Individuals must not be impoverished of their constitutional rights on a plea of military necessity that has neither substance nor support. . . . The military claim must subject itself to the judicial process of having its reasonableness determined. . . . The action [must] have some reasonable relation to the removal of dangers of invasion, sabotage, and espionage. But the exclusion of all persons with Japanese blood in their veins has no such reasonable relation . . . because [it] must necessarily rely for its reasonableness on the assumption that *all* persons of Japanese ancestry may have a dangerous tendency to commit sabotage and espionage. . . . It is difficult to believe that reason, logic or experience could be marshalled in support of . . . this erroneous assumption of racial guilt. In [General DeWitt's] *Final Report* . . . he refers to all individuals of Japanese descent as "subversive," as belonging to an "enemy race" whose "racial strains are undiluted." . . . Justification for the exclusion is sought . . . mainly upon questionable racial and sociological grounds not ordinarily within the realm of expert military judgement. . . . A military judgement based upon such racial and sociological considerations is not entitled to the great weight ordinarily given the judgements based upon strict military considerations. . . . I dissent, therefore, from this legalization of racism.

---

8   *Justice Robert Jackson, Dissenting from the Majority*

In his six-page dissent, Justice Jackson challenged the relevance of *Hirabayashi* as a precedent and distinguished between the immediate decisions of the military and the precedent-setting decisions of the Supreme Court.

It is said that if the military commander had reasonable military grounds for promulgating the orders, they are constitutional and become law and the Court is required to enforce them. There are several reasons why I cannot subscribe to this doctrine.

It would be impracticable and dangerous idealism to expect or insist that each specific military command in an area of probable operations will conform to conventional tests of constitutionality. . . . But if we cannot confine military

Source: United States Reports, vol. 323: Cases Adjudged in the Supreme Court at October Term, 1944, 242–48.

expedients by the Constitution, neither would I distort the Constitution to approve all that the military may deem expedient. That is what the Court appears to be doing, whether consciously or not. I cannot say, from any evidence before me, that the orders of General DeWitt were not reasonably expedient military precautions, nor could I say that they were. But even if they were permissible military procedures, I deny that it follows that they were constitutional. . . .

Much is made of the danger to liberty from the Army program of deporting and detaining these citizens of Japanese extraction. But a judicial construction of the due process clause that will sustain this order is a far more subtle blow to liberty than the promulgation of the order itself. A military order, however constitutional, is not apt to last longer than the military emergency. . . . But once a judicial opinion rationalizes such an order to show that it conforms to the Constitution . . . the Court for all time has validated the principle of racial discrimination. . . . The principle then lies about like a loaded weapon ready for the hand of any authority that can bring forward a plausible claim of an urgent need. Every repetition imbeds that principle more deeply in our law and thinking and expands it to new purposes. . . . A military commander may overstep the bounds of constitutionality, and it is an incident. But if we review and approve, that passing incident becomes the doctrine of the Constitution. There it has a generative power of its own. . . . Nothing better illustrates this danger than does the Court's opinion in this case. It argues that we are bound to uphold the conviction of Korematsu because we upheld one in *Hirabayashi v. United States,* when we sustained these orders in so far as they applied a curfew requirement to a citizen of Japanese ancestry. . . . Now the principle of racial discrimination is pushed from support of mild measures to very harsh ones, from temporary deprivations to indeterminate ones. And the precedent which it is said requires us to do so is *Hirabayashi.* . . . Because we said that these citizens could be made to stay in their homes during the hours of dark, it is said we must require them to leave home entirely; and if that, we are told they may also be taken into custody for deportation; and if that, it is argued they may also be held for some undetermined time in detention camps. How far the principle of this case would be extended before plausible reasons would play out, I do not know.

Analyzing Supreme Court Records

1. What factual claims about the military necessity of Japanese American evacuation were in dispute in this case? Did any of the justices question the military's claims?

2. Why did Justice Black apply the precedent set in the *Hirabayashi* case to the ruling in the *Korematsu* case in his majority opinion? In his dissent, why did Justice Jackson reject the use of *Hirabayashi* as a precedent in this case?

3. Why did Justice Black argue that an evacuation order was not the same as a detention order? Why did Justice Roberts take a different view?

4. The majority opinion upheld "the exclusion order as of the time it was made." On what grounds did Justice Murphy feel that that order should not establish legal precedent?

5. Based on the majority opinion, can you speculate on why six justices of the U.S. Supreme Court announced the broad principle of "strict scrutiny" in all racial discrimination cases but then avoided the question of whether indefinite detention passed the "strict scrutiny" test in this case?

6. Fred Korematsu's conviction was overturned in 1984 (see "The Rest of the Story"), but the Supreme Court ruling in this case still stands. If you were Fred Korematsu, what argument would you make to have your conviction overturned? Why would you wait forty years?

7. Since the terrorist attacks of September 11, 2001, and the passage of the USA PATRIOT Act (Public Law 107-56), legal scholars have debated whether the Supreme Court's opinion in *Korematsu v. United States* might be used as a precedent for the categorical incarceration of Arab Americans as a military necessity in the war on terrorism. Write an argument for or against the use of *Korematsu* as a precedent justifying the evacuation or detention of Arab Americans in the name of national security.

The Rest of the Story

In April 1984, forty years after the Supreme Court declared Fred Korematsu guilty of disobeying a military order, his case was reconsidered in the U.S. District Court for Northern California, and his conviction was overturned. This was an extraordinary turn of events, unprecedented in U.S. legal history, and it occurred because a lawyer and legal historian, Peter Irons, conducted historical research and found evidence he never even dreamed existed.

Irons set out in 1981 to write a book about Japanese American cases involving curfew, evacuation, and internment during World War II. While digging through the unexamined records of the Justice Department, Irons happened upon written evidence that the Justice Department and the War Department knew that General John DeWitt had falsified data about Japanese subversive activity on the West Coast when he wrote his *Final Report*. Edward Ennis, the lawyer in the Justice Department charged with preparing the government's defense in the *Korematsu* case, did not receive DeWitt's report until after the Supreme Court had read it and relied on it as the factual basis for allowing curfews in the *Hirabayashi* decision. When Ennis read DeWitt's claims that Japanese Americans had used signaling equipment and radio transmissions to engage in acts of espionage, he began to ask questions. Ennis quickly learned that the Federal Bureau of Investigation, the Office of Naval Intelligence, and the Federal

Communications Commission had all told DeWitt that every rumor of such espionage had been thoroughly investigated and found false; all signals from the coast and all radio transmissions had been accounted for. By including the rumors of subversion but excluding the agencies' findings in his *Final Report*, DeWitt had knowingly fabricated claims to a "military necessity" for the evacuation of all Japanese Americans.

When he realized that the *Hirabayashi* decision was based on disproved rumors, Ennis alerted Solicitor General Charles Fahy and Assistant Secretary of War John McCloy that the Justice Department would be engaged in a suppression of evidence if it did not report these findings to the Supreme Court. Fahy and McCloy refused to inform the Supreme Court that the *Final Report* was falsified, but they did refrain from using that phony evidence in the written brief and did agree to include the footnote, which you read on page 204, subtly indicating limited confidence in DeWitt's report. A surviving outline of Fahy's oral argument indicates that he planned to quote from the *Final Report*'s espionage rumors in addressing the Supreme Court, but since the Justice Department has lost the transcript of Fahy's presentation, there is no proof that Fahy knowingly misled the Court on the matter of Japanese American espionage. In retrospect, Ennis regretted not resigning from his Justice Department position over this issue, but at the time he thought he could do more good on the inside. Indeed, he slipped his information to the lawyers for the ACLU, and you can see in their amicus curiae brief an effort to alert the Supreme Court to flaws in the *Final Report*.

When Peter Irons told sixty-two-year-old Fred Korematsu that the "military necessity" evidence used in his case had been falsified and that he had legal grounds to seek a reversal, Korematsu told Irons to go ahead with the case. Irons worked with a team of Japanese American lawyers, all children of citizens who had been interned during the war. The Justice Department offered to "pardon" Korematsu rather than face exposure of falsified evidence in open court. Korematsu replied that the Justice Department should instead seek a pardon from him.

Korematsu's lawyers decided to take their case to the federal district court rather than the Supreme Court. This less-risky strategy offered the best chance that Korematsu would be personally exonerated but meant that the precedent set at the Supreme Court level would not be altered. In 1984, after reviewing the evidence, U.S. District Court Judge Marilyn Hall Patel overturned Korematsu's conviction on the grounds that a "fundamental error" had occurred in the original trial. With Fred Korematsu sitting before her in court, Judge Patel said:

> *Korematsu* remains on the pages of our legal and political history. As a legal precedent it is now recognized as having very limited application. As a historical precedent it stands as a constant caution that in times of war or declared military necessity our institutions must be vigilant in protecting constitutional guarantees . . . and national security must not be used to protect governmental actions from close scrutiny and accountability. It stands as a

caution that in times of international hostility and antagonisms our institutions, legislative, executive, and judicial, must be prepared to protect all citizens from the petty fears and prejudices that are so easily aroused. (*Korematsu v. United States*, 584 F. Supp. 1406 [N.D. Cal. 1984]).

Between 1949 and 1980, very slow progress was made in the effort to compensate Japanese Americans for the financial losses resulting from relocation and detention. In 1980, due to pressure from the JACL and Japanese American elected officials, Congress established the Commission on Wartime Relocation and Internment of Civilians to review the facts surrounding implementation of Executive Order 9066 and to "recommend appropriate remedies." Peter Irons's research findings were among the facts available to this government commission. Still, progress was slow, but in 1988, four years after Fred Korematsu was exonerated, President Ronald Reagan signed the Civil Liberties Act, which provided for a $20,000 redress payment to each of the 60,000 surviving internees, including Fred Korematsu.

Before his conviction was overturned, Korematsu had not even told his children that he was a convicted criminal. After it was overturned, Korematsu welcomed opportunities to speak about his case. In an interview for the film *Of Civil Rights and Wrongs: The Fred Korematsu Story,* he said, "In order for things like this to never happen, we have to protest. Protest but not with violence, otherwise they won't listen to you, but you have to let them know, otherwise they're not going to hear you. So, don't be afraid to speak up." In 1998, when he was seventy-eight years old, Fred Korematsu was awarded the Medal of Freedom, the nation's highest civilian honor. He died of respiratory failure in 2005.

To Find Out More

The unabridged texts of the Supreme Court justices' majority opinion and three dissenting opinions in *Korematsu v. United States* are easily available on the Web at FindLaw (**caselaw.lp.findlaw.com**) and at the Touro Law Center (**tourolaw.edu/Patch/Korematsu***).

To read the full text of the lawyers' briefs and the amicus curiae briefs submitted to the Supreme Court in *Korematsu v. United States*, see pages 3–563 of *Landmark Briefs and Arguments of the Supreme Court of the United States: Constitutional Law*, volume 42, edited by Philip B. Kurland and Gerhard Casper (Washington, D.C.: University Publications of America, 1976). There are no transcripts of the lawyers' oral arguments in the *Korematsu* case before the Supreme Court. The Court did not provide for the recording and transcription of oral arguments until 1955.

There is a rich literature on Japanese American internment, including the personal experiences of those interned, the political conflicts outside and inside the camps, and the administration of the camps. A thorough bibliographical guide is included in Wendy Ng, *Japanese American Internment during World*

War II: A History and Reference Guide (Westport, Conn.: Greenwood Press, 2002). Among the best works on the subject are Roger Daniels, *Prisoners without Trial: Japanese Americans in World War II* (New York: Hill and Wang, 1993); Leslie T. Hatamiya, *Righting a Wrong: Japanese Americans and the Passage of the Civil Liberties Act of 1988* (Palo Alto, Calif.: Stanford University Press, 1993); John Tateishi, *And Justice for All: An Oral History of the Japanese American Detention Camps* (New York: Random House, 1984); Charles Kikuchi, *The Kikuchi Diary: Chronicles of an American Concentration Camp* (Urbana: University of Illinois Press, 1973); and Akemi Kikumura, *Through Harsh Winters: The Life of a Japanese Immigrant Woman* (Novato, Calif.: Chandler and Sharp, 1981).

Peter Irons traces the Supreme Court cases and the subsequent efforts to overturn them in two books: *Justice at War* (New York: Oxford University Press, 1983) and *Justice Delayed: The Record of the Japanese American Internment Cases* (Middletown, Conn.: Wesleyan University Press, 1989). *Personal Justice Denied*, the very informative report of the Commission on Wartime Relocation and Internment of Civilians, is widely available in a one-volume edition (Washington, D.C.: Civil Liberties Education Fund; and Seattle: University of Washington Press, 1997).

Among the many Web sites on Japanese American internment, see the Resource Page for Teachers sponsored by the History Institute at the University of Massachusetts, Amherst, at **umass.edu/history/institute_dir/internment .html**, which offers links to both documents and photographs. You can also find documents and photographs at the National Archives (**nara.gov**) by searching the keywords "Japanese internment." The University of Washington offers an excellent array of photographs and documents as part of its Japanese American Exhibit and Access Project, at **lib.washington.edu/exhibits/harmony**. Information on Japanese American internment in Arizona is available at **jeff .scott.tripod.com/japanese.html**, and information on internment in Utah is available at **lib.utah.edu/spc/photo/9066/9066.htm**.

Relevant films include *The Rabbit in the Moon,* Emiko Omori's beautiful and controversial examination of various ways in which Japanese Americans resisted internment, and *Of Civil Rights and Wrongs: The Fred Korematsu Story,* in which producer Eric Paul Fournier traces Korematsu's original case and the efforts by Peter Irons and a team of Japanese American lawyers to get the conviction overturned.

CHAPTER 10

Decision Making on the Brink

Presidential Recordings of the Cuban Missile Crisis

President John Kennedy was still in his bathrobe and slippers when his National Security advisor, McGeorge Bundy, brought him the photographs showing construction of nuclear missile sites on the island of Cuba—ninety miles off the Florida coast. It was Tuesday, October 16, 1962, Day One of the thirteen-day ordeal known as the Cuban missile crisis. Kennedy told Bundy to call a meeting that morning with fifteen of his trusted advisors, and he called his brother Robert, the attorney general. "We have some big trouble," announced the president. "I want you over here."

Fidel Castro had seized power in Cuba during the socialist revolution of 1959, just two years before Kennedy was sworn in as president in January 1961, and Cuba had been a thorn in Kennedy's side since the start of his administration. In April 1961, Kennedy had approved a plan by the Central Intelligence Agency (CIA) to secretly subsidize 1,500 Cuban exiles who believed they could invade their homeland by landing at the Bay of Pigs, incite a general uprising among the people, and overthrow Castro and his Soviet-friendly regime. The plan was doomed by biased information and poor planning; 51,000 of Castro's militia met the invaders, killing 115 and capturing 1,200. President Kennedy walked away from the humiliating incident determined to base future decisions on accurate information, thorough discussion, and candid advice from advisors he could trust.

Kennedy had run for president as a cold warrior who would close the unfavorable "missile gap" between U.S. and Soviet nuclear capacity and stand tough against Soviet-sponsored communism in satellite states such as Cuba. Once he came into office, Kennedy learned that there was no missile gap; the United States had many times more nuclear weapons than the Soviets, but

Soviet leader Nikita Khrushchev was a formidable political foe who was not cowed by U.S. military might. During the spring and summer of 1962, Khrushchev had been pressing the United States to give up West Berlin, the noncommunist half of a divided city that lay within Soviet-controlled East Germany; Khrushchev had told one American official that the Soviets could "swat your ass" if the United States chose to fight for Berlin. In Kennedy's judgment, Soviet actions in places like Cuba were merely tactical moves in the real cold war contest over control of Europe. The president believed that the Soviets would risk nuclear war for Berlin but would not risk war over Cuba. Indeed, in the eighteen months between the Bay of Pigs and the Cuban missile crisis, the Kennedy administration had developed Operation Mongoose, which included military plans to invade Cuba and assassinate Castro. When the Cubans and Soviets leveled charges of covert plans, the United States denied such activity but did not fear Soviet retaliation if these plans succeeded.

In the weeks leading up to the Cuban missile crisis, Kennedy had vigorously rejected Republican claims that the Soviets were pouring offensive weapons into Cuba. All of the CIA data supported the Soviets' public insistence that the weapons they were shipping to Cuba were purely "defensive," and Khrushchev's private assurances to Kennedy reinforced the president's view that the Soviets would not take unnecessary risks in the Western Hemisphere. Still, September polling data showed that while 80 percent of American respondents generally approved of Kennedy's foreign policy performance, 63 percent doubted that he was standing firm enough on the weapons situation in Cuba. Kennedy answered his critics and asserted his cold warrior credentials by publicly announcing that "if Cuba should possess the capacity to carry out offensive actions against the United States, then the United States would act." Confident that the Soviet Union would not be provocative in Cuba, Kennedy did not imagine he would ever have to match his warning with military action. A month later, he learned that just as his government had lied when denying subversive activity in Cuba, so had the Soviet government lied when denying the shipment of offensive nuclear weapons to Cuba.

Between October 16, when the U.S. government acquired evidence of nuclear weapons in Cuba, and October 28, when the Soviets agreed to remove those weapons, the world came as close as it had ever come to full-scale nuclear war. If the United States had chosen to abide by its word and "act" to remove the nuclear missiles on Cuba, the Soviets might have launched those missiles or its own missiles against U.S. cities, or the Soviets might have attacked Berlin or some other European capital. In either case, the United States might then have launched its nuclear missiles against the Soviets. As Kennedy noted at the time, any misstep could result in "the final failure"; Kennedy and Khrushchev would have presided over the end of the world.

The president's first decision in the crisis was to develop U.S. strategy in close consultation with the fifteen advisors he summoned to the White House on Day One. This group, called "ExComm"—the Executive Committee of the National Security Council—met every day, sometimes more than once a day, for the next twelve days. Determined not to repeat the mistakes of the Bay of

Figure 10.1 The Executive Committee of the National Security Council, 1962 This photo, taken during the Cuban missile crisis, shows the members of the Executive Committee. Seated to the president's left are Secretary of Defense Robert S. McNamara; Deputy Secretary of Defense Roswell Gilpatric; Chairman of the Joint Chiefs of Staff General Maxwell Taylor; Assistant Secretary of Defense Paul Nitze; Deputy United States Information Agency Director Donald Wilson; Special Counsel Theodore Sorensen; Special Assistant McGeorge Bundy; Secretary of the Treasury Douglas Dillon; Vice President Lyndon B. Johnson (hidden from view); Attorney General Robert F. Kennedy; Ambassador Llewellyn "Tommy" Thompson; Arms Control and Disarmament Agency Director William C. Foster; CIA Director John McCone (hidden from view); Under Secretary of State George Ball; and Secretary of State Dean Rusk. Source: Cecil Stoughton, White House/John Fitzgerald Kennedy Library.

Pigs, Kennedy sought a decision-making process that would provide him with candid debate on all possible options and outcomes using the most accurate data available. Kennedy participated fully in that debate, often pointing out how U.S. actions might appear to allies in Europe, who faced Soviet missiles every day and would think it a "mad act" to risk European security in order to remove a few missiles in Cuba. Kennedy never pointed out that the Soviet Union might be viewing covert U.S. action against Cuba as a sufficient threat to install missiles; he continued to think Berlin was the real issue. But he did coldly calculate that new missiles in Cuba did not actually alter the military balance of power. As the president put it, "It doesn't make any difference if you get blown up by an ICBM flying from the Soviet Union or one that was 90 miles away."

Still, Kennedy knew that the United States could not simply ignore the missiles. He had publicly stated that the United States would act if offensive weapons appeared in Cuba, so he had to either act or face a serious decline in U.S. prestige and power. In all of the debate over how to act, however, Kennedy was the person in the room most intent on eliminating the missiles from Cuba without sparking any armed conflict. Unlike his military advisors and, initially, his brother Robert, President Kennedy did not seek to use the crisis—and risk nuclear annihilation—to settle the score on Cuba.

For the first seven days of the crisis, the American people did not know about the missiles, and the Soviets and Cubans did not know that U.S. surveillance had detected them. Secrecy gave Kennedy a full week to deliberate with his advisors. They debated a range of responses, from a letter of protest to Khrushchev to an all-out surprise air strike and invasion. At the end of that clandestine week, the president went on national television to reveal the existence of Soviet missiles in Cuba and announce a measured response: the United States would "quarantine" Cuba through a naval blockade so that no more offensive weapons could be shipped in, and it would ask for a United Nations resolution demanding immediate elimination of all nuclear weapons on the island. In laying out this response, Kennedy made clear to the American public and to Khrushchev that the United States was prepared to take more aggressive action if necessary.

For the next four days, the world held its breath. The Soviets insisted that the weapons were a defensive deterrent against the constant threat of U.S. invasion, and United Nations diplomats shuttled between the U.S. and Soviet delegations. Meanwhile, some Cuban-bound Soviet ships seemed to be bowing to the blockade by turning around at sea, but construction on the nuclear missile sites in Cuba continued at an alarming pace. U.S. military maneuvers made clear to the Soviets that the White House was preparing for an attack on Cuba—and the Soviet Union. Kennedy was briefed on the (limited) civil defense aid available for citizens in urban areas in the event of a nuclear attack; there was no aid for rural citizens; only the Seattle region lay beyond the Cuban missiles' reach. Events seemed to be moving inexorably toward armed conflict.

Finally, late on Friday night, October 26, the eleventh day of the crisis, Kennedy received a thirteen-page private letter from Khrushchev offering to remove the missiles in exchange for a U.S. promise not to invade Cuba. The next morning, when Kennedy and his advisors were discussing how to respond to this offer, the news reported a public statement from Khrushchev offering to remove the Cuban missiles if the United States would remove fifteen Jupiter nuclear missiles stationed at the Turkish-Soviet border. To the men debating strategy in the White House, it appeared as if the fate of the planet rested on the response they fashioned to these mysteriously different offers. Saturday, October 27, Day Twelve of the crisis, was the longest and most difficult.

In popular culture treatments of the Cuban missile crisis—such as the Hollywood film *Thirteen Days*—a clever U.S. government finessed the crisis by simply ignoring Khrushchev's public demand for the trade of protective missiles in Turkey and responding only to the private request that the United States pledge not to invade Cuba. In real life, the resolution was more complicated.

President Kennedy advocated for acceptance of the Turkish missile deal, arguing that the United States planned to dismantle the outdated Jupiter missiles anyway and use newer missiles on Polaris submarines to protect Turkey. But ExComm members disagreed with the president; they disliked the political appearance of a Turkish-Cuban missile trade and pressed for acceptance only of Khrushchev's private demand that the United States vow not to invade Cuba.

While ExComm debated, Khrushchev became convinced that both the U.S. military and Fidel Castro were itching to go to war—even nuclear war. His alarm mounted with the Saturday afternoon news that his own Soviet officers in Cuba had violated no-shoot orders and had killed a U.S. Air Force surveillance pilot, thereby increasing pressure on the Kennedy administration to attack Cuba.

In the end, Kennedy and Khrushchev avoided war by agreeing to both of Khrushchev's offers. In a secret Saturday night meeting with the Soviet ambassador to the United States, Robert Kennedy followed up that day's public offer not to invade Cuba with private assurance that the United States would, in four or five months, remove the Jupiter missiles. Khrushchev publicly accepted the no-invasion offer on Sunday morning, even before he knew about the Jupiter missile offer. In April, the missiles were removed from the Turkish border, but the United States never signed a noninvasion agreement because Castro would not allow the United Nations to verify the absence of offensive weapons on his island.

On Monday, October 29, President Kennedy ordered the creation of a commemorative gift for his advisors; his secretary, Evelyn Lincoln; and his wife, Jacqueline. He asked for a small silver plaque simply displaying the month of October with a line highlighting the dates October 16 through October 28. For the moment, the crisis was over.

Using the Source: Presidential Tapes

The genuine threat of nuclear war in October 1962 provides ample reason for our continued interest in the Cuban missile crisis. But a companion reason is that the United States managed its side of this world crisis through a unique decision-making process: an ad hoc "ExComm" led by the president for a discrete period of time. Fortunately for those who study decision making, crucial portions of that process were preserved on tape recordings made in the Cabinet Room and the Oval Office. Presidential tape recordings became famous during Richard Nixon's Watergate scandal in the 1970s, but presidents had actually been taping selected Oval Office conversations since Franklin Roosevelt was in office in the 1930s.

John Kennedy installed a taping system in the summer before the missile crisis, probably to assist him in later writing his memoirs. To operate this simple system in either the Oval Office or the Cabinet Room, the president flipped switches hidden under his office desk or at his seat at the Cabinet Room table. Concealed microphones would then transmit conversations to the reel-to-reel tape recorder in the White House basement. The only people who knew about the system were the president, his brother Robert, Evelyn Lincoln, and the two Secret Service agents who had installed the system and changed the reels of tape when they ran out.

Over the course of the thirteen-day Cuban missile crisis, President Kennedy recorded close to forty hours of discussion with his ExComm. This group came together in seventeen tape-recorded meetings that lasted from thirty minutes to four hours. Between meetings, the president attempted to attend to other business, but ExComm members worked virtually around the clock on the missile crisis, consulting with military and diplomatic experts to gather information and explore alternatives, punctuating their days and nights with catnaps in their offices, but constantly preparing for their meetings with the president.

The Kennedy tapes, whose existence became public in 1973 during the Watergate scandal, have allowed scholars to explore the decision-making process used in the White House to avert nuclear war in 1962. The tapes support Kennedy's own claim that, as a chief executive, "the last thing I want around here is a mutual admiration society." Following the Bay of Pigs debacle, which Kennedy blamed on inadequate interrogation of the plan, the president encouraged debate among his aides, explaining, "I want all the input, but when they don't give it to me, I've got to dig in their minds." According to Robert Lovett, who had served as secretary of defense under Harry Truman, "President Kennedy had a quality which I have rarely seen in the holder of the chief executive office; that is, a willingness to have the person whose advice he sought answer with complete frankness and, if necessary, bluntness."

The tape recordings from the Cuban missile crisis reveal Kennedy presiding over meetings that lacked a rigid agenda; discussion often shifted rapidly from one issue to another, and participation was nonhierarchical. The president frequently pulled the discussion back to the topic of most immediate concern to him, but older ExComm members accustomed to a more structured approach worried that the seminar-like discussions of an impending nuclear holocaust were dangerously inefficient. Because the crisis ended peacefully, however, Kennedy's method earned respect as a way to air creative alternatives and devise solutions that best integrate different ideas.

What Can Presidential Tapes Tell Us?

The most obvious advantage of presidential tapes is that they are unscripted, candid, and in the moment. They capture as no other document could the actual process President Kennedy employed to elicit an array of strategic options from his expert, but very scared, advisors. Any effort to label some of Kennedy's debating advisors as warmongering "hawks" and others as conflict-averse "doves" is challenged by the evidence on the tapes, which show that different individuals took different stances at different times. The tapes show plans evolving in response to specific developments and reveal participants revising their positions in the face of new evidence or arguments. They also show the mounting fatigue and anxiety as the days wore on; sentence structure suffered, ExComm members increasingly interrupted one another, and shorthand references to previous discussions were more frequent. These qualities give the tapes an immediacy and authenticity missing from carefully written recollections.

Consider, for example, this set of exchanges on Saturday, October 27, the most stressful day of the crisis, when ExComm members were debating the merits of Khrushchev's two offers: either that the United States pledge not to invade Cuba or that the United States remove missiles from Turkey.

President Kennedy knows he is repeating his position

PRESIDENT KENNEDY: I think it would be better . . . to get clarification from the Soviet Union of what they're talking about. . . . As I say, you're going to find a lot of people think this [Turkish missile offer] is a rather reasonable position. . . .

Attorney General Robert Kennedy admits he is just working out the argument in his head

Before the crisis, and in the first two days of the crisis, Robert Kennedy was a staunch advocate for invading Cuba. Has he forgotten the invasion plans he helped design? Has he changed his mind?

ROBERT KENNEDY: . . . I haven't refined this at all—but he's [privately] offered us this arrangement in Cuba—that he will withdraw the bases in Cuba for assurances that we don't intend to invade Cuba. We've always given those assurances. We'd be glad to give them again. . . . The question of the Turkish bases . . . has nothing to do with the security of the Western Hemisphere . . . [but] we will withdraw the bases from Turkey if . . . you withdraw your invasion bases in the Soviet Union. . . .

Is the president's brother trying to expand U.S. gains by reducing the number of Soviet bases?

BUNDY: I think it's too complicated, Bobby.

What is happening to the free give-and-take of ideas?

ROBERT KENNEDY [sharply]: Well, I don't think it is.

PRESIDENT KENNEDY: . . . The first thing that you want to emphasize before you go into details is that the [unclear] 24 hours, that work's going to stop today before we talk about anything. . . . The other thing is not to have the Turks make any statement so that this thing— Khrushchev puts it out, and the next thing the Turks say they won't accept it. . . . Now, how long will it take for us to get in touch with the Turks?

How does this comment convey the president's response to his brother's proposal?

These unstructured and wide-ranging discussions offer a fascinating case of actual decision making but have a real disadvantage as a source of information: they are disorganized and repetitive. ExComm members might be exploring the air strike option one moment and then asking whether every ship's crew patrolling the quarantine zone included a Russian speaker and then speculating on developments at the United Nations. Sometimes, ExComm members discuss two or three things at once; often, they repeat points that have been made before and will be made again. As a result, it is difficult to track isolated topics through the 700-page written transcript of the missile crisis tapes.

Another disadvantage to these voluminous recordings is that they offer an incomplete record in at least two ways. First, not everything that transpired in the U.S. government during the crisis was taped: important meetings were held outside the Oval Office and Cabinet Room; President Kennedy did not flip on the tape recorder for every meeting in the Oval Office (though he did record all Cabinet Room meetings); and some discussions end abruptly because the Secret Service agents did not realize when a tape had run out. The tapes are also an incomplete record of the crisis because they cannot tell us what was going on in Moscow or in Havana; in order to get the Soviet and Cuban sides of the story, we must turn to the notes and recollections of non-American participants.

A final disadvantage of the tapes as a historical source is that the poor quality of the original recordings makes it difficult to decipher exact phrasings. This has caused considerable dispute among historians who use the tapes. Everyone agrees that mistakes are inevitable, even with our modern capacity to digitize and amplify, but there are legitimate disputes over the words spoken in particularly fuzzy sections and equally legitimate disputes over whether isolated transcription problems affect the overall record. In the last crunch of the crisis, for example, did Secretary McNamara suggest "an eye for an eye" or "half an eye for an eye?" Does it matter? Historians are still debating that moment on the tapes, as well as others.

Questions to Ask

In the excerpts from the tapes provided here, you can see the Kennedy decision-making process that still fascinates students of leadership style. You can also engage with two of the main issues that occupied ExComm's attention during the crisis: What course of immediate action will be strong and threatening but not ignite nuclear war? What response to Khrushchev's two offers is most likely to resolve the crisis in a way favorable to the United States and its European allies?

- What were ExComm's reasons for not immediately attacking the Cuban missile sites?
- Why did the United States not publicly agree to remove old Jupiter missiles in Turkey?
- How do tape recordings of conversation seem different from transcripts of a formal debate in, say, the U.S. Congress?
- What role did President Kennedy play in these discussions?
- Were ExComm members disrespectful of President Kennedy?

Source Analysis Table

The following table allows you to keep track of selected participants' views on the key debate in two early meetings (October 16 and October 18) and in two of the last ExComm meetings (October 27). Not all fifteen ExComm members are included in these excerpts.

ExComm Member	October 16 Should U.S. react to Cuban missiles? If so, how?	October 18 Should U.S. conduct air strikes? If not, what alternatives?	October 27 Should U.S. ignore second Khrushchev communication? Why? How?
President John Kennedy			
Robert McNamara, Secretary of Defense			
Dean Rusk, Secretary of State			
McGeorge Bundy, National Security Advisor			
Edwin Martin, Assistant Secretary of State for Inter-American Affairs			
General Maxwell Taylor, Chair, Joint Chiefs of Staff			

(continued)

ExComm Member	October 16 Should U.S. react to Cuban missiles? If so, how?	October 18 Should U.S. conduct air strikes? If not, what alternatives?	October 27 Should U.S. ignore second Khrushchev communication? Why? How?
Llewellyn "Tommy" Thompson, U.S. Ambassador-at-Large			
Robert F. Kennedy, Attorney General			
George W. Ball, Under Secretary of State			
Paul H. Nitze, Assistant Secretary of Defense for International Security Affairs			
Ted Sorensen, Kennedy aide and speechwriter			

To download and print this table, visit the book companion site at **bedfordstmartins.com/brownshannon**.

The Source: Presidential Tape Recordings from the Cuban Missile Crisis, 1962

The portions of the ExComm meetings included here have been excerpted from much broader, more lengthy discussions so that you can focus on particular topics and arguments.

1   *Tuesday, October 16, 6:30 P.M.* (Day One of the crisis; second ExComm meeting of the day)

> ExComm is trying to determine if the intelligence on the missiles in Cuba is accurate and what action, if any, to take. General Marshall "Pat" Carter (deputy director of the CIA) is briefing ExComm on the reconnaissance photos taken of the missile sites the night before.

PRESIDENT KENNEDY: General, how long would you say we had before these, at least to the best of your ability for the ones we now know, will be ready to fire?

GENERAL CARTER: Well, our people estimate that they could be fully operational within two weeks. . . .[1]

ROBERT MCNAMARA [Secretary of Defense]: That wouldn't rule out the possibility that one of them might be operational very much sooner.

[President Kennedy queries Carter on plans for more surveillance flights the next day. — Eds.]

PRESIDENT KENNEDY: There isn't any question in your mind, however, that it is a medium-range missile [MRBM]?

CARTER: No. There's no question in our minds at all. . . .

MCGEORGE BUNDY [National Security Advisor]: How do we really know what these missiles are, and what their range is, Pat? I don't mean to go behind your judgment here, except that there's one thing that would be really catastrophic, [which] would be to make a judgment here on a bad guess as to whether these things are — We mustn't do that. . . .

---

[1]In these excerpts, ellipses (i.e., . . .) tell you that words from the transcript have been deleted in order to condense the material for this chapter. Dashes (i.e., —) tell you that the speaker simply trailed off. Where the transcribers could not tell what the speaker was saying, you'll see [unclear].

Source: The Kennedy Tapes: Inside the White House during the Cuban Missile Crisis, edited by Philip Zelikow, Timothy Naftali, and Ernest R. May (Cambridge, Mass.: Belknap Press of Harvard University Press, 2001).

McNAMARA: I tried to prove today . . . that these were *not* MRBM's. And I worked long on it. I got our experts out, and I could not find evidence that would support any conclusion *other* than that they are MRBM's. . . .

[Discussion turns to the options for dealing with these new missile installations, including the possibility of a surprise air strike. — Eds.]

DEAN RUSK [Secretary of State]: I would not think they would use a nuclear weapon [in response to an air strike by the United States] unless they're prepared to generate a nuclear war. I don't think, I just don't see that possibility . . . we could be just utterly wrong—but we've never really believed that Khrushchev would take on a general nuclear war over Cuba.

BUNDY: May I ask a question in that context?

KENNEDY: We certainly have been wrong about what he [Khrushchev] is trying to do in Cuba. There isn't any doubt about that. Not many of us thought that he was going to put MRBM's on Cuba. . . .

BUNDY: But the question I would like to ask is . . . what is the strategic impact on the position of the United States of MRBM's in Cuba? How gravely does this change the strategic balance?

McNAMARA: Mac, I asked the Chiefs that this afternoon, in effect. And they said "substantially." My own personal view is: Not at all. . . .

KENNEDY: . . . It doesn't make any difference if you get blown up by an ICBM flying from the Soviet Union or one that was 90 miles away. Geography doesn't mean that much. . . .

EDWIN MARTIN [Assistant Secretary of State for Inter-American Affairs]: It's the psychological factor. . . .

KENNEDY: What's that again, Ed? What are you saying?

MARTIN: Well, it's the psychological factor that we have sat back and let them do it to us. That is more important than the direct threat. . . .

KENNEDY: Last month I said we weren't going to [allow Soviet missiles in Cuba]. Last month I *should* have said that we don't care. But when I said we're *not* going to [allow it], and then they go ahead and do it, and then we do nothing, then I would think that our risks increase. . . . What difference does it make? They've got enough to blow us up now anyway. I think it's just a question of—After all, this is a political struggle as much as military. Well, so where are we now? . . .

McNAMARA: Mr. President, we need to do two things, it seems to me. First we need to develop a specific [air] strike plan limited to the missiles and the nuclear storage sites. . . . Since you have indicated some interest in that possibility, we ought to provide you that option. . . . But that's an easy job to do. The second thing we ought to do, it seems to me, as a government, is to consider the consequences. I don't believe we have considered the consequences of any of these actions satisfactorily. And because we haven't considered the consequences, I'm not sure we're taking all the action we ought to take now to minimize those. I don't know quite what kind of a world we live in after we've struck Cuba, and we've started it. . . . How do we stop at that point? I don't know the answer to this. . . .

GENERAL MAXWELL TAYLOR [Chairman of the Joint Chiefs of Staff]: Mr. President, I should say that the Chiefs and the commanders feel so strongly about the dangers inherent in a limited strike that they would prefer taking *no* military action rather than take a limited strike. . . . My inclination is all against the invasion, but nonetheless trying to eliminate as effectively as possible every weapon that can strike the United States. . . .

ROBERT KENNEDY [arguing for invasion]: Assume we go in and knock these [missile] sites out. . . . Where are we six months from now? . . . If you're going to get into it at all . . . we should just get into it and get it over with, and take our losses. And if he wants to get into a war over this. . . .

McNAMARA: Mr. President, that is why we ought to put on paper the alternative plans and the probable, possible consequences. . . . Even if we disagree, then put in both views. Because the consequences of these actions have not been thought through clearly. The one that the Attorney General just mentioned is illustrative of that. . . .

TAYLOR: Mr. President, I personally would just urge you not to set a schedule . . . until all the intelligence that could be—

KENNEDY: That's right. I just wanted, I thought, we ought to be moving. I don't want to waste any time. . . . I just think we ought to be ready to do something, even if we decide not to do it.

2   *Thursday, October 18, 11:10 A.M.* (Day Three of the crisis; first ExComm meeting of the day)

ExComm is considering the military's advice to proceed with a massive air strike and debating whether this attack should be a surprise "first strike" or one preceded by a clear warning to Khrushchev.

RUSK: . . . I think the American people will willingly undertake great danger and, if necessary, great suffering, if they have the deep feeling that we've done everything that was reasonably possible to determine whether this trip was necessary . . . [all of which] will militate in favor of a consultation with Khrushchev. . . . There is the possibility, only a possibility, that Khrushchev might realize that he's got to back down on this. We can't be—I have no reason to expect that. This looks like a very serious and major commitment on his part. But at least it will take that point out of the way for the historical record, and just might have in it the seeds of prevention of a great conflict. . . .

LLEWELLYN E. "TOMMY" THOMPSON [U.S. Ambassador-at-Large]: . . . If you do give him [Khrushchev] notice, the thing I would fear the most is a threat to Turkey and Italy to take action, which would cause us considerable difficulty [unclear]. . . .

BUNDY: What is your preference, Tommy?

THOMPSON: My preference is this blockade plan. . . . I think it's highly doubtful the Russians would resist a blockade against military weapons, particularly offensive ones, if that's the way we pitched it to the world.

PRESIDENT KENNEDY: What do you do with the weapons already there?

THOMPSON: Demand they're dismantled, and say that we're going to maintain constant surveillance, and if they are armed, we would then take them out. . . .

PRESIDENT KENNEDY: Of course then he would say: "Well, if you do that, then we will—"

THOMPSON: I think [Khrushchev] would make a lot of threatening language but in very vague terms. . . .

PRESIDENT KENNEDY: Yeah. I think it more likely he would just grab Berlin. . . .

THOMPSON: I think that or, if we just made the first strike, then I think his answer would be, very probably, to take out one of our bases in Turkey, and make it quick too and then say that: "Now I want to talk." I think the whole purpose of this exercise is to build up to talks with you, in which we try to negotiate out the bases. There are a lot of things that point to that. One that struck me very much is, if it's so easy to camouflage these things or to hide them in the woods, why didn't they do it in the first place? They surely expected us to see them at some stage. That, it seems to me would point to the fact their purpose was for preparation of negotiations.

PRESIDENT KENNEDY: The only offer we could make, it seems to me, that would have any sense, according to him, would be the—giving him some out, would be our Turkey missiles. . . .

McNAMARA: If there is a strike without preliminary discussion with Khrushchev . . . I think we must assume we'll kill several hundred Soviet citizens [working at the missile sites]. Having killed several hundred Soviet citizens, what kind of response does Khrushchev have open to him?

GEORGE W. BALL [Under Secretary of State]: . . . [If we take] a course of action where we strike without warning, that's like Pearl Harbor. It's the kind of conduct that one might expect of the Soviet Union. It is not conduct that one expects of the United States. And I have a feeling that this 24 hours [warning] to Khrushchev is really indispensable.

PRESIDENT KENNEDY: Then if he says, "Well, if you do that, we're going to grab Berlin." The point is, he's probably going to grab Berlin anyway.

BALL: Sure. Go ahead.

PRESIDENT KENNEDY: He's going to take Berlin anyway. . . .

McNAMARA: Well, when you're talking about taking Berlin, what do you mean exactly? Does he take it with Soviet troops?

PRESIDENT KENNEDY: That's what it would seem to me.

McNAMARA: . . . We have U.S. troops there. What do they do?

TAYLOR: They fight.

McNAMARA: They fight. I think that's perfectly clear.

PRESIDENT KENNEDY: And they get overrun.

McNAMARA: Yes, they get overrun, exactly.

UNIDENTIFIED: Well, you have a direct confrontation.

ROBERT KENNEDY: Then what do you do? . . .

UNIDENTIFIED: It's then general war. Consider the use of—

PRESIDENT KENNEDY: You mean a nuclear exchange?

GENERAL TAYLOR: Guess you have to. . . .

KENNEDY: Now, the question really is what action we take which lessens the chances of a nuclear exchange, which obviously is the final failure. . . . Let's just think. We do the message to Khrushchev and tell him that if work continues, et cetera, et cetera. At the same time, launch the blockade. If the work continues, that we go in and take them out. . . .

3   *Saturday, October 27, 10:00* A.M. (Day Twelve of the crisis; first ExComm meeting of the day)

The naval quarantine of Cuba has been in effect since October 24. ExComm is meeting to discuss Premier Khrushchev's Friday night proposal that the Soviets remove the missiles from Cuba in exchange for a U.S. promise not to invade Cuba. Suddenly, the president is handed a news release that has just come over the wire.

PRESIDENT KENNEDY [reading from the news release]: "President Khrushchev told President Kennedy yesterday he would withdraw offensive weapons from Cuba if the United States withdrew rockets from Turkey."

BUNDY: No he didn't. . . .

TED SORENSEN [Kennedy aide and speechwriter]: He didn't really say that, did he?

PRESIDENT KENNEDY: That may not be—He may be putting out another letter. . . . Pierre, that wasn't the letter we received was it?

PIERRE SALINGER [Press Secretary]: No. I read it pretty carefully. It doesn't read that way to me either. . . .

RUSK: I really think we ought to talk about the political part of this thing. . . . The Turkish thing hasn't been injected into the conversation [at the United Nations], and it wasn't in the letter last night. It thus appears to be something quite new.

McNAMARA: This is what worries me about the whole deal. If you go through that letter, to a layman it looks to be full of holes. I think my proposal would be to keep—

BUNDY: Keeping the heat on. . . .

McNAMARA: Keep the heat on. This is why I would recommend the 2 daylight and one night [surveillance] mission. . . .

PRESIDENT KENNEDY: I think what I'd like to do is—I think we ought to go ahead, so it's all right with me. I think we might have one more conversation about [the nighttime mission] however, at about 6:00, just in case during the day we get something more. . . .

In case this [newly reported Khrushchev proposal] *is* an accurate statement, where are we with our conversations with the Turks about the withdrawal of these—

PAUL H. NITZE [Assistant Secretary of Defense for International Security Affairs]:
[The Turks] say this is absolutely anathema and is a matter of prestige and
politics. . . . I would suggest that what you do is to say that we're prepared
only to discuss *Cuba* at this time. After the Cuban thing is settled we can
be prepared to discuss anything. . . .

BUNDY: It's very odd, Mr. President. If he's changed his terms from a long letter to you . . . only last night, set in the purely Cuban context . . . there's
nothing wrong with our posture in sticking to that line.

PRESIDENT KENNEDY: But let's wait, and let's assume that this is an accurate report of what he's now proposing this morning. There may have been some
changes over there.

BUNDY: I still think he's in a difficult position to change it overnight, having
sent you a personal communication on the other line.

PRESIDENT KENNEDY: Well, now, let's say he has changed it. This is his latest
position.

BUNDY: Well, I would answer back saying that, "I would prefer to deal with
your—your interesting proposals of last night."

PRESIDENT KENNEDY: Well now. . . . We're going to be in an unsupportable position on this matter if this becomes his proposal. In the first place, last
year we tried to get the missiles out of there because they're not militarily
useful, number one. Number two, it's going to be—to any man at the
United Nations or any other rational man, it will look like a very fair trade.

NITZE: I don't think so. . . . I think you would get support from the United
Nations on the proposition: "Deal with this Cuban thing. We'll talk about
other things later." I think everybody else is worried that they'll be included in this great big trade if it goes beyond Cuba. . . .

PRESIDENT KENNEDY: Well, have we gone to the Turkish government before
this came out this week? I've talked about it now for a week. Have we had
any conversations in Turkey, with the Turks?

RUSK: . . . We've not actually talked to the Turks.

BALL: . . . If we talked to the Turks, I mean, this would be an extremely unsettling business.

PRESIDENT KENNEDY: Well, *this* is unsettling *now,* George, because he's got us
in a pretty good spot here. Because most people would regard this as not
an unreasonable proposal. I'll just tell you that. In fact, in many ways—

BUNDY: But what *most* people, Mr. President?

PRESIDENT KENNEDY: I think you're going to find it very difficult to explain
why we are going to take hostile military action in Cuba, against these
sites . . . [when] he's saying: "If you'll get yours out of Turkey, we'll get ours
out of Cuba." I think we've got a very touchy point here.

BUNDY: I don't see why we pick that track when he's offered us the other track
within the last 24 hours. You think the public one is serious?

PRESIDENT KENNEDY: I think you have to assume this is their new and latest
positions, and it's a public one. . . . I think we have to be thinking about

what our position is going to be on *this* one, because this is the one that's before us, and before the world.

SORENSEN: As between the two, I think it's clear that practically everyone here would favor the private proposal.

RUSK: We're not being offered a choice. . . .

PRESIDENT KENNEDY: But seriously, there are disadvantages to the private one, which is this guarantee of Cuba. But in any case, this is now his official one. . . .

NITZE: Isn't it possible that they are going on a dual track, one a public track and the other a private track? The private track is related to the Soviets and Cuba, and the public track is one that's in order to confuse the public scene with additional pressures.

PRESIDENT KENNEDY: It's possible.

THOMPSON: I think, personally, that [the public] statement is the one the Soviets take seriously.

NITZE: Fight the Turkish one with the best arguments we can. I'd handle this thing so we can continue on the real track, which is to try to get the missiles out of Cuba pursuant to the private negotiation. . . .

PRESIDENT KENNEDY: I think it would be better . . . to get clarification from the Soviet Union of what they're talking about. . . . As I say, you're going to find a lot of people think this is a rather reasonable position. . . .

ROBERT KENNEDY: . . . I haven't refined this at all—but he's [privately] offered us this arrangement in Cuba—that he will withdraw the bases in Cuba for assurances that we don't intend to invade Cuba. We've always given those assurances. We'd be glad to give them again. . . . The question of the Turkish bases . . . has nothing to do with the security of the Western Hemisphere . . . [but] we will withdraw the bases from Turkey if . . . you withdraw your invasion bases in the Soviet Union. . . .

BUNDY: I think it's too complicated, Bobby.

ROBERT KENNEDY [sharply]: Well, I don't think it is.

PRESIDENT KENNEDY: . . . The first thing that you want to emphasize before you go into details is that the [unclear] 24 hours, that work's going to stop today before we talk about anything. . . . The other thing is not to have the Turks make any statement so that this thing—Khrushchev puts it out, and the next thing the Turks say they won't accept it. . . . Now, how long will it take for us to get in touch with the Turks?

UNIDENTIFIED: I'll find out [unclear], Mr. President. We'll see.

BALL: I think it's going to be awfully hard to get the Turks not to say [that the Soviet offer is unacceptable].

PRESIDENT KENNEDY: No, but we can give them some guidance. . . .

BUNDY: I think it will be very important to say at least that the current threat to peace is not in Turkey; it is in Cuba. There's no pain in saying that, even if you're going to make a trade later on. Then I think we *should* say that the public . . . message is at variance with other proposals which have been put forward within the last 12 hours. . . .

PRESIDENT KENNEDY: Let's not kid ourselves. They've got a very good proposal, which is the reason they made it public—

BUNDY: . . . Last night's message was Khrushchev's. And this [public] one is his own hard-nosed people overruling him. They didn't like what he said to you last night. Nor would I, if I were a Soviet hard-nose. . . .

PRESIDENT KENNEDY: They've got a good product. This one is going to be very tough. . . . If we are forced to take action, this will be, in my opinion, not a blank check, but a pretty good check [for the Soviets] to take action in Berlin on the grounds that we are only unreasonable, emotional people, that this is a reasonable trade, and we ought to take advantage of it. . . .

4 *Saturday, October 27, 4:00 P.M.* (Day Twelve of the crisis; second ExComm meeting of the day)

In this four-hour meeting, ExComm members are working on the wording of a letter to Khrushchev and still debating whether the United States should address only the private offer to trade missiles for a noninvasion pledge or address the public offer to trade off missiles in Cuba for missiles in Turkey.

THOMPSON: Mr. President, if we go on the basis of a trade, which I gather is somewhat in your mind, we end up, it seems to me, with the Soviets still in Cuba with planes and technicians and so on, even though the missiles are out. And that would surely be unacceptable. . . .

PRESIDENT KENNEDY: Yeah, but . . . I'm just thinking about what we're going to have to do in a day or so, which is 500 [air] sorties . . . and possibly an invasion, all because we wouldn't take the missiles out of Turkey. We all know how quickly everybody's courage goes when the blood starts to flow, and that's what's going to happen . . . when we start these things and they grab Berlin. . . . Let's not kid ourselves. . . . Today it sounds great to reject [the Turkey deal], but it's not going to after we do something. . . .

THOMPSON: I don't agree Mr. President. I think there's still a chance that we can get this [noninvasion of Cuba] line going.

PRESIDENT KENNEDY: That he'll back down? . . . [But] this other [Turkish] one, it seems to me, has become their public position, hasn't it?

THOMPSON: This may be just pressure on us. I meant to accept the other . . . noninvasion of Cuba. . . . The important thing for Khrushchev, it seems to me, is to be able to say: "I saved Cuba. I stopped an invasion." And he can get away with that if he wants to, and he's had a go at this Turkey thing, and we'll discuss that later. . . .

SORENSEN: In other words, Mr. President, your position is that once he meets this condition of the halting work and the inoperability, you're then prepared to go ahead on either the specific Cuban track or what we call a general détente [Turkish missile] track?

PRESIDENT KENNEDY: Yeah, now it all comes down [to] . . . whether we have to agree to his position of tying [Cuba to Turkey]. Tommy doesn't think we do.

I think that, having made it public, how can he take these missiles out of Cuba if we do nothing about Turkey?

BALL: You give him something else. . . . And the promise that when this is all over there can be a larger [unclear].

PRESIDENT KENNEDY: He's going to want to have that spelled out a little.

THOMPSON: His position, even in the public statement, is that this all started by our threat to Cuba. Now he's [able to say he] removed that threat. . . .

ROBERT KENNEDY: Well, the only thing is, we are proposing here the abandonment [unclear].

PRESIDENT KENNEDY: What? What? What are we proposing?

ROBERT KENNEDY: The abandonment of Cuba.

SORENSEN: No, we're just promising not to invade. . . .

[They continue to discuss the specific language of the letter to Khrushchev. They are working from a draft letter written by Adlai Stevenson, U.S. ambassador to the United Nations, and a draft they have been developing in the meeting. At this exhausted moment, a younger brother's teasing of his older brother breaks the tension.—Eds.]

BALL: I tell you Mr. President . . . I think if we could take our letter, introduce some of the elements of Adlai's letter in the last part of it, that might do it. I'm not sure how yet.

ROBERT KENNEDY: Why do we bother you [President Kennedy] with it? Why don't you guys work it out?

PRESIDENT KENNEDY: . . . There's no question [of] bothering me. I just think we're going to have to decide which letter to send.

ROBERT KENNEDY: Why don't we try to work it out without you being able to pick it apart.

[Prolonged laughter] . . .

PRESIDENT KENNEDY: The one you're going to have to worry about is Adlai, so you might as well work it out with him.

[Louder laughter]

SORENSEN: Actually, I think Bobby's formula is a good one. . . .

BUNDY: That's right, Mr. President. I think Bobby's notion of a concrete acceptance on our part of how we read last night's telegram is very important. . . .

TAYLOR: Mr. President, the [Joint Chiefs of Staff] have been in session during the afternoon. . . . The recommendation they give is as follows: That the big [air] strike, Oplan [Operations Plan] 312, be executed no later than Monday morning, the 29th, unless there is irrefutable evidence in the meantime that offensive weapons are being dismantled and rendered inoperable. That the execution of the strike plan be followed by the execution of 316, the invasion plan, 7 days later. . . .

PRESIDENT KENNEDY: Well that's the next place to go. But let's get this letter [sent to Khrushchev].

[The final letter focuses on immediate cessation of missile construction and elimi-nation of the missiles in exchange for a U.S. promise not to invade. It says that dis-cussion of "other armaments" must involve U.S. allies in the North Atlantic Treaty Organization and can be discussed once the Cuban missile crisis is settled. In pri-vate, that evening, Attorney General Robert Kennedy assures Soviet ambassador Anatoly Dobrynin that the United States will remove the Jupiter missiles from Turkey in a few months. — Eds.]

Analyzing Presidential Tapes

1. On October 16, what were the arguments for and against a U.S. military reac-tion to the installation of Cuban missiles?

2. On October 18, what are the arguments for and against an unannounced U.S. air strike? What alternatives did ExComm members propose?

3. Why did ExComm members not want to respond publicly to Khrushchev's sec-ond communication?

4. Some say these tapes reveal an egalitarian decision-making style. Do you find President Kennedy operating as one among equals, or do you see him playing a stronger leadership role?

5. Ask older friends or relatives what they remember about the Cuban missile cri-sis. Did the family stock up on food? Did they have a bomb shelter? Were there more bomb drills at school? Do they recall Kennedy's televised address? Do they recall feeling afraid? Write up a brief summary of what you learned from your interviews.

The Rest of the Story

In November 2002, Cuban missile crisis participants from the United States, Russia, and Cuba marked the fortieth anniversary of the event with a confer-ence in Havana, Cuba. These government officials gathered for three days, as they had gathered five times before, since 1987, to compare their memories of the event and to test their memories against newly released government docu-ments. The conference proceedings, combined with documents from the time and participants' written recollections, have produced a rich record of the Cuban missile crisis, along with three basic conclusions. First and foremost, the world was even closer to a nuclear holocaust in October 1962 than anybody knew at the time. Second, the Kennedy decision-making process, while valu-able for its caution, was not entirely rational, as some political scientists have claimed. Third, ExComm's caution was not the sole reason that disaster was averted. Caution on Khrushchev's part was equally important. Although risky, aggressive action by both the U.S. government and the Soviets had caused the crisis, the leaders of both countries recognized the danger in the moment and took bold, sober action to avert it.

We now know that Cuba possessed missiles equipped with nuclear warheads before the crisis began and that those weapons were positioned to fire at the United States in the event of an invasion. We also now know that there were forty-two concealed nuclear warheads in Cuba and that U.S. surveillance had not been able to locate all of them, so an air strike would not have eliminated the threat. Finally, we know now, but did not know at the time, that the Cubans possessed tactical nuclear weapons that could be used in battle against an invading U.S. military and that U.S. estimates of 5,000 Soviet military personnel in Cuba was low—by a factor of ten. Khrushchev knew all of this in October 1962 and knew how close the United States was to taking military action. Indeed, unbeknownst to President Kennedy, the U.S. military was engaged in covert action on the ground in Cuba during the last weekend of the crisis.

Was ExComm's response to the information it did possess entirely rational? Was this a cool and calculated decision-making process as some have argued? James G. Blight, of Brown University, says no. Blight, a key organizer of the conferences for missile crisis participants, has concluded from those conference discussions, his own study of the ExComm tape transcripts, and government documents that the nonrational emotion of fear operated during the crisis in a beneficial way. Rather than causing the Americans to take rash action, genuine fear for the survival of the planet caused the members of ExComm to exercise more caution than they had in their pre-crisis calculations about how to maneuver in the cold war's global chess game. Cold logic could have caused the United States to follow the established military protocol in this situation and quickly attack. Logic could also have led to the conclusion that the Soviet Union would not risk war for Cuba. It was fear of others' irrationality and fear of the known outcome of nuclear war that caused ExComm to take a cautious approach.

Throughout the crisis, President Kennedy knew better than anyone that his decision-making process would be praised only if the human race survived to tell the tale. Afterward, he knew how important it was that Khrushchev had proved equally afraid of nuclear annihilation and was willing, at the crucial moment, to give up the Cuban missiles. But if he was not willing to defend those missiles, why had Khrushchev sent them to Cuba in the first place? Here, rationality and irrationality apparently cooperated. The Soviet leader rationally wanted to aid Castro, who had solid evidence of U.S. plans to invade; he wanted to use Cuba as a pawn in the Berlin chess game (just as Kennedy surmised); and he wanted to compensate for the deterrence gap between the Soviets' fifty intercontinental nuclear missiles and America's 500 comparable missiles by placing forty-two less-expensive medium-range nuclear missiles near the U.S. coastline. Khrushchev's irrational belief that he could secretly install those missiles in Cuba without causing conflict with the United States derived from his reliance on false intelligence reports, his failure to carefully analyze probable U.S. reactions, and his unwillingness to expose his plan to debate among his advisors. Fortunately, the irrationality that ExComm members feared did not carry Khrushchev beyond the brink.

Popular culture treatments of the Cuban missile crisis perpetuate the myth that the United States was an innocent victim in this story, rather than a mature combatant in global cold war politics, and obscure the importance of the Soviet Union in cutting the public and private deals that averted disaster. Exposure to the complex conversations on the ExComm tape recordings helps correct these errors and reminds us that open communication and decent humility are valuable weapons in a nation's arsenal.

To Find Out More

The Presidential Recordings: John F. Kennedy: Volumes 1–3, The Great Crises (New York: W. W. Norton, 2001), published with a CD, is currently the most complete and accurate transcription of the ExComm tapes. Large portions of this transcription are also available in a concise edition titled *The Kennedy Tapes: Inside the White House during the Cuban Missile Crisis* (Cambridge, Mass.: Belknap Press of Harvard University Press, 2001). Edited by Philip Zelikow, Timothy Naftali, and Ernest R. May, these two editions correct transcription errors in the 1997 edition of *The Kennedy Tapes: Inside the White House during the Cuban Missile Crisis*, which was edited by Philip Zelikow and Ernest R. May. Both of the 2001 editions were published under the auspices of the Presidential Recordings Program of the Miller Center of Public Affairs at the University of Virginia. For more information on this program, go to: **millercenter.virginia .edu/programs/prp**. For an accessible sample of presidential tape recordings from the 1930s through the 1990s, see William Doyle, *Inside the Oval Office: The White House Tapes from FDR to Clinton* (New York: Kodansha America, 1999).

A brief, gripping narrative of the crisis, which makes extensive use of the ExComm tapes, is Sheldon M. Stern's *The Week the World Stood Still: Inside the Secret Cuban Missile Crisis* (Stanford, Calif.: Stanford University Press, 2005). Two works on John F. Kennedy that capture the crisis as it was experienced in the White House are Lawrence Freedman, *Kennedy's Wars: Berlin, Cuba, Laos, and Vietnam* (New York: Oxford University Press, 2000) and Richard Reeves, *President Kennedy: Profile of Power* (New York: Simon and Schuster, 1993). In *Awaiting Armageddon: How Americans Faced the Cuban Missile Crisis* (Chapel Hill: University of North Carolina Press, 2003), Alice L. George examines the domestic experience during the crisis and in its aftermath.

The Soviet and Cuban perspectives on the crisis are presented in Aleksandr Fursenko and Timothy Naftali, *"One Hell of a Gamble": Khrushchev, Castro, and Kennedy, 1958–1964* (New York: W. W. Norton, 1997). A close look at the Cuban perspective can be found in James G. Brenner, Philip Blight, James G. Blight, and Philip Brenner, *Sad and Luminous Days: Cuba's Secret Struggle with the Superpower after the Missile Crisis* (Lanham, M.D.: Rowman and Littlefield, 2002). The 1992 conference involving participants in retrospective discussions of the crisis is analyzed in James G. Allyn, James G. Blight, and others, *Cuba on the Brink: Castro, the Missile Crisis, and the Soviet Collapse* (Lanham, Md.: Rowman and Littlefield, 2002). James G. Blight's argument for the beneficial role of fear in the crisis appeared first in his book *The Shattered Crystal Ball* (Savage, Md.: Rowman and Littlefield, 1990).

The most influential American memoir about the crisis is Robert F. Kennedy's *Thirteen Days* (New York: W. W. Norton), first published in 1968 and reissued in 1999. Although the tape recordings call into question some of the attorney general's constructions in that memoir, the book effectively captures the mood of the moment.

The Cuban Missile Crisis, 1962 (New York: New Press, 1992), edited by Laurence Chang and Peter Kornbluh, presents some tape transcripts along with dozens of memos, cables, meeting notes, letters, and briefing papers. For recently declassified documents, audio clips from the ExComm meetings, and some of the photographs taken by reconnaissance aircraft of the missile installations in Cuba, visit the National Security Archive's Web site at **www2.gwu .edu/~nsarchiv/nsa/cuba_mis_cri**. More audio files of the ExComm meetings are available at **hpol.org/jfk/cuban**. For various points of view on the decision-making process in the White House, see **cubanmissilecrisis.org**. All of the official U.S. Department of State documents dealing with the crisis can be found at **state.gov/www/about_state/history/frusXI/index.html**.

CHAPTER 11

Speaking of Equality

The Senate Debate on the Civil Rights Act of 1964

"Abraham Lincoln emancipated the slaves," declared President John F. Kennedy in 1962, on the one hundredth anniversary of the Emancipation Proclamation, "but in this century, our Negro citizens have emancipated themselves." It was just this sort of celebratory rhetoric that convinced civil rights activists across America that their dynamic, young, articulate president was on their side and that he supported their grassroots uprising against segregation, discrimination, and racial prejudice. In truth, Kennedy wanted an end to all the street demonstrations, sit-ins, and freedom rides that were disrupting the political order of his administration. Shocking photos of Southern sheriffs turning dogs and hoses on peaceful black marchers created just the sort of cold war propaganda for the Soviet Union in Africa and Asia that Kennedy sought to avoid. And public demands from leaders like Martin Luther King Jr. that the federal government take strong action on civil rights threatened Kennedy's plan to keep racial politics out of his legislative deal making with Southern Democrats in Congress.

As much as he wanted to, though, President Kennedy could not control or curtail the civil rights movement. His administration's record between 1961 and 1963 reveals a reluctance to take political risks for the cause of racial justice, but Kennedy's public image as a supporter of civil rights encouraged activists to believe that this was the moment when black history in America could be turned around. It was the people's confidence that they could create change, not Kennedy's own initiatives, that ultimately forced the president to catch up with the civil rights movement. On June 11, 1963, two and a half years after making his inaugural pledge to fight for human rights "at home," Kennedy went on national television to declare that "the time has come for this nation to fulfill its promise" of equal rights for all, and to announce that he was sending a new civil rights bill to Congress. This speech culminated a week in which the U.S. Justice Department deployed the National Guard so that two black citizens of Alabama could exercise their right to enroll at the state's public university, and black and white citizens throughout the segregated South staged 160 separate pro–civil rights demonstrations. The civil rights bill that Kennedy submitted to Congress following his televised speech included not only voting rights and educational access but also a highly controversial "public accommodations" provision that outlawed racial segregation in places such as restaurants, hotels, theaters, and restrooms.

No black leaders had been included in drafting this civil rights bill. In segregated America in 1963, there were no black citizens in the U.S. Senate, only four blacks in the House of Representatives, just one African American advisor to the president, and a handful of blacks in the executive branch. The thousands of black citizens who lobbied and demonstrated for civil rights in the early 1960s pressed their suit right up against the halls of power, but they did not have a seat in those halls. Although Kennedy's rhetoric about blacks emancipating themselves was encouraging, the reality of power was different. If the racial system was going to change, if African Americans were going to peacefully gain rights in the United States, then the whites in the U.S. Congress had to vote to make that happen. In the summer of 1963, Kennedy was not optimistic about the votes in Congress. He warned a gathering of civil rights leaders at the White House that "we may all go down the drain" with a doomed civil rights bill. A. Philip Randolph, the seventy-four-year-old black leader and veteran lobbyist, told Kennedy, "It's going to be a crusade, then. And I think that nobody can lead that crusade but you, Mr. President."

Three months later, John F. Kennedy was dead, and his assassination meant that Lyndon Baines Johnson, from the thoroughly segregated state of Texas, was now president. Those who feared that Johnson's ascendancy meant the end of the civil rights bill did not consider that before he became Kennedy's vice president, Johnson (popularly known as LBJ) had been the most canny and persuasive Senate majority leader in U.S. history. LBJ had led the Senate in passing the 1957 and 1960 civil rights bills, which created the Civil Rights Commission and the civil rights division in the Department of Justice. Those who doubted LBJ's civil rights credentials were unaware that he had advised President Kennedy to take the high ground by declaring racial justice a moral imperative. He had also advised the Kennedy Democrats to give up negotiating with the Senate's Southern segregationists, who were all Democrats, and instead build alliances with moderate Northern Republicans who supported civil rights legislation.

As a Southerner, LBJ knew about racism and segregation in a way that Kennedy never could. He also knew from experience, as Kennedy did not, that America's blacks could wait no longer; as he told a Kennedy aide, they were "tired of this patient stuff and tired of this piecemeal stuff"; it was time to "pull out the cannon." Johnson believed that almost any problem could be solved by legislation, and he was typically prepared to use any tool at his disposal to achieve a legislative goal. When Kennedy's assassination thrust Johnson into the presidency, he waited only five days to announce that "no memorial oration or eulogy could more eloquently honor President Kennedy's memory than the earliest possible passage of the Civil Rights bill for which he fought so long." Although Kennedy had actually fought less than six months for the bill, LBJ appealed to Americans' grief for their martyred president in expressing his hope "that the tragedy and torment of these terrible days will bind us together in a new fellowship, making us one people in our hour of sorrow."

When the second session of the Eighty-eighth Congress opened in January 1964, everyone—including the Southern segregationists in the House and Senate—knew that the political ground had shifted irrevocably. Now, polls showed that 62 percent of Americans supported civil rights legislation; the Johnson White House was choreographing what the *Congressional Quarterly* called "some of the most intensive and effective behind-the-scenes lobbying in modern legislative history"; dozens of organizations—from the NAACP and the AFL-CIO to the National Council of Churches of Christ and the National Council of Jewish Women—were lobbying for the bill; and both Democrats and Republicans in Congress were stepping over party lines to deliver the

Figure 11.1 Bus Station in Durham, North Carolina, May 1940 *This photograph depicts everyday life in the segregated South before U.S. entry into World War II. Wherever they went in the segregated region, African Americans faced an unrelenting array of signs designating "white" and "colored" spaces that reminded them that whites drew the lines that most blacks did not dare cross. One wonders if the photographer meant to capture the ironic ad for an article on "Hitler's Love Life." In the coming years, the U.S. fight against Nazi racism would cast segregation as un-American.* Source: Library of Congress.

legislation. In this new political atmosphere, Southern Democrats lost their traditional control over Northern Democrats. Since the start of the New Deal in 1932, Southern Democrats had supported a strong federal role in programs like Social Security and agricultural subsidies; in exchange, Northerners did not use federal power to challenge Southern states' prerogative to limit black voting rights and to limit blacks' access to public accommodations. Northern Democrats' obedience to this thirty-year political arrangement ceased in 1963 when the Kennedy and Johnson administrations advocated a new coalition with pro–civil rights Northern Republicans.

The Kennedy administration, on LBJ's advice, had urged the House of Representatives to take up the civil rights bill prior to the Senate considering it. The bill had a better chance in the House for two reasons: first, the House Judiciary Committee, which had to approve the bill before the whole House voted on it, was chaired by Emanuel Celler, a liberal Jew from New York who supported civil rights; and second, the House had rules limiting the length of debate on any bill, so consideration of the bill could not drag on and on. As a result, the bill that the House of Representatives sent to the Senate on February 10, 1964—less than three months after Kennedy's assassination—was actually stronger than the original bill. The tougher bill now included a prohibition against racial discrimination in employment in any workplace with more than twenty-five employees. In an attempt to defeat this "nefarious" legislation, Congressman Howard W. Smith, an eighty-year-old segregationist from Virginia, introduced an amendment to include "sex" along with race, creed, color, and national origin as a prohibited form of discrimination in employment or public life. Smith thought his colleagues in the House of Representatives would defeat the entire bill rather than give women equal rights, but he misjudged the historical moment. Smith's "sex" amendment was accepted, and the bill became an even more sweeping piece of legislation. With 152 Democrats and 138 Republicans in favor (and 96 Democrats and 34 Republicans against), the civil rights bill was passed from the House of Representatives over to the Senate for approval or defeat.

The Senate presented a much more difficult situation than the House. The Senate Judiciary Committee was chaired by James O. Eastland (D-Mississippi), whose belief in racial segregation was matched by his talent for killing civil rights bills in committee so they would never reach a full Senate vote. Moreover, the Senate had no rule limiting debate on a single bill. If a bill reached the full Senate for a vote, a handful of senators could choose to continue debating it as long as they had the strength to stand and draw breath. In that situation (known as a filibuster), debate continued until the other senators simply gave up and agreed to set aside the vexing bill so they could turn to other Senate business—or until sixty-seven of the Senate's one hundred members voted cloture, which meant that debate was over and a vote would be taken. Between 1917, when the Senate rules first allowed for cloture, and 1964, there had been only twenty-eight attempts to end a debate and force a vote on a bill; only five of those attempts at cloture had succeeded. Since 1937, Southern senators had defeated all eleven attempts to end their filibusters of civil rights bills, which meant those eleven bills had died without ever coming to a vote.

In 1964, pro–civil rights senators, under President Johnson's leadership, dodged segregationist obstructions by using an obscure Senate rule to bypass Eastland's Judiciary Committee and move the civil rights bill directly to the floor of the Senate. There, Democrats and Republicans worked as a team to keep the bill alive and craft compromise language. To strengthen their hand, President Johnson announced that he was not afraid of a filibuster. "I don't care how long it takes," he declared. "I don't care if the Senate doesn't do one other piece of business this year. . . . We are not going to have anything else hit the Senate floor until this bill is passed." The greatest threat of filibuster was always that no other Senate business would be conducted. To that threat the president (and one-time "master" of the Senate) said, in effect, "So what?"

As it turned out, the Eighty-eighth Congress did very little business between March 9 and March 26, when senators debated bypassing the Judiciary Committee, and virtually no other business between March 30 and June 19, when the members of the U.S. Senate held a continuous debate about the merits of the civil rights bill, formally known as House Resolution (H.R.) 7152. The high point of that debate came on June 10, when, for the first time in American history, the U.S. Senate was able to muster a two-thirds vote in favor of cloture on a civil rights bill, thereby ending the fifty-seven-day filibuster and forcing a vote. Senators then passed the bill by a vote of 73 to 27. The House quickly reapproved the slightly amended bill by a vote of 290 to 130, and it went immediately to the White House for President Johnson's signature on July 2, 1964. Before signing the bill, LBJ announced that the historic denial of "inalienable rights" to American citizens could no longer continue. "The law I sign tonight," he said, "forbids it."

Using the Source: Senate Speeches

The physical separation of blacks from whites in public places was one of the most tangible—and deliberately humiliating—aspects of racial discrimination in the United States between 1900 and 1964. Black protest alone could not end this undemocratic practice; only legislative action on the part of the U.S. Congress could end it nationally. For that reason, Senate speeches about segregation in public places are a vital piece of the civil rights movement's story. The purpose of that movement's demonstrations, sit-ins, and marches was to demand that those in power had to change the nation's racial system. The Senate debate over H.R. 7152 provides evidence of how those in power heard and responded to that message from the streets.

The one hundred whites who debated H.R. 7152 for fifty-seven days from the end of March, through April and May, and into June of 1964 were engaged in an unprecedented discussion of the U.S. Constitution and American race relations. On one level, they were arguing over just how far the federal government could legally go in prohibiting racial discrimination; at another level, they were debating whether racial discrimination was morally compatible with democracy. Supporters' strategic maneuver to bypass the Senate Judiciary

Committee meant that there was no committee "testimony" about the bill from constitutional lawyers, civil rights activists, African American citizens, or prosegregation citizens; any argument that a senator wanted to make for or against the legislation had to be introduced by that senator himself during the filibuster on the Senate floor.

In some filibusters in the past, senators had dragged out debate and exhausted their opponents by simply reading from the newspaper or the phone book, but that did not occur in this instance. The bill's opponents, who were staging the filibuster, chose to give long, serious speeches about the dangers of the civil rights bill, and its supporters chose to actively challenge the segregationist filibuster by delivering their own serious arguments about the necessity of a civil rights act. For fifty-seven days, all senators spoke directly to the racial and constitutional questions raised by H.R. 7152. Politics as usual was momentarily interrupted by the political idealism driving the civil rights movement from the street and onto the Senate floor.

What Can Senate Speeches Tell Us?

Like all political speeches, Senate speeches are designed to persuade. Rhetoric is the art of verbal persuasion; the goal is always to convince the listener to cast a vote or take an action or write a check on behalf of a particular partisan purpose. The great advantage of all political speeches is that no matter how many lies or distortions are uttered, speeches always reveal what the speaker truly believes to be the most persuasive approach to winning support from a particular audience. In the case of Senate speeches, every senator has two audiences to consider: voters back home and colleagues in the Senate.

Because senators design their remarks to please or persuade their constituents, we can use Senate speeches as an indirect guide to the attitudes of the voters that each senator was addressing. There is a particular advantage to Senate speeches in the high-profile 1964 civil rights debate: every senator knew that the words uttered in the nation's capital were being quoted in home state newspapers and could directly affect the next election. A speech in this debate had to appeal to popular opinion back home and had to be one the senator could defend on the stump. On this bill, no senator could casually trade a vote in exchange for a new bridge or highway; the stakes were too high. The result is that the speeches in this debate provide us with an unusually reliable record of the public positions senators were willing to take on these questions in 1964. That does not mean that we can assume the speeches necessarily reveal what every senator "really" believed about race. In some cases, the speeches were personally sincere; in other cases, they were not. Insight into every senator's heart is not what these public, political speeches offer us. Instead, these speeches tell us what every senator in 1964 regarded as winning arguments.

Consider, for example, this excerpt from a speech by Senator Sam Ervin, a prosegregation Democrat from North Carolina who opposed H.R. 7152. Senator Ervin's comments were made on March 18, 1964, during the debate over whether to bypass the Judiciary Committee. At this point, opponents like Ervin were trying to convince their colleagues that this bill needed a full committee investigation.

Raises the issue of states' loss of power under this federal legislation

This reference to a jurist from the early twentieth century highlights Ervin's expertise as a constitutional lawyer

This argument is meant to appeal to senators sympathetic to racial justice but worried about overextending federal powers

> If Congress enacts the bill it will say that a part of the legislative power is to be vested in the Department of Health, Education, and Welfare, that a part of the legislative power is to be vested in the Housing Administration, and that a part of the legislative power is to be vested in the Department of Commerce. . . . Is that what we wish to do with the legislative power of the United States? . . . Suffice it to say, Mr. President, that the bill undertakes to centralize in the Federal Government powers over the lives of the people, which the Constitution vests in the States or reserves to the people themselves. . . . As Chief Justice White declared, in substance, in *McCray v. United States,* 195 U.S. 27, 55, the safety of our institutions depends upon its strict observance by all those who hold offices created by the Constitution. That statement by Chief Justice White is something which Senators should take to heart.

Predicts that H.R. 7152 would endow agencies of the executive branch with powers that belong to Congress

Refers to the president of the Senate, who is the vice president of the United States; during this debate, however, "Mr. President" refers to the president pro tem of the Senate, the senator presiding "at the time" (pro tempore)

Senator Ervin's focus on the bill's threat to congressional power and its threat to states' powers does not give us dramatic prosegregationist rhetoric. In that sense, a disadvantage of Senate speeches is that they can appear legalistic and indirect. But Ervin's legalistic argument tells us what a smart, politically savvy segregationist regarded as the best rhetorical strategy for winning his argument.

Revealing as they are, the Senate speeches have the disadvantage of sounding well organized and professional. They do not reveal the tense drama and physical exhaustion accompanying this fifty-seven-day filibuster. They do not paint a picture of the arguments in the hallways or the sleeping cots set up in senatorial offices. To fully appreciate the dedication and stamina required to deliver these speeches, we need to grasp the rules of the filibuster game.

The pivotal rule is that it takes sixty-seven votes, two-thirds of the one-hundred-person Senate, to end a filibuster and bring a bill to a vote. So the twenty-seven Senate opponents of H.R. 7152 could keep the filibuster going, but the supporters had to gather sixty-seven votes to end it. In addition, the rules stipulate that a filibuster succeeds and the bill in question dies if, at the moment a senator demands a "quorum call," there are fewer than fifty-one senators on the floor. So the Democratic and Republican supporters of H.R. 7152 had to maintain disciplined cooperation for twelve weeks in order to make sure there were always fifty-one members on the floor of the Senate, day in and day out. During those twelve weeks, they had to convince sixty-seven senators to vote cloture in order to end the filibuster.

Because of these rules, a filibuster is the legislative equivalent of a military siege: it is physically as well as intellectually taxing. The goal of the bill's twenty-seven opponents was to win a quorum call by convincing twenty-four of their colleagues to just give up and go home. To achieve that goal, they did not have to convince those colleagues that racial discrimination was a good thing. They just needed to convince their colleagues that H.R. 7152 was a bad piece of legislation and should be abandoned. The Senate speeches can tell us what arguments some senators used to discredit H.R. 7152 and what arguments others used to insist that the Senate could not abandon the bill at this historic moment. But just as the speeches cannot reveal all the drama behind the scenes, neither can they give us an African American perspective on racial segregation in the United States in 1964. It was because of racism that no African Americans sat in the U.S. Senate when the Civil Rights Act was under debate. The disadvantage, as well as the advantage, of these particular speeches is that they reveal only how elite, white men were grappling with the issue of American racism. But since elite, white men were the ones passing the laws in the United States at that time, we can learn much about the political attitudes of the day by listening to the words they chose and the points they emphasized in the filibuster over H.R. 7152.

Questions to Ask

- What arguments did supporters of the bill make to justify the bill's use of federal power over the states?
- What arguments did opponents make to discredit H.R. 7152?
- What do the arguments tell us about the views of voters back home?
- How did the filibuster rules influence the types of arguments made by opponents?
- What was the "moral" issue for each side in this debate?

Source Analysis Table

The selection of speeches that follow were delivered on the floor of the Senate either during the filibuster or right before, when senators debated the proposal to bypass the Judiciary Committee. Most of the selections focus on the "public accommodations" aspect of H.R. 7152 (often referred to as Title II), which prohibited racial discrimination in privately owned businesses that were open to the general public. The speeches opposing the bill represent the Senate opponents' rhetorical emphasis on congressional, state, and private power, rather than racial segregation per se. The following table allows you to note and compare the racial and legislative arguments put forth in each speech.

Speaker	Position on H.R. 7152	Arguments Regarding Racial Discrimination	Arguments Regarding This Particular Bill
1. Senator Mike Mansfield			
2. Senator Richard Russell			
3. Senator John Stennis			
4. Senator Hubert Humphrey			
5. Senator Thomas Kuchel			

(continued)

Speaker	Position on H.R. 7152	Arguments Regarding Racial Discrimination	Arguments Regarding This Particular Bill
6. Senator Sam Ervin			
7. Senator Strom Thurmond			
8. Senator James O. Eastland			
9. Senator Everett Dirksen			
10. Senator Barry Goldwater			

To download and print this table, visit the book companion site at **bedfordstmartins.com/brownshannon**.

The Source: Speeches from the Senate Debate on the Civil Rights Act of 1964

1   *Majority Leader Mike Mansfield (D-Montana)*, February 17, 1964

> Senator Mansfield was the elected leader of the Democratic majority in the Senate. It was his job to shepherd the civil rights bill through the Senate to victory. In his opening address to the Senate on H.R. 7152, he named Senator Hubert Humphrey (D-Minnesota) and Senator Thomas Kuchel (R-California) as the senators with "direct responsibility" for handling the bill, and he defended his decision to procedurally bypass Senator Eastland's Judiciary Committee.

The civil rights bill has now arrived from the House. In the near future, the leadership will propose to the Senate that this measure be placed on the calendar, without referral to committee, and that, subsequently, the Senate as a body proceed to its consideration.

The procedures which the leadership will follow are not usual, but neither are they unprecedented. And the reasons for unusual procedures are too well known to require elaboration.

The substance of the bill has been discussed and debated, not for a week or a month, but for years. President Johnson has prescribed for civil rights legislation an urgency second to none. . . . Whatever any Senator may lack in understanding of the substance of the bill will, I am sure, be made up in extensive discussion on the floor of the Senate. . . . This approach is to be preferred in connection with a bill of such wide ramifications, for, in fact, the substance of the civil rights legislation falls with almost equal validity within the purview of several committees. . . . .

Mr. President, speaking for myself, let me say at the outset that I should have preferred it had the civil rights issue been resolved before my time as a Senator or had it not come to the floor until afterward. The Senator from Montana has no lust for conflict in connection with this matter. . . . But, Mr. President, great public issues are not subject to our personal timetables; they do not accommodate themselves to our individual preference or convenience. They emerge in their own way in their own time. . . . We hope in vain if we hope that this issue can be put over safely to another tomorrow, to be dealt with by another generation of Senators.

The time is now. The crossroads is here in the Senate. . . . If the Senate were to choose the course of evasion and denial, we would leave this body a less significant and less respected factor in the Government of the United States than it was when we entered it. I implore the Senate, therefore, to consider deeply the consequences of such a course. . . . The Senate's role [ought to be that of] a

Source: Senator Mike Mansfield, opening address to the Senate, on February 17, 1964, HR 7152, 88th Cong., 2nd sess., *Congressional Record* 110, pt. 3 (1964): 2882–2884.

leading participant, an essential and active participant, in shaping the continuing process of equalizing opportunities, that all Americans may share fully in the promise of the Constitution. . . . Senators would be well advised to search, not in the Senate rules book, but in the Golden Rule for the semblance of an adequate answer on this issue.

2 | *Senator Richard Russell (D-Georgia),*
February 25, 1964

> Senator Russell opposed Senator Mansfield's motion to move H.R. 7152 past the Judiciary Committee. President Kennedy's regard for Senator Russell as a friend and mentor had been one factor stalling his initiative on civil rights legislation.

I can understand the concern with the anticipated legislative situation on the so-called civil rights bill; but I hope, in this time of great pressure, that the Senators will not lose completely their sense of perspective. I hope Senators will look into the parliamentary question that would be involved, as to whether one member of the Senate . . . has the right by a single objection to bypass the committees of the Senate and bring a bill to the calendar. That is the issue that will be before the Senate from a parliamentary standpoint. . . . I hope Senators will not consider this a dilatory action on my part. It is not part of a filibuster. I am seeking only to remind the Senate of its responsibilities and of the desirability of not throwing its rules out the window when a certain type of legislation comes along. We should apply the same rule whether we are enthusiastically in favor of a piece of legislation or whether we are against it.

Source: Senator Richard Russell, February 25, 1964, HR 7152, 88th Cong., 2nd sess., *Congressional Record* 110, pt. 3 (1964): 3498.

3 | *Senator John Stennis (D-Mississippi),*
March 10, 1964

> The Senate did not vote to bypass hearings in the Judiciary Committee until March 26, more than a month after Senator Mansfield's opening remarks. But even before that procedural matter was settled, senators began debating the merits of the bill itself. In this speech, Senator Stennis was arguing against Title II of H.R. 7152, which prohibited racial segregation in public accommodations.

Source: Senator John Stennis, March 10, 1964, HR 7152, 88th Cong., 2nd sess., *Congressional Record* 110, pt. 4 (1964): 4818.

I recognize that Congress has great power in many fields but it should not—and I trust the Senate will not—attempt to use this power to wipe out and eradicate inherent and basic individual rights which are clearly beyond the reach of governmental control. Included in this is the right to acquire and own property and to use, or to restrict the use of it, as one sees fit; the right of an independent proprietor to operate his business as he sees fit; and the right of an individual to choose his own associates and customers.

I submit, Mr. President, that the basic constitutional issues involved in Title II of H.R. 7152 are of much greater significance and importance than our personal feelings and convictions about racial matters and the merits of integration.

Let us look at what Title II proposes to do. . . . Under the terms of the bill, the heavy hand of Federal control will extend to private business establishments. . . . The owners and operators of [these] establishments . . . will be divested of their long-recognized right to enjoy and utilize their property as they see fit. . . . These rights are fundamental and they cannot be impaired by the Federal Government under the guise of protecting the real or fancied rights of other individuals.

. . . I believe that the designation of the businesses covered in H.R. 7152 as public accommodations is itself a misnomer and is, therefore, calculated to deceive. The enterprises enumerated in the bill are in no sense public accommodations. . . . [They] are private enterprises and are privately owned and operated. No person has any vested right in them except the individual or individuals who own them. . . . All of this means that in considering H.R. 7152 . . . we must never forget that it is our own Constitution with which we are tinkering.

4   *Senator Hubert Humphrey (D-Minnesota),* March 30, 1964

> Senator Humphrey presented, as Democratic floor leader for H.R. 7152, a sixty-eight-page overview of the entire bill. Humphrey spoke for more than three hours in his opening remarks on the legislation he had been advocating for fifteen years.

I have been privileged to initiate this debate, and I would like my colleagues to know that it is my intention to address myself to all eleven titles of the bill. At the conclusion of my remarks, I shall be more than happy to attempt to answer questions or to engage in debate . . . but during my presentation I shall not yield. . . . I sincerely hope that Senators opposed to this legislation will be equally willing to permit the Senate to work its will, after an opportunity for searching examination and analysis of every provision. We issue this friendly

Source: Senator Hubert Humphrey, March 30, 1964, HR 7152, 88th Cong., 2nd sess., *Congressional Record* 110, pt. 5 (1964): 6528, 6531–6532.

challenge: we will join with you in debating the bill; will you join with us in voting on H.R. 7152 after the debate has been concluded? Will you permit the Senate and, in a sense, the Nation, to come to grips with these issues and decide them, one way or another? This is our respectful challenge. I devoutly hope it will be accepted. . . .

Mr. President, I turn now to Title II, one of the most important, significant, and necessary parts of the bill. This title deals with discrimination in places of public accommodation, a practice which vexes and torments our Negro citizens perhaps more than any other of the injustices they encounter. . . . It is difficult for most of us to fully comprehend the monstrous humiliations and inconveniences that racial discrimination imposes on our Negro fellow citizens. . . . He can never count on using a restroom, on getting a decent place to stay, on buying a good meal. These are trivial matters in the life of a white person, but for some 20 million American Negroes, they . . . must draw up travel plans much as a general advancing across hostile territory. . . . The Committee on Commerce has heard testimony from travel experts that if a Negro family wants to drive from Washington, D.C., to Miami, the average distance between places where it could expect to find sleeping accommodations is 141 miles. . . . What does such a family do if a child gets sick midway between towns where they will be accepted? What if there is no vacancy? . . .

Ironically, the very people who complain most bitterly at the prospect of Federal action are the ones who have made it inevitable. . . . This proposed legislation is here only because too many Americans have refused to permit the American Negro to enjoy all the privileges, duties, responsibilities and guarantees of the Constitution of the United States.

5   *Senator Thomas Kuchel (R-California),* March 30, 1964

In this speech, Senator Kuchel presented, as Republican floor leader for H.R. 7152, his economic analysis of the bill.

Discrimination has been demonstrated and documented in a long and sordid series of illegal and unconstitutional denials of equal treatment under law in almost every activity of many of our fellow men. Thus, such legislation as we now have before us cannot be ignored, nor can the issue be avoided, no matter from which State a Senator might come. . . .

Every American is aware that discrimination in public accommodations has motivated most of the 2,100 demonstrations which occurred in the last half of 1963. Public accommodations legislation is certainly nothing new. . . .

Source: Senator Thomas Kuchel, March 30, 1964, HR 7152, 88th Cong., 2nd sess., *Congressional Record* 110, pt. 5 (1964): 6556–6558.

Thirty of the fifty States and the District of Columbia have laws of this kind. . . .
There can be no question but that segregation in public accommodations ob-
structs and restricts interstate travel and the sale of related goods and services.
The market for national entertainment such as community concerts, athletic
competitions and motion pictures is surely restricted by such a situation.
National industries seeking new sources of manpower and availability to growing urban markets are inhibited from locating their offices and plants in areas
where racial strife is likely to occur.

. . . Logically and unquestionably, any businessman should have the right
to refuse to serve the drunk, the disorderly, the disreputable. He still will be free
to refuse to serve the drunk, the disorderly and the disreputable. He will still be
free to set standards for dress and conduct for persons in his establishment.
But, under the mandate of the Constitution, he would have to apply these
same standards to all customers and thus could not deny service to anyone
solely because of his race, religion, or national origin. What is wrong with that?

<table>
<tr><td>6</td></tr>
</table>

6   *Senator Sam Ervin (D-North Carolina),*
April 11, 1964

**In this speech, Senator Ervin argued against Title II of H.R. 7152, the pro-
hibition on racial segregation in public accommodations. Ervin would gain
new fame and popularity in 1973 when he chaired the special Senate committee investigating the Watergate burglary. Senate Leader Mike Mansfield
appointed Ervin to the chair because he was so strict about the Constitution.**

If the bill is passed in its present form, it will signal the destruction of constitutional government in the United States as we have known it. . . . There
would be a complete end of the Federal system which divides the powers of
government between the Federal government on the national level and the
States on the local level. . . . This bill, and especially the public accommodations provision of the bill . . . does not attempt to regulate interstate commerce
at all. It undertakes to regulate the use of privately owned property and the rendition of personal services within the borders of the States. It has been acknowledged from the very beginning of the establishment of the Republic to
this date by every court that has dealt with the subject that the power to regulate the use of privately owned property and the rendition of personal services
within the borders of the States is a power which belongs to the States, not to
Congress. . . .

I wish to call the attention of the Senate to the Federal Food, Drug and
Cosmetic Act of 1937. This act is based upon the power of Congress, under the

Source: Senator Sam Ervin, April 11, 1964, HR 7152, 88th Cong., 2nd sess., *Congressional
Record* 110, pt. 6 (1964): 7700, 7703.

interstate commerce clause [of the Constitution], to prohibit commerce in adulterated or deleterious or misbranded drugs, food, and the like. . . . In that respect, that act of Congress is entirely different from the proposals of the pending bill, for the pending bill does not constitute an effort to regulate or exclude the transmission across State lines of anything. Instead, the pending bill constitutes a brazen effort to regulate the use of privately owned property and the rendition of personal services within the borders of a State.

7   *Senator Strom Thurmond (D-South Carolina),* April 14, 1964

In this speech, Senator Thurmond argued against Title VII of H.R. 7152, the prohibition against racial or sexual discrimination in employment. Thurmond had led a prosegregation defection from the Democratic Party in 1948 when Senator Humphrey introduced a civil rights plank into the party platform. That year, Thurmond ran for president on the "Dixiecrat" ticket and won 2 percent of the vote.

I agree that a man should be permitted to operate his own private business in the way he wishes. He should also be permitted to hire all white people, if he wishes to do that; or all Chinese, or all Filipinos, or people of any other race; or to hire some of each. He should be permitted to hire people in whatever proportion he wants to hire them. Our Government was founded on the theory of freedom. . . . When we deny a man the right to choose his own employees for his own business, we are denying him a very vital right of freedom. He knows better than anyone else what kind of people he wants to have work with him in his line of work. . . .

I believe most Negroes are happier among their own people. . . . I believe people generally are happier among their own kind. Arabs are probably happier among other groups of Arabs. I think the Jews are happier among their own people. I believe that white people are happier among their own people. It does not mean they dislike anybody. It does not mean that they have prejudice against anybody. Nature made us like that. The white men inhabit Europe; the yellow men, Asia; the red men inhabited America; the black men, Africa. I do not know what God had in mind; but He must have had something in mind. . . .

The southern people have warm affection for the Negro. They understand the Negroes and have tried to help them. . . . The Negroes are much better off as a result of their coming to this country. The progress they have made has not been the result of activities on the part of people who are seeking votes by defending the so-called civil rights legislation. The people who are primarily responsible for the progress of the Negroes are the southern people, because the South is where most of the Negroes have lived until recent years. The South has

Source: Senator Strom Thurmond, April 14, 1964, HR 7152, 88th Cong., 2nd sess., *Congressional Record* 110, pt. 6 (1964): 7903.

had this problem. It is familiar with it and has had to bear it. The people of the South have borne up bravely. They have done much for the Negroes.

8   *Senator James O. Eastland (D-Mississippi),*
April 18, 1964

> It was Senator Eastland's Judiciary Committee that Senator Mansfield navigated past in order to get the civil rights bill heard on the floor of the Senate. Here Eastland argued against H.R. 7152 in general and Title II in particular.

Mr. President, H.R. 7152 . . . is, in my judgement, the most monstrous and heinous piece of legislation that has ever been proposed in the entire history of the U.S. Congress. It is inconceivable that the great mass of American people would not repudiate this bill out of hand if they were advised and understood its exact character and nature. . . . It is my duty to resist enactment. . . . Government by force and intimidation either borders on or crosses the border into anarchy, and today in many areas of the United States we are witnessing . . . a concerted and deliberate effort by certain minority groups to frighten and intimidate elected and appointed representatives of the people into giving them advantages, privileges, jobs and preferment. . . . We are witnessing a character of conduct that is lawless in its nature and designed to teach the children of this country to be disrespectful of authority; to violate the law; to invade the private and personal property of others, and to take by force that which they do not own and have no right to acquire. We can say what we please, but the proposed Civil Rights Act is a direct result of this widespread unlawful agitation, and those who would give it their whole-hearted support are, in a very real sense, unwittingly supporting anarchy itself. Appeasement was the road that led to World War II.

Source: Senator James O. Eastland, April 18, 1964, HR 7152, 88th Cong., 2nd sess., *Congressional Record* 110, pt. 6 (1964): 8355–8356.

9   *Senator Everett Dirksen (R-Illinois),*
June 10, 1964

> Though Senator Kuchel was technically in charge of persuading Republicans to support H.R. 7152, Senator Dirksen proved to be the pivotal Republican figure in the debate. For weeks, he negotiated revisions in the bill's federal powers that made it more acceptable to rural Republican voters. In this speech, Senator Dirksen argued, after fifty-seven days of Senate filibuster, to end the debate on H.R. 7152 by voting for cloture.

Source: Senator Everett Dirksen, June 10, 1964, HR 7152, 88th Cong., 2nd sess., *Congressional Record* 110, pt. 10 (1964): 13319–13320.

When he spoke these words in his deep, melodious voice, every member of the Senate was present to hear him.

Mr. President, it is a year ago this month that the late President Kennedy sent his civil rights bill and message to the Congress. For two years, we had been chiding him about failure to act in this field. At long last, and after many conferences, it became a reality. . . . Today, the Senate is stalemated in its efforts to enact a civil rights bill. . . . To argue that cloture is unwarranted or unjustified is to assert that in 1917, the Senate adopted a rule which it did not intend to use. . . . It was adopted as an instrument for action when all other efforts failed. . . . There are many good reasons why cloture should be invoked and a good civil rights measure enacted. . . .

First. It is said that on the night he died, Victor Hugo wrote in his diary, substantially this sentiment: "Stronger than all the armies is an idea whose time has come." The time has come for equality of opportunity in sharing in government, in education, and in employment. It will not be stayed or denied. It is here. . . .

Second. Years ago, a professor who thought he had developed an incontrovertible scientific premise submitted it to his faculty associates. Quickly they picked it apart. In agony he cried out, "Is nothing eternal?" To this one of his associates replied, "Nothing is eternal except change." . . . America grows. America changes. And on the civil rights issue we must rise with the occasion. That calls for cloture and for enactment of a civil rights bill. . . .

Third. There is another reason—our covenant with the people. For many years, each political party has given major consideration to a civil rights plank in its platform. Go back and reexamine our pledges to the people as we sought a grant of authority to manage and direct their affairs. Were these pledges so much campaign stuff or did we mean it? Were these promises on civil rights but idle words for vote-getting purposes or were they a covenant meant to be kept? If all this was mere pretense, let us confess the sin of hypocrisy now and vow not to delude the people again. . . .

Fourth. . . . There is another reason why we dare not temporize with the issue which is before us. It is essentially moral in character. It must be resolved. It will not go away. Its time has come. Nor is it the first time in our history that an issue with moral connotations and implications has swept away the resistance, the fulminations, the legalistic speeches, the ardent but dubious arguments, the lamentations and the thought patterns of an earlier generation and pushed forward to fruition. . . .

Pending before us is another moral issue. Basically it deals with equality of opportunity in exercising the franchise, in securing an education, in making a livelihood, in enjoying the mantle of protection of the law. It has been a long, hard furrow and each generation must plow its share. . . . Today is the one-hundredth anniversary of the nomination of Abraham Lincoln for a second term for the presidency on the Republican ticket. . . . At Gettysburg 101 years ago he spoke of "a new nation, conceived in liberty and dedicated to the proposition that all men are created equal." . . .

That has been the living faith of our party. Do we forsake this article of faith, now that the time for our decision has come?

There is no substitute for a basic ideal. We have a firm duty to use the instrument at hand; namely, the cloture rule, to bring about the enactment of a good civil rights bill.

I appeal to all Senators. We are confronted with a moral issue. Today let us not be found wanting in whatever it takes by way of moral and spiritual substance to face up to the issue and to vote cloture.

10   *Senator Barry Goldwater (R-Arizona),*
June 18, 1964

In this speech, Senator Goldwater explained his decision to vote against H.R. 7152 the day before the final vote was taken and the bill passed, 73 to 27. Senator Goldwater led a conservative resurgence within the Republican Party in 1964 and, just a few weeks after delivering this speech, was nominated to run as the Republican candidate for president against the Democrats' President Johnson. He won only 39 percent of the vote, doing best in the southern states.

Mr. President, there have been few, if any, occasions when the searching of my conscience and the reexamination of my views of our constitutional system have played a greater part in the determination of my vote than they have on this occasion.

I am unalterably opposed to discrimination or segregation on the basis of race, color, or creed, or on any other basis; not only my words, but more importantly my actions through the years have repeatedly demonstrated the sincerity of my feeling in this regard. . . . .

I realize fully that the Federal Government has a responsibility in the field of civil rights. . . . My public utterances during the debates [on the 1957 and 1960 civil rights acts] reveal clearly the areas in which I feel that Federal responsibility lies and Federal legislation on this subject can be both effective and appropriate. Many of those areas are encompassed in this bill and to that extent, I favor it. . . . The two portions of this bill to which I have constantly and consistently voiced objections, and which are of such overriding significance that they are determinative of my vote on the entire measure, are those which would embark the Federal Government on a regulatory course of action with regard to private enterprise in the area of so-called public accommodations and in the area of employment—to be more specific, titles II and VII of the bill. I find no constitutional basis for the exercise of Federal regulatory

Source: Senator Barry Goldwater, June 18, 1964, HR 7152, 88th Cong., 2nd sess., *Congressional Record* 110, pt. 11 (1964): 14318–14319.

authority in either of these areas; and I believe the attempted usurpation of such power to be a grave threat to the very essence of our basic system of government; namely, that of a constitutional republic in which 50 sovereign States have reserved to themselves and to the people those powers not specifically granted to the Central or Federal Government. . . . .

I repeat again: I am unalterably opposed to discrimination of any sort and I believe . . . some law can help—but not law that embodies features like these, provisions which fly in the face of the Constitution and which require for their effective execution the creation of a police state. . . . If my vote is misconstrued, let it be, and let me suffer its consequences. Just let me be judged by the real concern I have voiced here. . . . My concern is for the entire Nation, for the freedom of all who live in it and for all who will be born into it.

Analyzing Senate Speeches

1. What were the supporters' arguments in favor of H.R. 7152? Did they focus on the general evils of race discrimination or on the particular features of this bill?

2. What were the opponents' arguments against H.R. 7152? Did they focus on the merits of race discrimination or the problems they see in this bill?

3. How do you think the rules of the filibuster game shaped the differences in emphasis between supporters and opponents of the bill?

4. What evidence can you locate in the speeches to show that members of the U.S. Senate were paying attention to the civil rights movement in the streets?

5. Do you have any reason to think that opponents or supporters of H.R. 7152 were emphasizing different points in their Senate speeches than they would emphasize in political speeches back home? What other types of sources would you use to test your hypothesis?

6. Before 1964, the South voted solidly for the Democratic Party. After 1964, Southerners began to vote Republican. Write a short essay on the role you think the civil rights debate played in this important political realignment in the United States.

The Rest of the Story

The most immediate and dramatic effect of the 1964 Civil Rights Act was in the desegregation of public accommodations throughout the southern states. Many had predicted violent resistance to the integration of restaurants, swimming pools, hotels, and movie theaters, but a survey of fifty-three southern cities in the summer of 1964 found "widespread compliance" and only scattered cases in which whites assaulted blacks for integrating a public place.

Resistance was quelled in December 1964, when the Supreme Court ruled unanimously in *Heart of Atlanta Motel v. United States* that the commerce clause of the U.S. Constitution empowered Congress to enact Title II of the 1964 Civil Rights Act, which proscribed racial segregation in public accommodations throughout the nation. Since 1964, no one has mounted a credible legal challenge to Title II; those who desire racial segregation of public places have no credibility in American political debate.

Other sections of the 1964 Civil Rights Act, however, have continued to spark controversy, both in the courts and in Congress. Title VII, for example, barred employment discrimination based on race, color, religion, sex, or national origin and created the Equal Employment Opportunity Commission (EEOC) to implement the law. This meant that businesses that employed fifteen or more workers were not supposed to use social categories when determining an individual job applicant's qualifications for a position or when deciding which employees to promote within the business.

Employment discrimination is more difficult to prove than discrimination in public accommodations. It is quite obvious when a restaurant owner or theater manager refuses to serve an African American family or a woman alone or a Sikh. No restaurant owner can claim that white patrons are more qualified to eat the food on the menu; no theater manager can claim that native-born patrons perform better as audience members. Any court would dismiss such claims as nonsensical. But when a business is charged with racial discrimination because it employs very few African Americans, the business owner will typically argue that the problem is not race but that African American applicants lack the qualifications for the jobs, and that it is not the business owner's responsibility to make up for the educational or training deficit in the local black community.

In 1971, the Supreme Court issued a ruling on employment discrimination in *Griggs v. Duke Power Company*. In that case the Court established that when a complaint charged hiring discrimination, the burden of proof was on the business owners to show that their hiring criteria were legitimately and rationally based on the qualifications for the job. Duke Power Company lost the 1971 case because it required janitors to have a high school degree, a rule that had a "disparate impact" on African Americans in the local community who at the time were less likely to have high school degrees. Duke Power Company could not show that a high school degree was a bona fide occupational qualification for performing the duties of a janitor.

In the two decades following the *Griggs v. Duke Power Company* case, political debate and legal disputes continued over how to determine disparate impact and how to define bona fide occupational qualifications. Spurred by five Supreme Court rulings in the 1988–89 session that limited federal authority in employment discrimination cases, Congress passed the 1991 Civil Rights Act in order to clarify the rules governing employment discrimination. Of particular concern to Senator Edward Kennedy (D-Massachusetts) and other legislators who sponsored the 1991 law was the Supreme Court's 1989 decision in *Wards Cove Packing v. Atonio*. In that decision, passed by a 5–4 vote, the majority overturned the *Griggs v. Duke Power Company* precedent and ruled that the burden of proof in discrimination lawsuits rests with the complainant, not the employer. The majority also ruled that Atonio and his fellow workers at the Wards Cove salmon-processing plant in Alaska had failed to prove that the company's hiring practices were racially discriminatory, even though most of the positions on the cannery floor were held by nonwhites and all of the office positions were held by whites. The four justices who dissented in this case argued that Wards Cove Packing Company used practices that had a disparate impact on the nonwhite pool of potential employees. For example, cannery workers were housed in separate dormitories from office workers, and openings for office jobs were publicized only by word of mouth, so potentially qualified cannery workers were unlikely to hear about office positions.

The Civil Rights Act of 1991 did not dictate how courts should rule in any particular case, but the Democratic-controlled Congress did say that the burden of proof in such cases rests with the employer, not the complainant. Business practices could have a disparate impact (that is, a company could legitimately hire a disproportionate number of whites or men), but only if the employers could show that their hiring rules were rationally tied to the job in question.

President George H. W. Bush had successfully vetoed the Civil Rights Act of 1990 on the grounds that it would force companies to establish racial hiring quotas in order to avoid discrimination lawsuits. President Bush and his allies argued that complainants used statistics alone to prove disparate impact; if the local community was 45 percent black, then complainants could charge discrimination if only 20 percent of a company's workforce was black. Following another year of debate, President Bush signed the Civil Rights Act of 1991 because, like the 1990 bill, it said that specific business practices, not statistics, were the deciding issue in any individual discrimination case. Amid the rancorous debate over this bill, there was universal agreement that better education for all Americans would improve every worker's job qualifications and bring greater racial equality to the job market.

To Find Out More

All speeches delivered in the U.S. Senate and the U.S. House of Representatives are published in the *Congressional Record,* which can be found in any federal depository library (a library that automatically receives the federal documents printed and published by the U.S. Government Printing Office). To find the federal depository library nearest you, consult "GPO Access" at **access.gpo.gov**. For sessions since 1994, the *Congressional Record* is available online; an online index to the *Congressional Record* going back to 1983 can be found at **gpoaccess.gov/databases.html**.

The *Congressional Record* is published every day, and congressional rules dictate that every issue contains "a substantially verbatim account of remarks made during the proceedings" of that date. Members can make technical or grammatical changes in the printed record if they are submitted by midnight of that day's session, and they can submit an "Extension of Remarks" within thirty days of a session. According to congressional rules, however, "in no event would actually uttered remarks be removable" from the day's record.

The 3,000 pages of Senate debate on H.R. 7152 are spread out over six volumes of the *Congressional Record,* from February 17, 1964, to June 19, 1964. The Congress publishes a very complete index to each session of the *Record,* so you can look up specific terms or names, such as "public accommodations" or "Sam Ervin," and find all the pages on which the term or person appears in that congressional session.

The Congressional Quarterly, a weekly magazine that focuses on the Senate and House of Representatives and legislation pending in Congress, is an excellent source of information on weekly developments in Congress.

In the last thirty years, American historians have produced an impressive body of literature on the civil rights movement of the 1950s and 1960s. Within that literature, two books focus on the history of the Civil Rights Act of 1964. Charles and Barbara Whalen's *The Longest Debate: A Legislative History of the 1964 Civil Rights Act* (Washington, D.C.: Seven Locks Press, 1985) is a very accessible narrative written in a journalistic style that pays close attention to the political maneuvering in the both the House and Senate. In *To End All Segregation: The Politics of the Passage of the Civil Rights Act of 1964* (Albany: State University of New York Press, 1990), Robert D. Loevy presents similar material but from the more analytical standpoint of a political scientist. Loevy has also edited *The Civil Rights Act of 1964: The Passage of the Law That Ended Racial Segregation* (Albany: State University of New York Press, 1997), which includes essays by key participants.

For readable books that place the story of the Civil Rights Act of 1964 in the context of the larger civil rights movement, see Richard Reeves, *President Kennedy: Profile of Power* (New York: Simon and Schuster, 1993); Robert Mann, *The Walls of Jericho: Lyndon Johnson, Hubert Humphrey, Richard Russell, and the Struggle for Civil Rights* (New York: Harcourt Brace, 1996); Taylor Branch, *Pillar of Fire: America in the King Years, 1963–65* (New York: Simon and Schuster, 1998); and David Garrow, *Bearing the Cross: Martin Luther King, Jr., and the Southern Christian Leadership Conference* (New York: William Morrow, 1986).

For more information online, see the Civil Rights Documentation project at **usm.edu/crdp**, which provides dozens of oral histories by Mississippi residents who were active in the civil rights movement, and **congresslink.org/civil/cr10.html**, which offers a legislative history of the bill. The entire text of the law can be found at **usinfo.state.gov/usa/infousa/laws/majorlaw/civilr19.htm**.

CHAPTER 12

A Son Writes Home

Letters from the Vietnam War

"The longer I'm over here, the more I think we should get out quickly, almost no matter how." Jeff Rogers announced that hopeless view in a letter to his parents on April 20, 1969, after serving five months as a naval officer on board a hospital ship anchored off the coast of Vietnam. Jeff's despair over the war was not unusual among those serving "in country" in 1969; nor was it unusual for servicemen and -women to write home expressing their despair. Jeff Rogers's letters home are notable only because his father was William P. Rogers, secretary of state in Richard Nixon's administration. In fact, Jeff Rogers was the only child of a high-ranking administration official to serve in Vietnam during the Nixon years. Over the course of Jeff's one-year tour of duty in Vietnam, from early November 1968 through October 1969, he provided his father with a more direct, candid view of the war than a secretary of state typically gets in military reports or intelligence briefings.

Jeff Rogers did not go to Vietnam enthusiastically, but he did go willingly. He enlisted in the navy in 1968 after a year at Harvard Medical School convinced him that he did not want to be a doctor. Up until that moment in his life, the twenty-four-year-old Rogers had enjoyed all the privileges his father's success could afford. When Jeff, his sister, and his two brothers were children in Washington, D.C., their father was serving as attorney general in President Dwight Eisenhower's administration. Later, when William Rogers was influencing public policy as a partner in a powerful Washington, D.C., law firm, Jeff attended Sidwell Friends' School with Nixon's daughters and then went to Dartmouth College, from which he graduated in 1966. That was the year after President Lyndon Johnson had authorized the initial escalation in Vietnam and the year before an energetic antiwar movement coalesced on college campuses. Jeff avoided the early disruptions of the war, gliding smoothly from Dartmouth to Harvard Medical School. His decision to withdraw from Harvard put Jeff at unfamiliar risk.

In America in 1968, any young man who left school was likely to be drafted into the army, and William P. Rogers's son was no exception. Jeff had to immediately weigh all the options that his peers were weighing: get drafted, enlist, apply for conscientious objector status, or move to Canada to escape the draft. Jeff even had a physician's offer to write him a bogus medical excuse. In the end, he chose to enlist in the navy, as his father had done in World War II, and went to officer candidate school (OCS), where he trained to be a ship's navigator. Family privilege did not keep Jeff out of Vietnam; indeed, he was one of the few from his OCS class to be assigned to the war zone. But his job was less dangerous than many others: he was to serve as a navigator on the USS *Repose,* a 520-foot navy hospital ship anchored off the coast of South Vietnam.

The same week Jeff arrived in Vietnam, Richard Nixon, a Republican, won the 1968 presidential election, defeating Lyndon Johnson's vice president, Hubert Humphrey. During the campaign, Nixon railed against U.S. policy in Vietnam, blaming Vice President Humphrey along with President Johnson for not bringing "peace with honor." Nixon began his presidency believing that within a year he could disentangle the United States from the war, withdraw

Figure 12.1 Ensign Jeff Rogers with His Father, Secretary of State William P. Rogers
This photograph was taken in May 1969, when the secretary of state made an official tour of Vietnam. Source: Courtesy of Jeff Rogers.

the 540,000 troops fighting there, and still somehow "win the peace." To achieve that ambitious goal, Nixon appointed three key advisors: Melvin Laird to head up the Defense Department; Jeff's father, William P. Rogers, to lead the State Department; and Henry Kissinger to serve as chair of the National Security Council. Nixon did not care that his old friend Bill Rogers lacked foreign policy expertise. Nixon wanted a loyal ally taking care of global business in the State Department so that he and Kissinger were free to manage Vietnam strategy.

Nixon believed that the battle to establish a noncommunist South Vietnam was a vital part of the cold war with the Soviet Union. So while he wanted to extricate the United States from Vietnam, he also wanted to leave behind a secure, independent, democratic, pro-U.S. government in Saigon, the capital of South Vietnam. This was Nixon's meaning when he spoke of "peace with honor." The key problem with Nixon's plan was that the mass of South Vietnamese people did not see the situation in his cold war terms. They had not been consulted in 1954 when the Western powers divided Vietnam into a communist "North" Vietnam and a pro-U.S. "South" Vietnam; their cultural and historical identity was as "Vietnamese" people who were always struggling against outside powers to achieve national sovereignty (see Map 12.1). From their standpoint, Vietnam's traditional capital, Hanoi, located in the north, was the symbol of national independence, while the U.S.-supported capital in the

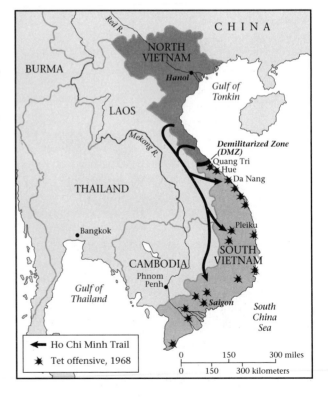

Map 12.1 The Vietnam War, 1954–1975 In 1969, Jeff Rogers's ship was based between the South Vietnamese city of Da Nang and the demilitarized zone at the 17th parallel, which had been established by the Geneva Conference of 1954 as the dividing line between North and South Vietnam. This map shows the Ho Chi Minh Trail, the key supply line for the North Vietnamese into the south. President Nixon justified the bombing of Cambodia as necessary to cut this supply line.

south, Saigon, was a symbol of foreign intervention. Regardless of their views on communism, many Vietnamese living in the south supported Hanoi's claim that the war was about national reunification. As a result, southern civilians often aided the North Vietnamese army and their southern military allies, known as the Vietcong.

Jeff Rogers was one of many Americans who wrote letters home from Vietnam expressing their shock, their anger, and even their shame at discovering that the Vietnamese people did not regard the United States as their champions and did not trust the U.S.-backed government in Saigon. The in-country experience of these Americans contradicted the claims of Presidents Johnson and Nixon that U.S. goals in Vietnam were within reach. By 1969, when Jeff Rogers was in Vietnam and his father was in the State Department, the majority of Americans doubted that an independent, democratic government in South Vietnam could emerge from the war, and they did not want to lose more American lives in a futile military effort. Already, 32,000 Americans had died in Vietnam and more than two million had done a tour of duty there. Nixon won the 1968 election largely because of his promise to end the war without sacrificing American honor, and 1969 was supposed to be the year that promise was fulfilled.

As Ensign Jeff Rogers settled into his navigator's post on board the USS *Repose,* just off the coast of Vietnam, his father joined a debate within the Nixon administration about how to achieve peace with honor in Vietnam. National Security advisor Henry Kissinger focused on the "honor" aspect of Nixon's goal. He argued that the United States should escalate the war by increasing the bombing of North Vietnam. This would pressure Hanoi into accepting peace terms that preserved a pro-U.S. government in Saigon and thus protected America's global dignity. Secretary of State Rogers and Secretary of Defense Laird focused on the "peace" aspect of Nixon's goal and opposed any bombing increases that would jeopardize ongoing peace talks in Paris or increase political divisions at home.

Although Nixon expected Rogers to defer to Kissinger on Vietnam policy, Rogers allied with Laird to advocate for withdrawal from Vietnam through a policy called Vietnamization. In theory, this meant training and equipping the Army of the Republic of [South] Vietnam to wage its own war for an independent democracy against the Democratic Republic of [North] Vietnam. In reality, Vietnamization meant replacing American casualties with South Vietnamese casualties.

In the spring of 1969, Nixon publicly endorsed the Vietnamization policy and responded to Americans' war weariness by scheduling the withdrawal of 125,000 troops by April 1970. It was true that 434,000 Americans remained in country, and Americans suffered 60,000 casualties, including 11,000 deaths, in Vietnam in 1969. Still, Vietnamization and troop reductions pointed in the direction the majority of the American people desired: de-escalation of the U.S. role in Vietnam. Unbeknownst to the American people, President Nixon simultaneously endorsed Kissinger's plan to escalate the war through increased bombing. Kissinger feared that a policy of Vietnamization would encourage

Hanoi to simply wait out American withdrawal before taking over the south; he wanted to force a peace agreement that would prevent that outcome. Without the congressional authorization required by the Constitution, and against the advice of both Secretary Rogers and Secretary Laird, Nixon ordered the secret bombing of Hanoi's supply lines running north to south through Cambodia, Vietnam's neutral neighbor. Five years later, during the Watergate scandal, the House of Representatives debated whether this three-month, secret bombing campaign should be among the "articles" justifying impeachment of President Nixon for violating the Constitution. It was not included in the final articles of impeachment but continued to be a controversial course of action.

Jeff Rogers did not know about the secret bombing of Cambodia; the secretary of state did not reveal government secrets to his son, nor did he dwell on his disagreements with Henry Kissinger. Jeff knew only what he read in the press, heard from others in the military, and saw for himself. His letters home gave the nation's secretary of state an intimate view of one young American's growing doubts about the American mission in Vietnam.

Using the Source: Personal Letters

Americans who were alive during the Vietnam War look back on that controversial historical event through inevitably distorted lenses. Subsequent political developments, personal experiences, and military involvements can cause us to remember ourselves as having been more—or less—supportive of the war than we actually were. When we have access to our own letters from this era, or can read others' letters, we are reminded of the mix of feelings at the time and also are reminded that we did not know how the war was going to turn out. Letters capture human beings in the messy midst of life, when we are part of history, not looking back on it. So when we set out to reconstruct the history of an event as layered with memory as the Vietnam War, letters give us an honesty and authenticity about what the war felt like in the moment. For this event, as for so many others in the past, we turn to letters in order to "hear" how participants at the time felt, spoke, and communicated with one another on the most momentous and the most trivial aspects of their lives.

What Can Personal Letters Tell Us?

The great advantage of letters is their immediacy. Unlike memoirs, the author's construction of a letter is not filtered through the leaky sieve of memory, nor have events and reactions been edited by subsequent experiences and reinterpreted through lessons the writer learned later. What is on the page in a letter constitutes some representation of what the author was thinking and feeling at the time the letter was written. Letters also give us the author's "voice," through their use of language, level of formality or informality, and general mode of self-presentation. But it is their overall immediacy that draws us to letters from the past. Even when the past we are studying is fairly recent, even when we have film footage, home movies, tape recordings, and face-to-face interviews, we still appreciate the direct, candid connection that letters seem to offer.

Letters can be misleading, however. Their immediacy suggests transparency, and we can be seduced into believing that everything the letter writer wrote was exactly what he or she thought and felt at the time. When using letters to understand the past, we must keep in mind that they are a construction of words on the page, and those who write letters bring multiple, often unspoken, sometimes unconscious, motives to their correspondence. So we ask, for example, to whom was the letter directed—and how that might have shaped the letter's contents and purpose. In the case of Vietnam War letters, for example, did soldiers write differently to their mothers than to their girlfriends or to friends who had already done a tour of duty in country? Did soldiers who agreed with their parents about the war write more candidly than those who felt their parents did not understand the situation? Did soldiers employ one tone of voice or another in order to persuade their particular reader of the sincerity and accuracy of their view of the war? Did they write to shock, to convince, to gain sympathy, or to vent anger?

Letters, like all human utterances, invite multiple interpretations. Consider the letter Jeff Rogers wrote to his parents on March 14, 1969, in which he complained about the inaccuracy of intelligence reports coming out of Vietnam. The three short paragraphs here raise a number of questions about why Jeff chose to construct the letter as he did.

Even his father, the secretary of state?

So if intelligence reports and press reports have such little relation to what really is happening, who does one believe? Worse, I really wonder if <u>anyone</u> knows what the true story is. The war is too fragmented, too spread out, and too multi-faceted to really be understood as far as who is accomplishing what.

Is Jeff lecturing his father or warning him?

Does he change the subject to avoid offending?

About income tax. We don't have to file as long as we're in the Vietnam combat zone, so I'll wait until I get back to do that.

Is Jeff trying to show that his opinions on the war are based on in-country experience?

Yes, we occasionally have beach parties and I've gotten to swim once or twice. But we just got word that there had been a sniper incident at the beach we've been using so beach parties may be out.

We can read a great deal into Rogers's particular construction of comments here. In fact, we can read too much into them. A young man lying on his bunk on a humid Friday afternoon in the South China Sea is probably not plotting his letters precisely enough to warrant microscopic analysis. When we study letters for historical insight, we have to maintain a balance between under-interpreting and overinterpreting them. We can never retrieve the multiple motives shaping a single letter. Indeed, Jeff himself now finds that "like any reader, I ponder what in the world I meant by some of what I wrote, and why I wrote as I did in those moments. As I read my own letters, I feel much like an historian doing research." In the case of this particular letter, what we do find is evidence that a sailor on board a ship off the coast of Vietnam heard enough press reports and eyewitness accounts to conclude that the two seldom matched, alongside evidence that a sailor's daily life was a confusing mix of beach parties and sniper attacks. However, we do not know from this one letter whether Jeff's arrangement of comments reflected a pattern of blending war commentary with mundane details of life, nor do we know if that pattern was motivated by the desire to telegraph some subtext to his parents.

Because letters are such immediate, highly individualistic expressions, it is risky to make too many claims about the past on the basis of a single surviving letter by an author whose situation and background are unknown. Without any context, we might exaggerate the meaning of a comment or completely misunderstand the meaning. There are two ways around this problem: we can read a lot of letters from a number of individuals in the same situation and look for recurring themes and attitudes in the letters, even if we do not know much about the authors of those letters; or we can study a set of letters from one individual whose situation and background we know, drawing on patterns of expression and our information about the author to understand the significance of the comments in the letters. This chapter's source allows you to take the second approach.

We know a great deal about Ensign Jeff Rogers, who, between November 1968 and August 1969, wrote the dozen letters included here to his father, Secretary of State William P. Rogers; his mother, Adele Langston Rogers; and his sister, Dale Rogers Marshall. We can provide context for these letters because of the public record on William P. Rogers and because Jeff Rogers himself is alive and able to supply background information. But, as is often the case with collections of letters, we have only one side of the correspondence: Jeff's parents saved his letters, but Jeff did not save the letters from his parents. This common disadvantage forces us to infer what was being said by one correspondent based on the letters from another correspondent. In the case of the Rogers letters, the public record suggests (and Jeff confirms) that his father was quite circumspect in what he said to his son about Vietnam policymaking in the White House. It was only later, and largely through his mother, that Jeff learned of the ways in which the Nixon-Kissinger team excluded Rogers from decisions, hid secrets from him, and ignored his advice in policymaking. Press reports at the time and later studies of the Nixon war policy have confirmed this pattern, but Secretary Rogers never publicly complained about his treatment. Adele Rogers, on the other hand, was willing to telegraph her own views on the role she wanted her husband to play in the war and was even willing to paraphrase her son's letters in order to make her own point. In an interview for the *New York Times Magazine* on July 27, 1969, she told a reporter that Jeff's letters from Vietnam kept saying, "This is a very good war to end, Daddy, and you'd be a good man to end it."

Jeff Rogers's letters from Vietnam highlight the advantages and disadvantages that come with all correspondence as a historical source, but Jeff Rogers was obviously not typical of the Vietnam serviceman. At age twenty-five, this son of the secretary of state was five or six years older than the average soldier or sailor. As a white, college-educated volunteer who had been through OCS, he was notably more educated and economically privileged than the tens of thousands of disproportionately nonwhite draftees coming out of high school to serve in this war. Like those drafted for Vietnam duty, Jeff served for just one year, but as a navigator on a hospital ship, he was not with the mass of men (and women nurses) attached to infantry units and engaged in combat operations in the country's dense mountains and jungles. Jeff's posting on the USS *Repose* put him at sea off the coast of South Vietnam, between the city of Da Nang and the demilitarized zone, which marked the border between the northern and southern halves of the country (see Map 12.1 on p. 266). Jeff's letters, unlike many from Vietnam, do not include reports of dangerous missions, ambushes in the jungle, or sudden grenade attacks. In contrast to those in battle units, Jeff did not have to hide fear and danger to protect the feelings of those at home. He wrote candidly about his boredom (a common theme in Vietnam letters), his worries about his own future, and his pride in his work. He also wrote about the strange contrasts between American luxuries, wartime horrors, military corruption, and Vietnamese survival. And he wrote about his changing views on the U.S. mission in Vietnam.

Questions to Ask

- What was Jeff Rogers's attitude toward the war and toward President Nixon when he arrived in Vietnam?

- When and how do his letters suggest a change in his views on the war?

- In what way do the letters reveal Jeff's relatively privileged status in society?

- What do letters like these allow you to conclude about Jeff's feelings about his privileged status?

- What can you confidently conclude from these twelve letters about Jeff's relationship with his parents?

Source Analysis Table

The twelve letters excerpted here stretch from Jeff Rogers's first letter home after arriving in Vietnam to one of his last letters before returning to the United States. This span of time allows you to trace changes in his attitudes and to link those changes to experiences he recounted in the letters. Use the following table to keep track of Rogers's views on the war and the reasons that he held those views or changed his views. As you watch for experiences and observations that indicate changes in his thinking, pay attention to comments that reflect unchanged attitudes as well. Both are important for understanding how the war experience affected Jeff Rogers's opinions on the war.

Letter	Reasons for Supporting U.S. Mission in Vietnam	Reasons for Doubting U.S. Mission in Vietnam
1. November 10, 1968		
2. November 24, 1968		
3. December 7, 1968		
4. December 30, 1968		
5. February 18, 1969		
6. March 14, 1969		

(continued)

Letter	Reasons for Supporting U.S. Mission in Vietnam	Reasons for Doubting U.S. Mission in Vietnam
7. April 20, 1969		
8. May 24, 1969		
9. May 31, 1969		
10. June 10, 1969		
11. June 23, 1969		
12. August 28, 1969		

To download and print this table, visit the book companion site at **bedfordstmartins.com/brownshannon**.

The Source: Jeff Rogers's Letters from Vietnam, November 10, 1968–August 28, 1969

1 *November 10, 1968*

> Jeff Rogers left Travis Air Force Base, northeast of San Francisco, California, on Friday, November 1, 1968, and after a series of airplane flights, he arrived in Vietnam on Tuesday, November 5, the day Richard Nixon was elected president. He devoted most of his first letter home to his parents to describing life on aboard his hospital ship, the USS *Repose*.

Dear Mother and Dad,

. . . I'm quite impressed with and already proud of what this ship does. As they say, it's not about the traditional Navy—a lot of the stuff about secrecy, about protocol, about routine, and of course about weapons is irrelevant here. But it's obvious we do a vital job and a greatly appreciated one. Some statistics: in 1968 so far, 5,571 patients (2,624 battle casualties, 485 non-battle casualties, 2,590 disease) only 152 deaths and returned 2,834 to combat. We've had a total of 8,763 helicopter landings since we got on station in February, 1966 and not one accident.[1] . . . It's a little "heavy" at times directing down a helo [helicopter] that extends almost the full length of the landing pad onto a small area which is moving up and down ten feet or more, especially when you know that there may be someone close to dead already inside—minutes count. All kinds of patients are brought aboard—about 15–20 helos per day . . . [by boat] quite a few Vietnamese—some combat victims but many others for elective surgery or general care.

I feel good about doing something relatively positive in this war. But it's also a strange feeling of being almost farther from the war here. Standing on the bridge at night and watching flares, gunfire, and occasional ships firing in the distance while drinking coke or coffee, BS'ing with the men on watch, and thinking about going back to bed in an air conditioned room after eating a midnight breakfast if wanted—the two things contrast so much. And then supervising the carrying from the helos of bleeding, dying, sick patients. It's hard to know what my reaction to it all is yet. Mostly I've been too busy so far to have time to form a reaction. And we get so little news out here. Just occasional Armed Forces Radio and week or two old papers and magazines. Right now anyway somehow for me personally the war seemed worse when I was watching it on TV—maybe partly because of feeling frustrated to only be able to sit there. But for the guys brought aboard (and women civilians too), the war is <u>here</u> and a helluva lot worse than it is on TV. And for the doctors—they seem

---

[1] Later in the letter, Rogers noted that he just learned that these statistics, though available in newsmagazines, were supposed to be secret, so he added, "HUSH HUSH."

much more tired than the crew. . . . I was pleased with the outcome of the election. . . . I'm not surprised it was so close. Just like in '60. Another couple of weeks and it might have been reversed. Have you talked with Mr. Nixon, Dad? Must be kind of an awesome feeling for him now. . . .

Love, Jeff

2   *November 24, 1968*

Dear Dale and Don [Jeff's older sister and her husband],
. . . You speak of having trouble imagining me over here. Well, in a way, it's difficult to comprehend being over here. The American presence is so overwhelming here, it doesn't seem halfway around the world. . . . In the military, it's as if a portion of the U.S. had been transplanted over here and stuck in amongst little bits and pieces of a foreign, oriental country called Vietnam. Here I live with Americans, eat American food, drink fresh water (distilled aboard ship), watch occasional taped U.S. TV, listen to U.S. radio . . . and watch American military power fire at an invisible enemy. Never once in three weeks here have I even been aware of hearing Vietnamese talked. . . . The Vietnamese I have interacted with so far are either fluent in English or are too wounded or sick to talk. It's a strange war, but as attested to by the 34 guys we flew out yesterday by helicopter on stretchers on their way back home—a real one.

Love, Jeff

3   *December 7, 1968*

> Jeff's job was to position the USS *Repose* at offshore locations as close as possible to battle areas so that helicopters carrying the wounded had quick access to the hospital. He also helped to direct the highly skilled helicopter pilots onto the ship's small landing pad and aided in the transfer of the wounded from the helicopters to the operating room.

Dear Dad,
. . . I was pleased to hear that Chief Justice Warren agreed to stay on. I assume that was your work—congratulations.[1] My major news is that I have taken

---

[1] Chief Justice Earl Warren was appointed to the Supreme Court by President Eisenhower, when William Rogers was attorney general. Warren led the Court in the *Brown v. Board of Education* decision, which desegregated public schools in 1954. Rogers approved this decision, but it was one that created enforcement problems for the Eisenhower administration, in which Richard Nixon served as vice president.

over as navigator of the *Repose*. This won't change my job much because I've been doing the navigator work anyway. But . . . this gives me more leeway in making decisions. . . . So the *Repose* has definite advantages for a junior officer. It is one of the very few large ships on which an Ensign can become OOD ("officer of the deck") after only a month aboard (this is nothing great to my credit, as other Ensigns have made it in equal or less time, though some in much more). . . . Other advantages of the *Repose* for officers are the good living conditions, and the preferred treatment you get on next duty. I toured the crew's living quarters the other day, really for the first time—and they're pretty bad. Four small "bunks" in a stack, all very close together, and inadequate toilet and shower facilities. Compare to my two-room stateroom, bathroom shared by two people, and quiet. . . .

Disadvantages of the *Repose* are the full unbroken year over here and the unNavy-like nature of the ship—no weapons, unique organization, etc. . . . The biggest disadvantage of this ship is its monotonous and repetitious operating schedule. Pretty much the same times, same places, same operations. This simplifies navigation and much else but increases the tedium of a year over here. . . .

I really appreciate your letters too.

Love, Jeff

4   *December 30, 1968*

Dear Mother and Dad,

. . . The *Newsweeks* just started arriving; getting here when they are still current, which is great. . . . Mail time both ways varies a lot. We've been spending three days in Da Nang harbor, where we get mail quickly; followed by three days off the DMZ,[1] where we get mail slowly or not at all. . . . We are scheduled to be off the DMZ on the 25th. We go to Subic [Bay Naval Base] in the Philippines on the 27th so at least we'll be in a little better shape for the New Year. On the way to Subic celestial navigation becomes important, so I should get some experience using a sextant with stars and the sun. We go to Subic four times a year for 5 or 6 days each time. But the ship hasn't gone anyplace else for 1½ years. . . . So unless the war changes, we stay right here. . . .

Since I stopped writing yesterday, the following things happened—all fairly typical of life on the *Repose*. I stood a 12 noon to 1600 OOD[2] watch during which we sent away various of the ship's boats to the Da Nang area for milk, mail, to take some of the crew to beach parties, to transport the Captain and other brass to play tennis or amuse themselves. . . . Like a lot on the *Repose*, things often

---

[1] The "DMZ" was the demilitarized zone, which marked the border between the northern and southern halves of the country.

[2] According to the twenty-four-hour clock used in the military, "1600" is 4:00 P.M.; "OOD," as Jeff noted in a previous letter, means "officer of the deck."

seem to be done haphazardly and the little things sometimes seem more important to the brass aboard (5 captains, 4 medical) than the big things, which is frustrating. The captain gets much madder if you are 5 minutes late with a boat for tennis than if a helicopter with 16 seriously wounded medevac (medical evacuation patients) is mistakenly sent one hour out of its way—both have happened.

Rogers then described his first trip ashore with thirty other officers to have dinner and drinks at the Officers Club at the naval base in Da Nang.

You feel a little foreign walking from the boat to the club. Mud streets, dodging motor scooters, being saluted by little Vietnamese military men, and almost being run over by little Vietnamese civilians. Then into the club and back to the pseudo-America where the Vietnamese waiters and waitresses seem to be the foreigners there to serve the big Americans. These parties are cherished by the Captain, Exec, and the doctors—but they turn off almost all of the junior officers in the ship's company—including me definitely. They take up time better used sleeping and the "regulars" become so obsessed with their little ventures that they become a real burden for those who have to prepare boats for them and see that everyone gets there and back . . . quite a lot of trivia to take up the time we don't have between the important things. . . . This month promised to be very quiet—just administrative, with lookout for small craft and swimmers (patrol boats in the harbor, after dropping percussion grenades to keep away any Viet Cong swimmers who have a liking for sabotaging ships). . . .

Being on the periphery of a hospital here . . . I'm more convinced than ever that I was correct in leaving medicine. But I'm also less sure than ever of just what I want to do. One thing I've eliminated is a career in the Navy. . . .

Yes, we see some of the firing around Da Nang and near the DMZ. And we anchor close to the piers which have been shelled occasionally—but still we are relatively quite safe. . . .

Love, Jeff

5   *February 18, 1969*

Dear Mother and Dad,

Though it's been quite a while since I wrote, not much new has happened in the interim. . . . Thirty days straight of floating with only a sandy, barren, low coastline in the distance. . . . There have been some kind of depressing times for me since Subic in that the initial excitement of the ship and activity of learning has worn off and now it's the prospect of 8? more months of the same plus questions still about what I want to do in the future and about myself in general. But my spirits are pretty good now. I've been spending some time with the nurses, which is something of a diversion, though even there the conversation often revolves around the frustration of one year at sea, the frustration of this war, and the condition of the dead and dying patients. . . .

Everyone has been prepared for a large Tet offensive (Tet began yesterday, the 17th), though so far only minor increases in fighting seem to have occurred.[1] I've doubted all along that they would have a major offensive at this time. They are too smart to do so when we are all prepared for one. We'll see.

Seems like Nixon is doing a good job so far. I've heard only positive comments even from self-proclaimed "liberals." Seems to me the two basic elements are his air of calm, quiet efficiency and his open honesty with the press and public about his opinion. I think the latter is <u>very</u> important. The fact that no one in the administration seems disturbed by such trivial things as everyone knowing who the cabinet would be a day or two early is a hugely refreshing contrast to Johnson. As is his directness about his hopes and himself: i.e. "hope to win the respect and eventually the friendship of Negroes." If he can just keep speaking openly and honestly and acting on his own beliefs even when he starts to be criticized, as is inevitable, he should be a damn good president, I think.

I received and enjoyed the tapes you sent. It was reassuring to know you're still having ice cream with butterscotch sauce for dinner. . . . In your last letter, it annoyed me a little what you said about Dad not being able to ask about job suggestions for me. I'm not asking any special favors, in fact I've made it clear I don't want them. All I'm asking is that you keep your eyes open for possibilities. . . . I can't believe that any mention of the subject [of Jeff's search for a post after Vietnam] would be taken as an "order" as Mother suggests. . . . Which brings me to the whole subject of not using pull. I agree in general, but I think it's easy to be so sensitive to it (as I've been in the past) as to pass up opportunities and thus perhaps the chance to do something worthwhile for others. . . . Dad and I were talking once about families and Dad pointed out that an alternative to rejecting the parents, in effect, and starting on your own was to build on what the parents are and have done, and he used the Kennedys as an example. Well, one of the reasons the Kennedys have done so much is that they haven't been afraid to use their own and each other's influence. Though I, too, find the extremes they carry it to distasteful, there is definitely something to be said for not being afraid to use "pull" if one honestly believes it will be for the good of all. . . . So I repeat my original request made months ago: I'd appreciate it if Dad would let me know if he hears of any good Junior Naval Officer billets that exist in the D.C. area. . . . I don't think it's an unreasonable request to ask of my father, Secretary of State or not. Thanks. . . .

I found the following headline in the *Wall Street Journal* and it now is on my desk:

Cruise Ship Staves Off Ennui With Good Food and Endless Activities.

Love, Jeff

[1] Tet Nguyen Dan is the lunar New Year festival and marks the most important holiday in Vietnamese culture. This celebration of the beginning of spring is a time for family visiting, feasting, and gift giving. A year earlier, in 1968, the North Vietnamese and Vietcong had staged a dramatic assault on the south during Tet. They inflicted so much damage that polls showed a majority of the American public doubted the United States was making progress in the war.

6   *March 14, 1969*

Jeff wrote this letter just three days before Nixon ordered secret bombing of Cambodia.

Dear Mother and Dad,

Nothing much new to report. Things stay the same here—which is one of the most discouraging aspects of this war. No apparent motion or progress, just a steady influx of dead and dying men. For the first time, yesterday, I felt a little sick to my stomach watching a helo land with six Marines straight off the battle-field—they looked pretty badly mangled when they took them off the helo. Soon found out I was right: 5 out of 6 were dead on arrival, the 6th died shortly after. Not that I'm not expecting to see death in a war, but all of it we see here seems harder to accept because we see or sense no progress towards any goal.

Another thing that bothers me about the war is the so-called "intelligence." First of all it seems to have little relation to what really happens. A case in point is the intelligence about the recent offensive. We were told a month before Tet they expected a big attack on Quang Tri during Tet, etc., etc. As far as I know there has still been no sizeable attack on Quang Tri, and the offensive began after Tet is not the same type of offensive as was predicted, etc. Every few days we get classified intelligence messages saying that "tonite will be the big attack." Never happens.

And on the other side our press releases both exaggerate and underplay events. *Newsweek* described the attack on Da Nang as something like: "bombs raining in on the city, fires and secondary explosions throughout the city." We got there several hours after the attack and saw three fires, widely scattered, and little else. In general, things looked normal and only moderate damage was done to several military installations. Or another example was the explosion in the landing craft in Da Nang—an explosion we could see, hear, smell. Military press releases as reported on American Forces Vietnam radio network said one killed and 30 injured. In truth, over 30 were killed instantly and the whole landing area was a shambles.

So if intelligence reports and press reports have such little relation to what really is happening, who does one believe? Worse, I really wonder if <u>anyone</u> knows what the true story is. The war is too fragmented, too spread out, and too multi-faceted to really be understood as far as who is accomplishing what.

About income tax. We don't have to file as long as we're in the Vietnam combat zone, so I'll wait until I get back to do that.

Yes, we occasionally have beach parties and I've gotten to swim once or twice. But we just got word that there had been a sniper incident at the beach we've been using so beach parties may be out.

We have a change of command next month. Should be interesting to adjust to a new Captain. . . . This Captain now is quite lax and so we have things pretty easy, but I dislike him strongly, to be frank. His priority list is 1. His reputation and social status 2. Other niceties (but not necessities) like parties, uninterrupted church services, and short hair 3. The welfare and safety of patients. His attitude bothers me a lot. . . .

Love, Jeff

7 · *April 20, 1969*

Secretary of State Rogers and his wife were scheduled to make an inspection trip to Vietnam in the spring of 1969. Although Rogers was often frozen out of strategic planning for the war, his trip was intended to demonstrate the Nixon administration's continuing support for the war even as it laid plans to announce the Vietnamization policy.

Dear Mother and Dad,

. . . I've been wondering, Dad, if you plan to travel at all around Vietnam when you're here—if you still plan to come. It's a shame to be over here a year and see only the coastline and bits of Da Nang. I don't know if it's possible or ethical for me to travel around with you (or your entourage, that is) for a day or so, but it would be great if it would. If it's impossible, I certainly understand.

The longer I'm over here, the more I think we should get out quickly, almost no matter how. Even an initial small unilateral withdrawal might both demonstrate our ultimate peace goal and scare the South Vietnamese into doing a little more for themselves. As I've said before the thing that bothers me most about it all are the sickening sameness of each day, of the news reports, of the "battles," of the intelligence briefings, of the dead and dying people—there seems to be *no* progress or even change—just more dead and destroyed. The other aspect that makes me doubt that we should stay is the very strong impression that NO ONE REALLY KNOWS what's happening over here. . . . Our Captain says "the allies have really been winning a great victory in the A Shaw Valley" and Marines who have been wounded in the A Shaw Valley say we are getting wiped out there. . . . The government since '65 predicts changes that never occur, and doesn't predict the few that do, etc. It's not that there's a conspiracy to deceive, or a plan to keep the war going by the Vietnamese capitalists or the U.S. militarists or expansionist plans by the U.S.—as the radicals would have one believe. It's not that intentions are bad—it's just that knowledge of what's really happening is abysmal, and given the nature of the war and the country it's probably impossible to ever attain a complete, accurate picture. And if no one can really understand what's happening now, how can anyone decide what should happen or how to get there. Maybe I'm saying that the whole thing is beyond our control and we should stop trying to control it, because all we do meanwhile is waste men and money. The loss of men is obvious. The loss of money becomes clearer when you watch millions spent on the battleship *New Jersey,* then see it sit off the coast here, firing maybe 50 rounds a day far inland and read reports that it "destroyed 4 enemy bunkers and 2 tunnels, no known enemy killed." In fact, I think every U.S. Navy combatant ship over here could be pulled out without any noticeable effect on the war. (Supply ships and hospital ships are different.)

I like what the administration has been saying so far but, as you pointed out, it seems awfully important that results be "forthcoming," not just talk. Look forward to seeing maybe both of you next month.

Love, Jeff

P.S. If troops are pulled out of Vietnam, an excellent way to get them back would be on big white ships.

8   *May 24, 1969*

William and Adele Rogers made an official State Department visit to Vietnam between May 14 and May 19. On the first day of their visit, President Nixon went on national television to announce the new Vietnamization policy. Jeff Rogers was able to travel around the country with his parents for three or four days. Today, Jeff recalls visiting Hue with them and seeing some young recruits preparing to go out on their first mission, looking "petrified." He says his parents were deeply affected by the trip, including their visit on board the USS *Repose.*

Dear Dad,

I'm enclosing the death report on Forbes, the man with the blistered amputation you gave the purple heart to. They didn't think he would die, but he did. The hospital people also wanted you to know so you could take it into account if you write letters to families.

Love, Jeff

9   *May 31, 1969*

Dear Mother and Dad,

Hope the rest of your trip went well. As I wrote to Dad earlier, it was great to see both of you and a really good chance to see more of the country. . . . Am working on a collection of pictures of our trip to the *Repose,* some of which Mother would particularly like I suspect. . . . Don't know if you ever heard, also, that just before you went into the Intensive Care Unit to give purple hearts another patient died. Apparently they just covered him with a sheet while you were there and removed him later. But to most of the men over here and to their families that's what this war is about—not the pacification re-settlement stuff you were shown on your trip.[1]

Love, Jeff

[1] "Pacification resettlement" was a wartime term for U.S. efforts to move South Vietnamese villagers away from areas controlled by the north or the Vietcong and to persuade them that allegiance to the United States and Saigon promised greater political and economic freedom.

10   *June 10, 1969*

Dear Mother and Dad,

Generally things are the same. . . . Of course, people are standing by to see if there'll be any major changes in our operations with the beginning of with-drawal [crossed out] replacement, though it's probably doubtful I realize. If troops continue to be removed, it's going to be harder than ever for those who remain—and for the families of those wounded or killed. Also for those who are sent over here. Wonder if there's some way to stop sending any combat troops over here and use the natural end of men's tours to phase out our com-bat troops. Probably will be necessary to send replacement advisory and sup-port military types for some time. But to send replacement frontline Marines, for example, who may have a 20% chance of getting killed or permanently maimed over here while troops are being withdrawn will be hard as hell on everyone. Anyway, I am pleased about the first move and hope that the process goes as quickly as possible or quicker. . . .

Mother, let me put in a correction. As long as you think it's a good story (I do too) and are going to be telling it, let me tell you how it really goes: This nurse did <u>not</u> say, as you said, "No it doesn't matter to me that your father is Secretary of——what is he secretary of?" This implies that she didn't know his position. She did. What really was said is as follows: Me: "Does my father's position make any difference to you one way or the other?" Her: "No, it doesn't matter to me that your father is Secretary of——(brief pause while her mind went blank for a second before she completed the sentence) Me (interrupting quickly during the pause): "Okay, okay, you've convinced me." The point is not that she didn't know what Dad is Secretary of, but that her mind went blank for a second just at the appropriate time. (Which perhaps indicated indeed that Dad's position was not in the forefront of her impression of me, which is what I was trying to ascertain.)

Love, Jeff

11   *June 23, 1969*

Dear Mother and Dad,

As always, things are the same. So there really is no news. There is very little talk about the replacement <——> withdrawal—obviously it doesn't affect at all the lives of most people over here. As a matter of fact, there is in general little talk about the general situation over here and what should be done. People just seem to have given up on the whole mess and only look forward to finishing their year (this is not a new development, having been that way since I arrived). . . .

Love, Jeff

12   *August 28, 1969*

Dear Mother and Dad,

Got back from R&R a few days ago. It was great—especially the days of leave I took afterward to visit Pleiku. I was off the ship 13 days—somewhat longer than most R&R's to say the least. Six days in Tokyo . . . then back to Vietnam and up to the Pleiku area for three days. I was with an Army major I'd met in Saigon. He is really fine and was great to me—as were all his friends and associates, from the Commanding General on down (or "up" depending on what you think of Generals). I spent two days traveling in helicopters around the various Montagnard[1] villages that the U.S. civic action people are working in. It is one of the most fascinating things I've seen. The people are truly primitive, yet truly appreciative of the Americans—in both respects quite unlike Vietnamese. Again it confirmed my impression that one's attitude towards our involvement in Vietnam is conditioned <u>very</u> strongly by one's experience here, because there is a huge variety of possible types of experiences: from getting killed, which we see on the ship every day—to political involvement which I saw in Saigon—to the grateful smiles of some Montagnard chief—to obscene gestures towards and thievery from GI's that I see in Da Nang.

Watching the civic action work with the Montagnards raises again the moot question of whether we should be here at all—and the vital question of what to do now—abandoning some of these people too abruptly would be criminal now—but having Americans killed every day is equally criminal. . . . The chance to go into the villages and talk to the people leisurely and actually

---

[1] Term from the era of French colonial rule in Vietnam that refers to the independent group of mountain people who lived in the central highlands of Vietnam and did not align with the Hanoi government during the war. The Montagnards were not strong supporters of Saigon, either, but were friendly toward the Americans, who often hired them to do U.S. Army reconnaissance work.

see what's going on was a good complement to my field trips with Dad in which we saw a great variety of places—but one felt it was all staged in the showplaces of Vietnam. This visit was the real places where the war is going on. . . .

I, for one, have been really pleased with all the major directions that you and the President have been steering policy, as well as pleased with the President's domestic plans. Do hope though that the next withdrawal from here isn't postponed too long. I worry that the administration will fall into the LBJ trap of trying too hard to save face for the U.S., i.e., not withdrawing in the face of enemy action. When in reality "face" is much less important than lives. See you in two months.

Love, Jeff

Analyzing Personal Letters

1. Rogers arrived in Vietnam in November 1968. On what date do you find the first evidence that he was developing some skepticism about the war? What personal experiences caused these first doubts about the mission? Which six paragraphs from these twelve letters would you select to illustrate the evolution in Rogers's view of the war while in Vietnam?

2. What were Rogers's opinions about the Vietnamese people? Do you see any connection between those opinions and his growing doubts about the U.S. mission in Vietnam?

3. The sons of two of William Rogers's predecessors in Vietnam policymaking, Secretary of State Dean Rusk and Secretary of Defense Robert McNamara, developed stress-related illnesses while their fathers were presiding over the Vietnam War. Based on the letters excerpted here, how would you describe Jeff Rogers's reaction to his father's position in the Nixon administration? Do these letters provide you with enough evidence to characterize this father-son relationship?

4. Jeff Rogers said that the United States should get out of Vietnam "quickly, almost no matter how" (Source 7). But shortly after the Vietnamization program began, Jeff complained that it made things "harder than ever for those who remain" (Source 10). What were his concerns about Vietnamization? Did those concerns make a good argument for getting out of Vietnam quickly or for staying in country longer?

5. Jeff Rogers enjoyed privileged status in American society and was relatively protected from danger while in Vietnam. Does this information make his increasing opposition to the war more significant or less valid? Why?

6. Write a one-paragraph interpretation of the letters Rogers wrote on May 24 and May 31 (Sources 8 and 9), immediately after his parents' visit to Vietnam. How does your reading of all of the other letters in this chapter influence your interpretation of these two short letters?

The Rest of the Story

Jeff Rogers left Vietnam in late October 1969, a year after arriving. He spent the second year of his navy service in Washington, D.C., in a naval division charged with training foreign naval officers. Because of his job in the navy, in 1970 Jeff was able to accompany his father on a second State Department trip to Vietnam, where both father and son were investigating the progress of Vietnamization. The secretary of state approved his son's inclusion on the trip only because the navy had a legitimate job for him to do. In retrospect, Jeff regards this trip as "another indication of Dad's integrity."

At the end of his tour of duty with the navy in 1970, Jeff Rogers enrolled at Yale University Law School, where he was a classmate of Bill and Hillary Clinton. In 1973, he moved to Portland, Oregon, and began to practice law. That same year, President Nixon asked William P. Rogers for his resignation and named Henry Kissinger as the new secretary of state.

Before Rogers left office, the war in Vietnam officially ended in Paris in January 1973. Secretary of State Rogers, along with the representatives of North and South Vietnam, signed the formal "Agreement on Ending the War and Restoring Peace in Vietnam." The real end to the war came two years later, in April 1975, when troops from North Vietnam took over Saigon, forcing South Vietnamese and U.S. embassy officials to escape by scurrying on board helicopters and squeezing into airplanes. This chaotic, undignified end to America's involvement in Vietnam was precisely the nightmare that Nixon had hoped to avoid when he dreamed of "peace with honor."

Between 1969, when Jeff Rogers was serving in Vietnam, and 1973, when his father signed the official peace agreement, the Nixon administration pursued Henry Kissinger's plan to use "brutal unpredictability" in aerial bombing to force Hanoi into a peace agreement that retained a separate government in the south and removed all North Vietnamese troops from the south. The bombing campaign of those years included an open renewal of bombing in Cambodia in the spring of 1970 and expanded bombing of the neighboring nation of Laos. In the spring of 1972, with only 95,000 U.S. troops left in Vietnam, the government launched a massive bombing campaign over North Vietnam and placed mines in North Vietnamese harbors. Then, after winning reelection in November 1972 on the promise that peace was at hand, Nixon ordered the most massive bombing campaign yet against Hanoi, destroying factories, hospitals, and residential neighborhoods. These escalations of violence from the air did not elicit substantial concessions from Hanoi but significantly increased U.S. antiwar sentiment. With more than 70 percent of Americans agreeing that it had been a mistake to send troops to Vietnam, Nixon and Kissinger finally acquiesced to a peace agreement that was strikingly similar to the terms Hanoi had offered back in 1969, before all the bombing. There was to be a coalition government in the south in which the Vietcong would be legitimate participants, and the United States was to withdraw all of its troops without requiring a similar withdrawal of North Vietnamese troops. The humiliating debacle that occurred in April 1975 marked the final triumph of these northern troops and the end to all hope for an independent coalition government in the south as the country was reunited under the Hanoi government.

In the four years between Hanoi's original proposal of peace terms in 1969 and U.S. acceptance of those terms in 1973, 25,000 Americans died along with several hundred thousand Vietnamese, for a total of 58,000 American deaths and 1.7 million Vietnamese deaths between U.S. escalation of the war in 1965 and its end in 1973.

After resigning as secretary of state, William Rogers returned to his law practice in Washington, D.C., and only once returned to public life, to chair the commission investigating the explosion of the *Challenger* space shuttle in 1986. When William Rogers died in January 2001, journalist and former antiwar activist Howard Fineman wrote an editorial in the *New York Times* in which he recalled being invited into the secretary of state's office for a conversation while an antiwar protest was under way outside the White House gates. According to Fineman, Secretary Rogers was the one man in the administration who treated peace protestors with respect, even though he feared that outspoken opposition prolonged the war. Other commentators at the time of his death noted that William P. Rogers was never associated with any of the scandals that tainted the Nixon administration.

While in Vietnam, Jeff Rogers had predicted that Richard Nixon would be "a damn good president" if he "can just keep speaking openly and honestly and acting on his own beliefs even when he starts to be criticized." Over the years, however, the Nixon administration's paranoia over the antiwar movement and leaks to the press about war plans fostered increasing secrecy and illegal behavior. This pattern culminated in a desperate effort to control the election of 1972; since Nixon could not run as the president who had "won the peace" in Vietnam, he felt he had to manipulate the election in his favor. In retrospect, even Nixon's closest advisors have admitted that without Vietnam, there would have been no Watergate scandal. It was his persistent failures in Vietnam and his inability to accept failure that led Nixon to authorize the illegal actions that eventually ended in his resignation in August 1974, after facing nearly certain impeachment.

Jeff Rogers never left Portland after setting up his law practice there in 1973. He raised his two children there, served as an assistant U.S. attorney in Portland during the Clinton administration, and was Portland's city attorney from 1985 to 2004. Although he and his father held different political allegiances in the 1970s and 1980s, they continued to respect each other and to enjoy an active exchange of views through phone calls and, of course, letters.

To Find Out More

Jeff Rogers's letters are among the millions of letters in the hands of private Americans. His were sitting in a box in his attic until his son asked permission to use them in a college paper, and that request led to their presentation here. The sheer chance involved with moving Jeff Rogers's letters from his attic to this book is not all that unusual in historical research. Sometimes, finding un-published letters can be as easy as cleaning out a grandparent's basement and as difficult as placing ads in local newspapers and then traveling around the country to follow up on leads. In between those two poles, you will find that there are millions of unpublished letters, dealing with every conceivable topic, deposited in historical archives all across the United States. Imagination and the aid of a librarian and a Web browser can help you discover if a person or topic of interest has relevant letters on file in any archive in the United States.

There are many published collections of letters, including several devoted to the letters of those who served in Vietnam. Collections that feature letters written by a wide variety of Americans in Vietnam include *Dear America: Letters Home from Vietnam,* edited by Bernard Edelman (New York: New York Veterans Memorial Commission and Simon and Schuster, 1985); *Letters from Vietnam,* edited by Bill Adler (New York: Presidio Press, 2003); *Letters from Vietnam,* edited by Glenn Munson (New York: Parallax Publishing, 1966); and *Dear Dr. Spock: Letters about the Vietnam War to America's Favorite Baby Doctor* (New York: New York University Press, 2005). *War Letters: Extraordinary Correspondence from American Wars,* edited by Andrew Carroll (New York: Washington Square Press, 2002), includes letters from various wars, including Vietnam. Published vol-umes that feature just one individual's letters from Vietnam include Paul J. Raisig Jr., *Letters from a Distant War: Vietnam from a Soldier's Perspective* (North Carolina: Pentland Press, 2004); Rick St. John, *Circle of Helmets: Poetry and Letters of the Vietnam War* (Authorhouse, 2002); Daniel H. Fitzgibbon, *To Bear Any Burden: A Hoosier Green Beret's Letters from Vietnam* (Indianapolis: Indiana Historical Society, 2005); James G. Rowe, *Love to All, Jim: A Young Man's Letters from Vietnam* (Strawberry Hill Press, 1989); Oscar Herrgesell, *Dear Margaret, Today I Died—Letters from Vietnam* (San Antonio: Naylor Co., 1974); John Derral Hargroder, *Love Always US54607898: Letters from an American Soldier in Vietnam to His Wife Back in the World* (Authorhouse, 2005). See, too, Lynda Van Devanter's *Home before Morning: The Story of an Army Nurse in Vietnam* (Amherst: University of Massachusetts Press, 2001), which uses letters to evoke a woman's experience in the war. *Shrapnel in the Heart: Letters and Remembrances from the Vietnam Veterans Memorial,* edited by Laura Palmer (New York: Vintage, 1988) and *Letters on the Wall: A Collection of Letters Left at the Vietnam Veterans Memorial* (New York: Collins, 2006) are both collections of letters left at the me-morial in Washington, D.C.

The historical literature on the Vietnam War is voluminous. In *Nixon's Vietnam War* (Lawrence: University Press of Kansas, 1988), Jeffrey Kimball ex-amines the last five years of the war. Broader accounts can be found in George C. Herring, *America's Longest War: The United States and Vietnam, 1950–1975* (Philadelphia: Temple University Press, 1986); Marilyn Young, *The Vietnam Wars, 1945–1990* (New York: Harper Perennial, 1991); Stanley Karnow, *Vietnam: A History* (New York: Viking Press, 1983); and Neil Sheehan, *A Bright Shining Lie: John Paul Vann and America in Vietnam* (New York: Vintage Books, 1989). See, too, Keith Beattie, *The Scar That Binds: American Culture and the Vietnam War* (New York: New York University Press, 2000); Andrew E. Hunt, *The Turning: A History of Vietnam Veterans against the War* (New York: New York University

Press, 1999); and Christian G. Appy, *Working-Class War: American Combat Soldiers and Vietnam* (Chapel Hill: University of North Carolina Press, 1993).

Vietnam veterans have published a number of remarkable memoirs, including Philip Caputo, *Rumor of War* (New York: Holt, Rinehart, and Winston, 1977); Michael Herr, *Dispatches* (New York: Knopf, 1977); Tim O'Brien, *If I Die in a Combat Zone* (New York: Dell, 1973); and Ron Kovic, *Born on the Fourth of July* (New York: McGraw-Hill, 1976).

Three Web sites offer excellent documents and bibliographies on the Vietnam War: the Vietnam Project, sponsored by Texas Tech University, at **vietnam .ttu.edu**; **vietnamwar.net**, a nonacademic site that offers extensive leads to resources; and the Vietnam War Bibliography, provided by Dr. Edwin Moise of Clemson University at **clemson.edu/caah/history/FacultyPages/EdMoise/ bibliography.html**.

CHAPTER 13

Declarations for Changing Times

Student Protest Manifestos from the 1960s

"My God, they're killing us!" The young woman's cry rang out across the Commons at Kent State University on May 4, 1970. Four students lay dead and nine others were wounded after members of the Ohio National Guard opened fire on a noontime protest against President Nixon's expansion of the Vietnam War into Cambodia. The killings at Kent State reverberated across the nation's campuses. In response, 80 percent of all U.S. colleges and universities experienced some sort of student protest against those who were "killing us," and nearly five million students at 900 colleges and universities went on strike to end classes, cancel exams, and focus all attention on the meaning of Kent State.

American students used that moment to underscore their generational alienation from powerful adults who controlled the government, the military, the political parties, the economy — and the nation's colleges and universities. Only 13 percent of American students identified with "radical" political ideas in a 1969 poll, but 80 percent identified with "my generation." Even though students were not the only ones calling for an end to the Vietnam War, a national commitment to racial equality, and a war on poverty in the 1960s and 1970s, they saw themselves as the vanguard of change; indeed, by 1970, they trusted no one over the age of thirty to have the courage for change. Ironically, youth's rebellion in this era grew out of their training in elementary and high school, where cold war–inspired curricula taught students to believe that America was the greatest nation on earth because it ensured political liberty and economic opportunity to all its citizens. When developments in the civil rights movement and the Vietnam War caused young people to doubt those school lessons, they protested — in great numbers.

The United States had experienced a "baby boom" in the post-Depression, postwar years between 1946 and 1964; at the end of that reproductive explosion, almost 40 percent of the population was under age nineteen. The postwar prosperity of the 1950s and the postwar expansion of public universities meant that millions of families could afford to send their children to college. By the end of the 1960s, almost half of all Americans between the ages of eighteen and twenty-one were attending college, and 75 percent of them were enrolled in public institutions. The college population grew from three million in 1960 to five million in 1964, and then doubled to ten million in 1973, producing bulging dormitories, crowded classes, huge demands on state legislatures to fund higher education, and a strong sense among America's youth that they were a demographic force to be reckoned with.

Looking back on the sixties, we can identify two waves of student protest. The first wave, between 1960 and 1968, involved a few thousand intensely idealistic students determined to make American institutions live up to the nation's democratic promises. The second, much larger wave, beginning in 1968 and lasting until 1974, drew millions of mainstream students who engaged in citizen protests, like the one at Kent State. But the second wave was not simply bigger and louder; it was inflected with the new voices of counter-culture youth alienated from established institutions and divided by the violent tactics of radical revolutionaries. In the fourteen years between John Kennedy's optimistic election in 1960, Lyndon Baines Johnson's escalation of the Vietnam War, and Richard Nixon's disgraced resignation in 1974, fourteen new classes of young people entered American colleges and universities, and each class raised the decibel level of student outcry.

The first wave of the student protest movement reflected students' commitment to working within the existing system. Black students who began lunch counter sit-ins in Greensboro, North Carolina, early in 1960 formed the Student Nonviolent Coordinating Committee (SNCC, pronounced "snick"). They agreed with Dr. Martin Luther King Jr.'s philosophy of nonviolence but sought independence from King's Southern Christian Leadership Council (SCLC). As an autonomous organization, SNCC participated in the 1961 Freedom Rides, which integrated interstate buses in the South. SNCC members then took up the dangerous work of registering Southern blacks to vote.

In these early years, SNCC included blacks and whites who believed they could work together, under the protection of the Kennedy administration, to bring about racial democracy. SNCC's interracial volunteer teams persevered amid hatred and violence—and with scant government protection. Up north, in 1962, liberal white students formed the Students for a Democratic Society (SDS) to voice their opposition to nuclear weapons and class inequality. SDS founders rejected both the anticommunist paranoia of the 1950s and the pro-Marxist rigidities of the "Old Left." In defining their generation's "New Left," they optimistically embraced the 1950s faith that established U.S. institutions could be used to reform the nation's military and diplomatic strategies and to promote equitable racial and economic policies.

The male-dominated membership of SDS and SNCC also embraced 1950s assumptions about women. Men in both organizations praised individual dignity and human equality but expected female members to make coffee, type minutes, and demonstrate their political commitment through sexual availability. When a handful of college women questioned this contradiction within the movement in 1965, they were silenced by the macho leadership of SNCC and SDS. Women's revolt awaited the second wave of student protest.

In the fall of 1964, students shifted their focus from national and international issues to their right to political protest at their home campuses. The Free Speech Movement (FSM) emerged at the University of California–Berkeley (UC–Berkeley) when the university administration shut down a traditional campus site for political speeches and recruitment. Berkeley students ultimately compelled the university administration to honor the Constitution's First Amendment, but that took four months of sustained demonstrations, bloody confrontations with local police, the arrest of 800 demonstrators, and the resignation of the university's chancellor.

Events at Berkeley ignited a national student critique of college policies governing students' personal lives and launched a debate over traditional teaching practices and traditional course offerings. The old tradition of "in loco parentis," whereby college administrators served "in place of a parent," came under fire for rules governing what time students had to be in their dorms at night, what clothing they could wear to class or to meals, how long their hair could be, and where and for how long they could kiss goodnight. Opponents of in loco parentis argued successfully that such petty personal infringements infantilized students rather than training them for self-governing autonomy.

As the second wave began to break over American campuses, fights over dorm curfews would seem quaint to incoming college students. Those who started college in the fall of 1968 came with a very different set of experiences than had their predecessors in 1960 or 1964. Watching television at home, this vanguard of the second wave had already seen the early promises of the sixties unraveling. By 1968, President Johnson's three-year escalation of the war in Vietnam looked to many like a waste of lives and money, and as the war drained funds and attention away from Johnson's optimistic civil rights and antipoverty programs, student activists grew bitter.

Urban race riots in the summers of 1965, 1966, and 1967 revealed the government's impotence and the power of violence. Black students in SNCC were frustrated by their elders' counsel to be patient when more than two dozen civil rights workers had been killed since 1960, and they were angry that their voter registration progress in Mississippi had been compromised by deals within President Johnson's Democratic Party. In 1966, SNCC turned youth's call for autonomy and self-determination into a racial call for Black Power, which required the expulsion of all whites from SNCC activities. Malcolm X, a hero to those in SNCC, had articulated the logic of black separatism before he began to shift toward a policy of racial cooperation; however, Malcolm's assassination in 1965 deprived young people of his leadership.

While the majority of American students still supported the Vietnam War in 1966 and 1967, they were being challenged by antiwar classmates to renounce the safe privilege of a student deferment from the military draft and jungle warfare. Many in the draft resistance movement turned in or even publicly burned their draft cards in protest against both the war and the Selective Service System that administered the draft. In October 1967, 50,000 people,

*Figure 13.1 **This Is the Sixties?*** *This photo was taken during the Free Speech Movement at the University of California–Berkeley. Students in the photo were marching on December 7, 1965, to protest the arrest of 800 student demonstrators. Their hairstyles and clothing remind us that the first wave of student activists looked more like children of the 1950s than counterculture rebels. Their signs remind us that they had faith in American traditions of free speech, individual conscience, and labor protest and viewed their professors as their allies.*

Source: The Bancroft Library, University of California–Berkeley.

including antiwar students, joined in a Stop the Draft demonstration at the Pentagon. Their peaceful protest ended at midnight when paratroopers stormed the crowd, bashing heads and clubbing bodies. As was so often the case in the 1960s, this violent crackdown by government authorities recruited new adherents to the protest movement. Back on campus, more students listened to antiwar classmates' claims that the government was not to be trusted.

The year 1968 is the turning point in every narrative of the sixties. One writer described it as "the year when history came off its leash." For students entering or returning to college, 1968 unfolded at a dizzying speed. In January, the Tet offensive in Vietnam revealed the United States was not as close to victory as the government claimed, and in February CBS news anchor Walter Cronkite publicly expressed his doubt that the war could ever be won. In March, Minnesota's antiwar senator, Eugene McCarthy, aided by hundreds of student campaigners, made a strong showing against President Johnson in the New Hampshire presidential primary. Two weeks later, President Johnson announced he would not seek reelection, and New York senator Robert F. Kennedy announced that he would run—as an antiwar candidate. In early April, Martin Luther King Jr. was assassinated, depriving young people of a powerful voice for peace and moral change.

Later that month, students at Columbia University in New York City protested the university's plan to make room for a new gymnasium by tearing down a nearby black neighborhood. Student protesters occupied five buildings for seven days, held three school officials hostage, ransacked the president's files, and demanded thorough reform of the university's financial policies and educational curriculum. When police stormed Columbia's campus, 10 percent of the student body of 7,000 was placed under arrest, but their weeklong protest had galvanized a national discussion of college curricula. In the wake of the Columbia incident, students across the nation began to demand courses in which they could learn to analyze and discuss controversial social issues, not simply take lecture notes on safe subjects.

The summer of 1968 offered no respite. In June, Robert Kennedy won the California primary with the help of black activists, Mexican American workers, and college students but was tragically assassinated the same day. And in August, 10,000 young people clashed with Chicago police in a week of bloody street demonstrations outside the Democratic national convention. Around the globe in that same year, students rose up against war, repression, and economic privilege in Paris, Mexico City, and Prague.

These international developments produced a broad population of protest sympathizers and participants on American college campuses. On the surface, they looked more radical than earlier protesters because they wore "hippie" clothes, used recreational drugs, played psychedelic music, and boasted about a dramatic loosening of sexual mores. But these pot-smoking peace marchers seemed naive to that radical fringe of college students, black and white, who had moved beyond protesting. The second wave's militant radicals believed that the U.S. government was impervious to reform and deserved a violent revolution; they did not believe that a peaceful counterculture could ever bring peace. Meanwhile, at the nonviolent end of the spectrum, there emerged the most enduring legacy of sixties student protest: the women's liberation movement. Part counterculture, part militant, part mainstream, this female protest against male supremacy found its voice in 1968 and took full advantage of the decade's pro-equality, prorevolutionary rhetoric. By linking personal and political freedom, women's liberation wrought fundamental changes in the distribution of power in private and public life.

Student protests in the 1960s and 1970s bore all the marks of youth: they were loud, impatient, arrogant, sometimes naive, sometimes violent. Generational identity was partly an illusion since young people chose many different routes to protest and reform, and the outcome of their efforts was inevitably different from what many imagined. Ultimately, however, the influence of the student movements is evident in the fact that college students in most U.S. colleges and universities today still live according to the principles of free speech, personal autonomy, and classroom attention to social issues that were established by students in the 1960s.

Using the Source: Manifestos from the Sixties

The United States of America was created by political manifestos. Thomas Paine's *Common Sense* and Thomas Jefferson's Declaration of Independence are prime examples of public proclamations of ideals, purposes, and intentions that served to rally supporters, persuade doubters, and warn opponents. When the founders listed freedom of speech first in the Bill of Rights, they were protecting the right of any American to publish and distribute a manifesto as much as they were protecting the right to stand on a street corner and deliver a spoken address.

The tradition of manifestos has persisted in American history; individuals and groups have printed and circulated millions of statements declaring both political conviction and intended actions. The right to do so has been threatened by laws and the courts, most notably during World War I, when the government passed the Espionage Act of 1917 and then used it to convict and imprison Charles Schenck for distributing a leaflet challenging wartime military conscription and to imprison Eugene Debs for a wartime speech against militarism. Using that precedent, Congress and the courts between 1920 and 1960 mounted various efforts to limit the dissemination of unpopular ideas that the state deemed dangerous.

Ironically, the Supreme Court in the 1960s was aggressive in overturning restrictive precedents in order to protect free speech. So just at the time that protesters were denouncing the Establishment as antidemocratic, the Supreme Court was actively shielding protesters' right to such dissent. Except for its 1968 decision in *United States v. O'Brien* that burning draft cards was an unprotected interference with the "smooth and efficient functioning" of the Selective Service System, the Supreme Court took no opportunity to limit sixties protest, and Congress never used the Vietnam War as a reason to silence published or spoken criticism of the government.

Manifesto writers in the 1960s operated in a moment of technological transition when it came to actually printing their leaflets and pamphlets. Xerox machines were appearing in private business, in government, and at universities, but cheap, convenient copy centers were not widespread: to Xerox one hundred copies of a six-page manifesto would have been a prohibitively slow and expensive process for student protesters whose parents were not funding their activism. Employing a print shop to set the type for a manifesto was similarly expensive, and many professional printers refused to handle student protest materials. Typically, then, students typed up their manifestos on widely available "ditto" or "mimeograph" forms, which produced an inked template that could be used to run off a few hundred copies from a ditto or mimeograph machine onto inexpensive paper. Countless young women took risks by staying late at their part-time clerical jobs to secretly use their employers' mimeograph equipment, and plenty of middle-aged opponents of the war contributed money so that student groups could purchase equipment to print manifestos, newsletters, and "underground" (or alternative) newspapers.

It is important to keep in mind that during the 1960s participants conducted nationwide political protests without benefit of the Internet. Manifestos occasionally appeared as news items in mainstream newspapers and on television (neither political talk radio nor National Public Radio was a major news source in the 1960s); they were published in campus newspapers and in the underground press; and they were printed as leaflets, flyers, and pamphlets that circulated via the U.S. mail and were passed hand to hand from campus to campus.

What Can Sixties Manifestos Tell Us?

One way to determine what sixties manifestos *can* tell us is to establish what they *cannot* tell us. No manifesto can tell us how many people read it, much less how many people agreed with it. A printed pronouncement cannot report whether it changed any reader's mind, won converts, turned off followers, convinced someone to attend a rally or burn a draft card, or persuaded someone to vote or not to vote. A single document does not in itself reveal whether its author or authors even intended to persuade readers to join a particular movement. Political manifestos are unlike popular culture media, which are always intended to sell something and therefore appeal to mainstream values. Manifestos, by contrast, may not be intended for popular appeal. A particular manifesto may have been meant solely to solidify the shared values of an already established cadre, to shock and intimidate readers outside the movement, or to push an existing movement in a more radical direction by proclaiming a new set of beliefs and intentions. Memoirs by individuals who either produced or read sixties manifestos can help us grasp the purpose or effect of a particular text, but the manifesto itself does not typically yield information on persuasiveness, popularity, or purpose.

In some cases, we can calculate a manifesto's influence because we know the identity of the authors, we know that they repeated the manifesto's message in many venues, and we know that they gained organizational authority on the basis of that manifesto's message. This was true of the authors of the 1962 Port Huron Statement (Source 2). But many manifestos from the sixties, reflecting the era's experiments with communalism, do not identify their authors; they present themselves as the product of a collective, whether they were or not.

When we know that a particular ideology, such as Black Power, was politically influential, we can look at manifestos to see how its adherents defined that ideology. The historical record makes clear that the Black Power approach replaced earlier approaches to racial issues, so even though we lack distribution figures for Black Power manifestos, their rhetoric can guide us to the tenor of the times and to the reasoning that produced new alignments on matters of race and community autonomy.

Some manifestos, such as those calling for revolution in the post-1968 second wave, express attitudes that never gained a wide following but attracted significant public attention and were thus influential. For some, frustration with the Vietnam War, racism, and global poverty bred increasingly radical analyses of the causes and solutions to these problems. Second-wave manifestos often exhibited a macho bravado, a threatening claim to independence from the Establishment, a proud rejection of any desire to work within the existing system of beliefs or procedures, and a willingness to use violence. Did the authors of these texts hope to persuade, warn, or frighten their readers? Were they announcing the existence of a mass movement or hoping to write one into reality? Consider, for example, this excerpt from a 1969 document distributed by a radical offshoot of SDS that aligned itself with a group called the Revolutionary Youth Movement (RYM):

Generational identification inflates the size of RYM

Swear words reinforce the rejection of societal norms

More distance from antiwar Americans working within the existing political system

Kids used to try to beat the system from inside the army or from inside the schools; now they desert from the army and burn down the schools. . . . There develops a "generation gap" and a "youth problem." Our heroes are no longer struggling businessmen, and we also begin to reject the ideal career of the professional and look to Mao, Che, the Panthers, the Third World, for our models, for motion. We reject the elitist, technocratic bullshit that tells us only experts can rule, and look instead to leadership from the people's war of the Vietnamese. . . . The most important task for us toward making the revolution, and the work our collectives should engage in, is the creation of a mass revolutionary movement . . . different from the traditional revisionist mass base of "sympathizers." Rather, it is akin to the Red Guard in China, based on the full involvement of masses of people . . . with a full willingness to participate in the violent and illegal struggle.

Does "our" mean all youth or simply this manifesto's authors?

Alignment with anti-American forces distances RYM far from the majority of antiwar Americans, who identified with U.S. national interests

No single manifesto represented all students' views in the sixties, but an array of manifestos from that decade is invaluable for capturing the rhetorical climate in which students operated, whatever their own views. These grassroots expressions of philosophy and intention form an important body of surviving evidence from the era that helps us see the breadth of attitudes and the tone and pace of change over the course of the decade. Manifestos offer us direct engagement with student protests, whether they were calling for reform or revolution.

Questions to Ask

The sixties manifestos in this chapter are only from student groups; they do not represent all student positions at all points in time but do reflect an evolving spectrum of student protest positions between 1960 and 1969. As you read these manifestos within the context of all that unfolded in the 1960s, try to balance evidence of change with signs that some attitudes persisted over time.

- Were the authors of these sixties manifestos consistently aware of their generational identity, or did that change over time?
- Do the authors of these manifestos appear motivated by worry over their own future financial security, or do they presume their own prosperity amid others' deprivation?
- What can this collection of manifestos tell you about the relationship between the antiracism movements of the sixties and the anti–Vietnam War movement?
- Do concerns about gender inequity appear in any of the antiracism or antiwar manifestos?
- Authors of these manifestos believed they were rejecting rigid cold war notions that divided the world between "us" and "them." Is there evidence, however, that the manifesto authors had been raised during the cold war?

Source Analysis Table

This sample of student manifestos addresses issues of race, education, poverty, the Vietnam War and military conscription, and sexism. Use the following table to trace trends in alienation and radicalism among different groups and at different moments.

Source	Advocates Reform of Governing Systems	Challenges Legitimacy of Governing Systems	Calls for Creation of New Governing Systems
1. SNCC Founding Statement (1960)			
2. SDS Port Huron Statement (1962)			
3. Free Speech and the Factory (1964)			
4. Sex and Caste: A Kind of Memo (1965)			
5. Call for a March on Washington (1965)			
6. The Basis of Black Power (1966)			

(continued)

Source	Advocates Reform of Governing Systems	Challenges Legitimacy of Governing Systems	Calls for Creation of New Governing Systems
7. We Refuse (1967)			
8. Columbia Liberated (1968)			
9. Lilith's Manifesto (1969)			
10. Vietnam and the Draft (1969)			
11. You Don't Need to Be a Weatherman to Know Which Way the Wind Blows (1969)			

To download and print this table, visit the book companion site at **bedfordstmartins.com/brownshannon**.

The Source: Student Manifestos
from the Sixties

Political enthusiasm often produces lengthy documents. The students who authored these manifestos typically put more time and energy into their political writing than into their class assignments. As a result, most of these manifestos have been excerpted to focus on the core point in each and to allow you to compare several manifestos over time.

1 | *Student Nonviolent Coordinating Committee Founding Statement,* 1960

> Student sit-ins at segregated lunch counters in 1960 resulted in a conference of black student leaders on April 16–18, 1960, in Raleigh, North Carolina. Ella Baker, executive director of the Southern Christian Leadership Conference, organized the meeting to provide newly politicized young people with the philosophical and organizational skills they would need to broaden and sustain their movement. Others in SCLC, including Dr. Martin Luther King Jr., were tempted to control the students' activities, but Baker encouraged the students to be independent and to make sure that their organizing be about "more than just a hamburger." It was at this Raleigh conference that the black students decided to form their own organization, separate from SCLC. This statement was SNCC's first act as an independent organization.

We affirm the philosophical or religious ideal of nonviolence as the foundation of our purpose, the presupposition of our belief, and the manner of our action. Nonviolence, as it grows from the Judeo-Christian tradition, seeks a social order of justice permeated by love. Integration of human endeavor represents the crucial first step towards such a society.

Through nonviolence, courage displaces fear. Love transcends hate. Acceptance dissipates prejudice; hope ends despair. Faith reconciles doubt. Peace dominates war. Mutual regards cancel enmity. Justice for all overthrows injustice. The redemptive community supersedes systems of gross social immorality.

Love is the central motif of nonviolence. Love is the force by which God binds man to Himself and man to man. Such love goes to the extreme; it remains loving and forgiving even in the midst of hostility. It matches the capacity of evil to inflict suffering with an even more enduring capacity to absorb evil, all the while persisting in love.

Source: Reprinted in Joanne Grant, editor, *Black Protest: History, Documents, and Analyses, 1619 to the Present* (New York: Fawcett, 1968), 290.

By appealing to conscience and standing on the moral nature of human existence, nonviolence nurtures the atmosphere in which reconciliation and justice become actual possibilities.

2   *Port Huron Statement, Students for a Democratic Society,* 1962

University of Michigan student Tom Hayden drafted this mission statement for Students for a Democratic Society, which was debated and revised in June 1962, when SDS members convened at a campground owned by the United Auto Workers of America on the shores of Lake Huron. When finally adopted, the full manifesto was forty pages long.

Introduction: Agenda for a Generation

We are people of this generation, bred in at least modest comfort, housed now in universities, looking uncomfortably to the world we inherit. When we were kids the United States was the wealthiest and strongest country in the world; the only one with the atom bomb, the least scarred by modern war, an initiator of the United Nations that we thought would distribute Western influence throughout the world. Freedom and equality for each individual, government of, by, and for the people—these American values we found good, principles by which we could live as men.[1] Many of us began maturing in complacency.

As we grew, however, our comfort was penetrated by events too troubling to dismiss. First, the permeating and victimizing fact of human degradation, symbolized by the Southern struggle against racial bigotry, compelled most of us from silence to activism. Second, the enclosing fact of the Cold War, symbolized by the presence of the Bomb, brought awareness that we ourselves, and our friends, and millions of abstract "others" we knew more directly because of our common peril, might die at any time. We might deliberately ignore, or avoid, or fail to feel all other human problems, but not these two, for these were too immediate and crushing in their impact, too challenging in the demand that we as individuals take the responsibility for encounter and resolution. . . . Although mankind desperately needs revolutionary leadership, America rests in national stalemate, its goals ambiguous and tradition-bound instead of informed and clear, its democratic system apathetic and manipulated rather than "of, by, and for the people." . . .

---

[1] The use of "men" to mean all people was common among male activists, who questioned all social hierarchies except male dominance.

Source: Reprinted in Alexander Bloom and Wini Breines, editors, *"Takin' it to the streets": A Sixties Reader* (New York: Oxford University Press, 2003), 50–55.

Our work is guided by the sense that we may be the last generation in the experiment with living. But we are a minority—the vast majority of our people regard the temporary equilibriums of our society and world as eternally functional parts. In this is perhaps the outstanding paradox; we ourselves are imbued with urgency, yet the message of our society is that there is no viable alternative to the present. . . . For most Americans, all crusades are suspect, threatening. The fact that each individual sees apathy in his fellows perpetuates the common reluctance to organize for change. The dominant institutions are complex enough to blunt the minds of their potential critics, and entrenched enough to swiftly dissipate or entirely repel the energies of protest and reform, thus limiting human expectancies. Then, too, we are a materially improved society, and by our own improvements we seem to have weakened the case for further change. . . .

The search for truly democratic alternatives to the present, and a commitment to social experimentation with them, is a worthy and fulfilling human enterprise, one which moves us and, we hope, others today. . . . We would replace power rooted in possession, privilege, or circumstance by power and uniqueness rooted in love, reflectiveness, reason, and creativity. As a social system we seek the establishment of a democracy of individual participation, governed by two central aims: that the individual share in those social decisions determining the quality and direction of his life; that society be organized to encourage independence in men and provide the media for their common participation.

3 *Free Speech and the Factory, Free Speech Movement,* 1964

This statement was part of a seven-page document titled "We Want a University," written by unnamed activists in the UC–Berkeley Free Speech Movement at the end of the tumultuous fall semester of 1964. On September 14, the dean of students declared that the sidewalk in front of the campus could no longer be used for political activity. On September 30, five students were arrested for ignoring the new rule; two days later, 2,000 students protested those arrests. Police swarmed the campus in subsequent weeks amid continual negotiations between students and the administration, culminating in a December 1 sit-in by 1,000 students at the main administration building and the arrest of more than 800 demonstrators. By mid-December, both the Faculty Senate and Associated Students had voted in support of the protesters, and on January 2 a new chancellor was brought in to oversee reforms on campus—and the reinstatement of the political activity area at the campus gates.

Source: Original pamphlet posted online at the Free Speech Movement Archives at **www.fsm-a.org**.

No one can presume to explain why so many thousands have become part of the Free Speech Movement. All we can say is what each of us felt: something was wrong; something had to be done. . . . In our fight for free speech we said the "machine" must stop. We said that we must put our bodies on the line, on the machinery, on the wheels and gears, and that the "knowledge factory" must be brought to a halt. Now we must begin to clarify, for ourselves, what we mean by "factory." . . .

The best way to identify the parts of our multiversity machinery is simply to observe it "stripped down" to the bare essentials . . . eight semesters, forty courses, one hundred twenty or more "units," ten to fifteen impersonal lectures per week, one to three oversized discussion meetings per week led by poorly paid graduate student "teachers." . . . The course-grade-unit system structure . . . produces knowledge for the student-cog which has been exploded into thousands of bits and is force-fed by the coercion of grades. . . .

The Free Speech Movement has given us an extraordinary taste of what it means to be part of something organic. Jumping off the conveyor belt [of lectures, exams, grades], we have become a community of furiously talking, feeling, and thinking human beings. If we take seriously our common agreement that we stopped a "machine" how can we be accused of conspiring to destroy a "great university." Where? . . .

We would like to establish the availability of a revolutionary experience in education. If we succeed, we will accomplish a feat more radical and significant than anything the Free Speech Movement has attempted. We will succeed in beginning to bring humanity to campus.

4

Sex and Caste: A Kind of Memo, Casey Hayden and Mary King, 1965

This document can be read as an intentional alternative to the manifesto style that characterized men's leadership in 1960s protest movements. Based on their experiences working on civil rights with SNCC and on welfare issues with SDS, Mary King and Casey Hayden became convinced that women had a valuable perspective to offer in the political debate over equality and justice. This memo, mailed to women in New Left organizations in 1965 and reprinted in *Liberation* magazine the following year, inspired many young women to define women's liberation on their own terms.

There seem to be many parallels that can be drawn between treatment of Negroes and treatment of women in our society as a whole. . . . Women seem

Source: Reprinted in Sara Evans, *Personal Politics: The Origins of Women's Liberation in the Civil Rights Movement and the New Left* (New York: Vintage, 1979), 235–38.

to be placed in the same position of assumed subordination in personal situations too. It is a caste system[1] which, at its worst, uses and exploits women. . . . Many people who are very hip to the implications of the racial caste system, even people in the movement, don't seem to be able to see the sexual caste system and if the question is raised they respond with: "That's the way it's supposed to be. There are biological differences." Or with other statements which recall a white segregationist confronted with integration.

The caste system perspective dictates the roles assigned to women in the movement, and certainly even more to women outside the movement. Within the movement, questions arise in situations ranging from relationships of women organizers to men in the community, to who cleans the freedom house, to who holds leadership positions, to who does secretarial work, and who acts as spokesman for groups. . . .

Having learned from the movement to think radically about the personal worth and abilities of people whose role in society had gone unchallenged before, a lot of women in the movement have begun trying to apply those lessons to their own relations with men. . . . When they hear conversations involving these problems . . . very few men can respond non-defensively, since the whole idea is either beyond their comprehension or threatens and exposes them. The usual response is laughter. That inability to see the whole issue as serious, as the straitjacketing of both sexes, and as societally determined often shapes our own response so that we learn to think in their terms about ourselves and to feel silly rather than trust our inner feelings. . . .

Nobody is writing, or organizing or talking publicly about women, in any way that reflects the problems that various women in the movement come across. . . . Objectively, the chances seem nil that we could start a movement based on anything as distant to general American thought as a sex-caste system. Therefore, most of us will probably want to work full time on problems such as war, poverty, race. The very fact that the country can't face, much less deal with, the questions we're raising means that the movement is one place to look for some relief. Real efforts at dialogue within the movement and with whatever liberal groups, community women, or students might listen are justified. That is, all the problems between men and women and all the problems of women functioning in society as equal human beings are among the most basic that people face. We've talked in the movement about trying to build a society which would see basic human problems (which are now seen as private troubles), as public problems and would try to shape institutions to meet human needs rather than shaping people to meet the needs of those with power.

[1] A caste system divides society into groups with different ranks and different amounts of power and status based on sex, race, religion, wealth, occupation, or heredity.

5   *Call for a March on Washington for Peace, Students for a Democratic Society,* 1965

SDS issued this call for a march on Washington, D.C., in November 1965 on the heels of a nationwide antiwar demonstration on October 15, 1965, in which more than 100,000 Americans had marched against the war in eighty cities and on campuses across the country. In 1965, the majority of college students still supported the Vietnam War, but large demonstrations helped to bring opposition from the margin to the center of political discussion. Approximately 20,000 protesters gathered in front of the White House in response to this call.

In the name of freedom, America is mutilating Vietnam. In the name of peace, America turns that fertile country into a wasteland. And in the name of democracy, America is burying its own dreams and suffocating its own potential. . . . Our aim in Vietnam is the same as our aim in the United States: that oligarchic rule and privileged power be replaced by popular democracy where the people make the decisions which affect their lives and share in the abundance and opportunity that modern technology makes possible. This is the only solution for Vietnam in which Americans can find honor and take pride. Perhaps the war has already so embittered and devastated the Vietnamese that that ideal will require years of rebuilding. But the war cannot achieve it, nor can American military presence, nor our support of repressive unrepresentative governments.

The war must be stopped. There must be an immediate cease fire and demobilization in South Vietnam. There must be withdrawal of American troops. . . . Only the Vietnamese have the right of nationhood to make their government democratic or not, free or not, neutral or not. It is not America's role to deny them the chance to be what they will make of themselves. That chance grows more remote with every American bomb that explodes in a Vietnamese village. But our hopes extend not only to Vietnam. Our chance is the first in a generation to organize the powerless and the voiceless at home, to confront America with its racial injustice, its apathy, and its poverty, and with the same vision we dream for Vietnam: a vision of a society in which all can control their own destinies.

We are convinced that the only way to stop this and future wars is to organize a domestic social movement which challenges the very legitimacy of our foreign policy; this movement must also fight to end racism, to end the paternalism of our welfare system, to guarantee decent incomes for all, and to

Source: Reprinted in Alexander Bloom and Wini Breines, editors, *"Takin' it to the streets": A Sixties Reader* (New York: Oxford University Press, 2003), 183–84.

supplant the authoritarian control of our universities with a community of scholars. . . . SDS urges everyone who believes that our war-making must be ended and our democracy-building must begin, to join in a March on Washington on November 27, at 11 A.M. in front of the White House.

6 | *The Basis of Black Power, SNCC,* 1966

By the spring of 1966, many SNCC members resented Martin Luther King Jr.'s nonviolent approach, which had not prevented the murders of more than two dozen civil rights workers in the previous five years. By electing Stokely Carmichael as their new chair that spring, SNCC members shifted away from a pro-integration civil rights strategy to a more separatist Black Power strategy. Carmichael wrote and circulated this manifesto to explain the new position; he displayed his media savvy by also publishing it in the *New York Times* on August 5, 1966.

The myth that the Negro is somehow incapable of liberating himself, is lazy, etc., came out of the American experience. . . . Any white person who comes into the movement has these concepts in his mind about black people, if only subconsciously. He cannot escape them because the whole society has geared his subconscious in that direction. . . .

Negroes in this country have never been allowed to organize themselves because of white interference. As a result of this, the stereotype has been reinforced that blacks cannot organize themselves. The white psychology that blacks have to be watched, also reinforces this stereotype. Blacks, in fact, feel intimidated by the presence of whites, because of their knowledge of the power that whites have over their lives. . . .

The reasons that whites must be excluded is not that one is anti-white, but because the effects that one is trying to achieve cannot succeed because whites have an intimidating effect. . . .

It must be offered that white people who desire change in this country should go where that problem (racism) is most manifest. The problem is not in the black community. The white people should go into white communities where the whites have created power for the express purpose of denying blacks human dignity and self-determination. . . . What does it mean if black people, once having the right to organize, are not allowed to organize themselves? It means that blacks' ideas about inferiority are being reinforced.

If we are to proceed toward true liberation, we must cut ourselves off from white people. We must form our own institutions, credit unions, co-ops, political parties, write our own histories. . . . These facts do not mean that whites

Source: Reprinted in Alexander Bloom and Wini Breines, editors, *"Takin' it to the streets": A Sixties Reader* (New York: Oxford University Press, 2003), 116–21.

cannot help. They can participate on a voluntary basis. We can contract work out to them, but in no way can they participate on a policy-making level. . . .

In an attempt to find a solution to our dilemma, we propose that our organization (SNCC) should be black-staffed, black-controlled, and black-financed. We do not want to fall into a similar dilemma that other civil rights organizations have fallen into. If we continue to rely upon white financial support we will find ourselves entwined in the tentacles of the white power complex that controls this country. . . . We are not, after all, the ones who are responsible for a genocidal war in Vietnam; we are not the ones who are responsible for neocolonialism in Africa and Latin America; we are not the ones who held a people in animalistic bondage over 400 years. We reject the American dream as defined by white people and must work to construct an American reality defined by Afro-Americans. . . .

A thorough re-examination must be made by black people concerning the contributions that we have made in shaping this country. If this re-examination and re-evaluation is not made, and black people are not given their proper due and respect, then the antagonisms and contradictions are going to become more and more glaring, more and more intense, until a national explosion may result. . . .

7   *We Refuse, The Draft Resistance,* 1967

The organized effort to encourage noncompliance with the Selective Service System began in San Francisco in 1967. This public statement of purpose was issued by a semi-underground group called the Resistance in advance of Stop the Draft Week, held October 14–21, 1967. The weeklong demonstrations culminated in the March on the Pentagon, where 50,000 protesters assembled and were attacked at midnight by paratroopers from the Eighty-second Army Division.

The Resistance is a group of men who are bound together by one single and clear commitment: on October 16 we will hand in our draft cards and refuse any further cooperation with the Selective Service System. By doing so we will actively challenge the government's right to draft American men for its criminal war against the people of Vietnam. We of the Resistance feel that we can no longer passively acquiesce to the Selective Service System by accepting its deferments. . . . Those opposed to the war are dealt with quietly, individually and on the government's terms. If they do not get the deferments, they must individually find some extra-legal alternative. A popular last resort is Canada,

Source: Reprinted in Marvin E. Gettleman, Jane Franklin, Marilyn B. Young, and H. Bruce Franklin, editors, *Vietnam and America: A Documented History,* 2nd ed. (New York: Grove Press, 1995), 307.

and those who go to Canada must be politically silent in order to stay there. Legal draft alternatives are kept within reach of elite groups—good students, those who are able to express objection to all war on religious grounds, and those with the money to hire good lawyers. For the majority of American guys the only alternatives are jail or the army. . . .

Many who wish to avoid the draft will, of course, choose to accept deferments; many, however, wish to do more than avoid the draft. Resistance means that if the government is to continue its crimes against humanity, it must first deal with our opposition. We do not seek jail, but we do this because as individuals we know of no justifiable alternative and we believe that in time many other American men will also choose to resist the crimes done in their names.

8   *Columbia Liberated, Columbia University Strike Committee,* 1968

This statement was issued in the fall of 1968, almost six months after the seven-day strike in April at Columbia University. In addition to setting out the strikers' philosophical stance, the manifesto reiterated the original demand that Columbia terminate plans to replace a black neighborhood with a gymnasium and sever all ties with the Institute for Defense Analysis, which provides research for the Defense Department. It also demanded that the university drop all charges against those who participated in the springtime demonstrations and sit-in.

The most important fact about the Columbia strike is that Columbia exists within American society. . . . Striking students are responding to the totality of the conditions of our society, not just one small part of it, the university. We are disgusted with the war, with racism, with being a part of a system over which we have no control, a system which demands gross inequalities of wealth and power, a system which denies personal and social freedom and potential, a system which has to manipulate and repress us in order to exist. The university can only be seen as a cog in this machine; or, more accurately, a factory whose product is knowledge and personnel (us) useful to the functioning of the system. . . . And the policies of the university—expansion into the community, exploitation of blacks and Puerto Ricans, support for imperialist wars—also serve the interests of banks, corporations, government, and military represented on the Columbia Board of Trustees and the ruling class of our society. In every way, the university is "society's child." Our attack upon the university is really an attack upon this society and its effects upon us. We have never said otherwise. . . .

Source: Reprinted in Alexander Bloom and Wini Breines, editors, *"Takin' it to the streets": A Sixties Reader* (New York: Oxford University Press, 2003), 387–91.

People now know that they are fighting the forces behind Columbia, the power of the ruling class in this society, not just the institution. And they have the commitment to keep fighting. The Democratic National Convention killed electoral politics for young people in this country and the Chicago Police Dept. provided an alternative—to fight. So did Columbia in the spring. So does it now, along with every other university in this country. The struggle goes on. Create two, three, many Columbias, that is the watchword!

9 *Lilith's Manifesto, Louise Crowley,* 1969

By 1968, women active in various protest movements had begun organizing separate "women's liberation" groups out of frustration with the sexism of male activists. Louise Crowley, a member of the Women's Majority Union in Seattle, attended a conference sponsored by the prosocialist United Front against War and Fascism in Oakland, California, in the spring of 1969 and was enraged when women's critique of male dominance was mocked and denounced. Crowley wrote this manifesto and published it in the first issue of *Lilith,* the newspaper of the Women's Majority Union. It was signed by sixteen women and two men.

Once upon a time, I've been told, there was a woman in the then-vanguard party who felt a need deeper than that of spot welding a superficial unity around current issues. She disappeared and has never been heard from since. Presumably the earth has swallowed her or maybe it was the East River. At any rate, such foolhardy hubris was not repeated, and radical women have since disciplined themselves, with only minor grumblings ("bitchings"), to accept . . . a promissory note on pie to be granted in some future socialist sky, reward for humble performance of their allotted tasks in kitchens of radical halls and at the typewriters of radical offices or for their zeal for organizing their fellow-women to support prevailing campaigns.

So, in Oakland, we get told again to go the back of the bus. . . . Well, damn it, I'm not going back, because I've no faith in the unity that's sought through yielding; and I'm not going to walk away because I'm as much a part of this revolution as you are and maybe, at this moment in history, more. Here I stand. You're going to have to cope with me, brother. Now.

THEREFORE BE IT MANIFEST:

- The biological dichotomy of sex needs no reinforcement by differential cultural mores. Whatever qualities pertain to humanity pertain to it as a species. If assertiveness, for example, is a virtue in man, it is a virtue also in women; if forebearance is a virtue in woman, it is likewise a virtue in

Source: Robin Morgan, editor, *Sisterhood Is Powerful: An Anthology of Writings from the Women's Liberation Movement* (New York: Random House, 1970), 527–29.

man. (If you brother, can't get a hard-on for a woman who doesn't grovel at your feet, that's *your* hangup; and sister, if you can't turn on to a man who won't club you and drag you off by the hair, that's yours. Keep your hangups the hell out of this revolution.)

- The mutilation of individual whole human beings to fit the half-sized procrustes' bed[1] society assigns selectively to "men" and "women" serves a purpose far more contrary to the pursuit of freedom than simple divisiveness: because *all* persons can be consigned to one or the other category and their personalities trimmed . . . to fit the mold considered appropriate to their sex, *none* can escape; half the human race receives indoctrination and training in the exercise of dominance over others, while the other half receives reciprocal conditioning to servility, all being given to presuppose that a pattern of authority and submission to authority is the universal, inevitable, and biologically determined order of social relationships.

- All known societies have thus utilized the clear and all-inclusive dichotomy of sex as the chief vehicle for early and continuous limitation on the essentially liberatory free play of human imaginings and aspirations, perverting a benign natural phenomenon to service of the social status quo.

- Should leadership be retained by forces of but limited vision, the revolution must be cut tragically short of its full potential. . . . It is unthinkable that the revolution now in progress be allowed to suffer such curtailment. . . . We can afford no less than total liberation. *This* revolution has got to go for broke: Power to no one, and to everyone: to each the power over his/her own life, and no others.

[1] In Greek mythology, Procrustes made every guest fit his adjustable bed by stretching those who were too short and amputating the legs of those who were too tall. A "procrustean bed" has come to mean an arbitrary standard that forces individuals to conform.

10   *Vietnam and the Draft,* 1969

This second-wave antiwar manifesto was signed by 250 student body presidents representing an array of American colleges and universities. It was published in campus newspapers across the country and may have been sent to President Nixon's secretary of defense, Melvin Laird.

In June of 1967, our predecessors submitted . . . a petition signed by over 10,000 draft-eligible students from nine campuses, calling for alternative ser-

Source: Reprinted in Alexander Bloom and Wini Breines, editors, *"Takin' it to the streets": A Sixties Reader* (New York: Oxford University Press, 2003), 196–97.

vice for those who cannot fight in Vietnam. There have been many other similar attempts to influence Congress and the Administration. Nonetheless, despite all our efforts, the Selective Service System remains impervious to change. Presently, thousands of fellow students face the probability of immediate induction into the armed forces.

Most of us have worked in electoral politics and through other channels to change the course of America's foreign policy and to remove the inequities of the draft system. We will continue to work in these ways, but the possible results of these efforts will come too late for those whose deferments will soon expire. We must make an agonizing choice: to accept induction into the armed forces, which we feel would be irresponsible to ourselves, our country, and our fellow man; or to refuse induction, which is contrary to our respect for law and involves injury to our personal lives and careers.

Left without a third alternative, we will act according to our conscience. Along with thousands of our fellow students, we campus leaders cannot participate in a way which we believe to be immoral and unjust. Although this, for each of us, is an intensely personal decision, we publicly and collectively express our intention to refuse induction and to aid and support those who decide to refuse. We will not serve in the military as long as the war in Vietnam continues.

11 *You Don't Need to Be a Weatherman to Know Which Way the Wind Blows,* 1969

This mimeographed manifesto was published by members of the Weatherman Underground, a break-off group from the Revolutionary Youth Movement, which in turn had splintered from the Students for a Democratic Society. As SDS dissolved into factions, each claiming to be more radical than the next, it demonstrated the alienation and bitterness produced by years of protest against a war that would not end until 1973. A year after publishing this statement, three of its signers accidentally blew themselves up while making bombs in a Greenwich Village apartment.

People ask, what is the nature of the revolution that we talk about? Who will it be made by, and for, and what are its goals and strategy? . . . The main struggle going on in the world today is between U.S. imperialism and the national liberation struggles against it. . . . Every other empire and petty dictator is in the long run dependent on U.S. imperialism, which has unified, allied with, and defended all of the reactionary forces of the whole world. . . . The U.S. empire, as a world-wide system, channels wealth, based upon the labor and resources of the rest of the world, into the United States. The relative affluence

Source: Reprinted from William H. Chafe and Harvard Sitkoff, editors, *A History of Our Time: Readings on Postwar America* (New York: Oxford University Press, 1999), 313–16.

existing in the United States is directly dependent upon the labor and natural resources of the Vietnamese, the Angolans, the Bolivians, and the rest of the peoples of the Third World. . . .

The goal is the destruction of U.S. imperialism and the achievement of a classless world: world communism. Winning state power in the U.S. will occur as a result of the military forces of the U.S. overextending themselves around the world and being defeated piecemeal; struggle within the U.S. will be a vital part of this process, but when the revolution triumphs in the U.S. it will have been made by the people of the whole world. . . .

In this context, why an emphasis on youth? Why should young people be willing to fight on the side of Third World peoples? . . . As imperialism struggles to hold together this decaying social fabric, it inevitably resorts to brute force and authoritarian ideology. People, especially young people, more and more find themselves in the iron grip of authoritarian institutions. Reaction against the pigs or teachers in the schools, welfare pigs or the army is generalizable and extends beyond the particular repressive institution to the society and the State as a whole. The legitimacy of the State is called into question . . . and the anti-authoritarianism which characterizes the youth rebellion turns into rejection of the State, a refusal to be socialized by American society. Kids used to try to beat the system from inside the army or from inside the schools; now they desert from the army and burn down the schools. . . . There develops a "generation gap" and a "youth problem." Our heroes are no longer struggling businessmen, and we also begin to reject the ideal career of the professional and look to Mao, Che, the Panthers,[1] the Third World, for our models, for motion. We reject the elitist, technocratic bullshit that tells us only experts can rule, and look instead to leadership from the people's war of the Vietnamese. . . . The most important task for us toward making the revolution, and the work our collectives should engage in, is the creation of a mass revolutionary movement . . . different from the traditional revisionist mass base of "sympathizers." Rather, it is akin to the Red Guard[2] in China, based on the full involvement of masses of people . . . with a full willingness to participate in the violent and illegal struggle. . . .

The strategy of the Revolutionary Youth Movement for developing an active mass base . . . fits with the world strategy for winning the revolution, builds a movement oriented toward the power, and will become one division of the International Liberation Army, while its battlefields are added to the many Vietnams which will dismember and dispose of U.S. imperialism. Long Live the Victory of People's War!

[1] References are to Mao Tse-tung, Chinese communist leader, 1945–1976; Che Guevara, an Argentine Marxist revolutionary; and the Black Panther Party, a radical black nationalist organization.

[2] The Red Guard was a paramilitary youth organization in China in the 1960s.

Analyzing Student Manifestos

1. What changes in tone and philosophy do you see in the SDS and SNCC manifestos? For SDS, how does the Port Huron Statement (Source 2) differ from the Weatherman document (Source 11)? For SNCC, how does the founding statement (Source 1) differ from "The Basis of Black Power" (Source 6)?

2. What are the similarities and the differences between "Sex and Caste: A Kind of Memo" (Source 4) and Lilith's Manifesto (Source 9)? What seems to have changed for activist student women in just three years?

3. The manifestos from the Berkeley Free Speech Movement (Source 3) and the Columbia University uprising (Source 8) are both concerned about American universities. How does the expression of that concern change between 1964 and 1968?

4. Based on the two manifestos from 1969, what do you think the antiwar student body presidents (Source 10) would say about the Weathermen (Source 11)? What do you think the Weathermen would say about the student body presidents?

5. Memories of the sixties still influence American public life. In reading the manifestos, do you find that the issues raised and opinions expressed feel familiar to you or remote? Do you find yourself agreeing with some of the manifestos and disagreeing with others? Write a brief essay in which you express the relevance of these manifestos from the sixties to your political experience today.

The Rest of the Story

In 1967 and 1968, San Francisco State University was wracked by violence as members of the Black Student Union fought with the administration over the structure and autonomy of a proposed black studies program. Black students trashed the campus cafeteria, the board of trustees opposed hiring faculty members who were perceived as black radicals, the president refused to negotiate with students, and protests were quelled with severe police action. No one behaved well because no one knew how to behave in such a situation. There were no traditions or mechanisms in place for setting up civil negotiations among administrators, faculty, and students. The campus riots of the sixties made clear that university governance had to mean more than unquestioned student obedience—or student-police violence.

In the five years following the chaos at San Francisco State, more than 500 colleges and universities established black studies programs, departments, research centers, and libraries. As historian Karen Miller points out in her essay in *Long Time Gone: Sixties America Then and Now,* most of these programs "did not require the kinds of extremes that had occurred at San Francisco State precisely because there *was* a San Francisco State."

A parallel development in the area of women's studies at San Diego State University (SDSU) was not marked by violence. In 1969, students involved in women's liberation allied with faculty and community women to collect 600 signatures on a petition calling for a women's studies program. The following year, SDSU became the first institution of higher education to establish a Women's Studies Department, which was governed by a board that included ten students, six faculty, and three administrators. By 1980, Women's Studies, like Black Studies, had spread across the country, and 500 institutions offered classes or programs in this new scholarly field.

The second wave of student protest is often remembered for its rhetorical excesses, its use of bullying means to democratic ends, and its hypocritical use of violence to oppose war. It is easy to forget that student protesters also made lasting reforms on their campuses in the late 1960s and early 1970s. In retrospect, the disruptive actions by many students seem unnecessarily radical because the goals they sought now appear to be so natural and obvious: a contractual, not parental, relationship between campus administrators and students; a student role in campus governance, including faculty hiring and curricular decisions; a dynamic approach to curricular development so that new pedagogical approaches and contemporary issues are continually integrated into course offerings and individual students' interests influence students' course plans; assertive policies to ensure diversity in a campus student body and faculty; and serious, critical scholarly attention to issues of race, gender, sexuality, and economic class. Fundamental to all of these reforms was the protesters' success in establishing that political activism and social criticism are not separate from, or necessarily at odds with, educational endeavor and that students are not citizens-in-waiting; they are legitimate members of the body politic who enjoy all the constitutional rights of nonstudents and have a legitimate interest in learning about the social problems they will inherit. Since the sixties, these demands have become basic principles in higher education.

As the San Francisco State episode illustrates, the process for achieving campus reform was neither smooth nor elegant. Rigid or dismissive responses by those in power frustrated students who had been raised to trust their leaders. That frustration produced wild demonstrations, resulting in such extreme police action that administrators had to make amends by granting many students' demands. Students at other schools were thereby encouraged to break a few windows in order to get a student seat at the decision-making table. There was no clear plan for any of this, but a pattern emerges in retrospect and has since informed more than one administrative workshop on how to handle student demonstrations.

Curricular programs in African American Studies and Women's Studies, as well as in Asian and Asian American Studies, Mexican American Studies, and Ethnic Studies, are among the most tangible legacies of student protest in the sixties. Incorporation of these new areas of study into the curriculum served three simultaneous purposes: campus resources were devoted to areas of study that had previously been ignored; people of color and women, who were grossly underrepresented on the faculties of U.S. colleges and universities, gained employment opportunities in these new curricular areas; and students of color and female students felt that academia recognized, for the first time in history, the contributions and struggles of people who were not white or not male. In the last three decades, these programs have contributed substantially to the diversity of knowledge and personnel in higher education. Just as significantly, they have served as a model for other curricular programs, such as Environmental Studies and Queer Studies. Today, the interaction between these programs and traditional disciplines has produced more interdisciplinary approaches to knowledge and serves as a testament to an important achievement of student protest in the sixties: the creation of a tradition of curricular innovation, responsiveness, and timely engagement with the world.

To Find Out More

The most useful and reliable histories of the sixties are Terry H. Anderson, *Movement and the Sixties: Protest in America from Greensboro to Wounded Knee* (New York: Oxford University Press, 1995); Mark Hamilton Lytle, *America's Uncivil Wars: The Sixties Era from Elvis to the Fall of Richard Nixon* (New York: Oxford University Press, 2006); Todd Gitlin, *The Sixties: Years of Hope, Days of Rage* (New York: Bantam Books, 1987); Maurice Isserman and Michael Kazin, *America Divided: The Civil War of the 1960s* (New York: Oxford University Press, 2000); Mark Kurlansky, *1968: The Year That Rocked the World* (New York: Ballantine Books, 2003); and David Farber, *The Age of Great Dreams: America in the 1960s* (New York: Hill and Wang, 1994). Farber also edited a collection of topical essays by historians, *The Sixties: From Memory to History* (Chapel Hill: University of North Carolina Press, 1994), and Alexander Bloom edited a collection of articles, *Long Time Gone: Sixties America Then and Now* (New York: Oxford University Press, 2001).

There are a number of excellent collections of primary documents from the sixties, which include manifestos, eyewitness accounts, poems and songs, posters, letters, news articles from the time, and government reports on protest movements. See, for example, Van Gosse, *The Movements of the New Left, 1950–1975: A Brief History with Documents* (Boston: Bedford Books, 2005); Alexander Bloom and Wini Breines, editors, *"Takin' it to the streets": A Sixties Reader* (New York: Oxford University Press, 2003); and Peter B. Levy, editor, *America in the Sixties: Right, Left, and Center* (Westport, Conn.: Praeger Publishers, 1998).

Participant memoirs are a rich source of information about the experience of the sixties. Tom Hayden, one of the founders of SDS and an author of the Port Huron Statement, wrote *Reunion: A Memoir* (New York: Random House, 1988). John Lewis, an early leader of SNCC and later a congressional representative from Georgia, recalled his encounter with Black Power in *Walking with the Wind: A Memoir of the Movement* (New York: Simon and Schuster, 1998). Mary King, one of the authors of "Sex and Caste: A Kind of Memo," looked back on her experiences as a white woman in SNCC in *Freedom Song: A Personal Story of the 1960s Civil Rights Movement* (New York: William Morrow, 1988). Susan Brownmiller recalled the early days of the women's liberation movement in *In Our Time: Memoir of a Revolution* (New York: Dial Press, 1999).

The "Manifesto Project" within the online Sixties Project offers an array of manifestos by students and nonstudents; see **www3.iath.virginia.edu/sixties/ HTML_docs/Resources/Primary.html**. The Pacifica Radio/UC–Berkeley Social Activism Sound Recording Project makes available primary source audio interviews, photographs, news articles, and video clips covering a wide array of topics and participants, including harsh critics of student protest activism, at **lib.berkeley.edu/MRC/pacificaviet**. The Bobst Library at New York University has an online exhibit, organized by month and year, tracking both national and campus events through photographs and brief texts that illustrate the changing times, at **nyu.edu/library/bobst/collections/exhibits/arch/1965/ Index.html**. For the SNCC Web site, see **ibiblio.org/sncc;** for the archives of the Free Speech Movement, see **fsm-a.org;** for the SDS archives, see **sds.revolt .org/index.htm;** for a description and discussion of the Kent State shootings by two faculty members at Kent State University, go to **dept.kent.edu/sociology/ lewis/LEWIHEN.htm;** and for a recollection of events at Columbia University during the 1968 strike, see **columbia.edu/acis/history/1968.html**.

Full versions of some of the manifestos cited in this chapter are available at the following sites:

- Port Huron Statement (Source 2): **coursesa.matrix.msu.edu/~hst306/ documents/huron.html**
- Free Speech and the Factory (Source 3): **fsm-a.org/stacks/wewantuniv.html**
- Sex and Caste (Source 4): **cwluherstory.com/CWLUArchive/memo.html**
- Call for a March on Washington (Source 5): **lib.berkeley.edu/MRC/ pacificaviet/sdsmarchondc.html**
- The Basis of Black Power (Source 6): **historyisaweapon.com/defcon1/ blackpower.html**
- Columbia Liberated (Source 8): **www.personal.umd.umich.edu/ ~ppennock/doc-Columbia.htm**
- Lilith's Manifesto (Source 9): **historylink.org/essays/printer_friendly/ index.cfm?file_id=2321**

CHAPTER 14

Drawn to Summits

Political Cartoons on President Reagan and the Arms Race

"My fellow Americans, I am pleased to tell you I just signed legislation which outlaws Russia forever. The bombing will begin in five minutes." President Ronald Reagan was joking, of course. It was a Saturday morning in the late summer of 1984; he was vacationing at his ranch in Santa Barbara, California, and having a bit of fun while he tested the sound levels on the microphone set up to record his weekly radio message. The president was, in effect, drawing an oral cartoon of himself: his joke grossly exaggerated his critics' view of him as a "commie hater" and warmonger, making the criticism so ridiculous that even the radio technicians in the room laughed. The only problem was that the microphone was on—and broadcasting. The whole world, including officials in the Soviet Union, heard the "joke," and they took it as evidence of the president's genuine feelings; his humor, they said, revealed his authentic hatred for the Russian people and his desire to destroy them. Some of Reagan's critics in the United States agreed with that analysis; other critics viewed the gaffe as proof that the president was too clumsy and simpleminded to handle delicate diplomacy.

The irony in the story is that 1984, the year that Reagan ran for reelection, marks a turning point in his relationship with the Soviet Union and the start of Reagan's open dialogue with the Soviet leadership on the subject of nuclear arms limitation. In his first term, the president had reversed a twenty-year trend toward "détente"—the relaxing of tensions between the world's two military superpowers—and had emphasized instead his ideological view of communism as a corrupt political and economic system bent on global domination. In that first term, Reagan had used aggressive rhetoric to describe the Soviet Union, calling it an "evil empire" and promising that the West would not simply contain communism, which had been its policy since the 1940s, but would "transcend communism" and relegate the Soviet system to the "ash heap of history." Beyond the warlike language, Reagan's first term in office was marked by the first complete breakdown of arms limitations talks in twenty years and was the first time since Harry Truman's presidency that there was no "summit," or top-level meeting between the two superpower leaders. Those who worried about this pattern in Reagan's first term had trouble dismissing as a "joke" his accidental on-air remark about bombing the Russians.

What critics could not imagine in 1984 — indeed, what no one could imagine in 1984 — was that Reagan's second term would be punctuated by four substantive summit meetings with the Soviet Union's new leader, Mikhail Gorbachev, and that Reagan and Gorbachev would make progress in reducing the threat of nuclear war between their two nations. This surprising turn of events was brought about by several coinciding factors, including President Reagan's mounting fear of nuclear war and General Secretary Gorbachev's conviction that the arms race was destroying the USSR's hopes of creating prosperity for its people under a communist economy.

Ronald Reagan brought to the presidency two long-standing convictions: that Soviet military power was a grave threat to the United States and to world peace and that the Soviet economic system was on the verge of collapse. To address these two beliefs, he pushed through massive increases in military spending. In his first year in office, for example, he won congressional authorization for a 25 percent increase in the military budget, producing the largest military authorization bill in U.S. history. By the end of Reagan's two terms, his administration's highly publicized weapons expenditures had expanded the defense budget by 40 percent. Reagan argued that a buildup of U.S. military power either would scare the Soviets into negotiating for arms control or would ignite increases in Soviet defense spending that would destroy that nation's fragile economy. "We must keep the heat on these people," he told one political ally in 1982. "What I want is to bring them to their knees so that they will disarm and let us disarm; but we have got to do it by keeping the heat on."

The American people had mixed feelings about Reagan's "heat on" strategy. While applauding his rhetorical denunciations of Soviet communism, his supporters also applauded the president's promises to cut taxes and reduce federal deficit spending. The dramatic expansion in military spending, however, when coupled with Reagan's tax cuts for upper-income earners, produced soaring federal budget deficits as well as a barrage of criticism for "Reaganomics." Massive cuts in social spending for the poor, elderly, and children did not offset increases in military expenditures, and tax cuts intended to spur the economy failed to generate enough revenue to pay for all the new weapons (see Source 3). In 1981, Reagan's first year in office, only 20 percent of Americans responding to one poll said that the United States spent "too much" on defense; by 1985, that figure had risen to 66 percent. By that time, the federal deficit had grown 134 percent, from $907 billion to more than $2 trillion, and many feared that Reaganomics would bring the United States to its own economic knees.

Impervious to public opinion on foreign and military policy, President Reagan continued to pursue his own agenda of peace through military strength. In early 1983, he announced that his Defense Department would pursue an expensive line of research and development on a Strategic Defense Initiative (SDI)—quickly dubbed "Star Wars"—which the president envisioned as a space-based shield against nuclear attack. For President Reagan, SDI was the ultimate expression of his desire to avoid nuclear war. But opponents of nuclear weapons did not perceive this hard-line, anticommunist, promilitary president as their ally; they scoffed when he promised to share SDI with the Soviets. Many in the scientific community, meanwhile, regarded SDI as science fiction, a product of the president's experience as a Hollywood actor (see Source 12).

Few were aware in 1983 that President Reagan was increasingly convinced of the need for arms control talks with the "evil empire." The United States military buildup had, as intended, frightened the Soviets—but not into submission, only into greater certitude that the United States was about to attack. Events in the fall of 1983 impressed upon Reagan the high stakes of his military gamble: the Soviets accidentally shot down a civilian Korean airliner, the Pentagon forced the president to listen to briefings on possible nuclear war scenarios, and the Soviets' near-fatal overreaction to a large-scale U.S.-led military war game made those scenarios more plausible. The screening of a television drama, *The Day After,* which imagined life in Lawrence, Kansas, following a nuclear war, spoke to the former actor in his own language about the human dimension of superpower confrontation. In a major address favoring nuclear arms control in January 1984, Reagan signaled that his priorities were shifting away from defeating the Soviet Union and toward reducing nuclear weapons. Some questioned the sincerity of his call for talks to "begin now," noting that it coincided with his run for reelection. But historians with access to internal memos and Reagan's own diary find that Reagan was indeed reordering his priorities.

No American president can single-handedly bend world events to his will. Reagan's new priorities would not have mattered if there had not been, simultaneously, a remarkable series of developments in the Soviet Union. Leonid Brezhnev, the leader of the Soviet Union since 1964, died in 1982 at age seventy-six. He was followed by two equally elderly, equally conservative representatives of the communist regime: Yuri Andropov, who came into office at age sixty-eight and died two years later, was followed by Constantin Chernenko, who came into office at age seventy-three and died a year later (see Source 7). American jokes about the graying of the Soviet leadership were not muted by the fact that President Reagan was the same age as Chernenko, but those jokes were silenced by the Soviet Politburo's election of Mikhail Gorbachev to the government's top post in March 1985. Gorbachev was twenty years younger than Reagan and represented a wholly new perspective on the future of the Soviet Union and its relations in the world. In stunning speeches during his first year as the USSR's new leader, Gorbachev emphasized *glasnost* (openness) and *perestroika* (economic restructuring), insisting that reduced military

Figure 14.1 Ronald Reagan and Mikhail Gorbachev Meet in Geneva, 1985 This
*photograph captures the mood at the first Reagan-Gorbachev summit in Geneva, Switzerland,
on November 19, 1985. The two men met with only interpreters for an hour in the morning
and then participated in more public discussions. In the late afternoon, they walked alone to
a pool house on the shore of Lake Geneva and, with only interpreters present, held a genuine
conversation about their mutual need for trust and a reduction in weapons. At the end of the
day, Reagan told a diplomatic aide, "You're right, I did like him."* Source: Courtesy of the
Ronald Reagan Library.

spending was vital to make the communist economic system more globally
competitive with U.S. capitalism and calling for a negotiated end to the arms
race. The American public responded positively to Gorbachev's vision as well
as to his winning personal style. The Soviet leader's open face and broad smile,
topped by his bald head and forehead birthmark, made him instantly recog-
nizable and a real personality match for America's famously charming president.

In November 1985, Reagan and Gorbachev held their first summit meeting
in Geneva, Switzerland. The great achievement of that summit was that the
two world leaders actually talked alone, with only two translators in the room,
for more than two hours, engaging in the most honest exchange of ideas, pro-

posals, hopes, and fears in U.S.-Soviet history. They spoke seriously of a 50 per-cent reduction in strategic arms—the long-range missiles that one country could launch from homeland bases against the other—and of drastic reduc-tions in "intermediate" weapons—those based all around Europe. The two leaders learned two things in Geneva: first, they liked each other and believed they could work together productively; second, Reagan's commitment to pur-suing a still-untested Strategic Defense Initiative was unacceptable to Gorbachev. Reagan viewed SDI as a guarantor of peace: both sides would have a shield ren-dering nuclear weapons useless. Gorbachev viewed SDI as a costly extension of the arms race, arguing that eliminating nuclear weapons would make SDI un-necessary. Still, they ended their first meeting with the remarkable joint state-ment that nuclear war "cannot be won and must never be fought" and with the promise that neither nation would "seek to achieve military superiority" (see Source 10).

The Reagan-Gorbachev summit meeting in Reykjavik, Iceland, just one year later, brought the two nations to the brink of peace; the two leaders seri-ously negotiated a plan to eliminate all nuclear weapons. Private conversations between the two leaders and group meetings between arms negotiators were bold, innovative, and rather impetuous. Conservative participants on both sides feared that the euphoric momentum of the meeting was headed toward a 50 percent cut in strategic weapons, an elimination of Soviet and U.S. inter-mediate weapons in Europe, and a commitment to more reductions in the fu-ture. Reagan told his aides that "a miracle is happening" and felt confident that his strategy of massive arms spending had forced the Soviets to accept his goal. The two-day meeting was scheduled to end at noon on the second day, but Reagan and Gorbachev, and their negotiating teams, kept working until 7:30 P.M., believing a deal was imminent. In the end, however, the two leaders left Reykjavik with nothing to show for their labors (see Source 11). The whole package unraveled over SDI: Reagan insisted that the United States be allowed to continue research and development of this still-hypothetical system, both in laboratories and in space, and Gorbachev insisted that research be limited to laboratories. Neither leader would budge on this point. Politically, Gorbachev felt he could not persuade his already skeptical colleagues in Moscow that the United States would share SDI with the Soviet Union, and his economic plans did not allow for the Soviets to launch their own SDI project. Reagan was right: the USSR could not afford to keep up with U.S. military spending. But Reagan's fascination with the image of a nuclear shield in space blinded him to Gorbachev's arguments against pursuing SDI (see Source 12).

The collapse of the Reykjavik summit did not mean the end of U.S.-Soviet discussions over arms control or the end of Reagan-Gorbachev summits. The two leaders met again in Washington, D.C., in December 1987, at a time when both were in political trouble at home and in need of a foreign policy success. Reagan's stature had been diminished by a political scandal involving il-legal weapons deals with Iran and Nicaraguan "contra" fighters. Meanwhile, Gorbachev was becoming increasingly unpopular with antireformist Soviet politicians, and he faced a costly quagmire in Afghanistan, where the Soviet attempt to control that country was losing to U.S.-funded Islamic fundamentalists. The Washington summit produced an agreement to eliminate certain intermediate nuclear weapons, accounting for just 4 percent of each nation's arsenals. It was a small step toward START (Strategic Arms Reduction Talks), a step aided by the fact that Gorbachev now regarded SDI as a technical impossibility. He was quite willing to let the United States waste billions of dollars on a defense shield that could be breached for far less money.

Ronald Reagan and his wife, Nancy, traveled to Moscow, Russia, in May 1988 for his fourth summit with Gorbachev. The U.S. president had eight months left in office. Dreams of eliminating all nuclear weapons had been replaced by modest arms control talks, and Congress and the Joint Chiefs of Staff had agreed to shelve SDI and write off the $12 billion spent on exploring that failed idea. The Moscow summit was more a celebration of four years' worth of good intentions than a true negotiating session. At a well-staged walkabout for photographers in Red Square, Reagan told reporters that he no longer thought of the Soviet Union as the "evil empire" that he had described just five years earlier. He had used such language, he said, when "talking about another time in another era." Now, in 1988, Reagan joined Gorbachev in a Moscow toast to "the hope of holding out for a better way of settling things."

Using the Source: Political Cartoons

Jeff MacNelly was a prize-winning political cartoonist facing professional trouble when his candidate, Ronald Reagan, emerged victorious from the 1980 election. MacNelly later admitted, "That was hard for me because I can't go around saying, 'Gee, isn't the president doing a great job?' That's not what a political cartoonist does."

What a political cartoonist "does" in a democratic society is to provide citizens with pointed, pictorial satire. Ever since Ben Franklin published the first American political cartoon in 1754 (admonishing the colonies to unite in fighting the French and Indian War), journalists have been using irony, sarcasm, ridicule, and exaggeration to stimulate readers' engagement with current events. Certainly since the late nineteenth century, when Thomas Nast's drawings mocked political corruption, cartoonists have been using visual humor to provoke citizen outrage and action. Provocation is their job; that is what newspapers and magazines pay them to do; that is why the public pays attention to them. No matter what their political position, all political cartoonists agree with one of the profession's great figures, Bill Mauldin, who said his role was to "jar, shake, needle people out of their fat-headedness."

Political cartoons are printed proof of free speech and a free press, and political cartoonists are the annoying artists in our daily newspapers who remind us that freedom brings both laughter *and* aggravation. In a democracy, any public figure and any public policy can be "drawn and quartered" by a political cartoon, and cartoonists' duty is to put politicians and citizens on notice that their hypocrisies, conceits, and missteps are subject to visual ridicule and graphic mockery. When Florida governor Jeb Bush warned Gary Trudeau to "walk softly" in his *Doonesbury* cartoons, Trudeau commented that "telling a cartoonist to walk softly is like asking a professional wrestler to show a little class. It's just not a productive suggestion."

To be effective, a political cartoon must capture the essence of a complex situation in a clever drawing that the viewer can understand in about twenty seconds. Political cartoonists do not have the luxury of a newspaper editorial's qualifying clauses and explanatory background. Cartoonists must grab the reader's attention, must make a serious editorial statement, must make that statement both visually interesting and immediately comprehensible, and must be funny. Cartoonists are the high-wire artists in the editorial circus. When they succeed at making a strong, clear point in an aesthetic and humorous way, it is thrilling to the crowd; when they fail, it is obvious to every viewer. So great is the cartoonist's potential to make a powerful statement that the acerbic editor H. L. Mencken once announced, "Give me a good cartoonist and I can throw out half the editorial staff."

The key to effective political cartooning is "caricature"; cartoonists must draw an image of a person or place or thing so realistically that viewers instantly recognize it, but cartoonists must, at the same time, distort their subject, exaggerate its features, and transform it in a way that is not only funny but also meaningful. In deciding which features to distort, which visual qualities to exaggerate, the cartoonist must be guided by the editorial point of the cartoon. "Caricature does not deal merely with faces and forms," explained the nineteenth-century cartoonist Joseph Keppler. "It has to deal with character as well. If a man is notoriously stingy, that stinginess must be pictured in his caricature, and pictured extravagantly so that it will stand out as the most prominent feature of the portrait."

Cartoonists make their arguments by drawing the most ridiculous, most absurd, most extreme version of a political situation; they illuminate their sober editorial points with the aid of outrageous drawings and comedic devices. Included in the cartoonist's tool kit are sight gags, puns, dialogue, labels, stereotypes, cultural references, and clichés. Each of these tools is useful to the cartoonist, but each has its flaws. For example, clichés are, by definition, quickly understood, which is desirable for a cartoonist. But, also by definition, clichés lack originality, and viewers are not impressed by predictable cartoons. Thus, the cartoonist who depicted Ronald Reagan carrying a briefcase in the shape of a gunboat was recycling a cliché from the nineteenth century about "gunboat diplomacy" and was therefore probably not as effective as cartoonists who found more original ways to critique the president's military buildup. Likewise, the cartoonist who labels specific objects in a drawing may be helping the viewer get the point but may also be admitting that the drawing is not clever enough to be self-explanatory. And the cartoonist who makes a cultural reference to a historical event or a pop culture icon may connect well with viewers who know history or pop culture but may leave other viewers confused about the meaning of the reference.

Above all, every cartoonist must assume that viewers are sufficiently informed about current events to have some idea of what a particular cartoon is about, even if they don't grasp every reference or gag. When Adrian Raeside, the cartoonist for *The Colonist* in Victoria, British Columbia, drew the cartoon you see here, he was obviously assuming that his Canadian viewers knew that President Reagan's joke about bombing Russia had been mistakenly broadcast over the radio airwaves one August morning in 1984. Raeside greatly exaggerated the event in order to mock Reagan's attempt at humor but also to make a serious point about the potential effect of such gaffes by an American president.

Source: Charles Brooks, editor, *The Best Editorial Cartoons of the Year: 1985 Edition* (Greta: Pelican Publishing, 1985), 20.

What Can Political Cartoons Tell Us?

Political cartoons must be accessible to a broad spectrum of the public; a wide variety of viewers must be able to "get" them—and get them quickly. For that reason, cartoons from past decades can give us a window on what ideas and images were widely available and widely shared in the popular culture. If a cartoonist in 1981 used the image of jellybeans in a cartoon about Reagan, we can conclude that it was well known that the president loved jellybeans and kept a jar of them on his desk; otherwise, that cartoonist's editor might have said the reference to jellybeans was just too obscure. Similarly, if cartoonists in the 1980s typically drew Mikhail Gorbachev with a birthmark on his forehead, we can conclude that Americans were quite familiar with the Soviet leader's visage. So the most obvious advantage to political cartoons as a source of information about the past is that they offer us a quick, entertaining index to popular culture.

Political cartoons also offer an accessible guide to political developments and debates that were so well known that they could be abbreviated into a single drawing using few, if any, words. If a cartoonist in the 1980s could use the abbreviation "SDI" in a drawing, or simply refer to "Star Wars," without further explanation, then we can conclude that the debate about Reagan's Strategic Defense Initiative was a frequent topic in political debate and that these shorthand references were widely used and understood.

Public reaction to political cartoons is often an index to the limits or points of tension in public discourse. For example, less than six months after the terrorist attack on the World Trade Center on September 11, 2001, cartoonist Mike Marland outraged many subscribers to the *Concord (N.H.) Monitor* because of a drawing he used to criticize President George W. Bush's Social Security proposals. Marland depicted the president flying a plane labeled "Bush Budget" into twin towers labeled "Social" and "Security." To quell the public outcry, the *Monitor* apologized to its readers. But strong public reactions are part of the history and daily life of political cartooning. Back in 1983, Paul Szep drew a verbal exchange over military weapons between President Reagan and then–Soviet President Yuri Andropov in which Andropov uttered a two-word Russian obscenity. Szep's employer, the *Boston Globe,* published the cartoon, but when subscribers complained about it, the newspaper suspended Szep for two weeks.

At least Szep was able to publish his editorial view. That is not always the case. We cannot assume that the spectrum of editorial views expressed in a collection of political cartoons from a particular year or era reflects the whole span of views in U.S. political debate. Traditionally, cartoonists' work had to be published by a newspaper or a magazine, and despite the First Amendment there have often been limits on how far an editor was willing to go in ridiculing a public figure or mocking a political proposal. Since cartoonists' job is to be outrageous, they endeavor not to censor themselves; but since their job depends on getting published, cartoonists must consider whether an editor will accept a particularly biting image, especially when the political climate is not open to dissent.

Today there are fewer and fewer political cartoonists on the permanent editorial staffs of daily newspapers; increasingly, cartoonists work as freelancers who must try to sell their work to a wide array of news outlets. This can give them greater freedom of expression but can also leave them without any guarantee of being published. Will this shift in the relationship between political cartoonists and news outlets produce a greater diversity of views we see expressed in cartoons, or will it narrow such views as outlets pick only cartoons that won't offend? How will the explosion of news outlets on the Web change the public's access to political cartoonists' zany visions of history as it is being made? Newspaper readers in the past opened the editorial page and were confronted with political cartoons with which they did not agree. Will Internet users choose to visit only those cartoon sites that confirm their opinions? Will political cartoonists in the future be able to "jar, shake, needle people out of their fat-headedness"? Only time will tell.

Questions to Ask

The cartoons here are arranged chronologically from 1981, when Ronald Reagan first became president, to 1988, when he was about to leave office. They allow you to trace the evolution of political debates over President Reagan's military policy and his foreign policy toward the Soviet Union and to examine the array of techniques that political cartoonists use to convey their points.

- Which cartoons do you "get" instantly, and which ones do you have to think about for a little while?

- What changes do you see here in the depiction of Ronald Reagan's Soviet policy?

- Do the cartoons that praise Reagan and Gorbachev for progress toward peace actually qualify as political "cartoons"?

- Which cartooning techniques are most effective: visual gags or clever use of language? references to popular culture? moral appeals?

- Is it possible to separate your agreement or disagreement with the political message of a cartoon from your assessment of its success as a cartoon?

Source Analysis Table

You can use check marks in the boxes to track changes in the story of Reagan's foreign policy and to record different tools that cartoonists use to make their points.

Source	Reagan Promilitary	Reagan Pro–Arms Control	Physical Exaggeration	Pop Culture References	Spoken Words	Labels
1. "Can't you see . . ." (1981)						
2. "Let's negotiate . . ." (1981)						
3. "He's got to eat . . ." (1982)						
4. "Surely they'll not be so stupid . . ." (1982)						
5. "I'm surprised . . ." (1983)						
6. "Go on, Yuri . . ." (1984)						
7. "Say, here comes the new blood . . ." (1984)						

(continued)

Source	Reagan Promilitary	Reagan Pro–Arms Control	Physical Exaggeration	Pop Culture References	Spoken Words	Labels
8. "The U.S. bargaining chip . . ." (1985)						
9. "The Soviets are a bunch of . . ." (1985)						
10. "Hey, maybe we should do this . . ." (1985)						
11. Reykjavik summit (1986)						
12. "Little Ronnie . . ." (1987)						
13. Two doves (1987)						
14. "Evolution" (1988)						

To download and print this table, visit the book companion site at **bedfordstmartins.com/brownshannon**.

The Source: Political Cartoons from the Reagan Era, 1981–1988

CARTOONS FROM 1981

<table>
<tr><td>1</td><td></td></tr>
</table>

"Can't you see I'm trying to fill a hole?"
by Bill Sanders, *Milwaukee Journal*, 1981

In his first year as president, Ronald Reagan pleased some Americans and angered others by advocating sharp increases in defense spending and large cuts in spending on social services. In October 1981, Reagan advocated an expensive speedup in the deployment of the "MX" missile, a land-based intercontinental ballistic missile approved under President Jimmy Carter. This proposal, which involved redesigning the basing plan for the MX, was hotly debated in Congress and in the press throughout 1981. Ultimately, Congress rejected the new basing plan.

Source: Charles Brooks, editor, *The Best Editorial Cartoons of the Year: 1982 Edition* (Greta: Pelican Publishing, 1982), 41.

2

"There's nothing to negotiate!"
"Let's negotiate!"
by Al Liederman, Rothco Syndicate, 1981

In the same year that President Reagan was pressing to speed up MX missile deployment, he also ordered production of the neutron bomb, which had been halted under President Jimmy Carter. The neutron bomb was designed to reduce the amount of blast, so that fewer buildings would be destroyed, while increasing the amount of radiation, so that more people would be killed. The Reagan administration's strategic argument was that production of these weapons would bring the Soviet Union to the bargaining table.

Source: Charles Brooks, editor, *The Best Editorial Cartoons of the Year: 1982 Edition* (Greta: Pelican Publishing, 1982), 44.

CARTOONS FROM 1982

3   ***"He's got to eat to have strength to start reducing"***
by Jim Mazzotta, *Fort Myers News Press*, 1982

In February 1982, President Reagan submitted a federal budget that included $200 billion in defense spending, alongside reductions of $63 billion in programs such as food stamps, Medicare, and Medicaid. The 1982 budget projected a federal deficit of $91.5 billion. Reagan argued that cuts in social spending would reduce waste and fraud in social programs, while increases in defense spending would bring victory in the cold war and an end to the need for large defense budgets.

Source: Charles Brooks, editor, *The Best Editorial Cartoons of the Year: 1983 Edition* (Greta: Pelican Publishing, 1983), 43.

"HE'S GOT TO EAT TO HAVE THE STRENGTH TO START REDUCING..."

4

"Surely they'll not be so stupid as to keep coming!"

by Bob Artley, *Worthington Daily Globe*, 1982

The Reagan administration argued that a large defense buildup was a spending strategy to defeat the Soviet Union, either economically or militarily. Critics argued that the strategy fueled a risky arms competition in which neither country could back down.

Source: Charles Brooks, editor, *The Best Editorial Cartoons of the Year: 1983 Edition* (Greta: Pelican Publishing, 1983), 44.

The nuclear arms race

CARTOONS FROM 1983

5

"I'm surprised at how the president dealt with the Russians . . ."
by Walt Handelsman, *Catonville Times*, 1983

On September 1, 1983, a Soviet fighter shot down Korean Air Lines Flight 007 when the civilian plane mistakenly flew 500 kilometers off course into Soviet airspace. All 269 passengers and crew were killed, including Congressman Lawrence McDonald (D-Georgia). Four days later, President Reagan denounced the shooting as "an act of barbarism" and revoked the license of Aeroflot Soviet Airlines to operate in and out of the United States but ordered no further retaliation. Cartoonists had lampooned President Reagan's tough stance toward the Soviet Union during his first three years in office, but this incident offered a chance to mock anti-Soviet conservatives who were disappointed in Reagan.

Source: Charles Brooks, editor, *The Best Editorial Cartoons of the Year: 1984 Edition* (Greta: Pelican Publishing, 1984), 39.

CARTOONS FROM 1984

6   *"Go on, Yuri, make my day . . ."*
by Mike Peters, *Dayton Daily News,* 1984

Sudden Impact, the fourth of Clint Eastwood's Dirty Harry movies was a big hit in early 1984. In the film, Detective Harry Callahan aims his gun at the head of a thief who is holding a gun at a hostage's head and growls, "Go ahead, make my day." By referencing that quote, cartoonist Mike Peters was playing on some Americans' perception of President Reagan as a tough leader and on others' perception of Reagan as someone who would relish a confrontation with the Soviets. At the same time, Peters was invoking the president's own Hollywood career as an actor who had made fifty-three movies between 1937 and 1964.

Source: Charles Brooks, editor, *The Best Editorial Cartoons of the Year: 1985 Edition* (Greta: Pelican Publishing, 1985), 55.

7

"Say, here comes the new blood now . . ."
by Jack Higgins, *Chicago Sun-Times*, 1984

Constantin Chernenko, age seventy-two, was immediately appointed to replace Yuri Andropov as the Soviet president after the seventy-year-old Andropov died in February 1984. Chernenko was the same age as President Reagan, but he did not enjoy Reagan's robust health. Many, including cartoonists, viewed the physical contrast between the two leaders as a metaphor for U.S. strength and Soviet weakness. Indeed, Chernenko died in office in March 1985.

Source: Charles Brooks, editor, *The Best Editorial Cartoons of the Year: 1985 Edition* (Greta: Pelican Publishing, 1985), 2.

CARTOONS FROM 1985

8   *"The U.S. bargaining chip! The Soviet bargaining chip, chip, chip, chip!"*
by Chuck Asay, *Colorado Springs Sun*, 1985

This cartoon, which appeared just a few days after Gorbachev came to power in the USSR, indicates that the press was immediately expecting some attempt at arms negotiations between President Reagan and this new, young Soviet leader. Chuck Asay, who drew this cartoon, was a supporter of Reagan's SDI. He believed that because Gorbachev lacked any new weapons system he could trade away in order to eliminate SDI, he would simply try to prevent the United States from developing a defense system.

Source: Charles Brooks, editor, *The Best Editorial Cartoons of the Year: 1986 Edition* (Greta: Pelican Publishing, 1986), 28.

9

"The Soviets are a bunch of rabid, murdering . . ."
by Mike Graston, *Windsor Star,* 1985

In July 1985, just four months after Mikhail Gorbachev became the leader of the USSR, he and President Reagan announced that they would hold a summit in Geneva, Switzerland, in November of that year. This was President Reagan's first meeting with a Soviet leader since taking office, and his four years as president had been marked by angry rhetoric from both cold war enemies. As a result, there was considerable skepticism about whether the summit was a serious meeting or merely a diplomatic performance by both politicians in response to public pressure to meet.

Source: Charles Brooks, editor, *The Best Editorial Cartoons of the Year: 1986 Edition* (Greta: Pelican Publishing, 1986), 25.

10   *"Hey, maybe we should do this more often"*
by Hy Rosen, *Albany Times-Union*, 1985

Ronald Reagan's 1984 reelection campaign theme, "It's morning in America," suggested a new start for an incumbent president. Hy Rosen may have been invoking that theme in this cartoon, which appeared immediately after the Geneva summit, amid optimistic reports of genuine discussions between Reagan and Gorbachev.

Source: Charles Brooks, editor, *The Best Editorial Cartoons of the Year: 1986 Edition* (Greta: Pelican Publishing, 1986), 25.

CARTOONS FROM 1986

11 *Reykjavik summit destroyed by Star Wars*

by Jerry Fearing, *St. Paul Dispatch–Pioneer Press*, 1986

Ronald Reagan and Mikhail Gorbachev held their second summit in October 1986. The news coming out of the first day of meetings on October 11 raised high hopes for dramatic reductions in the number of intermediate-range missiles in Europe and the intercontinental ballistic missiles in the United States and Soviet Union. But hopes were dashed on October 12 when the two leaders could not agree on a plan for research and deployment of Reagan's Strategic Defense Initiative, which skeptics of the hypothetical system dubbed "Star Wars."

Source: Charles Brooks, editor, *The Best Editorial Cartoons of the Year: 1987 Edition* (Greta: Pelican Publishing, 1987), 40.

CARTOONS FROM 1987

12   *"Little Ronnie Reagan and his imaginary friend"*
by Mike Keefe, *Denver Post,* 1987

In the aftermath of the Reykjavik summit, commentators continued to fear that Reagan's commitment to SDI and Gorbachev's resistance to it would ruin the potential for arms limitation that the two leaders' relationship seemed to promise. Only in retrospect, with the aid of documents and recollections, is it clear that in 1987 Gorbachev came to the conclusion that SDI would never be a viable defense shield and that he did not need to link arms limitation to controls on SDI development.

Source: Charles Brooks, editor, *The Best Editorial Cartoons of the Year: 1988 Edition* (Greta: Pelican Publishing, 1988), 63.

13 | *Reagan and Gorbachev emerging from a missile as doves*

by Dick Wallmeyer, *Long Beach Press-Telegram*, 1987

The third Reagan-Gorbachev summit in Washington, D.C., in early December 1987, was less ambitious in its goals for arms reduction than the Reykjavik summit, but it did successfully achieve some reductions in actual nuclear weapons. More important for the mood of the time, the summit made clear that the two leaders of the world's nuclear superpowers were still committed to arms reductions and that the failure at Reykjavik had not spoiled the Reagan-Gorbachev partnership for peace. At the start of the summit, President Reagan said, "Americans believe people should be able to disagree and still respect one another, still live in peace with one another. That is the spirit, the democratic spirit, that I will bring to our meetings."

Source: Charles Brooks, editor, *The Best Editorial Cartoons of the Year: 1988 Edition* (Greta: Pelican Publishing, 1988), 2.

CARTOONS FROM 1988

14   *"Evolution"*

by Joe Majeski, *Wilkes-Barre Times-Leader,* 1988

By the time of the fourth Reagan-Gorbachev summit in Moscow in May 1988, even Ronald Reagan's critics were admitting that he had made great strides in mending the relationship with the USSR. The president who had called the Soviet Union the "evil empire" and revived production of the neutron bomb now referred to the Soviets as "allies" and sought to eliminate all nuclear weapons.

Source: Charles Brooks, editor, *The Best Editorial Cartoons of the Year: 1989 Edition* (Greta: Pelican Publishing, 1989), 45.

Analyzing Political Cartoons

1. Exaggeration and distortion are basic tools that cartoonists use to make their editorial points. Which of Ronald Reagan's physical features were typically exaggerated in these political cartoons, and what messages did the cartoonists convey with their distorted drawings?

2. Cartoonists argue about artistic techniques among themselves. Some take the view that a cartoonist who draws labels on people or objects in a cartoon is somehow cheating or insulting the reader's intelligence. Look over the cartoons in this set that include labels. Do you think they detract from or enhance the impact of these cartoons?

3. If this set of cartoons were your *only* source of information on U.S. military policy and Soviet policy during the Reagan administration, what story would you be able to construct from the cartoons?

4. Cartoonists' work must be readily accessible to viewers, but cartoonists must also assume that their audience is somewhat informed about political events. Which cartoons in this set could have been grasped by a person who did not pay much attention to the news? Which cartoons required a more advanced knowledge of current events?

5. The cartoons in this chapter were all selected from a series of books published annually entitled *The Best Editorial Cartoons of the Year*. Which cartoon do *you* think is the "best" in this set? Write an explanation of your choice. Be sure to discuss the mix of content and style that influences your evaluation. Is your selection based on the editorial opinion expressed in the cartoon or on the cartoonist's use of exaggerated visual imagery to make a point? Does your favorite cartoon include a lot of detail, or is it very spare? Do you pay more attention to the words in the cartoon or to the drawing?

The Rest of the Story

Three years after Ronald Reagan left office, the Union of Soviet Socialist Republics ceased to exist, its presidency was eliminated, and Mikhail Gorbachev no longer held any official power. The fifteen republics that made up the USSR all became independent states in December 1991. Two years earlier, the Warsaw Pact nations of East Germany, Poland, Bulgaria, Czechoslovakia, Hungary, and Romania (which had operated under Soviet control since 1955) had all declared independence from Moscow. At the same time, the Berlin Wall came down, and the reunification of East Germany and West Germany began. As one historian put it, "A political avalanche had changed the face of Europe" in the space of just over two years, and only in the case of Romania was any blood spilled.

The American president who witnessed these dramatic events and devised U.S. foreign policy in response to them was George Herbert Walker Bush, formerly Ronald Reagan's vice president and a public official whose experience in foreign affairs included appointments as U.S. ambassador to the United Nations, chief U.S. diplomatic representative in China, and director of the Central Intelligence Agency. As a product of the U.S. foreign affairs establishment, Vice President Bush had been uncomfortable with President Reagan's harsh denunciations of the Soviet Union and equally uncomfortable with Reagan's wide swing toward eliminating nuclear weapons. When George H. W. Bush moved into the Oval Office, he intended to deal slowly and cautiously with the Soviet Union, Gorbachev, and the apparent thaw in the cold war.

In its first year, the Bush administration articulated a U.S. policy that looked beyond cold war "containment" of the Soviet Union and its Warsaw Pact countries and proposed "integration" of the USSR and its satellites "into the community of nations." Even as that new U.S. policy was being devised, the Warsaw Pact was unraveling. Commentators at the time criticized Bush for being too reserved in his reaction to the demise of Soviet power in eastern Europe, but the president believed that prudence dictated a fairly closed-mouth approach. Because independence movements within the Warsaw Pact put President Gorbachev in political danger inside the USSR, Bush believed that he should avoid any celebratory comments that conservatives in Moscow could interpret as a U.S. declaration of victory in the cold war. Rather than gloat over the Soviet loss of regional power, Bush sought to protect Gorbachev from his internal enemies and to assist Gorbachev's democratizing efforts by staying out of the way. Bush announced major cuts in conventional weapons and military forces stationed in Europe but did not otherwise interfere in the eastern Europeans' tumultuous political process.

Despite the fact that the international ground was shifting below their feet, George Bush and Mikhail Gorbachev did hold four summit meetings—the last four of a total of sixteen summits ever held between a U.S. president and a Soviet leader. The agendas at each of those summits reveal a shift from the cold war to what President Bush optimistically described as the "new world order."

The first summit was held on a ship off the island of Malta in December 1989, just as Soviet control over eastern Europe was collapsing. While the agenda focused on old, familiar issues—strategic arms limitation plans and military installations in Europe—the whole thrust was new. Gorbachev told Bush that the USSR's stability relied on continued U.S. military presence in Europe; faced with the prospect of a reunited, independent Germany, Gorbachev told Bush, "We don't consider you an enemy any more. Things have changed."

Indeed, things had changed so much that by the time of the second summit in the United States in 1990, the focus of discussion was not on weapons but on trade and Gorbachev's need for economic assistance from the United States in order to survive the political and economic dislocations resulting from Soviet policies of *glasnost* and *perestroika*. But it was the third summit, a one-day meeting in Helsinki, Finland, in early September 1990, that marked for many observers the end of the cold war and a new chapter in international history. Bush and Gorbachev met at Helsinki for one purpose: to solidify their shared opposition to Saddam Hussein's recent invasion of Kuwait. Gorbachev agreed to vote with the United States at the United Nations to denounce the Soviets' former ally, Iraq, but did not agree to join a military attack on Iraq should diplomacy fail. Gorbachev warned Bush that invasion of Iraq could lead to the sort of quagmire the Soviets had faced in Afghanistan and the United States had faced in Vietnam. Still, they spoke as partners in Helsinki, not as rivals.

Viewed from the perspective of the cold war, the cooperation around the Iraq problem looked to George H. W. Bush like the start of a new world order in which the two world powers, working together through the United Nations, would be able to guarantee world peace. So great was Bush's desire to stabilize this new world order that his final summit with Gorbachev in Moscow in the summer of 1991 was most notable for the American president's efforts to hold the Soviet Union together by discouraging the independence movement in Ukraine.

President Bush's new world order did not evolve out of the cold war as he had envisioned it. A cautious approach to the Soviet Union did not prevent the demise of that world power or the end of Gorbachev's influence; a decision not to invade Iraq did not prevent later U.S. adventures in that country. The four Bush-Gorbachev summits did mark the end of the cold war, but the new world order was beyond these two leaders' reach.

To Find Out More

The story of Mikhail Gorbachev's summit-based relationships with Presidents Ronald Reagan and George H. W. Bush is clearly narrated by *Washington Post* diplomatic correspondent Don Oberdorfer in *From the Cold War to a New Era: The United States and the Soviet Union, 1983–1991* (Baltimore: Johns Hopkins University Press, 1998).

Additional works that look back on the Reagan-Gorbachev relationship and arms negotiations from a post–cold war perspective include: Beth A. Fischer, *The Reagan Reversal: Foreign Policy and the End of the Cold War* (Columbia: University of Missouri Press, 1997); Raymond Garthoff, *Great Transition: American-Soviet Relations and the End of the Cold War* (Washington, D.C.: Brookings Institution, 1994); Peter Schweizer, *Victory: The Reagan Administration's Secret Strategy That Hastened the Collapse of the Soviet Union* (New York: Atlantic Monthly Press, 1996); and Paul Lettow, *Ronald Reagan and His Quest to Abolish Nuclear Weapons* (New York: Random House, 2005). These books present different views on Reagan's role in ending the cold war and include bibliographies that point to related journal articles.

For a study of the role of the first Bush administration and the end of the cold war, see Robert L. Hutchings, *American Diplomacy and the End of the Cold War: An Insider's Account of U.S. Diplomacy in Europe, 1989–1992* (Baltimore:

Johns Hopkins University Press, 1998). There are numerous "insider" accounts of the Reagan-Gorbachev years; two of the best are *Reagan and Gorbachev: How the Cold War Ended* (New York: Random House, 2004) by Jack Matlock Jr., who was ambassador to the Soviet Union in these years, and *Turmoil and Triumph: My Years as Secretary of State* (New York: Charles Scribner's Sons, 1993) by George P. Shultz, the chief architect of Reagan's foreign policy.

Three Web sites that offer interesting primary documents related to the Reagan-Gorbachev era of the cold war are The Reykjavik File, which contains documents about that summit from the National Security Archive at George Washington University (**gwu.edu/~nsarchiv/NSAEBB/NSAEBB203**); Ten Years After: The Fall of Communism in East/Central Europe (**rferl.org/specials/communism/10years**), which presents primary sources regarding the fall of Soviet power in specific Warsaw Pact nations; and The Cold War, a CNN Web site (**cnn.com/SPECIALS/cold.war**) based on the network's twenty-four episode documentary, which offers text sources related to each episode. Episode 22, "Star Wars, 1980–1988," and Episode 23, "The Wall Comes Down: 1989," provide transcripts of interviews conducted for the documentary, selected text documents, and biographical profiles of key players.

The cartoons used in this chapter were taken from the series *Best Editorial Cartoons of the Year* (volumes for 1982–1989). This annual volume is edited by Charles Brooks and is published by Pelican Publishing Company. Daryl Cagle also publishes an annual collection of cartoons, *The Best Political Cartoons of the Year* (Indianapolis, Ind.: Que Publishing), and operates a Web site (**cagle.msnbc.com**) featuring cartoons that have recently appeared in newspapers across the United States.

The best recent study of political cartoonists and their editorial art form is Chris Lamb's *Drawn to Extremes: The Use and Abuse of Editorial Cartoons* (New York: Columbia University Press, 2004). For a history of political cartooning in America, see Stephen Hess and Sandy Northrup, *Drawn and Quartered: The History of American Political Cartoons* (Montgomery, Ala.: Elliott and Clark Publishing, 1996). In 2005, cartoonist Chip Bok published *The Recent History of the United States in Political Cartoons* (Akron, Ohio: University of Akron Press, 2005), which covers the years between the Nixon presidency and the George W. Bush presidency.

Avoiding Plagiarism

Acknowledging the Source

Adapted from The St. Martin's Tutorial on Avoiding Plagiarism *by Margaret Price, University of Massachusetts–Amherst*

If you have taken classes that involve writing, particularly writing and research, chances are good that you have heard the term *plagiarism* before. You may have received syllabi that mention plagiarism and describe the penalties for it, such as a failing grade in the course or even suspension from school. You also may have read your school's plagiarism policy, which most likely offers a brief definition of plagiarism and issues dire warnings about what will happen if you plagiarize. And if you read or watch the news, you may have noticed that plagiarism is an important issue not only within academic settings but in the larger world as well. Clearly, plagiarism is serious business. But what is it, exactly? And how do you avoid doing it?

Defined simply, plagiarism is the unattributed use of someone else's words or ideas. However, this apparently simple definition can be quite complicated. It tends to change across contexts and may be understood differently by different readers. Despite the slipperiness of the definition, every writer has the responsibility to learn how to navigate it and to attribute sources accurately and fully. Ethical researchers must acknowledge their sources because writers and readers depend on one another's honesty. To use someone else's words or ideas without sufficient acknowledgment breaks that trust. Writers in academia are interdependent, with each of us depending on everyone else to help uphold the integrity of the group. Every person engaged in academic writing, from the first-time research writer to the seasoned professor, shares this responsibility. For this reason, the penalties for an academic writer who fails to practice academic integrity are severe.

Why Acknowledgment of Sources Is Important

Within the Western academic tradition, new ideas are built on older ones. Writers give acknowledgment in writing to their sources for a number of reasons:

- **To indicate that you are a responsible and careful researcher.** Acknowledging your sources increases your credibility as a researcher.
- **To give your writing added relevance.** When you refer to others' ideas and show how your own ideas fit into that framework, readers can see more easily what is significant about your work.
- **To help define your research project.** Sources help indicate what topic you are addressing, what approach you are taking, with whose ideas you are aligning yourself and from whose ideas you are distancing yourself, and (in some cases) what discipline you are writing in. In sum, citation helps situate *you* as a unique researcher.
- **To give your work added authority.** Your argument is based not only on your own investigation but also on others' investigations.
- **To demonstrate your responsibility as a member of the academic community.** Each of us relies on the others to uphold the values of this community, one of which is attribution of sources.

Keeping Track of Source Materials: The Research Portfolio

As an ethical researcher, you should establish good research habits and stick to them. A research project, even a relatively small one involving only a few sources, quickly accumulates materials. There is no firm rule for how to keep these materials organized, but keeping some form of research portfolio is important. This portfolio should include

- photocopies or electronic copies of your source information
- your notes
- your annotated bibliography
- drafts of the paper or project you are working on
- any feedback you have received

Organize your portfolio so that it is both comprehensive (containing all your materials) and manageable (designed for easy retrieval of information). With experience, you will develop a type of research portfolio that works for you. However, as you collect data, keep in mind some basic principles that will help you organize your research materials and avoid inadvertent plagiarism. Recording your research findings precisely and accurately reduces the chances that you will unintentionally express and claim someone else's idea as your own.

1. Create a structure for your portfolio. One example is the folder system. Hanging file folders represent large categories that can be subdivided using folders to represent smaller categories. As you discover more information through your research, you will add more folders, or perhaps revise the categories altogether. Keep your working bibliography (see the next section) in a separate folder. Also, keep your notes and annotations for each source. Another possible structure for a research portfolio is the notebook system, in which materials are kept in a three-ring binder, with dividers separating the categories. The system you use will be governed by how much material you accumulate as well as your own organizational preferences.

2. Keep backup materials. Your portfolio should include backup copies of everything to guard against loss or computer failure. If a lot of your information resides on a computer, keep hard copies of everything and at least one electronic backup.

3. Make a hard copy of each source for your own use. You should print out any articles that you download from an online periodical database, photocopy articles or chapters of books, and print out all Web sites. (Most printouts of Web sites will automatically note the URL and date of access. If this does not occur, note this information.) These printouts will be very useful for checking quotations, paraphrases, and bibliographic information.

4. Take notes on every source you collect. This step is crucial. If you simply read a source over and then later attempt to include some of its information in the draft of your paper, your chances of plagiarizing are much greater. You cannot truly digest a source's information unless you take notes on what you read. If you fail to take notes, your inclusion of the source's words is likely to sound choppy, with inadequate connectors between the source's ideas and your own.

Maintaining a Working Bibliography

A working bibliography is a list of all the sources you consult as you work on a research project. You may not need to include every source in your project, but you should keep a list of every work you have consulted so that your records are complete. If you develop this habit, you will avoid the problem of wondering where you found certain facts and ideas. A working bibliography also may come in handy for future research projects. After you complete your research, keep your working bibliography so that you can consult it again if necessary.

Your working bibliography should include complete information for each source so that you can write your citations easily (see Appendix II: Documenting the Source). This information includes the author's name, the title of the work, the title of the book or periodical it comes from (if applicable), the volume or issue number, the place of publication, the publishing company, the date of publication, and inclusive page numbers. Note any other information that pertains to the work's publication, such as whether it is a volume in a series, an edition other than the first, or a translation. Write down the information for each source as you begin using it. You can also keep your working bibliography on a computer file; this technique allows you to easily transfer the bibliography into your final draft later on.

Taking Notes: Knowing Where Each Idea and Word Comes From

It is easy to assume that the research process and the writing process are separate—"first I research, and then I write." But in fact, researching and writing should be intimately intertwined. As you read and research, new ideas occur to you. Your research question begins to change shape and sometimes to change direction. The development of your own thoughts in turn leads to a different reading of your sources. Taking notes and writing drafts while you research are essential. If you wait to begin note-taking and drafting until you have "finished" your research, the rich mixture of ideas and thoughts you created while researching will never be captured on paper.

You may be surprised to learn that research involves so much writing before you begin writing your "real" paper. But note-taking is not an optional or extra step. All responsible researchers write notes before (and while) drafting their projects. In fact, you can think of your notes as a first draft, or pre-draft, of your paper. They are crucial building blocks of an effective research project. A detailed note-taking system makes writing a paper much easier.

Taking careful notes while you are researching also makes it easier to figure out which ideas are your own. Any plagiarism policy that you read will say that plagiarism is the act of representing someone else's words or ideas as your own. Summarizing or paraphrasing requires that you take another person's idea and put it into your own words.

Clearly, then, it is better to write as you go rather than to save the writing for the end of a research project. But how do you go about doing it? Here are some concrete note-taking strategies.

- **Write an instant draft.** Before you begin researching, or as early in the research process as possible, write a draft that describes what argument you want to make or what question you want to explore. Writing professors Charles Moran and Anne Herrington call this an "instant draft." An instant draft will be a tentative, somewhat disorganized piece of writing, since you have not yet done your research. Its purpose is to capture what you know about a subject before you begin consulting other people's ideas. In your instant draft, address the following questions: *What do I* *already know about this topic? Where have I gotten my information from so far? Do I have a strong feeling or stance on this topic? What questions do I have about the topic? What is (are) the main thing(s) I want to find out through my research? Where will I begin looking for this information? What do I need help with? Whom can I ask for that help?* An instant draft is a research memo to yourself and is enormously helpful in providing a recorded baseline for your knowledge. As you learn more and more through your research, you will always know where you started out—and hence, which ideas you have acquired through researching.

- **Annotate each source.** Before you begin taking more detailed notes, annotate each source you have just read. That is, write a brief summary of the source's main point and key ideas. It is helpful to include annotations in your working bibliography (which turns it into an *annotated bibliography*). Some instructors will ask you to turn in an annotated bibliography with your final draft.

- **Practice taking notes to avoid patchwriting.** "Patchwriting," a term coined by writing professor Rebecca Moore Howard, means taking notes that are not exact quotations, but that are quite close to the original source's wording. Howard suggests the following system for avoiding patchwriting: First, read a source quickly, just enough to get its main point. Then read it through again, more slowly, taking notes in the margin (perhaps quick questions or key terms) as you go. Wait a bit before moving on to the next step (Howard suggests that half an hour is sufficient). Then, *without looking at the source again*, write a summary of it. Finally, check your summary against the original source. Have you duplicated any of the author's phrases? If so, quote the author directly or adjust the phrasing of your summary. The more often you do this exercise, the more adept you will become at summarizing sources.

Summarizing, Paraphrasing, and Quoting

You can record someone else's words or ideas in your notes by using three techniques: summarizing, paraphrasing, and quoting. Summarizing and paraphrasing involve putting a source's words into your own; quoting involves recording a source's exact words. After you practice these independently, it is a good idea to show your notes to your instructor and to ask for his or her comments on the effectiveness of your note-taking. Is it complete? Is it accurate? When summarizing and paraphrasing, do you put other authors' ideas into your own words effectively?

   1. Summarizing. To summarize is to rephrase a relatively large amount of information into a short statement in your own words. While some information will inevitably be lost, your job is to record what you see as the main idea of the passage. Summarizing is useful when you want to give a reader the gist of a relatively lengthy passage without going into every detail.

2. Paraphrasing. To paraphrase is to restate something with your own words and sentence structure. Unlike a summary, a paraphrase is generally about as long as the original passage. Because you are changing the language, you will also inevitably change the meaning of the passage *slightly*, but your job is to keep the meaning as intact as possible. Paraphrasing is useful when you want to convey another author's exact idea, but not his or her exact words—perhaps because the language is highly technical, or perhaps because a quote would be distracting.

3. Quoting. To quote is to state a source's exact words, signaled by the use of quotation marks. If you change a quotation in any way, you must indicate this by including ellipsis points (when you omit part of a quotation) or square brackets (when you make a slight change or addition for clarification). In a final draft, quotations are often less useful than summaries or paraphrases because quotations break up the flow of your writing and often require fairly extensive explanation. Quotations are useful, however, when you want to capture a source's exact wording.

Knowing Which Sources to Acknowledge

Beginning researchers often ask, "Do I have to cite *everything*?" This is a good question because not every piece of information in a research paper must be cited. Figuring out what to cite can be difficult, even for experienced researchers. Generally, if you are unsure, include a citation. It is always better to have an unnecessary citation in your paper than to omit one that is necessary.

Materials That Do Not Require Acknowledgment

Here are some types of materials that usually do not require acknowledgment in research projects:

- **Common knowledge.** It is often easy to spot pieces of common knowledge. The sky is blue, the United States has fifty states, the 1996 presidential candidates were Bill Clinton and Bob Dole—these are all pieces of information that appear in various sources, but because they are known to just about everyone, you do not need to cite a source. Sometimes, however, recognizing common knowledge becomes tricky because common knowledge for one person may not be common knowledge for another. Identifying your audience is the key to recognizing common knowledge. If you know what audience you are writing to, you will have a clearer idea of what your readers would consider common knowledge. As always, if you are unsure, be more conservative rather than less so.

- **Fact.** Uncontested pieces of information that can be found in many different sources—particularly reference sources such as encyclopedias—do not require acknowledgment. In *The St. Martin's Handbook*, writing professor Andrea Lunsford gives an example of one such fact: that most of the Pearl Harbor military base, except oil tanks and submarines, was destroyed on December 7, 1941, by Japanese bombers. She adds an example of information on the same topic that *does* require citation: "a source that argued that the failure to destroy the submarines meant that Japan was destined to lose the subsequent war with the United States" (394). The distinction Lunsford makes here is between fact (something commonly accepted as true) and opinion (something that is arguable).

- **Your own ideas.** Recognizing that an idea is your own can sometimes be difficult, especially during the research process, when you are reading and absorbing so many others' ideas. A good way to capture your own ideas is to write a draft *before* you begin researching.

- **Your own field research.** Knowledge that you create by conducting a field study such as a survey, an interview, or an observation is considered your own work. You do not need to cite this sort of information. However, another kind of ethics guides the field researcher. You should be clear about how you collected the information. In addition, you should be scrupulous about protecting your participants' autonomy (be sure to quote them accurately, and ask for their feedback when possible).

Materials That Do Require Acknowledgment

Anything that you draw from another source, unless it falls into one of the categories described above (common knowledge, fact, your own ideas, and your own field research), must be cited. Your citations should appear in two places: in the body of your paper and in a list at the end of the paper. The style of citation your instructor has asked you to use will affect the formatting of these citations. Complete bibliographic information for each source will appear in a section titled "Bibliography" (see Appendix II: Documenting the Source).

The following list is suggestive, but not exhaustive. New kinds of information are always emerging. Generally speaking, however, here are the types of materials that require acknowledgment in academic writing:

- **Another person's words.** Direct quotations must always be cited.

- **Another person's ideas.** Even if you rephrase someone else's idea by paraphrasing or summarizing it, you must cite it. Citations for paraphrases and summaries look just like citations for quotations, except that no quotation marks are used.

- **Judgments, opinions, and arguments.** Arguable information, such as the idea about the effect of the Pearl Harbor bombing discussed previously, must be cited. Whenever you offer an idea from another source that could be argued, acknowledge that it is this individual's point of view. You should do this even if you thought of the idea and *then* encountered it through your research. You can indicate in your writing that you came to the idea independently of the other author, but you cannot omit mention of the other author.

- **Visual information.** If you use a chart, graph, or picture from another source—or if you use the information from that chart, graph, or picture—acknowledge the source.

- **Information that can be attributed to a company or organization rather than a single person.** Web pages and corporate publications often do not list individual authors. In this case, the organization that sponsored the Web site or publication should be listed as the author. If the author is unknown, your citation should indicate that.

- **Information gathered from class lectures or from another aural source.** If you heard information rather than saw it, you must still cite it. You can cite information you have heard in various ways, including as a lecture, as a personal communication, or as an interview.

- **General help offered by readers.** Sometimes the feedback you receive from readers (such as your teacher, classmates, and friends) will affect the shape of your work, but not its content. For instance, a classmate might offer a suggestion for making your introduction more interesting. In this case, the best way to acknowledge your classmate's contribution is in a note of thanks appended to the paper. Such "Acknowledgments" notes generally appear at the end of academic papers or in a footnote added to the title or first paragraph. If you look at a refereed history journal, you will see examples of less formal acknowledgments of this kind.

Learning these rules and following them appropriately is one of your responsibilities as a member of an academic or writing community. Even if you plagiarize unintentionally, the penalties for plagiarism—which can be very severe—still apply to you. For more information on plagiarism, consult your school's or your department's guidelines. For more detailed and constructive information, speak with your instructor, who probably has a pretty good idea of what sort of citation is expected. You should also find out if your school has a writing center with tutoring available. Tutors can discuss ways of citing information and often can refer you to other sources of information if you need additional help. A third resource to consider is a writing handbook that includes the rules of academic citation as well as guidelines on conducting research, managing information, and citing sources responsibly. For an interactive tutorial on avoiding plagiarism, go to **bedfordstmartins.com/plagiarismtutorial**.

Documenting the Source

Whenever you use another researcher's work as a source in your own writing, whether you quote the researcher's words directly or rely on the researcher's evidence and theories to support your arguments, you must include documentation for that source. This is equally true when using a map, photograph, table, or graph created by someone else. The reasons for this are twofold. First, to avoid any possibility of plagiarism, you must always include proper documentation for *all* source materials (see Appendix I). Second, a proper citation gives important information to your reader about where to find a particular source, be it on a Web site, in a book at the library, or in an archive in your local community.

When documenting sources, historians use a standard form based on the recommendations published in *The Chicago Manual of Style*. All of the following documentation models are based on the guidelines published in the fifteenth edition of *The Chicago Manual of Style* (Chicago: The University of Chicago Press, 2003). These examples are based on the sources that appear in both volumes of *Going to the Source*. The diversity of the examples will give you some sense of the variety of source types that you may encounter in your research. For each source type, you will see a citation style that can be used for either a footnote, which appears at the bottom of the page of text, or an endnote, which appears at the end of a chapter or at the end of the whole text. This will be followed by an example of how this source type would be cited in a bibliography. Two examples are provided because footnote/endnote citation style is slightly different from bibliography citation style.

The examples provided here will help you address many of the documentation issues associated with source types that you come across in your research. However, this guide is not a comprehensive list, and as you dig further into the past, you may uncover source types that are not covered in this brief guide. For additional information about documenting sources in the *Chicago* style, please see **bedfordstmartins.com/resdoc**.

Documentation Basics

The question to keep in mind when you are wondering what to include in a citation is this: what does my reader need to know in order to *find* this source? When citing sources internally, you should use the footnote or endnote style. Footnotes and endnotes are used to document specific instances of borrowed text, ideas, or information. The first time you cite a source, you need to include the full publication information for that source—the author's full name, source title (and subtitle, if there is one), and facts of publication (city, publisher, and date)—along with the specific page number that you are referencing.

> 1. David Paul Nord, *Communities of Journalism: A History of American Newspapers and Their Readers* (Urbana: University of Illinois Press, 2001), 78.

If you refer to that source later in your paper, you need to include only the author's last name, an abbreviated version of the title, and the page or pages cited.

> 4. Nord, *Communities of Journalism,* 110–12.

A bibliography is used in addition to footnotes or endnotes to list all of the works you consulted in completing your paper, even those not directly cited in your footnotes. The sources included in your bibliography should be listed alphabetically, so the citation style for a bibliographic entry begins with the author's last name first.

> Nord, David Paul. *Communities of Journalism*: A History of American Newspapers and Their Readers. Urbana: University of Illinois Press, 2001.

BOOKS

■ *Standard format for a book*

The standard form for citing a book is the same whether there is an editor or an author, the only difference being the inclusion of "ed." to indicate that an editor compiled the work.

FOOTNOTE/ENDNOTE:

1. Tim Johnson, ed., *Spirit Capture: Photographs from the National Museum of the American Indian* (Washington, DC: Smithsonian Institution Press, 1998), 102.

BIBLIOGRAPHY ENTRY:

Johnson, Tim, ed. *Spirit Capture: Photographs from the National Museum of the American Indian.* Washington, DC: Smithsonian Institution Press, 1998.

■ *Book with two or more authors or editors*

When citing a source from a book with two or three authors or editors, you need to include the names of all of the authors (or editors) in the order that they appear on the title page. If a work has more than three authors, you need to include all of the names in your bibliography. However, in your footnotes or endnotes, you need only include the name of the lead author followed by "and others" or "et al.," with no intervening comma.

FOOTNOTE/ENDNOTE:

2. Graham Russell Hodges and Alan Edward Brown, eds., *"Pretends to Be Free": Runaway Slave Advertisements from Colonial and Revolutionary New York and New Jersey* (New York: Garland, 1994), 58.

BIBLIOGRAPHY ENTRY:

Hodges, Graham Russell, and Alan Edward Brown, eds. *"Pretends to Be Free": Runaway Slave Advertisements from Colonial and Revolutionary New York and New Jersey.* New York: Garland, 1994.

■ *Edited book with an author*

Sometimes a book will have an author and an editor. In that case, you need to include both the author's and the editor's names.

FOOTNOTE/ENDNOTE:

3. Hilda Satt Polacheck, *I Came a Stranger: The Story of a Hull-House Girl*, ed. Dena J. Polacheck Epstein (Urbana: University of Illinois Press, 1991), 36.

BIBLIOGRAPHY ENTRY:

Polacheck, Hilda Satt. *I Came a Stranger: The Story of a Hull-House Girl.* Edited by Dena J. Polacheck Epstein. Urbana: University of Illinois Press, 1991.

■ *Multivolume book*

If you are referring to a specific volume in a multivolume work, you need to specify which volume you used. This information should come before the page reference toward the end of the citation.

FOOTNOTE/ENDNOTE:

4. Bernard Bailyn, ed., *The Debate on the Constitution: Federalist and Anti-Federalist Speeches, Articles, and Letters during the Struggle over Ratification* (New York: Library of America, 1993), 2:759–61.

BIBLIOGRAPHY ENTRY:

Bailyn, Bernard, ed. *The Debate on the Constitution: Federalist and Anti-Federalist Speeches, Articles, and Letters during the Struggle over Ratification.* 2 vols. New York: Library of America, 1993.

Sometimes individual volumes in a multivolume work have separate volume titles. When citing a particular volume, you should include the volume title first followed by the name of the complete work.

■ *Book with an anonymous author*

Many books printed in the nineteenth century were published anonymously. If the author was omitted on the title page, but you know from your research who the author is, insert the name in square brackets; if you do not know who the actual author is, begin the citation with the work's title. Avoid using "Anonymous" or "Anon." in citations. As originally published, the author of *The Mother's Book* was listed as "Mrs. Child," so this citation includes that information along with the full name in brackets.

FOOTNOTE/ENDNOTE:

5. Mrs. [Lydia Maria] Child, *The Mother's Book* (Boston: Carter, Hendee, and Babcock, 1831), 23.

BIBLIOGRAPHY ENTRY:

Child, [Lydia Maria]. *The Mother's Book*. Boston: Carter, Hendee, and Babcock, 1831.

■ *Book-length work within a book*

Sometimes, the source that you are using may be a book-length work that has been reprinted within a longer work. In that case, you need to include both titles along with the editor of the longer work.

FOOTNOTE/ENDNOTE:

6. Álvar Núñez Cabeza de Vaca, *The Narrative of Cabeza de Vaca*, in *Spanish Explorers in the Southern United States, 1528–1543*, ed. Frederick W. Hodge (New York: Charles Scribner's Sons, 1907), 52–54, 76–78, 81–82.

BIBLIOGRAPHY ENTRY:

Cabeza de Vaca, Álvar Núñez. *The Narrative of Cabeza de Vaca*. In *Spanish Explorers in the Southern United States, 1528–1543*, edited by Frederick W. Hodge. New York: Charles Scribner's Sons, 1907.

■ *Chapter from a book*

If you want to cite a particular chapter from a book, you should include the title of the chapter in quotation marks before the title of the book.

FOOTNOTE/ENDNOTE:

7. Vicki L. Ruiz, "The Flapper and the Chaperone," in *From Out of the Shadows: Mexican Women in Twentieth-Century America* (New York: Oxford University Press, 1998), 12–26.

BIBLIOGRAPHY ENTRY:

Ruiz, Vicki L. "The Flapper and the Chaperone." In *From Out of the Shadows: Mexican Women in Twentieth-Century America*. New York: Oxford University Press, 1998.

PERIODICALS

Journals are scholarly publications that are usually published a few times a year. Popular magazines are written for the general public and are most often published on a monthly or weekly basis. Most newspapers are published daily, although some small local papers are published weekly. The following examples demonstrate the style for citing each type of periodical. If you consult an online periodical, the style for citing this source would be the same, with the addition of the URL at the end of your citation.

■ *Journal articles*

When citing an article from a journal, you need to include the volume number, issue number (when given), and date of publication.

FOOTNOTE/ENDNOTE:

8. Elizabeth A. Fenn, "Biological Warfare in Eighteenth-Century North America: Beyond Jeffery Amherst," *Journal of American History* 86, no. 4 (2000): 1552–80.

BIBLIOGRAPHY ENTRY:

Fenn, Elizabeth A. "Biological Warfare in Eighteenth-Century North America: Beyond Jeffery Amherst." *Journal of American History* 86, no. 4 (2000): 1552–80.

■ *Popular magazines*

When citing material from a popular magazine, you need to include only the magazine title followed by the date of publication and the page number(s) for the material. If you are citing from a regular feature of the magazine, you should include the title of the feature in the citation. If there is an author of the magazine article or the magazine's regular feature, the author's name would appear first in your citation, followed by the name of the feature.

FOOTNOTE/ENDNOTE:

9. Advertisement for International Realty Corporation, *The Crisis*, October 1911, 262.

BIBLIOGRAPHY ENTRY:

The Crisis. Advertisement for International Realty Corporation. October 1911.

■ *Newspaper articles*

When citing newspaper articles, you must include the day, month, and year of publication, and the author if the article had a byline. *Chicago* style allows for page numbers to be omitted because newspapers often publish several editions each day and these editions are generally paginated differently.

FOOTNOTE/ENDNOTE:

10. John Dickinson, "The Liberty Song," *Boston Gazette*, July 18, 1768.

BIBLIOGRAPHY ENTRY:

Dickinson, John. "The Liberty Song." *Boston Gazette*, July 18, 1768.

INTERNET SOURCES

■ *Internet archives*

Because many older sources like newspapers and letters are rare and fragile, researchers often turn to Internet archives such as that of the Library of Congress through which digital copies of these documents are made available. Access to documents on the Internet also allows you to examine materials without having to travel to the archives in which they are housed. To cite a document found on an Internet Web site, you need to provide as much of the following information as possible: the author, the name of the document with original date of publication, the name of the site, the sponsor or owner of the site, and the URL. Sometimes a Web archive will include a document number; when available, you should include this cataloging number as well.

FOOTNOTE/ENDNOTE:

11. Civil Rights Act of 1964, Document PL 88-352, *International Information Programs*, U.S. State Department, http://usinfo.state.gov/usa/infousa/laws/majorlaw/civilr19.htm.

BIBLIOGRAPHY ENTRY:

Civil Rights Act of 1964. Document PL 88-352. *International Information Programs*, U.S. State Department. http://usinfo.state.gov/usa/infousa/laws/majorlaw/civilr19.htm.

■ *An entire Web site*

To cite an entire Web site, you need include only the author of the site (if known), the name of the site, the sponsor or owner of the site, and the URL.

FOOTNOTE/ENDNOTE:

12. University of Minnesota College of Liberal Arts, *Immigration History Research Center*, University of Minnesota, http://www.ihrc.umn.edu.

BIBLIOGRAPHY ENTRY:

University of Minnesota College of Liberal Arts. *Immigration History Research Center*. University of Minnesota. http://www.ihrc.umn.edu.

OTHER SOURCES

■ *Published letters and other forms of correspondence*

When citing letters, memoranda, telegrams, and the like, you need to include the name of the sender and the recipient along with the date of the correspondence. Memoranda, telegrams, and other forms of communication should be noted as such in your citation after the recipient's name and before the date, but letters do not need to be specifically noted as such.

FOOTNOTE/ENDNOTE:

13. James Buchanan to Juan N. Almonte, March 10, 1845, in *Diplomatic Correspondence of the United States: Inter-American Affairs, 1831–1860*, ed. William R. Manning (Washington, DC: Carnegie Endowment for International Peace, 1937), 8:163.

BIBLIOGRAPHY ENTRY:

Buchanan, James. James Buchanan to Juan N. Almonte, March 10, 1845. In *Diplomatic Correspondence of ther United States: Inter-American Affairs, 1831–1860*, edited by William R. Manning. Washington, DC: Carnegie Endowment for International Peace, 1937.

■ *Unpublished letters and other forms of correspondence*

Unpublished letters and those that have not been archived should include some indication of this fact, such as "in the author's possession" or "private collection." If the letter was found in an archive, the location of the depository would be included as well. (For information on how to cite material found in an archive, see the section "Photos and other material found in an archive or depository" on p. 363.)

FOOTNOTE/ENDNOTE:

14. Jeff Rogers to William and Adele Rogers, November 10, 1968, in the author's possession.

BIBLIOGRAPHY ENTRY:

Rogers, Jeff. Jeff Rogers to William and Adele Rogers, November 10, 1968. In the author's possession.

■ *Court records*

When you are citing legal cases in historical writing, the name of the plaintiff appears first, followed by the name of the defendant, and both names are italicized. The first time you cite the case, you should also include the court and year in which the case was decided. Supreme Court decisions are published by the government in a series called *United States Reports*. When citing Supreme Court decisions, you need to include the name of the case in italics followed by the number of the volume that contains the particular case, the abbreviation "U.S." for *United States Reports,* page numbers, and the date of the decision.

FOOTNOTE/ENDNOTE:

15. *Korematsu v. United States,* 323 U.S. 242, 242–48 (1944).

BIBLIOGRAPHY ENTRY:

Korematsu v. United States. 323 U.S. 242, 242–48. 1944.

■ *Tables, graphs, and charts*

Whenever you incorporate statistical data into your work, it is important to document your evidence. If you borrow a table, graph, or chart from another source, you must cite it just as you would quoted material in your text. Include a citation in appropriate footnote format to the source of the borrowed information directly below it. If you change the table, graph, or chart in any way (for example, eliminating unnecessary information or adding another element such as a percent calculation to it), use the phrase "adapted from" in your citation, which signals to the reader that you have altered the original. If a number is used to identify the data in the original source, that information should be included as well at the end of the citation.

FOOTNOTE/ENDNOTE:

16. Adapted from Hinton R. Helper, *The Impending Crisis of the South: How to Meet It* (New York: Burdick Brothers, 1857), 71, table XVIII.

Because you wouldn't cite any one particular table in your bibliography, you would follow the style for citing the book, periodical, or Web site where the data you consulted first appeared.

■ *Paintings*

When citing paintings that appear in a catalog, archive, or database, you need to include the artwork's catalog or accession number if available. This documentation will allow other researchers to locate the original source more easily. Generally, specific works of art are not included in your bibliography. However, if a particular painting is important to your research, you may list it in your bibliography by the painter's name first.

FOOTNOTE/ENDNOTE:

17. George Catlin, *Shón-Ka-Ki-He-Ga, Horse Chief, Grand Pawnee Head Chief* (1832, Smithsonian American Art Museum: 1985.66.99).

BIBLIOGRAPHY ENTRY:

Catlin, George. *Shón-Ka-Ki-He-Ga, Horse Chief, Grand Pawnee Head Chief.* 1832.
    Smithsonian American Art Museum: 1985.66.99.

■ *Photos and other material found in an archive or depository*

Any material found in an archive or depository, be it a photograph, diary, letter, or map, needs to be cited just as published material would be. The name of the author (or photographer, in the case of photographs) should appear first, followed by the title of the image or document being cited in quotation marks, the date, and the name of the archive or depository. If a source from a collection is important enough to your work, you can mention that source specifically in your bibliography. However, if you make use of more than one photograph or other type of source from a particular collection, you need only cite them generally in your bibliography.

FOOTNOTE/ENDNOTE:

18. George P. Barnard, "Ruins of Charleston, S.C.," 1866, Beinecke Rare Book and Manuscript Library, Yale University.

BIBLIOGRAPHY ENTRY:

Photographs. Beinecke Rare Book and Manuscript Library, Yale University.

■ *Government publications*

The government publishes thousands of pages of documents every year. The format for citing these documents varies slightly from source to source depending on the format of the publication and the source being cited. For example, any testimony given before a congressional committee is usually published in a book. Here the exact name of the committee is given in the title of the work in which the testimony appears. When citing government publications in your bibliography, you would substitute the agency that published the work for the author, unless, of course, a particular author has been specified.

FOOTNOTE/ENDNOTE:

19. United States Congress, *Report of the Joint Select Committee to Inquire into the Condition of Affairs in the Late Insurrectionary States,* vol. 2, *South Carolina, Part I* (Washington, DC: Government Printing Office, 1872), 25–28, 33–34.

BIBLIOGRAPHY ENTRY:

United States Congress. *Report of the Joint Select Committee to Inquire into the Condition of Affairs in the Late Insurrectionary States.* Vol. 2, *South Carolina, Part I.* Washington, DC: Government Printing Office, 1872.

Acknowledgments (continued)

Page 44 (Source 5): "Two Guns White Calf Reading," date unknown. Great Northern Railway Company Advertising and Publicity Department Photos, Minnesota Historical Society.

Page 45 (Source 6): "Old Ration Place," date unknown. Courtesy of the Montana Historical Society.

Page 46 (Source 7): "Blackfeet Performance," c. 1930. Great Northern Railway Company Advertising and Publicity Department Photos, Minnesota Historical Society.

Page 47 (Source 8): "Family at Sun Dance Encampment," 1908. Courtesy of Browning Public Schools.

Page 48 (Source 9): "Students with Their Harvest," 1912. Courtesy of Browning Public Schools.

Page 48 (Source 10): "Mad Plume Family Harvest," c. 1920. Courtesy of Browning Public Schools.

Page 49 (Source 11): "Blackfeet Girl at Glacier National Park Switchboard," c. 1920. Great Northern Railway Company Advertising and Publicity Department Photos, Minnesota Historical Society.

Page 50 (Source 12): "Sewing Class at the Cut Bank Boarding School," 1907. Courtesy of the Sherburne Collection, University of Montana Archives.

Chapter 4

Page 81 (Figure 4.1): Portrait of Hilda Satt Polacheck as a young girl. Courtesy of the University of Illinois at Chicago, University Archives, Hilda Satt Polacheck Papers, HSP neg. 2.

Pages 88–97: "I Discover Hull-House," "The Oasis in the Desert," "The Ghetto Market," "The University," and "New Horizons" from Hilda Satt Polacheck, *I Came a Stranger: The Story of a Hull-House Girl*, edited by Dena J. Polacheck Epstein. Copyright 1989 by the Board of Trustees of the University of Illinois. Used with permission of the University of Illinois Press.

Chapter 5

Page 104 (Figure 5.1): Anonymous, "W. E. B. DuBois, editor of *Crisis* magazine, 1920s." Courtesy of the Schomburg Center, New York Public Library, SC-CN-83-0034.

Chapter 6

Page 127 (Figure 6.1): "The 3rd Div. on the move toward the front through ruins of Esnes." Library of Congress, LC-USZ62-49473.

Pages 134–138: From the diary of Corporal Eugene Kennedy at Hoover Institution on War, Revolution, and Peace, Stanford University. Courtesy of David M. Kennedy.

Pages 138–141: From the diary of John Metcalf Trible, Captain M.C., U.S. Army, in Tulane University Manuscripts Division. Courtesy of Special Collections, Tulane University.

Chapter 7

Page 152 (Figure 7.1): Photograph of Luisa Espinal. Used with permission of the Arizona Historical Society, #69493.

Pages 159–170: Vicki L. Ruiz, "The Flapper and the Chaperone: Historical Memory among Mexican American Women," in *Seeking Common Ground: A Multidisciplinary Reader on Immigrant Women in the United States,* edited by Donna Gabaccia, 141–157. Copyright 1992. Reproduced with permission of Greenwood Publishing Group, Inc., Westport, Conn.

Chapter 8

Page 176 (Figure 8.1): "Installation of Nicolai Cikovsky mural." Courtesy National Archives, photo no. 121-PS-1522.

Page 178: William Gropper, *Automobile Industry*, Detroit, Michigan, Northwestern Post Office, 1941. Smithsonian American Art Museum, Washington, D.C./Art Resource, N.Y.

Page 182 (Source 1): Ben Shahn, *The Riveter*, Bronx, New York, 1938. Smithsonian American Art Museum, Washington, D.C./Art Resource, N.Y.

Page 183 (Source 2): Elsa Jemne, *Development of the Land,* Ladysmith, Wisconsin, 1938. Smithsonian American Art Museum, Washington, D.C./Art Resource, N.Y.

Page 184 (Source 3): Robert Tabor, *Postman in a Storm*, Independence, Iowa, 1938. Smithsonian American Art Museum, Washington, D.C./Art Resource, N.Y.

Page 185 (Source 4): Stevan Dohanos, *Legend of James Edward Hamilton—Barefoot Mailman,* West Palm Beach, Florida, 1940. Smithsonian American Art Museum, Washington, D.C./Art Resource, N.Y.

Page 186 (Source 5): Xavier Gonzalez, *Tennessee Valley Authority*, Huntsville, Alabama, 1937. Courtesy of the General Services Administration, Public Building Service, Fine Arts Collection.

Page 187 (Source 6): Edward Millman, *Plowshare Manufacturing*, Moline, Illinois, 1937. Smithsonian American Art Museum, Washington, D.C./Art Resource, N.Y.

Page 188 (Source 7): Reginald March, *Assorting the Mail*, Washington, D.C., 1936. Courtesy of the General Services Administration, Public Building Service, Fine Arts Collection.

Page 189 (Source 8): Michael Lenson, *Mining*, Mount Hope, West Virginia, 1942. Courtesy of the General Services Administration, Public Building Service, Fine Arts Collection.

Pages 190–191 (Source 9): Paul Hull Julian, *Orange Picking*, Fullerton, California, 1942. Smithsonian American Art Museum, Washington, D.C./Art Resource, N.Y.

Pages 190–191 (Source 10): Lee Gatch, *Tobacco Industry*, Mullins, South Carolina, 1940. Courtesy of the General Services Administration, Public Building Service, Fine Arts Collection.

Chapter 9

Page 198 (Figure 9.1): Photograph of Fred Korematsu and family. From *Of Civil Wrongs and Rights: The Fred Korematsu Story*. Used with permission.

Chapter 10

Page 219 (Figure 10.1): Cecil Stoughton, "Executive Committee of the National Security Council meeting," White House/John Fitzgerald Kennedy Library. ST-A26-25-62.

Chapter 11

Page 243 (Figure 11.1): Jack Delano, "At the Bus Station," Durham, North Carolina, May 1940. Library of Congress, LC-USF33-20522-M5.

Chapter 12

Page 265 (Figure 12.1): Photograph of Jeff and William Rogers. Courtesy of Jeff Rogers and family.

Pages 274–275 (Source 1): Jeff Rogers to Adele and William Rogers, November 10, 1968. Courtesy of Jeff Rogers and family.

Page 275 (Source 2): Jeff Rogers to Dale Rogers Marshall, November 24, 1968. Courtesy of Jeff Rogers and family.

Pages 275–276 (Source 3): Jeff Rogers to William Rogers, December 7, 1968. Courtesy of Jeff Rogers and family.

Pages 276–277 (Source 4): Jeff Rogers to William Rogers, December 30, 1968. Courtesy of Jeff Rogers and family.

Pages 277–278 (Source 5): Jeff Rogers to Adele and William Rogers, February 18, 1969. Courtesy of Jeff Rogers and family.

Pages 279–280 (Source 6): Jeff Rogers to Adele and William Rogers, March 14, 1969. Courtesy of Jeff Rogers and family.

Pages 280–281 (Source 7): Jeff Rogers to Adele and William Rogers, April 20, 1969. Courtesy of Jeff Rogers and family.

Page 281 (Source 8): Jeff Rogers to William Rogers, May 24, 1969. Courtesy of Jeff Rogers and family.

Pages 281–282 (Source 9): Jeff Rogers to Adele and William Rogers, May 31, 1969. Courtesy of Jeff Rogers and family.

Page 282 (Source 10): Jeff Rogers to Adele and William Rogers, June 10, 1969. Courtesy of Jeff Rogers and family.

Page 283 (Source 11): Jeff Rogers to Adele and William Rogers, June 23, 1969. Courtesy of Jeff Rogers and family.

Pages 283–284 (Source 12): Jeff Rogers to Adele and William Rogers, August 28, 1969. Courtesy of Jeff Rogers and family.

Chapter 13

Page 292 (Figure 13.1): "Faces of Protest: Student pickets support the student-faculty strike protesting demonstrators' arrests on December 7." Courtesy of the Bancroft Library, University of California, Berkeley, UARC PIC 24B: 1: 19.

Pages 301–302 (Source 2): "Port Huron Statement," Students for a Democratic Society, 1962. Courtesy of Tom Hayden.

Page 303 (Source 3): "Free Speech and the Factory," Free Speech Movement, 1964. With kind permission of Michael Rossman, Free Speech Movement Archives, www.fsm-a.org.

Pages 303–304 (Source 4): "Sex and Caste: A Kind of Memo." Courtesy of Sandra Cason and Mary King.

Pages 307–308 (Source 7): "We Refuse," The Draft Resistance, 1967, from *Vietnam and America: A Documented History*, Second Edition, edited by Marvin E. Gettleman, Jane Franklin, Marilyn B. Young, and H. Bruce Franklin. Copyright © by Marvin E. Gettleman, Jane Franklin, Marilyn B. Young, and H. Bruce Franklin. Used by permission of Grove/Atlantic, Inc.

Pages 311–312 (Source 11): "You don't need to be a Weatherman to Know Which Way the Wind Blows," 1969, from *A History of Our Time: Readings on Postwar America*, edited by William H. Chafe and Harvard Sitkoff (New York: Oxford University Press, 1999). Used by permission of Oxford University Press, Inc.

Chapter 14

Page 320 (Figure 14.1): "President Reagan and Gorbachev at First Summit in Geneva, Switzerland, 1985." Photograph courtesy of the Ronald Reagan Library.

Page 324 (Figure 14.2): "Well if it isn't the microphone switch, what the heck is it?" Cartoon courtesy of Adrian Raeside.

Page 329 (Source 1): "Can't you see I'm trying to fill a hole?" Cartoon courtesy of Bill Sanders.

Page 330 (Source 2): "There's nothing to negotiate!" "Let's negotiate!" Cartoon courtesy of Liederman/Rothco.

Page 331 (Source 3): "He's got to eat to have the strength to start reducing . . ." Cartoon courtesy of Jim Mazzotta.

Page 332 (Source 4): "Surely they'll not be so stupid as to keep coming!" Cartoon courtesy of Bob Artley.

Page 333 (Source 5): "I'm surprised at how the president dealt with the Russians." Cartoon courtesy of Walt Handelsman.

Page 334 (Source 6): "Go on, Yuri, make my day . . ." Cartoon courtesy of Mike Peters.

Page 335 (Source 7): "Say, here comes the new blood now . . ." Cartoon courtesy of Jack Higgins.

Page 336 (Source 8): "The U.S. bargaining chip! The Soviet bargaining chip, chip . . ." Cartoon courtesy of Chuck Asay.

Page 337 (Source 9): "The Soviets are a bunch of rabid, murdering . . ." Cartoon courtesy of Mike Graston.

Page 338 (Source 10): "Hey, maybe we should do this more often." Cartoon courtesy of Hy Rosen.

Page 339 (Source 11): "Reykjavik." Cartoon courtesy of Jerry Fearing.

Page 340 (Source 12): "Little Ronnie and his imaginary friend." Cartoon courtesy of Mike Keefe.

Page 341 (Source 13): Untitled cartoon of Reagan and Gorbachev emerging from missile as doves. Cartoon courtesy of Dick Wallmeyer.

Page 342 (Source 14): "Evolution." Cartoon courtesy of Joe Majeski.

Index

Letters in parentheses following page numbers refer to:
(i)   illustrations
(f)   figures, including charts and graphs
(m)   maps